D1648576

Coming to Mind

Coming to Mind

The Soul and Its Body

LENN E. GOODMAN
D. GREGORY CARAMENICO

The University of Chicago Press
Chicago and London

Lenn E. Goodman is professor of philosophy and Andrew W. Mellon Professor in the Humanities at Vanderbilt University. His books include *Creation and Evolution, Islamic Humanism, In Defense of Truth, Jewish and Islamic Philosophy: Crosspollinations in the Classic Age, Avicenna, On Justice,* and *Love Thy Neighbor as Thyself.* He lives in Nashville, Tennessee.

D. Gregory Caramenico is an independent scholar and researcher in New York City.

The University of Chicago Press, Chicago 60637
The University of Chicago Press, Ltd., London
© 2013 by The University of Chicago
All rights reserved. Published 2013.
Printed in the United States of America

22 21 20 19 18 17 16 15 14 13   1 2 3 4 5

ISBN-13: 978-0-226-06106-1 (cloth)
ISBN-13: 978-0-226-06123-8 (e-book)

Library of Congress Cataloging-in-Publication Data

Goodman, Lenn Evan, 1944–
    Coming to mind : the soul and its body / Lenn E. Goodman and D. Gregory Caramenico.
        pages. cm.
    Includes bibliographical references and index.
    ISBN 978 0 226 06106-1 (cloth : alk. paper)—ISBN 978-0-226-06123-8 (e-book) 1. Soul. 2. Mind and body. I. Caramenico, Dennis Gregory. II. Title.
    BD421.G66 2013
    128ʹ.1—dc23
                                                            2013005905

♾ This paper meets the requirements of ANSI/NISO Z39.48-1992 (Permanence of Paper).

CONTENTS

ACKNOWLEDGMENTS

We owe thanks to many friends and colleagues for their thoughtful advice. Among them: Scott Aikin, Alejandro Arango, David Miguel Gray, Owen Jones, Jaideep Prabhu, Jeff Schall, and Catherine Weir.

We owe a debt to many others with whom we did not interact in person while preparing our study—both the reductionists with whom we take issue and their rivals who essay a more integrated view of personhood. The clarity and candor of reductionist thinkers like John Bickle, Paul and Patricia Churchill, Daniel Dennett, and Jaegwon Kim are whetstones to our argument. But other voices chime with it, striking harmonies, if never quite resolving to dull unison with us or with each other.

Brain scientists like Humberto Maturana, Francisco Varela, Evan Thompson, Gerald Edelman, Endel Tulving, and Roger Sperry have shown in their writings and their empiric work just how misguided reduction of persons to machinery proves to be—although that reductive project has long been advertised as inevitable and is still widely presumed to be the consummate and achievable goal of brain science. The late Ulric Neisser, a humanist and a probing theorist in experimental psychology, reminded several generations of researchers that cognitive psychology, essential as it is, never has the whole story and is never an end in itself. His constant awareness of natural and specifically social contexts remains an inspiration.

Biologists like Theodosius Dobzhansky, chief architect of the neodarwinian synthesis of modern genetics and evolution, has shown cogently why reduction is insufficient, and reductionism unworkable, in biology. Harold Morowitz has tracked emergence in the universe at a wide variety of levels. Raymond Tallis continues trenchantly to reveal just how sterile reductive models prove to be in describing human nature. Frans de Waal has used his vast ethological experience to allow animals to be seen as more than mere aggression-monsters. Susan Barry, poignantly telling her own story, has shown vividly how top-down, culturally mediated interventions can modify the givens of a seemingly hard-wired brain.

Consciousness, volition, intention and intentionality, memory, subjectivity and subjecthood, social awareness and concern are foregrounded by the work of neuroscientists and psychologists like the inimitable V. S. Ramachandran, Wilder Penfield, Albert Bandura, Simon Bar-Cohen, Roy Baumeister, Terrence Deacon, Michael Gazzaniga, Rachel Herz, Eddy Nahmias, David Premack, Robert Remez and J. D. Trout, Eleanor Rosch, Henry Roediger, Yadin Dudai, and their colleagues. Antonio Damasio, working at the interface of neuroscience and philosophy has complemented Spinoza's work by seeking the bodily links between thought and emotion, purpose, interest, and idea. These workers and many others whose investigations inform our own have been setting the parameters of the new understanding that grounds our synthesis.

Sound conceptual foundations are critical to an adequate grasp of personhood. Phenomenology has massively contributed here, outliving the positivism and out-maneuvering the scientism that once seemed confident of overriding it. By taking seriously the embodied self, philosophers like Franz Brentano, Edmund Husserl, and Maurice Merleau-Ponty kept clear the channels in which human action and experience are to be encountered.

The Gestalt school of psychology, inspired by the thinking of the art historian Christian von Ehrenfels, a student of Brentano's, uncovered extensive evidence of the integrative workings of thought, emotion, and perception. Gestalt psychologists, many of them exiled by the Nazis, saw their ideas sidelined for decades in Anglophone countries by the long dominance of Behaviorism. But their work has enjoyed dramatic vindication in recent decades as brain science and cognitive psychology repeatedly confirm their observations and experimental findings. Wolfgang Köhler, Rudolf Arnheim, Walter Ehrenstein, David Katz, Wolfgang Metzger, and Max Wertheimer win places of honor in our work, alongside artists like Josef Albers and color theorists like Johannes Itten, who learned from Gestalt explorations and whose creative vision complemented the insights and discoveries of the Gestalt pioneers.

Philosophers like Thomas Nagel and Roderick Chisholm also built on Brentano's work in framing their defenses of subjectivity and subjecthood. We owe them a debt, but we owe other debts as well to contemporary philosophers: to Sharon Bailin for her sage and sane examination of creativity; to Lynne Rudder Baker for her spirited, measured, and effective response to the Churchlands; to Philip Clayton, for defending and solidifying the idea of emergence; to C. L. Hardin, for his sparkling account of color; to Luca Turin and Tania Sanchez for witty and delightful words about scent; to Tim Crane for his clarity of exposition and analysis; to John Searle, who boldly recaptures and doggedly champions intentionality; to Ned Block, who, like Searle, has met Dennett on his own ground; to Anthony Kenny, for his ever lucid resistance to reductionism; to Nick Rescher, for his rigorously argued defense of free will and compatibilism; and to Roger Scruton, for his unmatched knowledge and wisdom about music, and many another subject.

The questions we address in this book are hardly new-hatched. We owe special thanks to historians of ideas like Robert Richards for his brilliant treatment of post-Darwinian theories of the mind, and to Richard Sorabji for his erudite, wide ranging, and engaged account of theories of the self, East and West. Kurt Danziger's incisive treatments of experimental psychology and memory have enriched our understanding. His concern with linguistic discipline and social context has been a special boon to all who grapple with the sometimes slippery concepts in play in these areas.

The time has come, we think, for an end to timidity and intimidation about the very mention of the human soul. The reality that the insights and discoveries of all these scientists and thinkers illuminate, from many different angles, is the conscious and active subject, emergent self or soul, not as a rival to the body it depends on yet also not describable in its terms or explainable by reference solely to the body's simplest constituents or the elemental principles of its construction. Not all of the investigators we cite would draw the same conclusion we have or use the same language we've chosen. But our argument is anchored in the evidence their work represents. So they deserve to be acknowledged here.

We owe special thanks to Dean Carolyn Dever of the Vanderbilt College of Arts and Science. Nicholas Schaser was a big help with the index and bibliography. Kathryn Krug has been an exemplary, sensitive, and thoughtful copy editor. At the University of Chicago Press, Tim McGovern has been a conscientious and attentive presence. Douglas Mitchell, our editor at the Press, was with us from the outset, reading, responding, and resonating with our efforts to construct a humanistic account that is ready to learn from ancient and more recent philosophic insights as well as the historic discoveries and contemporary findings of neuroscience, brain science, cognitive science, and psychology. His learning and skill, philosophical warmth and intellectual vigor are a model to his entire profession.

Greg Caramenico wishes to thank Caroline Cazes, *per tutto*. And Lenn Goodman thanks Roberta for her goodness, grace, and love of truth.

ONE

Bodies and Souls

It's a commonplace today to treat souls as relics of an obsolete metaphysics. But this book will argue for the reality of the soul. In speaking of souls rather than just minds, we're thinking of the affective as well as the cognitive dimensions of experience, active as well as passive, unconscious as well as conscious. Soul is the link connecting the ideas of personhood, subjecthood, consciousness, and all the backstage work that underwrites consciousness and agency.

Classically, the mind was one facet of the soul, the rational or cognitive side. Souls were what distinguished living from nonliving beings. So philosophers could speak of the animal and even vegetative as well as the rational soul, as if these were separate entities—all the while acknowledging that the soul was really one. Plato, in addressing questions about legitimate decision making, partitioned the human soul by one's objects of desire: appetitive, spirited, or intellectual. But he, like his wisest successors, recognized that in the end there's just one soul: What animates and motivates a living being, focuses attention, learns, remembers, cares, and guides, must be one reality. It's all very well to distinguish functions and assign them notionally to diverse "faculties," as many did in the Middle Ages. But, ultimately, functions must jibe if we're to function at all. And "faculties" are best conceived not as agencies but as place holders for realities whose workings neuroscience has now begun to understand.

It's natural, in the flight from hypostatic faculties, for thinkers to fight free of substantive reference altogether, preferring to speak of processes, or the stream of consciousness, or bundles of impressions and ideas. But souls are not just happenings. They are active beings, as natural to us as the skin that marks a boundary between our bodies and their environment. Souls speak up as our identity from the catbird seat of consciousness. They coordinate our experience, take charge of our memories. And, since we have ownership of our actions, souls make us willingly or grudgingly responsible for our choices.

Souls make us subjects, not by pouring some elixir into an otherwise dead body but by interweaving the activities of life and awareness, perception and imagination, memory and inspiration, allowing us to think, plan, and act. Souls make us persons, in a word; and, as such, capable of building relationships with one another and of modifying our surroundings physically, socially, intellectually, and culturally.

The terrain to which souls lay claim is vast, much of it still uncharted. Our aim in this book, however, is not encyclopedic. The insights and discoveries of thousands of inquirers in a wide array of disciplines have bearing on our case—psychologists, neurophysiologists, cognitive and brain scientists, philosophers, mystics, and theologians of many eras and cultures. We could hardly hope to capture all that matters in their work. But our thesis is straightforward if hardly uncontroversial. In arguing that human beings have souls we hope to show the perennial relevance of the human subject. We humans are selves, conscious much of the time, and capable of thought, action, and deliberation. We bear the marks of our history but also contribute to the formation of our own character. We frame values and plot a course. We can do such things because we are not complex machines. Souls are not computers. Nor are we mere playthings of chance. Souls, we argue, are emergent beings. They arise developmentally but outstrip and in some measure take charge of the bodies in which they arise. As we interpret experience, shape and reshape our memories, and labor to make sense of things, we often move creatively beyond the given to discover and invent, initiate actions, and think new thoughts.

Thinkers who challenge the uniqueness of the soul may turn to animals or machines in search of the counterparts Adam could not find even in Eden. We welcome their experiments in the lab, in the field, in cybernetics and linguistics, and in the thought experiments that human imagination builds. It is not our aim to challenge such efforts, or any honest inquiry. We only stress that any success in simulating what is distinctive in human intelligence or noting its analogues will come not simply from building bigger memory banks and faster switching mechanisms, listening to whale songs, or staking out elephant burial grounds, but from finding those facets of action and experience that are integrative and originative.

We humans have traveled a rocky evolutionary road to the arête we hold. We traverse similar paths as individuals, aided by the trailblazes of those who've gone before. We can make discoveries and tackle projects, in part because we've learned how. Our genes promote the growth of neural structures that make thought possible and let our memories work as dynamically and interactively as they do. But not all brain passages are hardwired. So learning does not await genetic change. We respond far more swiftly and reliably by cultural means. Minds are quicker still, to learn, appraise, critique, and respond. The messages travel at electrochemical speeds in the highly neuro-plastic networks of the brain.

It is not uncommon for mind and brain, body and soul, to be played off against each other as adversaries in a zero-sum explanatory game. That's not our approach. We find different sorts of questions addressed in talk of souls and bodies. We don't see souls as a special kind of body, fleeting but also eternal. Souls are not bodies of finer, filmier stuff. They're not stuff at all, not airy, quasi-physical wisps of smoke. It's incoherent to call souls spiritual beings, and thus not physical, but then imagine spirituality as implying that souls can pass through walls or float in midair, invisible by daylight but glimpsed, perhaps, in twilight, if the light is right, their traces captured on a photographic plate. It's no sounder to impute an aura or magnetic properties to a soul than to assign an aura to the grammar of this sentence or magnetic properties to the Australian ethos. Since souls are not bodies, it won't do to call them spiritual but then picture them as ethereal wraiths, physical as a lead sinker, only flimsier—yet somehow more robust.

Images of souls as quasi-physical entities persist and feed the bonfires of debunkers, as if exposure of the pretensions of a medium or mind reader amply proved that human beings are mere packets of chemicals; and minds, mere bundles of appearances – finessing any question as to how a packet of chemicals could *have* ideas, let alone make choices, feel sorrow, change plans, or write a poem. In the polemical woods that surround soultalk, one can't help recalling Carl Sagan's garage dragon, immense and fire-breathing but undetectable to the senses. That piece of theater, latterly embraced by our "new" atheists, is the kabuki caricature of ghosts and gods. But thought-ful theists have long held God's reality to be radically unlike that of finite creatures. Souls, too, we think, are quite unlike the bodily particulars that furnish our familiar world.

Souls are not bodies with magical properties. They won't answer to the tests for bodies. But only a dogmatic metaphysics excludes anything non-physical out of hand. Time, too, isn't physical; nor are facts, or numbers. Yet there are truths about numbers and other posits like perfect gases, perfect markets, or the figures Euclid studied, made up of lines that have no thick-ness. Ideas make their mark without ever being seen. And time passes with-out leaving tracks like those that only bodies make. It's hard to make a case (although it's often tried) that nations don't exist, or that armies are power-less since the individuals who compose them are the *real* beings. But nations can be united by an idea and dissolved or riven by the stumbling or fall of an idea. And armies can and do act in ways that no individual or mob can.

We're not claiming, to be sure, that persons are collectives. On the contrary, if individuals have ontic primacy over states or gangs or armies, that's because persons *are not collectives*. They establish an identity and modes of action and experience entirely inapplicable to groups—but equally inapposite in describing organs, cells, or molecules. That, precisely, is our point: Human individuals claim an ontic standing set apart from the bodily constituents that contribute to their personhood. Soul is the name for all that makes persons as such distinctive—our cognitive and affective, active and creative, appetitive and moral capabilities. The word 'mind,' often used in recent anglophone philosophy as a stand-in or euphemism for the French *esprit* or the German *Geist*, does not capture the same lively richness. That's probably one reason why epistemic puritans have made it their buckler.

'Mind' is a rich word. Its main valence is cognitive, as we've noted. We speak of paying mind to a person, fact, or idea—and, thus, colloquially, of minding someone's orders, or minding one's business, minding the store, or minding the baby. But 'mind' does not enjoy the full richness of the word 'soul,' with its moral, aesthetic, and spiritual overtones. Positivists worked hard to still such notes. We think it's pretty clear by now that their efforts did not succeed, any more than they succeeded in debarring value judgments. The Behaviorists, similarly, failed in permanently outlawing the idea of the mind, despite its rather slimmer profile than that of soul. We think there's an enduring place in human life for moral, aesthetic, and, yes, spiritual experience, and for the rich and sometimes challenging complexity of action, freedom, and creativity. But whether or not we're right about that, we doubt that linguistic fiats are the proper way to settle such questions. Philosophical dogmatism is a contradiction in terms.

When polemicists pit body against soul, or soul against body, it's usually in service to an agenda: sensual or ascetic, moralizing or libertine. That's not our game. We're not interested in making physicality a sump of guilt or an excuse for self-indulgence. Nor do we intend to address immortality or ensoulment, two issues long affixed to talk of souls. In many ways those preoccupations distract from efforts to understand what souls are. It's more helpful, we think, to recognize that trying to reduce thoughts, emotions, motives, insights, choices, and preferences to their bodily substrates systematically misconstrues human action and experience.

The insistent interest in separate souls is usually an entry ramp to talk about death. But human flourishing links up more naturally with life. The intimate nexus of souls with bodies grounds our case for the soul. It is through our embodiment that we live as individuals and members of a community. The senses spark our reflections and prompt our actions. Survival without a body (or some imagined bodily surrogate), if conceivable at all, would be pretty dead—nothing felt or undertaken. One might as well be π for all the life in immortality of that kind.

Beyond hopes or fears of immortality and atavistic thoughts of gifts or curses from the dead, a more compelling tradition sees the soul as the realization of a living being's potential. That perspective gives the word 'soul' a more descriptive, less fraught utility, not linked to Halloween, more at home with our embodiment. Aristotle spoke of entelechies in this sense, meaning nothing eerie but the natural expression of a specific sort of being. To Aristotelians the soul was an organism's form or organizing principle; organ systems were material and efficient causes. So memory could be described functionally as retaining experience and at the same time, in a more physiological image, as a ripple on the brain's liquid surface. Embodiment was not the enemy here, any more than when biblical texts located an animal's soul in the blood or used the words for breath or wind to name the soul, or called the heart the seat of human understanding and artistic skill and vision.

Despite the siren song of reductionism, humanistic discourse since ancient times has counted selves as primary realities. It's within this broad tradition that we situate our argument: Humans are subjects and agents. We engage with our environment and seek to shelter within it, make the best of it, and turn it to our advantage. It's because we act and choose, take initiatives, discover and invent, interpret experience, and reckon with our memories that human beings will continue to speak of souls. Our hope in this book is not to breathe new life into the human soul. That work was done by God. But we do hope to help restore the confidence of modern readers and thinkers about using the word 'soul,' much as Alasdair MacIntyre rescued the word 'virtue' and thereby helped revive a mode of moral philosophy sorely neglected until then. Our task here is not chiefly semantic but ontological. Our method is simple reasoning, not quite as fractal and convoluted as the scholastic modes that have proliferated in recent years, but with frequent reference to the work of brain scientists, whose findings, against all vulgar expectations, make them increasingly the allies of the substantive and active soul.

The Talmud likes to picture Judah the Prince (ca. 138–217), the redactor of the Mishnah, in dialogue with Antoninus Pius. How, the emperor asks, does God pass judgment when the body is no more? A soulless body, surely, can no more act than a rock. But souls might answer that only bodies drag them into sin; freed from physical trammels, they fly free as birds and just as blameless. The Rabbi answers with a parable: A lame and a blind watchman were plundering figs from the royal orchard. Both pled innocence when charged, one protesting that he could not even see the fruit, the other that he could never manage the orchard wall. But, seeing through their ruse, the king mounted the lame thief on the blind one's back and punished them together.[1]

Our core concern here is complementarity, not accountability. Afterworlds hardly stand alone in giving prominence to souls. Richard Sorabji invokes this-worldly moral thoughts in answering challenges to the self: Can dismissive theories adequately "accommodate compassion, punishment, compensation, relief, commitment, rights, duties, praise, and blame"?[2] Our own questions center on learning and memory, desire and intention, sociability and perception. Body and soul, we argue, work in tandem, linked even more tightly than the Talmudic parable suggests. For a living being is nothing without its life processes. Jam those spokes, and it's a corpse. Steady processes make the difference. Such processes can't be species-wide, Sorabji argues, "or we would all write like Shakespeare, since we can all produce the letters of the alphabet."[3] Processes and patterns are not bodies. By themselves they're just abstractions. At work in a living human body they open doors to personhood.

But if psychic processes animate our bodies, why speak of souls or call them substances? One reason, as Sorabji argues, speaking for an old tradition: A stream of consciousness, bundle of qualities, or palimpsest of impressions can't take ownership of thoughts or actions. A bundle of phenomena is not a subject: "an individual owns properties rather than consisting in them."[4] Unlike the V of wild geese in flight, the soul is no epiphenomenon. It has interests and a point of view, deeply invested in the body but not identical with it. Perception lays a groundwork.[5] But perception is no mere imprint or impression. It is not passive and atomic, as once imagined, but active and engaged, electro-mechanical at one end, conscious and social at the other. Memory, similarly, is not dead storage but lively, synthetic activity, both presupposing and constructive of a sense of self. Creativity, again, is not chance or copying. And human agency is no mere reflexive response to stimuli. It invokes and helps mold a self.

It's not unfashionable today to displace souls in favor of a computational metaphor. But computers, as the neuroscientist Terrence Deacon writes, "are conduits through which people (programmers) express themselves."[6] Thinking, unlike computation, is rarely deductive but often ampliative, completing a pattern, extrapolating, responding but also initiating. It doesn't just close a circuit. Reflecting on the dawn of computer electronics, the anthropologist Gregory Bateson wrote, "Thirty years ago we used to ask: Can a computer simulate all the processes of logic? The answer was 'yes,' but the question was surely wrong. We should have asked: Can logic simulate all sequences of cause and effect? The answer would have been 'no.'"[7]

Human thoughts are typically *about* something, and this aboutness is a mark of subjecthood. Our perspectives orient and are oriented by our interests. Computing, by contrast, once machines are programmed and turned on, "just happens," as Deacon puts it: There's no one and nothing, "outside of this system of embodied algorithms needed to watch over it, to initiate changes in its operation, or to register that anything at all is happening."[8] The same pulses might mean many different things, or nothing at all. Human subjecthood brings subjectivity: For better *and* for worse, our thoughts are ours. They arise in and reflect an identity. Electric currents and chemical surges may simulate the effect—as a novel might. But they can't *constitute* an identity.

Psychology deals with causes and effects not found in chemistry or physics: motives, reasons, concepts, intentions. So, as Freud and many another explorer of the psyche saw, psychology needs its own explanatory toolbox. Even assuming that only matter is real, Philip Clayton argues, physics can't explain everything. A science apt at making sense of atoms fails in speaking about minds just as badly as psychology would fail in trying to account for molecular bonding or ionizing radiation.[9] Myth is rife with similarly misplaced agencies, ascribing intentions and attitudes to thunder, fever, or plague. That's not just working at the wrong level of complexity. It's appealing to entirely the wrong sort of explanations.

Polemics often hurl actual or anticipated discoveries of neuroscience against moral or religious ideas. Romantics sometimes seek shelter in the lee of imagined alternatives to causality or rationality. That's not the tack we take. We don't see knowledge of the brain as inimical to understanding souls. On the contrary, brain science, as we'll show, increasingly enhances the idea of souls as subjects. Many of its most recent and robust findings broaden the realization that human experience is not explained without remainder in the terms descriptive of objects we can handle. So the familiar turf battles between human subjecthood and neuroscience seem increasingly misguided, whether waged in the name of science or spurred by discontent with nature's disenchantment.

We see no competition between body and soul. So we don't see a threat to humanity, morality, or spirituality, in uncovering the processes we use in making choices or through which our feelings take shape—any more than

it demeans Rembrandt or Mozart's work to learn about brushes and pigments or catgut and music stands. A Mozart symphony is not just a collection of notes, and a Rembrandt portrait is no mere mass of pigments. With
thoughts like these in mind, we don't share the eagerness of some writers
to stress a commitment to physicalism at the expense of all that emerges
from and transcends our bodies. Granted persons don't spring from the air.
We humans need our bodies. Brains matter. But tracking brain events won't
render objective what is quintessentially subjective.

If souls are nothing without their bodies, we won't be calling souls self-
sufficient. In the world we live in, not much is. Souls and their bodies alike
are rather empty notions in abstraction. Lulled by seeming familiarity, we
may privilege bodies. Yet the properties we sense or name belong not to
matter as such but to its varieties. Viewed traditionally, matter is inert and
ineffectual. But so are souls. The Midrash suggests an alternative to that dis-
empowering abstraction: Real is as real does. Souls act, but not alone. They
act *through* the body they organize.

Viewed with modern eyes, bodies are not impassive but active and interactive. Every body has a character manifested in its interactions. Ours is no
exception. Its activities are distinctive and complex. We're not just molecular
aggregates. We're persons, and persons don't just rust like iron cotter pins.
They hope, dream, remember, perceive, act, and create. Yet personhood, as
Jack Martin remarks, is a stunningly neglected subject in psychology—let
alone biology—although psychology "is about the behavior of persons."
Consider: "It is persons who exhibit self, agency, consciousness, and personal identity."[10] What kind of biology would methodically ignore features
so prominent in a species as these?

The body is built in ways that make our distinctively human life possible. The identity emergent from our bodily constitution is itself active. It
can, we've said, in some measure, take charge and make the body its instrument—seeing and sniffing with it, thinking by it, pursuing interests. As the
seat of our thoughts and emotions, moods and memories, the brain supports a self that thinks and cares, lays out the garden or plans the party. Souls
depend on bodies, but they're not dependent variables. We're not player
pianos plinking out pre-punched notes. A soul understands and undertakes
and proclaims a personality.

No one can doubt the brain's effects on behavior, in illness and health.
Hormones from within and outside it affect our emotions and capabilities. We can manage the effects, but only within limits. Fatigue and drugs
deflect or distort our judgment. Powerful feedback loops can turn pleasures
to compulsions or addictions. We're never wholly free. To imagine that is to

ignore how souls act and come to be. But souls can influence brains and potter with them. Talk therapy, counseling, training, and advice are examples.
There are many others: We can go on a diet or quit smoking, study clarinet,
learn a language. None of these is easy; none involves bending spoons by
telekinesis or staving off cancer with positive thinking. There are drugs that
can help with dieting or smoking or even psychotherapy—although they
don't help much without inner motivation. But there is no drug for learning
Czech or playing poker.

Souls, we think, are made, not born. In part, they're self-made—under-
writing their claim to substantiality. Freedom, spontaneity, and creativity confirm the claims of souls. Scientism, per contra, mates the kindly impulse to
excuse error and wrongdoing with cynical refusal to give credit where credit
is due. Fatalism, an offspring of this odd coupling of impulses, denies that
effort or intention make a difference. But the dependence of all natural events
on natural causes does not entail that all events are and always were unalterable. That faulty inference opens by celebrating natural causality but ends by
flouting it: Causes can't do their work if their effects are fixed from eternity.
The open future rests on the idea that causes operate in a temporal world.

Contingency comes into play whenever new causes arise. Human freedom finds its place with the recognition that we too are causes. We act not by
supernatural means, or slipping past the velvet causal rope by muttering the
name of Heisenberg. We do it by exercising volitions. Animals do that too;
but humans, more concertedly—weighing interests, assaying risks, prioritiz-
ing desiderata. Our ability, within certain tolerances, to predict what animals will do, or, in somewhat broader tolerances, what our fellow humans
may choose to do, does not diminish animal volition or human intention.
The choices and volitions are what any sound prediction must track. Such
prognostications do not preclude but presume the agent's role.

Agency, consciousness, and creativity warrant continued reference to souls,
not just in poetry or liturgy but in our common speech and thinking, and in
the scientific and philosophical explorations that seek to bring coherence,
even precision, to the understanding that ordinary discourse seeks to voice
and that religious and poetic discourse may strive to elevate. Memory is
of special interest here, being crucial in language acquisition, concept formation, problem solving, and learning of every sort. Creativity is an active
dialogue of insight and innovation with experience and tradition. From the
baldest natural metaphors to the most brilliant breakthroughs in science,
mathematics, poetry, or art, creativity is no mere happy accident but the
lively, constructive effort of a prepared mind, informed but not bound by
memory. Discoveries are won not despite the stable structures of the brain

but through their quiet work, not ignoring the horizon but expanding it, intellectually, aesthetically, pragmatically.

Five Arguments

In any serious brief for the reality of a thing, the argument sketches the quarry. So, in Thomas Aquinas's famous summary of five approaches philosophers use in arguing for God's reality, God is drawn as Prime Mover, First Cause, Necessary Being, Ultimate Perfection, and Author of governance and design. Denying that God is better known by faith than by reason and setting aside the thought that God is too manifest to be denied, Thomas reveals his approach to knowing God: Nature reflects the Creator's generosity and wisdom, despite the gulf between determinacy and infinity. Our arguments in this book (which by sheer chance also amount to five) may, similarly, help show both what we mean by 'soul' and how we understand 'reality.'

We open with perception. Today's neuroscience and cognitive psychology reveal active, integrative systems that belie the passive, atomistic story proposed by Locke and echoed by his Behaviorist avatars. In this seemingly familiar, perceptual context we find a paradigm case of embodied souls at work whenever we see, hear, touch, smell, or taste anything at all.

Our second argument focuses on consciousness. It's here that souls overtly declare themselves—as they do implicitly in our actions and perceptions.

In memory, too, subjecthood stands up to be counted, presupposed by memory, as William James urged, but increasingly constructed by it.

Agency is our fourth line of evidence and the key to our ontology: What acts is real. Souls are causes, not just effects—as though anything could be an effect without also being a cause!

Our fifth argument rests on creativity, the human penchant for adding fruitfully to the given. Again we see an active subject. In the ongoing bricolage of creative exploration, the mind takes its materials and tools opportunistically from unexpected realms, to fashion something new.

Many more arguments might be laid out, but these few may suffice. Adding to them would only stress the same conclusions and draw more detailed connections. All five lines of argument point to the same reality: the emergent human soul.

A Convenient Whipping Boy

Central among the issues about the soul is an old Cartesian riddle, how to connect physicality with subjectivity. Physical reductionists pronounce that case closed in principle, confident that science will soon present cutaway views exposing the machinery brains use to do our thinking. They're more skeptical about thoughts producing actions. But these doubts often come at the price of peopling the brain with "anthropomorphic gremlins" expected to work silently at tasks once thought the province of minds.[11] Avid reductionists here teeter on the brink of the fallacy of division, expecting genes or memes or neurons to accomplish what they are eager to claim that persons cannot do. The idea that thought and experience demand categories of their own rankled the Behaviorists. They shelved the very idea of consciousness on the grounds that subjectivity resists laboratory testing. Verificationism licensed the neglect: Why try to explain what can't be observed? How do we know that anyone has a mind? Introspection cuts no ice, since it cannot be shared.

Still, we're pretty good at determining when someone is conscious. And, *pace* strict dualists, minds and bodies do not seem utterly disconnected: We are aware of our bodies, and of many others. Thinking often does aid us in handling physical things. And, if we're hungry, food helps, not thinking about food. We feel a wound and don't just observe it. We smile at a friend and see our smile returned. We whack the puck and dry the dishes. So it won't do to cordon off consciousness in a world to itself—not when brain science is making such a promising start on getting to the roots of those processes that make thought possible.

Descartes is regularly a whipping boy in accounts of mind. Evidently not much resistance is expected from his quarter. But the ritual flagellation is a bit unfair. For, despite the troubles he bequeathed us, Descartes was hardly a committed dualist. He aimed to reconstruct knowledge on footings surer than he was raised on, using methodical doubt to clear the ground. Like the ancient Pyrrhonists he set aside any claim that could be denied—thus, any that could be doubted. But unlike those skeptics who sought peace of mind in suspending judgment about the rival speculations of "the dogmatists," Descartes made knowledge his goal, real answers about God, ideas, the emotions, and the world. He identified the essence of a thing with what cannot be denied of it and famously declared that he could not deny his own being. Not that dying was out of the question. But consciousness could not coherently disclaim itself. Doubt itself clinches the point: One's doubting cannot be doubted.[12] Consciousness gave Descartes his first existential proposition, the *I am* of his cogito. But it also told him *what* he was: *sum res cogitans*—consciousness was the essence of the self.

Bodies *can* coherently be doubted, even one's own. It was this Cartesian thought that Kant branded "Problematic Idealism," making knowledge of bodies dependent on other knowledge.[13] Methodical doubt allowed Descartes nothing real beyond the mind until he'd recognized that divine perfection rules out an omnipotent deceiver, one whose ruses cannot be detected. Only if God could be trusted could Descartes trust his senses—and then, only within the limits of their capacities. God's perfection allowed Descartes to call bodies real. But what were bodies? No sensory property proves essential, he reasoned: Since none is constant, any can be denied without denying the substance it represents. Any color, texture, sound, taste, or smell might yield to an alternative. But extension stands fast: No matter how its configuration changes, Descartes urged, a body must occupy space. Here, then, was the counterpart of consciousness: Extension was the essence of bodies.

That move opened nature to scientific study, using sensory reports, regimented by Descartes' own analytic geometry, which enabled free translation of spatial relations into and out of algebraic terms—allowing bodies to be described in terms of their reality, not just appearances. Substantial forms and "occult properties" would vanish. Extension would be mapped in sizes and shapes, motions and rests. Indeed, Cartesian analysis could accommodate as many dimensions as desired. So the new geometry could map any set of quantitative variables. Yet consciousness, Descartes reasoned, obeyed the laws of thought, not physics. The soul's fate belonged to the theologians, whose job it was to point the way to heaven.[14]

The price of the program was division of the world: souls to one side, bodies to the other. Animals fell to the physical domain, as if they were machines. *Any* body might share that fate. So thinkers like La Mettrie were soon calling humans, too, machines.[15] But Cartesian consciousness remained irreducible, and more immediate than matter. How, then, does thought know of bodies, or guide our own? Descartes had preserved no language in which to frame an answer. Thought and extension were what we know. No further essence presented itself. Ideas and emotions might affect other ideas and emotions; bodies, other bodies. Physics charted physical happenings; psychology, mental events. But no timber remained for a bridge between them.

Anxious about the sundered worlds, Descartes, notoriously, posited a kind of hydromatic transmission in the pineal gland, its function then unknown. Its central location in the brain seemed to position it ideally as the clearinghouse where "animal spirits" became fine enough to link body and soul.[16] Only the scheme's ingenuity, Spinoza wrote, gave any hint of its Cartesian authorship: "a philosopher committed to deduce nothing if not from self-evident principles" was appealing ad hoc to notions more occult than any Scholastic occult property.[17]

Descartes' ingenious failure has its counterpart in recurrent appeals to quantum phenomena in explanations of how minds might control bodies and brains. Just as Descartes sought a medium fine enough to verge or merge with the spiritual (and "spirits" robust enough to shift our limbs), some theorists today, rushing for the light, seek an opening for free will in quantum indeterminacy. Yet there is no evidence that subatomic events have purchase at the cellular level, and not much potential gain for our understanding of personhood. As with Descartes, there's little more to show for all the ingenuity than an inchoate hankering.

Still, dualism was hardly Descartes' final goal. He did see body and soul as irreducibly distinct. But when pressed about their interaction by the exiled Princess Elisabeth of Bohemia, he backed away from his sharp line of demarcation, calling his own *Meditations on First Philosophy* an exercise never meant for permanence. Difficult as it is to conceive the union of body and soul while keeping the two distinct, he wrote, a person is that union—just as we see ourselves in daily life.[18]

Despite his good intentions, Descartes' division left later thinkers at sea, often feeling forced to choose between mind and matter. Some turned to occasionalism or psycho-physical parallelism, denying interaction altogether. Many chose materialism or idealism. A whiff of hope survives the schism: Naturalist philosophers still situate minds at the core of metaphysics; and those who pursued idealism and its sequelae in the social construction of reality remain focused on our embodiment.

If the mind-body problem looms larger today than Descartes found it, however, it's not from any clinical or physiological advance—as if nature has only now heaved into view. Some philosophers have always thought souls physical. But the loss of substantial forms was a heavy blow to the tradition anchored in Plato's thought or in the Neoplatonic alloy of Stoic and Aristotelian ideas with Platonism. Neoplatonists might resemble dualists, given the polarity they see between matter and the intellectual. But Neoplatonic nature was infused with Mind. What reality it had was sprung from Form. Matter was just the "otherness" that harbors particularity. Mind, soul, and idea structured the world, imparting life to animals and consciousness to persons. But without substantial forms, matter seemed to go inert, consciousness lost its bodily moorings, and living beings began to look increasingly like machines.

Souls, as a result, became what Gilbert Ryle called ghosts in the machine. Invoking language analysis to lay those ghosts, Ryle called substantive use of words like 'mind' a category error: Only unregenerate dualists would ask how mechanism can explain subjectivity. Yet physics makes room for gravity, fields of force, radiation, and subatomic properties like spin, charm, and strangeness—notions that any good Cartesian would spurn as occult properties. Why does the wall between the physical and the mental still stand? Almost everything has been tried to make it disappear—magnetism, electricity, chemistry, mesmerism in the nineteenth century, quantum perturbations and chaos effects in the twentieth. Why won't souls just lie down and die, or behave like any ordinary physical thing?

The Cartesian reason is all too clear: Methodical doubt, applied like a polarizing lens, showed clearly not just that matter was extension but that the soul's self-affirmation has its privileges: If souls speak one must listen. For nothing takes precedence epistemically to consciousness. The radical difference between the self-presentation of awareness and the phenomenal presence of bodies left the two at odds. But the barrier between them was not strictly of Descartes' making. Like bodies and souls themselves, it's natural. Indeed, it has an evolutionary purpose. For the last thing we should be watching as we navigate a world of foreign objects, and friendly, hostile, or indifferent agencies, is the working of our brains.

Emergence and the Soul

It's not our aim, we've stressed, to sever souls from bodies. Souls, we believe, are emergent *in* our bodies. But souls are not well described in the terms most apt to bodies. Science won't gain precision by finessing the differences between thinking and the processes behind it. So Michael Gazzaniga, a founder of cognitive neuroscience, is a telling witness against the reductive slant so often given to its findings: Emergence, he writes, "is widely accepted in physics, chemistry, biology, sociology," yet neuroscientists resist it, "suspicious that this concept is sneaking a ghost into the machine." Gazzaniga accepts naturalism but not its reductionist extreme. He cautions against pushing explanatory categories beyond their limits: "It is lazy to stay locked into one layer of analysis and to dismiss the other."[19]

Reduction has its charms. Pierre-Simon Laplace (1749–1827) famously held that knowledge of all ultimate particles and the basic laws of physics would allow an absolute intelligence to predict any future state of the world. Laplace—delightfully—reduces everything to mechanism, only by imagining a higher sort of mind! What kind of knowledge would that mind possess? Would it know a priori all that we mortals must learn a posteriori? Just how heavily was Laplace leaning on ideas of God? Human knowledge is historical—emergent, in fact, not analytic. From Descartes' idea of matter as extension, could one predict the law of gravity? Extension implies nothing about forces. It cannot disclose the gravitational constant. Once we know the nature of matter more fully, we can treat gravity, inertia, momentum, and the like deductively. But, despite their inviting mathematical form, such inferences reflect natural, not logical, necessities. They rest on facts we had to discover. They're not true in all logically possible worlds.

Yet promises of predictability do cast their spell. Many a philosopher who cheerfully grants that symphonies don't translate neatly into words balks at admitting that talk of brain events won't displace ideas of human experience. But, as the neuroscientist Humberto Maturana observes, reducing thought and awareness, self-consciousness and language to neuroprocessing confounds experience with physiology. The dynamic, nonlinear, highly individual human mind is radically unlike a computer. Self-understanding and reflection are attributes of the psyche, not processes of the brain. Nor does our kinship with animals provide sufficient guidance. Maturana points to the allocation of work in the brain: "phenomenal domains are bound by a generative relation" far outstripping the inputs of diverse brain regions. The devastating impact of a brain lesion can lead even able experimentalists to mistake necessary for sufficient causes and leap from analogies to equivalences. But if evolution has brought us anywhere, experience in humans is very different from what occurs in other animals.[20]

Broad generalizations about cortical organization based on studies of a few model species—rats or macaques—Todd Preuss writes, rest on weak foundations.[21] Significant differences among species in neuronal shape and network density undercut the notion of a few familiar neuronal types and "operating systems" found in every brain. Histology shows significant variation. The VEN neuron, for example, a key subtype thought vital in cognition, is most prevalent in human adults, rarer in infants and small children, and minimal in other primates, although strongly represented in higher social species like elephants. Every species has its own evolutionary history, reflected in its anatomy and physiology. Superficial similarities in brains—hemispheric divisions, cell sizes and shapes, neurotransmitter modulation—don't establish larger equivalences. Human brains have more lateralized circuits and hemispheric asymmetries than the brains of many of our primate kin. Small initial differences in the cerebral cortex have evolved to underwrite major differences in mental capacity. Frontal lobe development is extensive, not least in the Wernicke's and Broca's areas that support our language use.

Thoughts, Gazzaniga writes, are not the same as neuronal firings. They're as invisible neuronally, he explains, invoking an image from Leibniz, as the work of a mill would be from scrutiny of its parts.[22] Billions of neurons, formed up in functional cohorts (not mere circuits), make thoughts possible. Consciousness, we add, likes to take the rudder. It can't perfectly control events within or outside the body or the brain, any more than sailors have absolute control of their skiff or the seas around them. But it does pursue control, tacitly or explicitly; and, with measured self-confidence, set a course. Neurons alone or in small groups, Gazzaniga explains, are bit players experientially: "we are people, not brains." So even detailed brain scans reveal little about the mind. "We now understand neurons and how they fire and a bit about neurotransmitters and so forth." But thoughts remain elusive. They "can't be described in terms of neuronal firings. They need to be understood in another vocabulary."[23]

The reductive aim is to map all thinking onto brain functions—and then, perhaps, erase the legend leading back to the mental world. But there's "no mapping possible," Maturana argues, between the operating syntax of the nervous system and the content of living experience. Content and meaning are contextual and personal. Thoughts arise in brain activity but can't be forced back into that box.[24] Does saying so impede discovery? On the contrary, Gazzaniga writes, it only reflects the layered interface of mind and brain. Science seeks to understand the interactions. But learning *how* brains generate experience won't erase the mind-brain distinction. If it did, it would trivialize the discoveries of how minds do their work—what makes souls real.

The Emergence of Emergence

G. H. Lewes, George Eliot's friend and lover, gave the word 'emergence' its present sense in 1875. But the idea is ancient. When Democritus and Leucippus sought to explain all qualities quantitatively, by reference to atoms, they gave new seriousness to the reductionism already implicit in the speculations of the Milesian *physikoi*. Thales had thought everything reduced to (and derived from) water. Anaximander made similar claims for "the indefinite." Anaximenes cast air in that role. The atomists, like the Milesians, relied on emergence alongside reduction. For the two notions interlock: One can't reduce all things to just one type without facing the challenge of rederiving complexity from that simplicity.

Democritean atomism was a brilliant riposte to the mystical monism of Parmenides (b. ca. 515 B.C.E.). The kernel of truth in Parmenides' view that the law of contradiction debars all change and multiplicity, Leucippus reasoned, could be saved, if every being were simple—hence, the atoms. Each indivisible being, in its pure positivity, would be changeless, as Parmenides asked. But phenomena, including phenomenal change, demand multiple atoms, and one sort of change must remain, namely motion. Democritean atoms, being pure solidity, had no give to them. Hence, a second great exception to Parmenides' way of truth: The void was real. Lest the atoms freeze in place, there must be space for them to move in.

From these simple posits, Democritus could reconstruct the world: Things are not as they appear. All things evident to the senses are aggregates whose properties and changes reflect the configuration of their atomic parts. Everything reduces to presence or absence. Hence the dream still alive in science: Find the simplest particles, learn their properties—ideally, few and simple— and all things become intelligible, from the scent of flowers and tastes of foods to animal instincts and human decisions. But notice the obverse: If the sounds we hear and savors we taste spring from the dance of atoms, they cannot be the same as those causes, or our explanations would collapse into tautologies. It's all very well to say that colors and scents are subjective and only atoms are real. But even to make the distinction, as Parmenides had, between truth and seeming, Democritus must distinguish atoms from appearances.

Reduction was the Democritean message absorbed in many a scientific and scientistic program: Atoms are the fact; the gross properties of aggregates are not. Subjectivities are not bone deep realities but mere flotsam from the "way of seeming." The question left for later generations: How do elemental particles project a complex, colorful world? That became an enduring agenda for science. But the question makes no sense if outcomes are identical with origins. That difficulty dogs reductionism as to the human person: Dualism can't connect the soul to its neural template. Strict mechanism doesn't try. Taken to its extreme, dualism abandons any claim to a physiology of mind. Reductionism at its purest rejects what was to be explained, spurning experience, as though the firm resolve to pay no mind to consciousness were not self-refuting. But neither the rupture nor the denial is supported by the evidence—as emergence is.

Emergence stands in tension with reduction. Yet the two are not alternatives but complementary perspectives, one looking upward or forward, at what is distinctive in a complex or outcome; the other, down or back at origins or parts. Reduction is vital to understanding. By simplifying and abstracting it seeks the roots of things, physically, conceptually, historically. But reduction goes limp when it's the only mode of explanation—as though parts revealed the full nature of a thing: Shakespeare's works, just ink on paper. Reduction becomes foolish when it pretends to replace what it explains. The elimination voids the explanation. Besides, reduction often slights something essential, or adds a sneer: Patriotism is mere territoriality; love, a surge of hormones; mercy, just resentment by another name.

Reductionism is not the same as reduction. It adds pretensions of totality and a bias against emergence. Those weaknesses are inflamed when reductionism examines life and minds: "Dynamical systems theories," Deacon writes, "are ultimately forced to explain away the end-directed and normative characteristics of organisms, because they implicitly assume that all causally relevant phenomena must be instantiated by some material substrate or energetic difference. Consequently, they are as limited in their power to deal with the representational and experiential features of mind as are simple mechanistic accounts."[25] Yet reductionism retains its appeal, partly for its irreverent air.

Emergence comes into its own in Darwin's wake. Plato had traced all diversity and multiplicity not to atoms but to a different sort of ultimate, the Form of the Good, which sheds being, truth, unity, goodness, and beauty on lesser beings, in the measure of their capacities. Ultimate simplicity was not in atoms. But what was one and changeless was still called on to explain the multifarious world. So, as Aristotle complained, Plato's explanations could not be specific: If unity and goodness underlie all things, what accounts for differences, and how can an unchanging cause explain natural change? Webbed feet benefit ducks, and horns help rams. The Good takes many forms. But we don't know much until we know that ducks use their feet for paddling and rams use their horns in their mating duels. That takes us beyond the universal good to the interests of each species, given its makeup and surroundings. What benefits one species wouldn't help another. Even 'being' won't mean the same for each type.

Darwin takes the story further, transforming the ancient idea of adaptation from a fact (fitness in a niche) to a process: Species are no longer fixed types but diverse populations with fuzzy boundaries, and fitness reflects the history of a lineage. For heritable differences that enhance reproductive success grow more prevalent, even if that means departure from the ancestral type. Many a Darwinian imagines that evolution precludes purpose or negates objective species differences. But it assumes such differences and explains them by reference to the differential success of diverse genetic salients in serving purposes. Plainly there's no physiology (or medicine!) without the idea that organs and organ systems have functions and perform well or poorly relative to the needs of a lineage.[26]

The reliance of modern species on a shared repertoire of physiological processes makes evolutionary sense by reference to the challenges ancestral populations faced. But organs and even organelles work in systems. It's no use having splendid molars without the digestive system to handle what the teeth grind up. Higher organisms preserve much from their unicellular heritage. The respiratory cycle, Krebs cycle, and citric cycle are at work in any animal cell, just as photosynthesis is the common heritage of green plants.

But differentiated cells, tissues, and organ systems have functions of their own. A mouse can do things an amoeba cannot.

Some explanations are organismic. They don't break down wholes to their least parts but regard the needs and capabilities of the whole, or the population. Even group size, as Darwin saw, has a critical impact on the survival of a type. So do mating opportunities, weather, food supply, competition, parasites, and diseases. Bias toward ever smaller, ever earlier, ever broader explanatory terms—"smallism," as Robert Wilson calls it[27]—hamstrings explanation. Just as organisms do many things that their parts cannot, there's much that individuals can't achieve alone. Sexual reproduction to start with, and many forms of nurture and protection—not to mention the projects of science, education, art, industry—any cultural enterprise.

When attributes or activities are not adequately explained by the elemental, one needs to speak of emergence and resist presuming that if we knew the makeup of things and the simplest properties of their simplest parts all natural mysteries would dissolve. That dream ignores the many ways in which complexity outstrips analysis. The strength of organisms and the action of evolution rest on that possibility. Bending too closely over the dissection tray can obscure the larger picture—development, environment, evolution.[28]

It was among chemists that the idea of emergence took hold most forcefully. Understandably. One can't describe water by reference to its elements, two colorless gases that combine explosively—now a potable liquid. Emergent systems have properties unseen in their constituents and beyond the givens of their past. Table salt, a necessity of animal life, resolves to chlorine and sodium—a greenish, poisonous gas, and a grayish metal so active chemically that it burns and explodes in water. Compounded, the two form a crystalline solid that gives flavor to meat and sweetness, in a way, to melons, the valences now neutralized that produced the distinctive properties of the elements. We know how this happens, but nothing at the start foretells the outcome. Even our distinction of compounds from mixtures rests on what we've learned from this experience and others like it.

C. Lloyd Morgan (1852–1936), a student of "Darwin's Bulldog," T. H. Huxley, introduced the term 'emergent evolution' in his Gifford Lectures of 1921–22. A biologist especially interested in animal mentation, Morgan was hardly unfriendly to reduction. His working rule, to ascribe animal behavior only as a last resort to powers like thinking, stirred the first Behaviorists, who called it "Morgan's canon." But Morgan was not blind to complexity. He rejected the Behaviorist taboo on consciousness, siding with open-minded evolutionists like Samuel Alexander, Henri Bergson, C. D. Broad, and R. W. Sellars. A thought from Mill's *Logic* spurred him on: The necessity of empiricism in science confirms (and reflects) the reality of emergence. Only experience can reveal the turns nature takes.

The periodic table was a case in point: New properties, as we now know, emerge with each new electron and orbital. The rise of life and mind, Morgan argued, clearly bespeak emergence—not vitalism, he insisted. No "elan" or "alien influence" disrupts "physico-chemical evolution." Emergence is "purely naturalistic"—yet spiritual in import, since it proclaims a duality Morgan saw heralded in Spinoza: Mind and matter as the "inner" and "outer" aspects of all things, leaving "no physical systems, of integral status, that are not also psychical systems; and no psychical systems that are not also physical systems."[29]

Emergence was humbler, perhaps, in Mill. But the idea itself has proved emergent, branching out, much as legal or constitutional rules do when they take directions unanticipated by their framers. Confident of the distinction between compounds and mixtures, Mill argued a fortiori for the distinctiveness of organisms: "To whatever degree we might imagine our knowledge of the properties of the several ingredients of a living body to be extended and perfected, it is certain that no mere summing up of the separate actions of those elements will ever amount to the action of a living body itself." Life is no mere sum of ingredients: The tongue "is, like all other parts of the animal frame, composed of gelatine, fibrin, and other products of the chemistry of digestion, but from no knowledge of the properties of those substances could we ever predict that it could taste, unless gelatine or fibrin could themselves taste; for no elementary fact can be in the conclusion which was not in the premises."[30]

Mill's argument foreshadows a parting of the ways about emergence: Is it just that we cannot predict how things will go? Or is there emergence in the nature of things? Is predictability the only problem here? By couching his argument in logical terms, Mill signals its comprehensiveness. Logic, for Mill, is psychological; but psychology mirrors the realities we know. So the failure of a priori predictions may reflect a reality in which emergent outcomes differ in their being from their precursors.

Today we can reason about how life might have arisen. We are beginning to see how the brain manages our familiar thoughts and doings. But the elementary properties of matter and the basic laws of physics presage nothing about the rise of life or the birth of intelligence—let alone the forms life takes or the decisions minds will make. Knowing a bit about the results, we feel our way back toward the roots. But elementary particles and elemental laws whisper not a word about life or consciousness. Perhaps global knowledge would permit Laplace's demon to make such prophecies. But it would need to know not just all of biochemistry, say, but all there is to know about the linkage of the living state to general chemistry and physics. Prediction, in such a case, might prove trivial. But only because those larger principles would presuppose the outcomes to be explained. Knowledge quite that comprehensive is not accessible to humans. Its laws would engulf all that we mortals must learn the hard way, a posteriori.

Examining Mill's case from another angle reveals the stronger, richer side of his thesis: Mill focuses on the differences of compounds from mixtures *and* from organisms. There's a structural analogy between the two distinctions, but no equivalence: Knowing how a compound differs from a mixture does not reveal how a canary differs from a geode. The biophysicist Harold Morowitz numbers over two dozen emergences in cosmic history.[31] Each gives emergence a different meaning. The survey illuminates Mill's point about distinguishing organic wholes from additive heaps—a distinction Lewes typified by contrasting resultants in physics with, say, organisms.[32] Arithmetic contains no notion of geometry. It motivates no idea of space. Life and thought, similarly, outreach the canon of physics—not that they violate its laws. Airplanes don't "defy" gravity, and organisms don't breach the Second Law of Thermodynamics. But neither life nor flight is deducible from Kelvin's or Newton's laws. We may, as Mill proposed, discover bridging laws that link diverse domains. But the content of those laws is as foreign to general chemistry or physics as biology itself is.

Recognizing the challenge to physicalism, Jaegwon Kim rejects emergence. His axiom is causal closure: "No physical event has a cause outside the physical domain."[33] To Kim this premise is tantamount to denying the efficacy of magic: Whatever a complex does must be explicable fully by reference to the physical properties of its simplest parts. So mental events must supervene on physical counterparts: no differences here without matching differences there. But the match is asymmetrical. Brain events don't just underwrite mental changes, they cause them. Everything is bottom-up. Top-down causality is redundant.

But nature is not quite so linear as that. A theorem, as Plotinus taught, is organic to its system, meaningless alone. The Stoics thought much the same about all things—as did Spinoza. Every natural thing, Leibniz argued, reflects and is reflected by every other. The quantum physicist David Bohm held similar views about the natural universe. It's not clear that bodies resolve to smallest bodies or that properties get ever simpler and halt at perfect simplicity.[34] There's more than one kind of causality, as Aristotle saw. And, as Democritus recognized, organization and arrangement matter. Roger Sperry, a Nobel laureate neuroscientist, drives home the point with the example of a wheel: Belonging to a larger whole determines much that happens to each part. Likewise with the brain: The whole does things its parts cannot, things it would be ludicrous to ascribe to neurons, let alone molecules or atoms.[35] What seems simplest does not always have causal primacy. A whole, in fact, may be able to direct itself and guide its parts.

Snowflakes take a vast variety of forms, so vast it's vanishingly unlikely that any two will ever be alike. That astounding uniqueness reflects an emergent complexity in each snowflake's history. Nothing in the chemistry of water or the physics of crystallization forecasts the forms swirling in any snowfall. But their ephemeral hexagonal doily patterns make snowflakes far simpler than the human genome, itself rich enough to guarantee that no two individuals—not even monozygotic twins—are genetically alike. Human brains are vastly more complex and history-prone than snowflakes. Each holds some 100 billion neurons and a million billion synapses. Ever growing and changing, strengthened or diminished, these links within each human brain far outnumber the elementary particles in the universe. Some are hardwired. But many dendrite tendrils are guided in their growth by microfilaments responsive to chemical stimuli, some of them externally prompted. Visual stimuli, for example, promote the growth of new dendritic spines in a frog's optical tectum. The new spines that spring up as a mouse learns can become permanent; old ones may atrophy.[36] The functional affinities of neurons are even more responsive. Hence the slogan: Neurons that fire together wire together. Constant selection broadens trafficked pathways and sidelines disused ones. That reveals much about learning, and a bit about forgetting.

The rich responsiveness of the brain renders its work far less reducible to the architecture of its parts than is a snowflake's form to the chemistry of water. The feedback loops typical of living systems, ramified to vast complexity, sustain the top-down causality that fosters an emergent personhood. Genetic, hormonal, and anatomical constituents lay the foundations. Experience, including social experience, paints the milieu. But even history at its most dynamic cannot complete the story of a human individual. Some determinants are existential. The brain's vast complexity underwrites the tiers of emergence. Small wonder that the Nobel neuroscientist Gerald Edelman takes the title of his study of consciousness from Emily Dickinson's lyric line, "The Brain—is wider than the sky."[37]

Social and Existential

For Aristotle, what rightfully says *I* is the mind that does the thinking and thoughtful choosing, since reason is the facet of the soul most distinctive of our species. For Epicurus, the *I* was closer to the will and rooted in desire; reason, more instrumental, was charged with making sure that our hedonic choices are not self-frustrating. For Locke, like Plutarch in antiquity, memory was what matters.[38] Leibniz here agrees: No one would wish to become king of China if it meant losing all touch with one's own past.[39] For the Stoics, the soul was the inner governing authority that discovers, with maturity, the real locus of value in the sound inclination of the will, an inviolable inner citadel, steadying one's identity not ontically or epistemically but morally.

That thought led Stoic philosophers to a further insight: Nature gives us room to choose the locus and focus of our identity. We adopt roles, the Stoic Hierocles argued, arrayed in concentric circles of commitment, defining who we are. They grow from the narrow, almost animal identity of the egoist to familial, communal, societal, and cosmopolitan senses of self.[40] Our roles, self-chosen in some measure, reflect what we ask of ourselves and what others, known and unknown, may expect of us. Cicero elaborates the implicit stage metaphor. Drawing on the now lost teachings of Panaetius, he cites historic and literary personalities and their personae, to reach a strikingly existentialist conclusion: What's right for Cato, even necessitated by moral consistency with the role that he's adopted, may not be right for others.[41]

Persons are selves. But, as Sorabji explains, the idea of persons can't always safely substitute for that of selves—or souls, we think. Epictetus can say, defiantly: "What did you say, man? Put *me* in chains? My leg you will put in chains, but my will [*prohairesis*] not even God can conquer."[42] Having been a slave, Epictetus knew more keenly than most what freedom means—and how to find the self that affirms its freedom. He "is not saying," Sorabji writes, "'you cannot chain the person, or human.' Of course you can. Nor is he saying 'there is an aspect of me you cannot chain, my will.' The tyrant knew that. He is rather saying 'the aspect of me you cannot chain is *me*.'"[43] Epictetus knew who he was. He chose who he would be. Again, when Plutarch says that memory weaves life into a whole, "he is not saying that a person or a human can be woven." The person, Sorabji argues, already exists.[44] But memory weaves something beyond the bare existent. Given the Stoic recognition that society is part of nature, not apart from it, Hierocles' concentric circles set individual souls into a constellation of roles, embraced or flouted, expressing and defining ever more explicitly who we are.

Nothing in the universe, the evolutionary biologist Ernst Mayr was fond of saying, is more interactive than living organisms. Minds all the more so. So, much of the conscious self is social. We empathize and emulate, evaluate, reject, or share actions and attitudes. Shared attention is an early stepping stone toward the emergent sense of self. Learning to speak depends on early shared attention—thus, the familiar social deficits of autistic children, tellingly mirrored in a stunted sense of self and attendant weaknesses in the use of language, our richest social medium and most powerful vehicle of personal expression.[45]

The mythic isolated self, then, would be the obverse of the pseudo-mystery of other minds. Social feedback modulates and enriches the shared and unique features of personality. Developmental psychology now charts what philosophers have long suspected: *I*, and *thou*, *he*, and *she*, and *they*, are mutually defining. Evidently those who hope to expunge the very idea of souls have not fully contemplated what they prophesy. Fortunately, their predictions are largely wishful thinking. Just as artificial languages, aiming to flush all ambiguity from discourse, founder on the centrality of ambiguity and its cousin, nuance, as bastions of privacy, sensitivity, and tact, so campaigns against souls and selves will fail, since experience belies them.

We humans are a symbol making, meaning seeking species. We inhabit a social environment, developing as individuals and evolving as a species within its parameters. The rise of agriculture and of cities long ago recalibrated our milieu, channeling the selection pressures to favor neuroplasticity over hardwiring.[46] Societies are funded by the capabilities of individuals. But social and cultural dynamics only partly resolve to the features of individual psychology. Just as mind and soul emerge from brains, societies and cultures emerge from the interactions of individuals and the groups they form. These too are more than the sum of their parts.

Persons, Albert Bandura observes, are both "producers and products of social systems." Yet such systems are rarely acknowledged in neurobiology.[47] Martin recaptures the Stoic contextualist spirit when he describes a person as an embodied individual, living and acting in a physical and sociocultural world that fosters self-understanding and enables reflective agency, guided by personal commitments and concerns. Even those facets of emergence most familiar in physical science and best tolerated by analytic philosophers fail adequately to reflect the agency of persons as social beings and bearers of meaning.[48] Nature, including those parts of nature that we call society and culture, has much to say about who we are, even from birth—even earlier. But history and our surroundings work in tandem with the existential choices, initiatives, and adjustments that each of us makes as we draw our own conclusions and form our own convictions about ourselves, our actions, and our history, framing a human life.

TWO

Perception

People love illusions, but illusions have a special interest for philosophers. Everyone enjoys the tickle of paradox when things are not as they seem. A related sense of discovery plays a role in the appeal of art. A painting, after all, is not a counterfeit. A portrait isn't meant to be mistaken for the sitter. It's the *likeness* we appreciate, capturing a character. The same goes for still lifes—the shimmer of the mirror, the glow of the pitcher on the table. Metaphors too aren't just descriptions. Their aptness is what's pleasing, the poet's skill and insight in evoking an idea or experience, not just naming things or listing their features. Likewise with illusions. Children love a magic show, not because they're fooled but because they see that something doesn't add up. They're curious and want to get behind the drapery, peer inside the box, feel around in the high silk hat to see where all those doves came from. The delight is in the mystery—and if grown-ups love the show, it's not because they're credulous. Gullibility would only dull the delight, turning virtuosity prosaic. We appreciate the sleight of hand and the devices that make the magic possible, even if we can't unpack the technicalities and figure out just how the tricks were done.

Philosophers have another interest in illusions, descended from the ancient project of parting truth from seeming. The aim is to discipline knowledge, break it in, as it were. Parmenides and Heraclitus were the pioneers—Parmenides learning from the goddess to sift pretentious appearances for a truth known best to reason; Heraclitus, warning of the flux of things and darkly cautioning the astute to keep to the common, for good sense's sake. Plato took that advice seriously, seeing the truth about knowledge as a gateway to reality—since knowledge must be of the real. Illusion became a prybar for loosening the hold of the senses, turning the mind away from changeable things toward the higher world of the Forms.

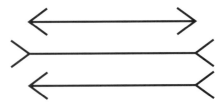

1. In the Müller-Lyer illusion, context makes one line look longer than the others. All, in fact, are equal.

Skeptical philosophers love illusions and keep a little box of them handy, not to elevate reason above perception, but to deflate knowledge claims they find troublesome. Other philosophers find other uses for illusions: Descartes to clear the ground; Hume, to double back on reason itself, not for perception's sake but to vindicate settled habits of the mind. Wittgenstein too calls on illusion, since sensory ambiguity brings interpretation to the fore and spotlights the scaffoldings of language and convention, the social side of the mental customs Hume spoke for.

Illusions are such immemorial founts of doubt and ambiguity it's almost a wonder that anyone still trusts the senses or expects reality to answer to their reports. Yet people continue to credit even film fictions. And philosophers who heartily deny that souls or God are real still use our native trust in sense perception to denounce what can't be seen, as though they hadn't, just a page before, invoked our proneness to illusions to undermine the senses and promote the view that every world, including that of science, is a social construct, a figment of myth and fantasy.

Optical illusions have better roles to play than promoting doubt. Many of the classics in the skeptic's box bespeak not fallibility but the value and versatility of the senses, at least in the functions they evolved to serve. In the Müller-Lyer illusion (fig. 1), for example, a line with inward pointing arrowheads naturally looks longer than an equal line with the points reversed. In the Fraser Spiral illusion, concentric circles viewed against a complex lattice seem to form a spiral or vortex. In the Poggendorf illusion, the continuation of an interrupted line is mislocated. The Union Jack compensates by shifting the red diagonals of St. Patrick's cross.

What these illusions show is that perception is interpretive. We see things in depth and gauge distances, sizes, and directions by clues and cues that may also mislead. We don't see the two-dimensional image painted on the retina. We see things and situations outside the eye. Perception is active, integrative, and holistic, not passive, linear, or atomic. That's been understood all the more vividly since the 1960s, when retinal images were stabilized for study. Our perception connects the dots, seeks and makes patterns, projects constancy, and corrects for all sorts of aberration and anomaly.

Doubts and Certainties

Few things at first blush seem clearer than sense presentations. But from the earliest days of Western thought, when science was largely speculative, sense reports have been called into question. Democritus wrote: "By convention sweet, by convention bitter, by convention hot, by convention cold, by convention color. In reality, atoms and void."[1] Aristotle, who prized perception, accordingly saw Democritus as a skeptic. Hadn't he said "either nothing is true or to us it is unclear"?[2] Trusting the senses was what made things unclear for Democritus, so Sextus, who really was a skeptic, could invoke him as an ally. But Democritus pursued doubt not for its own sake but to shatter an illusion that obscures things as they really are (cf. frg. 7).

Leucippus, the probable founder of atomism, like the monists Parmenides and Melissus, found change problematic, since it seemed to require a thing to become what it was not. Change could be saved, he reasoned, if all changes amount to the motions of tiny, unchanging parts. Hence atomism. The atoms' solidity guarantees their fixity, their determinate effects, and a perfect reductionism: Colors, sounds, and scents are just the impinging on our senses of some atomic swarm. Atomism had three corollaries: First, the reality of the void, opening up the space in which atoms could move. Second, strict determinism, shifting the rule that things must be what they are to the demand that aggregates change only as the motions of their parts dictate. "Nothing occurs by chance," Leucippus urged, "everything for a reason and by necessity" (frg. 2). That reason was atomic rearrangement. The critique of the senses came third. Atoms promised the clarity and constancy that the senses seemed to lack. But atoms are imperceptible: They cause sensations but remain unseen. So at the very dawn of systematic naturalism came a breach with the empiricism so often expected to support it.

What moderns first prized in Democritus was his atomism, then his determinism. But at issue for perception was the reduction of sensory qualities to atomic terms. Taking seriously Parmenides' caution about appearances, Democritus urged, "a person must learn he is sundered from reality" (6). Wisdom demands a winnowing: "Of knowledge there are two kinds, legitimate and bastard. To the bastard kind belong all these: sight, hearing, smell, taste, touch. The legitimate is different. When the bastard kind can see no smaller, nor hear, smell, taste, or touch—enter the finer" (11). We don't perceive atoms or the void. But atoms are reality: "I'd rather lay bare one cause," Democritus said, "than own the Persian empire" (118).

Hardly blind to the irony inherent in his position, Democritus pictures the senses reproving reason: "Wretched mind, would you take your beliefs from us and then discard us? That would be your ruin!"[3] Epicurus took the rebuke to heart and held fast to perception: The senses register atomic impacts. In the relative solidity of a rock or log we feel the hardness of the atoms. So we can infer their reality. All perception, ultimately, registers contact. That's clearest, perhaps, with smoke and scents, where the sense organs, as in the sense of touch, seem in direct contact with what they apprehend. But we taste flavors and smell odors not because the objects *have* such properties but because the particles reaching us cause what we feel.

Lucretius takes up the story in *De Rerum Natura*: The images or *eidōla* of Epicurus, now called *simulacra*, are "films, as it were, stripped from the outer surfaces of things" (4.30) like a shell or rind, the skin of a molting grasshopper or snake, or a calf's caul (4.50–63). Images are blocked by doors or walls but wriggle through glass, marvelously retaining their shape (4.68–74, 102–3). They shrink as they travel, and corners may rub off, so square towers look round in the distance (4.352–63). But each floating peel retains the nature of its source.

Still, naive realism, equating what we sense with what's out there in the world, soon turns to causal realism for Epicurus. Atoms, Lucretius urges, echoing Democritus, are not white or black or colored; their arrays produce the hues we see (2.730–38, 757–59).[4] The iridescence in a dove's neckring or peacock's tail is a light effect (2.795–817). Atoms have no scent or flavor, having no residues to yield up. They make no sound. For sounds are the resonance of larger bodies, spreading like ripples in a pond (4.550–614; 2.112). Atoms lack even warmth or coldness. All sensations are the effects of impacts (2.842–64).

Like other mechanists, Epicureans elide awareness, the plainest feature of the soul: "the bodies that strike the eye," Lucretius writes, are the same that "rouse our seeing" (4.217). We're assailed by voices, the salt savor as we walk by the sea, the flavor of wormwood as absinthe is mixed (4.221–24). Our hands in the dark confirm the shapes we saw by daylight (4.230–33). We judge distances, Lucretius conjectures, by the air currents each image drives before it (4.244–55). But how atoms are apprehended consciously as scents or savors is a question he has no tools to answer. He grants that a morsel may taste sweet or bitter to persons with diverse pores and palates (4.633–73). But he can't say how shapes become flavors.

Thoughts, Lucretius reasons, arise from images subtler than we sense. Unseen webs, woven in the air like gossamer threads or gold filigree, penetrate our pores, provoking thoughts of things we've never seen (4.722–48). No mind need weave these images. Thoughts are what the images themselves produce: "Suppose I perceive a lion when its image stirs the eyes. The mind must be moved similarly when it beholds the image of a lion or anything else, just as the eyes are, only the images are much finer" (4.750–56).

We may remember learning how images are focused on the retina and translated into electrical impulses from the optic nerve to the brain. Here the textbooks punted: How patterns become conscious and acquire meanings was not a question physiology texts tackled. Epicureans, similarly, papered over the gap from impact to awareness. The soul, for Lucretius, is physical, a spirit (*anima*), pervading the body but tightly linked with the mind or understanding (*animus*) anchored in the breast, "where fear and trembling throb, and joys caress." That throbbing, and the gentler touch of pleasures, prove the soul corporeal. So is the mind. "The rest of the soul, diffused all through the body, obeys its nod and sway" (3.138–46).

Placing the mind in charge, Lucretius even calls its cue *numen*, the name for Zeus's nod. Minds may savor a delight while the rest of the body holds still. But powerful emotions show that even this islet of tranquility is bodily. For "when the mind is shaken by some fear, we see the whole soul shudder with it in every member. Sweat and pallor flood the body, tongue stilled, voice checked, eyes glazed, ears ringing, limbs unhinged. Often we see men felled by mental terror. So anyone can see that mind connects with spirit, which, stricken by the mind, batters the body and topples it!" (3.151–60).

Sensations, images, and thoughts are passive here; ideas are the airy seeds of dreams (4.722–817). Minds are subtle stuff, "swifter than all we see" (3.185), responsive as liquid to the lightest touch. But still bodily. Lucretian souls are a fluid of fine atoms, rare as perfume or the subtle flavor of a wine, all but weightless, imperceptible, yet pervasive in effect (3.177–238). Souls are heat and air and breath, and something more with no common name. For "all these together are not enough to breed sensation" or set the limbs in motion. Only the fine atoms of the soul give blood, flesh, bones, and marrow the thrill of pleasure or shock of pain (3.239, with 240–50).

If anyone denies that bodies sense . . . he is battling plain facts. . . . It is captious to say that eyes see nothing, as if minds gaze out through an open door. The senses themselves recoil at that and return us to the eyeballs: Often we can't see gleaming things. The light dazzles our eyes. Not so with doorways. Doors feel no pain. Besides, if eyes were portals, wouldn't we see better if they were out, doorposts and all? (3.350–69)

Lucretius longs to catch the body-soul link. But the poverty of his native tongue, he laments, impedes him (3.257–60). The real obstacle, though, is not linguistic. The poet is inventive enough with words. The poverty belongs to his atomism. Soul is to body, he reasons, as scent is to spice (3.327), diffusing like warmth, or a flavor. The elements energize the emotions: Anger is heat, fear is chill, calm is the air. So fire prevails in the lion, wind in the deer, stolid calm in oxen. In humans these forces blend. Training may re-set the balance but can never wholly balance too strong or weak a mixture (3.256–313).

All sentient beings, Lucretius argues, are composed of insensate elements (2.865–67). Complexity makes dead parts a lively whole. But complexity just names the hope that what atoms cannot do their compounds can, without explaining how. What's hinted here is an idea of emergence, capabilities in a whole beyond the bare traits of its members. But reductionism pushes hard the other way. So the subjectivity Democritus cited in calling sense properties illusory remains unexplained. It took a Newton to discover that Democritus was wrong about colors. They aren't purely subjective. Nor are they mere occlusions of sunlight's simple whiteness. As Newton's prisms showed, colors are real.White light is a mixture:

> Colors are not qualifications of light derived from refractions or reflections of natural bodies (as it is generally believed) but original and connate proper-ties, which in divers rays are divers. Some rays are disposed to exhibit a red color and no other; some a yellow and no other, some a green and no other, and so the rest. Nor are there only rays proper and particular to the more eminent colors but even to all their intermediate gradations.[5]

A century after Newton wrote those words, Goethe, poet, thinker, and color theorist, still defended the simplicity of sunlight: colors only dyed it. Opposition to Newton's physics of light died hard. But the notion that colors are purely subjective died harder.

Simplicity

John Locke, who devised much that's now called common sense, saw per-ception as a lance to level against innate ideas—just as the social contract was a buckler against the divine right of kings. All ideas, Locke urged, stem from sense perception, "the first step and degree towards Knowledge, and the inlet of all the Materials of it."[6] General ideas are abstractions on sensations; the most general, abstractions upon abstractions. Abstraction here meant omission, *taking away*, as the etymology suggests. In generalizing, the story was, we drop out details distinctive to each sensation that we undergo. Undergo is the right word here. For "in bare naked *perception*," Locke wrote, "the mind is for the most part only passive."[7]

Only in reflection, Locke reasons, are minds active, working up what perception registers. Like Lucretius, Locke finesses the distinction between impact and awareness. He infers the passivity of perception from our powerlessness to control what we sense. Allowing mental work to structure perceptions might open a back door to innate ideas. We compare, say, the tastes of honey and sugar, Locke reasoned, and sweet things with salty, tastes with sounds. The ideas conveyed by words like 'like' are higher order abstractions.

But haven't we been using 'like' all along, even in our first comparisons? And can't much the same be said of all "abstract" ideas? At the root of general ideas like salt and sugar, Locke expected to find pure perceptions, the atoms of all thinking. The mind would be a *tabula rasa*, on which the senses inscribe their messages. But to *take* an impression even a blank slate must have its own nature. The mind for Locke was like a camera obscura, a darkened chamber where external images appear. But to function like a real camera, perception will need a receptive surface and a lens. And to compare sensations the mind cannot be passive.

Hume offers no specifics as to the origins of sensations, leaving such matters to anatomists and their confreres. But he too traces all ideas to sensations, "impressions," in his favored vocabulary. Ideas differ from impressions only in "force and vivacity." General ideas, "are nothing but particular ones annexed to a certain term which gives them a more extensive signification, and makes them recall upon occasion other individuals, which are similar to them."[8] So "all probable reasoning is nothing but a species of sensation."[9] As that last gives fair warning, the reduction of ideas to sensations was meant to set a match to rationalism. But the flames spread to his home turf when Hume argues that sensations are simple.

He can imagine Paris, he writes, although he's never seen it, and even "the *New Jerusalem*, whose pavement is gold and walls are rubies, tho' I never saw any such."[10] But, "after the most accurate examination of which I am capable, I venture to affirm . . . that every simple idea has a simple impression, which resembles it. . . . That idea of red, which we form in the dark, and that impression, which strikes our eyes in sun-shine, differ only in degree, not in nature." Hume challenges all comers to find a single countercase.[11] Motivating his strenuous embrace of the claim that every simple idea "is copied from a similar impression" are Hume's hopes for empiricism: "A blind man can form no notion of colours; a deaf man of sounds. . . . A man of mild manners can form no idea of inveterate revenge or cruelty."[12] Cruelty is hardly a simple sensation. But it's needed in the list if complex emotions are to be among the products human nature will construct.

Yet there is a rub. Could someone who'd never seen a certain shade of blue, Hume wonders, fill it in by comparing darker and lighter shades? It's hard to say one couldn't: "a proof that simple ideas are not always, in every instance, derived from the correspondent impressions."[13] Reneging on his boast two pages earlier that one countercase would upset his thesis, Hume calls the counterexample "so singular" as to be "scarcely worth our observing."[14] An awkward moment. Flagrant "effrontery," H. A. Pritchard calls it, since the objection raised "just the kind of fact which should have led Hume to revise his whole theory."[15]

Primal sensations might be saved if Hume gave up their simplicity, as many since have done. But there's a cost to pay: Complex sensations are subject to analysis. That makes room for pretty basic concepts with non-sensory components. We can distinguish hue from tone, say, as we must in choosing paints to fill in the missing shade. We can see when we've got it. But no one can see hue or tone by itself. "Abstract" ideas guide perception here.

It might seem wise at this point to ask ideas and impressions to join hands. But a doctrinaire empiricism resists, partly because atomic sense-data have long carried an aura of certainty in post-Cartesian philosophy: Panning for epistemic gold, empiricists saw sense intuitions like "BLUE PATCH," as perfect nuggets of knowledge. For even illusions indubitably do appear. Having no duration beyond their moment, no internal parts or external relations, sense intuitions, unlike judgments, have no truth value. But they're immune to doubt—epistemic counterparts to Democritean atoms. If error attacks the joints of judgment, where notion links to notion and might misconnect, pure sensations seem impervious. Epistemology need only find good ways of building judgments from them.

William James voices a broad consensus when he writes: "Sensations are the stable rock, the *terminus a quo* and the *terminus ad quem* of thought. To find such termini is our aim with all our theories."[16] Pragmatism, James urges, has discovered in sensation the "piers" that let us span the gap between thought and action: Sensation is the new alpha and omega. Simplicity is its strength. James has heard about experimental work showing how color perception calibrates itself by contrasts. But, finding philosophical idealists using that discovery to play up the relational character of perception at the expense of its material content, he plumps for simple sensa. He softens the dogma somewhat, by treating sensory simplicity in relative terms: Only in earliest infancy, before association links sensations with one another, are sensations simple. In an adult, *"A pure sensation is an abstraction."*[17] Hoping to compose the quarrel "between the sensationalists and the spiritualists" James presses his developmental account: "to a child the taste of lemonade comes at first as a simple quality." Only later in life do we learn "that many stimuli and many nerves are involved," much as we come "to perceive separately the sourness, the coolness, the sweet, the lemon aroma."[18]

James's Solomonic sundering of perception into sensuous and reflective moieties covers up his admission of the complexity of sensations and masks the debate about color vision that was flaring in his day. He turns over to a student, E. B. Delabarre, fourteen pages of his text, to explain the contrastive theory of color perception that was undercutting Hermann von Helmholtz's additive account. But James holds fast to a direct awareness of *"bare immediate natures"*—even if simplicity must be relegated to an ideal limit in infancy: "Before conceptions can come, sensations must have come, but before sensations come, no psychic fact need have existed, a nerve current is enough." That last prompts a prudent caution: "The nature and hidden causes of ideas will never be unraveled till the *nexus* between the brain and consciousness is cleared up." But then: "The brain is so made that all currents in it run one way."[19] Simple sensations must come first, as Locke demands. Distaste for idealism bars the path of inquiry, obscuring the active, synthetic work that turns electric pulses into a child's enjoyment of a glass of lemonade on a summer's day.

Simple sensations preoccupied Anglophone philosophers for much of the twentieth century.[20] The early Wittgenstein expected language to be built up of "atomic sentences." Bertrand Russell, like James alarmed by idealist contemporaries, singled out sense-data as potential building blocks in his logical atomism. Both philosophers ultimately abandoned the atomist approach. The work of the Gestalt psychologists mediated Wittgenstein's recognition that perceptions are more complex than Locke or Hume imagined: If a simple line drawing can be read as a picture of a rabbit or a duck, seeing is not so simple.

Our perception typically involves not just seeing but seeing *as*. Even childhood impressions are complex, laden with emotion and fraught with discovery. Sensations themselves, brain science shows, arise through complex, synthetic, and recursive processes. As the Gestalt psychologist Wolfgang Köhler saw, our experience, as infants, children, or adults, is holistic. Its objects have the natural properties familiar to us. Sense-data are the abstraction, as James suspected; their simplicity, a product of atomistic yearnings, and their placement between mind and matter, a byproduct of the dogmatic rigor that problematized realism about bodies even as it problematized realism about minds.[21] "In general," as Edelman reports, "it is impossible to experience a single quale—'red,' say—in isolation."[22]

Interpretation, we now know, goes hand in hand with perception. The sense-data wedged between perception and the world by philosophers like A. J. Ayer and H. H. Price, meant to safeguard against illusions, have the effect, as J. L. Austin put it, of "blinkering" philosophy and obscuring the ordinary sense of words like 'illusion'—ultimately undermining the very distinction they were meant to underwrite.[23] Yet some philosophers continue to set store in sense-data, in fear of naive realism. Some still view sensation as passive and even atomic.[24]

Clearly a round coin looks elliptical from most angles. Lacking X-ray vision, we generally see only surfaces of things, and only in part at that. We know there's more to things than we perceive. We say we see the books in the library, but stare as we might, we can't take in each page in every volume. So it's right to distinguish appearance from reality. The trick is to do so without substituting sensations for objects. That's just another road to skepticism, solipsism, or some form of idealism, denying things reality independent of thought. It's hard to say sometimes if sense-data theorists aren't simply targeting realism, intending to cut off the senses from the physical world. That's a no-win proposition. For realism of some sort is woven into the fabric of life. It's presupposed, as Austin argued, in the very distinction of being from seeming, since the idea of illusions makes no sense unless appearances are contrasted with realities.

Epistemically the weakness in what James called "sensationalism" was that in the search for certainty, philosophers retreated within the walls of subjectivity: The appearance BLUE PATCH NOW rests safe within the mind. The sincere report of a blue-patchy sensation, although hardly tautologous, secures certainty by hedging. Natural languages make room for many such qualifications. One can say, 'I seem to remember meeting you in Strasbourg,' or 'If I'm not mistaken . . .' All bets are covered—but at a price. The hunt for certainty won't bag much worth taking home with that blunderbuss. Self-consciously subjective judgments won't yield facts about what's in the world beyond the mind. There's no way of piling up impressions high enough to escape their subjectivity.

Psychologically the champions of sense-data accordioned the complexity of appearances and elided the active, integrative work of perception. There are appearances, of course. But none are atomic. Neither do they spring to our awareness ready made. Phenomena do have physiological roots. But that does not turn perceptions into pop-it beads. There's synthetic work at multiple levels, much of it preconscious. Raw stimuli are far too numerous and complex to make sense by themselves: We need to digest and marshal them, tease out signal from noise. That work presupposes interests as well as special equipment. But the brain, unlike a camera obscura or even a fine SLR, has much of what we need. Sensory atomists, following Locke and Hume, counted on the association of ideas to do the job, spontaneously linking sensations. But, as Köhler saw, brute association is unequal to the task: Unrelated sensa don't line up politely and pair off.[25] And, *pace* Hume, bare temporal contiguity can't help much. It might just make the rush of sensations more confusing.

Gestalt psychologists ascribed critical perceptual work to the mind's *bauplan*, its organizational structure. Experience is framed, as Kant saw it, in *his* response to epistemic atomism, by projecting pattern where mere stimuli are fragmentary. Just so with perception. Without such image enhancement, we'd have a hard time distinguishing objects at all.[26] Persons with visual agnosia take in sensations and know they must have some meaning; they may even trace an outline and *infer* that the figure before them is, say, a triangle. But they cannot see it as a triangle.[27] "No person blessed with a healthy nervous system," Rudolf Arnheim writes, "apprehends shape by patching it together through the tracing of its parts. . . . The normal sense of sight does nothing of the sort. Most of the time it grasps shape immediately." We needn't measure to see that a picture's askew, that one hand is larger than the other, that the piano's out of tune, or that this cocoa is sweeter than that. Gestalt research, Arnheim explains, "demanded a complete turnabout in the theory of perception."

> It seemed no longer possible to think of vision as proceeding from the particular to the general. On the contrary, it became evident that overall structural features are the primary data of perception, so that triangularity is not a late product of intellectual abstraction, but a direct and more elementary experience than the recording of individual detail. The young child sees 'doggishness' before he is able to distinguish one dog from another.[28]

Perception is relational, not atomistic. "The process of learning," J. J. Gibson wrote, is from indefinite to definite, not from sensation to percept."[29] Percepts are made, not just registered, scored, or chalked up. (Indeed, if they were, the mind would need far *more* elaborate innate categories than its normal operations seem to require.) So Russell's choice of a passive participle when he coined the term *sense-data* canonized a misleading premise. Sights and sounds, odors, flavors, and textures are taken in and taken up, related to our needs, personal histories, and evolved capabilities and limitations. Lucretius was right: Souls don't just face an open window.

Confronting the difficulties of the sense-data account, many an analytic philosopher turned not to neuroscience but to language for guidance. If artificial languages could not iron out the logical kinks and metaphysical confusions that had long troubled philosophy, the Oxford school hoped, perhaps resort to linguistic usage could clear things up. Hence the claim that philosophers need know nothing about the world or the brain to dissolve philosophical conundrums. Natural languages, after all, are rife with distinctions. Surely an astute umpire could use these to untangle philosophical disputes. Readily overlooked was the possibility that the subtleties enshrined in natural languages might reflect the same conflicting perspectives that spawn those disputes.

The notion of sense-data does help tease appearances loose from reality. It also tempts anti-realism: If all awareness is subjective, how can percepts vouch for a world independent of the mind? Epicureans may wobble between naive and causal realism. But Locke came down firmly on the causal side, opening doubts about how faithfully impressions represent the realities they announce. One response to such worries was for ordinary language philosophers (in the name of common sense) to press the recognition that perceptual terms are achievement words: 'I saw the game last night' does not imply the silent codicil, '– if I'm not mistaken.' It simply affirms having seen the game. Errors remain possible, of course. So are dreams, false memories, hallucinations. But, if so, no epistemic problems are solved by calling perceptual words success terms. If we want a way of controlling doubts, garden variety or hyperbolic, language analysis can't deliver.

It helps to see that hyperbolic doubt does get silly, leaning on the very distinction of veracity from error that anti-realism rejects. It's also worth noticing that doubt can grow disingenuous, presuming all sorts of worldly knowledge about projected sources of error in a world whose very existence it calls into question. Doubt gets downright ridiculous when inventing elaborate "possible world" scenarios that push the envelope of science fantasy and entertain any premise short of formal contradiction to invoke scientific sounding posits corrosive of experience while systematically sidelining actual knowledge about the limits of possibility. But no conjuror's trick can assure us that our senses deliver all they promise. If it could, our perceptual achievements—seeing a shooting star, hearing a mocking bird, smelling a rat, tasting a fig, touching a lover's cheek—would hardly be achievements.

Philosophically, the weakness of the sense-data idea lies in the competition it sets up between appearances and the world they represent. But in psychology, sensa put us on the wrong track by presenting as passive what is active and integrative. Eagerness to sideline the human subject neglects the constructive work of perception and discounts its complex, relational side, which is not fenced off from higher mental functions. We don't just record data. We pick out and identify objects and notice features that might matter. Our eyes scan the surroundings for salience, in rapid, coordinated movements, the saccades, first observed by Emile Javal (1839–1907) in the 1880s, using a mirror to track eye movements over a page of text. Saccades take as little as a fiftieth of a second, the swiftest motion we can make. But we see no blur. The brain corrects for that as it constructs the scene. If the light show stops, vision goes dead. It counts on change, eyes constantly searching out movements and contrasts that might disclose something new.[30]

G. E. Moore framed a celebrated argument aiming to explode all types of ethical naturalism. 'Good,' he argued, is undefinable, since any proposed definition is always open to question, whereas it makes no sense to question sound definitions:[31] Definitions are analytic, just spelling out the meaning of terms. Only someone unfamiliar with linguistic usages could intelligibly wonder about the correctness of a proper definition. For to question a claim is to hold it up to doubt, entertain its denial. But it makes no sense to doubt analytic sentences; their denial is contradictory. Moore prided himself on precision in reasoning and clarity in writing. He grounded his open question argument, characteristically, in linguistic usage. But rather than explain that words like 'good' are undefinable naturalistically because ideas of good resist reduction, tending to rise above all efforts to turn them into promises of pleasure or profit, or any natural state, Moore invoked an analogy: 'Good,' like 'yellow' is unanalyzable. He presumed 'yellow' and other basic color terms name simple intuitions, like the sense-data of Russell, his Cambridge colleague. But what people mean by 'good,' in fact, is often complex and variable with context. It's because our ideas of good are dynamic, not because they're simple, that they may outfly attempts to pin them down descriptively, although they often nestle among homely notions like happiness, beauty, virtue, or even home cooking, that win local or general approval.

As for 'yellow' and other color terms, what they name may look simple superficially. But colors too are achievements: The colors we see are made, not just given. That doesn't mean they're purely subjective, as if there were no real difference between the red and white stripes on the flag. It means there's work behind our seeing, starting in the eye, pursued in the oppositional channels of the optic nerve, and consummated in the brain, allowing us some pride in seeing things as they are. For the colors healthy people see match the wavelengths of the light coming from an object. That it makes no sense to look for colors at the atomic level is a red herring.

Five Senses?

Conventionally, we count five senses, each with its own portal and presentations: vision and the sights we see, hearing and the sounds we hear, smell and the odors we scent, taste and the savors we taste, touch and the objects we feel. We see with our eyes, hear with our ears, smell with our noses, taste with our tongues and palates, feel with our fingers and skin. Aristotle ranked the senses: Sight was noblest, being closest to the intellectual. Touch ranked last, seeming most physical. But touch was also most basic, found even in the lowest animals—although most sensitive, Aristotle thought, in human beings (*De Anima* 2.2.414a3; 414b3–9; 9.421a20–24). Aiming in *De Anima* to counter the physicalism of Democritus and Empedocles, Aristotle also voiced his preferences in the opening lines of the *Metaphysics*: "All men by nature desire to know. A sign of this is how we prize our senses, not just for their usefulness but for their own sake—vision above all. For even apart from practicality and with no action in view, we value seeing above the rest, since this sense best brings us knowledge and illuminates the diversity of things" (*Metaphysics* A 1.980a22–27).

Five is a nice round number. But physiology today allows us to do much better. Aristotle himself unsettles his count by noting all that we see: We see shapes as well as colors, we judge distances, group and distinguish objects, assay textures and even temperatures by eye before we venture a touch. Perhaps irritated by notions of an unaccountable sixth sense, Aristotle makes his case for stopping at five by subsuming several perceptual modalities under a single sense (*De Anima* 2.11.423b.27–29; 3.1.424b22–23). Yet Avicenna does not stray far in counting five *or eight* senses, like Aristotle allowing that touch distinguishes hot from cold, moist from dry, hard from soft, rough from smooth.[32]

Still, Aristotle's claim (*De Anima* 3.1.425a9–13) that no animal could have more than five senses—unless there were more than four elements!—is belied by the sense of the earth's magnetic field in some migratory birds and turtles, apparently some mammals, and even some bacteria—and by the specially adapted organs of echolocation in dolphins, the heat sensing pits of snakes, the remarkable chemoreceptors of fish, and the special sensors in their lateral line to water currents and vibrations—not to mention electric eels' judging the species, sex, and status of other eels by their electric currents.[33] The sensitivity of some animals differs so greatly from our own as to seem almost to add new senses. The keen noses of dogs and visual acuity of eagles and other raptors, the high-pitched sounds dogs hear, the ultra-low frequencies emitted and heard by whales, molluscs' visual compensation for refraction in water, and insects' vision in the ultraviolet or infrared don't fit readily in the human toolbox.

Humans, like other mammals, have a distinct vestibular sense, its organ in the inner ear, helping us keep our balance. We also have proprioception, the brain using somatic feedback to tell us how we're moving and where our limbs are. Interoception monitors our organs—stomach or muscle pain, bloating, heartburn, muscle flexing, breathing, even immune response and the vasodilation of inflamation or blushing, runner's high, and other effects of endogenous and exogenous opioids. The skin has its own receptors sensitive to ambient heat and distinct from those of tactile heat perception. Erotic pleasures, often described by the ancients in largely tactile terms, actually involve several perceptual systems linked to the brain's pleasure centers. Neuroscientists today readily count ten senses: the five classical ones, plus proprioception, thermoception, the interoceptive group, a sense of direction arising from the other senses, and the vestibular sense. Nor is it true that each sense has just one class of object. Our binaural hearing allows us to locate the source of a sound—not with the pinpoint accuracy of an arctic fox, but servicibly nonetheless. Binocular vision, similarly, imparts a sense of depth. All our perceptions are active, constantly filtering and integrating, charting rhythms and relationships.

Seeing

The proper object of vision, Aristotle says, is color (*De Anima* 2.7.418a27–29). So in discussing vision we'll turn to color first and then consider how vision discriminates objects and how we see in depth. The bodies we see typically get their color by absorbing or reflecting different segments of the spectrum. But our vision works with the light effects to generate meaningful and veridical values. The retina, as C. L. Hardin puts it, is "a bit of extruded brain."[34] Its photoreceptors, perhaps 100 million rods and some 5 million cones, if unstimulated, continuously release a neurotransmitter that inhibits signals from the bipolar cells that link each retina to its ganglion, the cluster of nerve cells whose axons form the optic nerve. The inhibition stops when light strikes. The light sensitive pigments in the photoreceptors—rhodopsin in rods, photopsin in cones—alter chemically and change molecular shape, yielding an electrical effect that signals the bipolar cells to release their neurotransmitter, exciting the synapses leading to the brain.

Rods specialize in peripheral and night vision. Their extended surface area makes them sensitive enough to detect a single photon, and their output is summed, maximizing response to light and movement. Rods are a hundred times more sensitive than cones, and their outputs are amplified biochemically. But they register only black and white and shades of gray. They react more slowly than cones, and the summing diminishes acuity: We can notice movement out of the corner of an eye, but we need to look to check out what was stirring.

Cones respond to colors as well as achromatic stimuli. They respond rapidly and register fine detail, essentially counting photons. But they need ten to a hundred times the light that rods do, so we can't make out colors in the dark. Individual cones, in fact, do not distinguish colors. They specialize. Humans have three types, called S, M, and L, for the short, medium, or long wavelengths of their optimal sensitivity. S is most sensitive to wavelengths centered around 430 nanometers (nm, billionths of a meter), a deep blue, almost violet; M, around 530 nm, a green; L around 560 nm, close to yellow, but bridging the range between green and something like red.

The colors cones respond to best still don't match the ones we see, nor do we blend colors as von Helmholtz conjectured. He had relied on Hermann Grassman's theory of how all colors might be built from just three light sources. But there was a fly in the ointment: It's true that purple can be made by mixing red and blue light. But yellow looks nothing like a red-green mixture. Purples may be redder or bluer, but we don't see reddish greens or greenish reds. Ewald Hering proposed an ingenious oppositional alternative to Helmholtz's model. But the additive approach held wide sway until the 1950s, when Leo Hurvich and Dorothea Jameson found evidence for an oppositional theory that could account for color vision without positing four chromatic processes, as Hering had, rather than the three suggested by our array of cones.

We know now that yellowish green light stimulates L and M cones but has little effect on S. Red light stimulates L cones more than M but affects S very little. Blue-green light stimulates M cones more than L and affects S somewhat more. Violet light stimulates L and S cones somewhat but has little effect on M. So our first responses gauge not simple colors but color differentials. Comparisons may begin as early as the bipolar cells. There are large-cell (magno) and small-cell (parvo) layers of these. Parvo cells are of two types: One type uses the discrepancies between L and M cone signals to gauge red-green differences; the other type gauges the blue-yellow opposition by summing L and M pulses and comparing S cone signals. It's the algebraic sum of the cone signals that is transmitted to the brain. The overlapping sensitivities of S, M, and L cones and the close comparisons of their output allow our vision to distinguish hundreds of thousands, even millions of colors.

The two optic nerves meet at the optic chiasma, their signals distributed largely to opposite sides of the brain and fed by the optic tracts into the lateral geniculate nucleus of the thalamus, the clearinghouse of most sensory inputs. Neurons here have receptive fields sensitive preferentially to signals from each type of cone. The resultant tuning refines our color comparisons. The optic tract passes on to the primary visual cortex (V1) in the brain's occipital lobe. Here, in the striate cortex, specialized cells sensitive to hue and brightness translate the red-green and blue-yellow differentials into color values. The information passes to the extrastriate V2, for further tuning, and then to V4, where for the first time the contrasts are related to the full range of visible hues, and on to the inferior temporal lobe, where color readings are coordinated with visual appraisals of form. Far from a tabula rasa, our color perception relies ultimately on a "color map" innate in the brain and progressively informed and elaborated by experience.

Given all this constructive work, color vision might be thought highly personal or culture bound. Language and associations do influence our responses to colors and our interest in specific color differences and combinations. But anyone who is not color blind can distinguish the same basic colors, and core color distinctions are remarkably steady from person to person and across cultures. Most languages spoken by good-sized populations name more than six and perhaps a dozen basic hues. Red, green, yellow, and blue, purple, orange, brown, pink, black, white, gray (and some say beige) are acknowledged in a wide diversity of cultures. As Brent Berlin and Paul Kay write, "Our essentially linguistic investigations"—since confirmed and expanded by others—"have led, seemingly inescapably, to the conclusion that the eleven basic color categories are pan-human perceptual universals."[35]

Hardin contrasts that finding with the views of the Wittgensteinian philosopher Rush Rhees and the social anthropologist H. A. Gleason, both writing in the 1950s, "when anthropological relativism and nonopponent color theory were in full flower"—as was the linguistic determinism inspired by Whorf and Wittgenstein. He finds relativism about color perception taken to its extreme when a 1950 text "solemnly assures us that the spectrum is the very paradigm of continuity and its division the product of cultural accident embedded in language"—although the frontispiece of the same book presents, "a pleasing photograph of a rainbow, whose most prominent feature is that it consists of a small set of clearly differentiated colored regions."

Tapping home his point, Hardin writes: "The perceptual salience of certain spectral hues suggests the existence of a natural, biologically induced set of hue categories which may in turn leave its traces in a variety of natural languages."[36] The structure of the lens of the eye, the reactions in the cone cells, the color processing in the cortex, the receptive fields of the neurons, and the brain's color map make color perception pretty uniform across the species. Color sensitivity does vary from person to person. But basic color categories match up with wavelengths on the visible spectrum.[37]

Meanings are another matter: It's one thing to perceive turquoise, oxblood, or mauve, quite another to have an attitude about it. Experience layers values on our perceptions, and conventions assign meanings to specific colors and combinations. Certain colors may evoke tranquility, irritation, pensiveness, or cheer in various individuals. The feelings may intensify as people employ favorite colors to express their identity or elicit an emotional response.[38] Children as young as three consistently associate specific colors with specific facial expressions, largely on a personal rather than conventional basis.[39]

Johannes Itten, who taught color theory at the Bauhaus, advised his students to find a favored palette and develop it as an artistic signature,[40] and many painters can be identified by their color choices, although some of the most versatile vary their palettes as their moods and interests change. Personal color preferences often reflect positive or negative experiences. Many people love blue, associating it with clear skies and pure, clean water. Most find green relaxing, thinking of forests or gardens. But some dislike it, since it reminds them of mold.[41] Differences in color preference, however, are not the same as differences in perception—or colors could not so readily be made expressive.

The brain compensates for a variety of conditions—chromatic aberration, for example, the color distortion caused by light's scattering in a lens. Perceptual constancy, sustained by such adjustments, regulates the "blooming, buzzing confusion" William James spoke of. As Lothar Spillmann notes, "the same object in our environment changes little in perception, despite large changes in illumination, distance, and viewpoint. These perceptual constancies (or invariances) are creative in the sense that they enable us to recognize objects and form experiences of the world around us regardless of the precise physical conditions under which stimuli occur."[42] Contributing to perceptual constancy is what we might call the "steadicam" effect: Our world does not bounce and sway as we walk. Color constancy is sustained by another adjustment our brains make: The wavelengths that reach the eye shift constantly, but the colors we see don't change as we move, say, from daylight to artificial light. They stay faithful to the reflectance spectrum that is invariant for each object.[43] Similarly, coal looks black even in bright sun; a silk scarf looks white even in the dark. It may be sending less light to the eyes than the coal does at noon, and our eyes can't distinguish reflectance from illumination. Illumination may vary, but it's the constant, the reflectance of a given surface (its albedo), that the brain registers. The brain teases out the mingled signals and compensates for ambient conditions by relying on contrasts. So ivory yellows next to swansdown, and objects at first unnoticed may glow with warmth and light in a Rembrandt painting.[44]

From the point of view of optics, image resolution within the eye peaks at the fovea, the square millimeter of the retina packed with some 50,000 cones. But it's the brain's work that turns retinal signals into perceptions. Each cone subtends just 30 seconds arc, but the brain resolves an image three times as fine, weaving a coherent scene from the information gathered as our eyes scan the visual field. The brain covers for the lack of receptors where the optic nerve exits the retina, a disk of some 6 degrees arc. There's no resulting blind spot, but without the compensatory work, an angle that large would leave a hole the size of twelve full moons. Nor do we normally see the macula, the yellowish spot shielding the fovea, or any shadow cast by the retinal blood vessels. Besides the far more rapid movements of the saccades, our eyes quiver every 30 to 80 seconds over some 10 to 30 seconds arc; they drift slowly by up to 6 minutes arc and make quick corrective movements of 1 to 20 minutes arc every .03 to 5 seconds. But no blurring results from all this motion.

Seeing, then, is more about how the mind reconstructs an environment than about light signals telegraphed to the brain. Yet the notion persists that perception is passive: colors, one philosopher writes, "are given." Were they products of our dispositions, "they would not be visible in the way they are."[45] Would the mind's active engagement really render color vision suspect, somehow unveridical? Granted the colors we see are constructed, they're constructed rather well. Color vision for most of us, most of the time, *is* an achievement, a dialogue of eyes, mind, and environment. Colors may look simple, and there is simplicity, as Newton showed, in each line of the visible spectrum; but each hue we see is forged in elaborate syntheses, making color perception a paradigm case of the active work of the human soul.

Color Contrasts

Itten reports numerous phenomena that undercut any notion of static, atomic, isolated, passively received sensations:

We know that a white square on a black ground will look larger than a black square of the same size on a white ground. The white reaches out and overflows the boundary, whereas the black contracts. A light-gray square looks dark on a white background; the same light-gray square looks light on a black ground.[46]

"In art," Errol Harris remarks, "this effect of context is unmistakable and indispensable. We react in general to gradients of light and shade and not to absolute intensities. . . . The glint of light on the water in Turner's *Dutch Fishing Boats*, and the sunlight on the distant cliffs are made luminous by their relation to the gloom of the threatening storm cloud."[47] Artists often achieve brilliant effects simply by leaving a patch of canvas unpainted. Hardin offers a nice experiment to demonstrate the effect: "look at the screen of your television set under normal room illumination when the power of the set is turned off. The screen will look to be a dark gray rather than black. Now turn on the set and find a noise-free picture with a good black in it. That black will be noticeably darker than the gray of the inactivated screen. But television pictures are brought into being by *adding* light to the screen, not by *subtracting* it." The black is a contrast effect.[48] Itten writes:

On white yellow looks darker, with an effect of fine, delicate warmth. On black yellow acquires extreme brilliance and a cold aggressive quality. . . . Red looks very dark on white, and its brilliance scarcely asserts itself. On black, however, red radiates luminous warmth. . . . On white, the effect of blue is one of darkness and depth. The surrounding white square looks brighter than in the case of yellow. On black, the blue takes on a brilliant character, with deep luminescence of hue . . . gray on ice blue looks reddish, while the same gray on red-orange looks bluish.[49]

The expressive language is not poetic license. Colors have expressive values for us from their personal and cultural associations and the constant interaction of perception with our cognitive and affective responses. Underlying the expressive impact is the dynamic of color relations. What we see is not just separate blotches. Colors get their vividness and character from the contrasts generated by competing neurons.[50] If our eyes are restricted to a single color, just as when their movements are halted, we soon "adapt" to what we're seeing and stop seeing anything at all. The visual field turns neutral gray, *eigengrau* as German researchers called it, "brain gray," to English speaking investigators. In this *ganzfeld* (whole field) effect, the brain is not receiving enough lively contrasts to register anything visual at all.[51] Hardin explains: "What the brain must settle for from the prototypical ganglion cells is the state of zero information, the sensation that corresponds to base-rate firing of the neural units."[52]

"Our sense organs," Itten writes, "can function only by means of comparisons."[53] Walter Ehrenstein, one of the Gestalt psychologists who first described how contrasts enable us to discriminate objects, now collaborating with Lothar Spillmann and Viktor Sarris, returns to the subject after nearly three quarters of a century:

> The receptive fields of retinal neurons are subdivided into a circular center and a concentric surround. The center and the surround are antagonistically organized, thus light falling onto the center activates the neuron, whereas light falling onto the surround inhibits it (*On*-center neuron). In the opposite type of receptive field all signs are reversed: Light in the center inhibits, whereas light in the surround activates the neuron (*Off*-center neuron). On-center neurons are assumed to mediate the sensation of "brighter," off-center neurons that of "darker." Similar receptive fields encode spectral or chromatic stimuli. Neurons with *double-opponent* receptive fields have been found to mediate color contrast.[54]

Itten notes seven kinds of color contrasts: of hue, light and dark, warm and cool, complementarity, and the contrasts of simultaneity, saturation, and extension.

Differences of hue are the primal differences among chromatic colors. Most prominent are the contrasts of the primaries, red, yellow, and blue: "The effect is always tonic, vigorous, and decided." The intensity of contrast diminishes for orange, green, and violet, and still more with tertiaries like yellow-orange or blue-violet. Contrasting hues are a natural vehicle for symbolism: "The undiluted primaries and secondaries always have a character of aboriginal cosmic splendor as well as concrete actuality. Therefore they serve equally well to portray a celestial coronation or a mundane still life. Contrast of hue is found in folk art of peoples everywhere. Gay embroidery, costume and pottery."[55] The impact of contrasting hues, Itten notes, is exploited in the stained glass of cathedrals, the paintings of Fra Angelico, Botticelli, Matisse, Picasso, Kandinsky, Leger, Miro, Franz Marc, and, of course, Mondrian.[56]

The contrast of light and dark traverses the range of shades between black and white. But when gray abuts a chromatic color we again see the effects of context and active comparison. "Neutral gray," Itten writes, "is a characterless, indifferent, achromatic color . . . mute, but easily excited to thrilling resonances. Any color will instantly transform gray . . . to a complementary color effect corresponding mathematically to the activating color." The reason: the response of photoreceptors in effect answering the signals received by nearby cells: "Gray is a sterile neuter, dependent on its neighboring colors for life and character. It attenuates their force and mellows them. It will reconcile violent oppositions by absorbing their strength and thereby, vampire-like, assuming a life of its own."[57]

Warm and cold, as applied to colors, are metaphors. But there are facts behind the figurative expressions. Itten even reported that people feel five to seven degrees cooler in a blue-green room than a red-orange one. Those two colors are typically called cold and warm respectively, but contrasts set the character of the intermediate colors.[58] Again relativity matters: "A bluish yellow or red tends to look cold, and so does a yellowish red or blue." But "a reddish yellow or blue seems warm."[59] Monet, as he turned increasingly to landscape painting *en plein air*, shifted from light-dark to warm-cold contrasts that seemed to him to capture "the shimmer of light in the air."[60]

Mixing complementary pigments yields a gray-black. But mingled light rays resolve to white, completing the visible spectrum. The afterimage that appears after intense visual stimulus complements the hue of the original image. The neurons responsive to the original color, all but exhausted, signal weakly, and nearby neurons take up the slack, often in the opponent channel.[61] By a similar effect, in the "simultaneous contrast," we spontaneously see the complements of colors still before us. The effects intensify the longer the opposing color is viewed and the more luminous it is. Similar effects occur in contrasts between a gray and a strong chromatic color and between any two colors not precisely complementary: Each tends to shift the other toward its complement. El Greco used this effect powerfully in *The Stripping of Christ* at the Pinakothek in Munich. "He has sacrificed 'beauty of color' to veracity of mood." Van Gogh, underscoring his color effects with textures, avoids direct complementarities. His off-rhymes intensify the expressive effects when he contrasts blue-violet rather than violet with the yellows and oranges in his *Café at Evening* in the Kroller-Müller Museum, setting "both the yellow and the orange in vibration . The yellow-green of the walls and the dark green of the tree generate another simultaneous contrast with the interspersed spots and streaks of red."[62]

Saturation is a measure of color purity. Colors cool when diluted with white. "Violet is extremely sensitive to white. Whereas saturated dark violet has something menacing about it, violet lightened with white—lilac—has an agreeable, and quietly cheerful effect." Mixing with black "deprives yellow of its brilliant character, turning it into something sickly or insidiously poisonous. Its splendor is gone. . . . Violet is enhanced by black. . . . Blue is eclipsed." Mixing with gray tones down a color: "Delacroix hated gray in a painting, and avoided it as much as possible." Dilution with a complement yields a variety of tones, brought to life by the contrasts: "A color may appear vivid beside a dull tone, and dull beside a more vivid tone."[63] As Delacroix remarked, "I can paint the skin of Venus with mud if you let me surround it as I like."[64]

Colors appear equally prominent in an artwork or a scene when they balance not just in area but in brilliance. It was Goethe who first estimated the luminosity of diverse hues, assigning numerical values not far off from those calibrated by instruments today: Yellow is the most brilliant, violet the least; red and green are closer in brilliance to yellow; blue is not far from violet. Goethe gave yellow a brilliance of 9; violet, 3. So, as a rule of thumb, artists say it takes three times as much violet as yellow in a painting if one is not to overpower the other.[65]

Beyond the seven contrast effects, as Itten explains, when red, yellow, blue, green, violet, and orange are seen against a black ground, "the light yellow plainly appears to advance, while the violet lurks in the depth of the black background. All the other hues are intermediate between yellow and violet." A white background reverses the effect.[66] Josef Albers (1888–1976), who came to the Bauhaus in 1920 and taught there from 1925 until the Nazis closed the school in 1933, explored and exploited color advance and retreat in his series *Homage to the Square*.[67]

Contrasts underlie the emotive and semiotic effects that artists evoke by the interplay of colors. Itten sketches some of the expressive values:

> Yellow is the most light-giving of all hues. . . . It loses the trait the moment we shade it with gray, black, or violet. . . . Yellow is used in the sense of celestial light in Altdorfer's *Madonna and Child with Angels*. . . . Just as there is but one truth, so there is only one yellow. Adulterated truth is vitiated truth, untruth. So the expressions of diluted yellow are envy, betrayal, falseness, doubt, distrust and unreason. . . . Passionate physical love glows forth in red-orange; blue-red purple connotes spiritual love. Thus Charonton portrayed the Father and the Son in crimson robes. . . . From demonic, sinister red-orange on black, to sweet angelic pink, red can express all intermediate degrees between the infernal and the sublime. Only the ethereal, transparent, aerial is barred to it, for there blue reigns supreme. . . . Blue is a power like that of nature in winter. . . . In the atmosphere of the earth, blue appears from lightest azure to the deepest blue-black of the night sky. . . . When blue is dimmed, it falls into superstition, fear, grief and perdition, but always it points to the realm of the transcendental. . . . Green is the color of the vegetable kingdom. . . . Incar-

nate sentience puts forth green. . . . When luminous green is dulled by gray, a sense of sad decay easily results. . . . Orange . . . has solar luminosity. . . . Festive orange readily becomes proud external ostentation. Whitened, it quickly loses character; diluted with black, it declines into dull, taciturn and withered brown. By lightening brown, we obtain beige tones, engendering a warm, beneficent atmosphere in quiet, intimate interiors. As the antipode of yellow, or consciousness, violet is the color of the unconscious—mysterious, impressive and sometimes oppressive, now menacing, now encouraging, according to contrast. When violet is present in large areas it can be distinctly terrifying, particularly towards the purple. "A light of this kind, cast upon a landscape," says Goethe, "suggests the terrors of the end of the world."[68]

Science fiction illustrators and film makers have not neglected the possibilities.

Violet is the hue of piety, and when darkened and dulled, of dark superstition. Lurking catastrophe bursts forth from dark violet. Once it is lightened, when light and understanding illuminate dark piety, delicate and lovely tints enchant us. Chaos, death and exaltation in violet, solitude and dedication in blue-violet, divine love and spiritual dominion in red-violet—these, in few words, are some of the expressive values of the violet band.[69]

Itten tests his scheme against the emotive values artists assign colors and their complements.[70] Color semiotics underscore the active engagement of the mind and thus speak for the reality of the soul: Perception is synthetic and never isolated but constantly in touch with personal and shared experience.

Picking Out Objects

Only differences of color and light are projected onto the retina. Transforming the signals based on those contrasts into a living picture of the world is the work of the brain. From the thalamus to the occipital lobe and beyond, varied information must be integrated and appraised. Visual information, scientists now believe, is processed in dedicated subsystems using separate neural pathways. A dorsal "where/how" stream terminating in the parietal lobe processes information about location, movement, and speed. The neurons in this pathway actively track objects and help coordinate muscular movement with visual information. A ventral pathway, the "what" stream, allows us to interpret what we see, classing and identifying objects. Information from the occipital lobe follows this pathway to the temporal lobe, where neurons determine if an object is recognizable and categorize it if it is. Strong links with the limbic system and structures in the medial temporal lobe connect the ventral pathway to processes that support memory and give emotional resonance to the image. The appraisal and the feed itself are much affected by attention, mood, and aspects of the scene that seem salient. Some scientists believe the two streams remain discrete until an object is consciously made out; others posit earlier feedback between the two.[71]

As the Gestalt psychologists suspected, our brains parse objects using constancy and change in shapes, angles, and colors to differentiate figure from ground. Cues from the motion of our heads and eyes help us in tracking.[72] Quiet brainwork reliant on "shape primitives," and "perceptual concepts" learned by tireless experimentation in infancy, privileges simple structures and foregrounds object types, singling out features and changes that might matter. The old mechanistic models of a passive, agglutinative perception moving stepwise from sensa to complexity prove unreliable.[73] As Arnheim writes, still sensitive to the old idea of the passivity of perception:

the world of images does not simply imprint itself upon a faithfully sensitive organ. Rather, in looking at an object, we reach out for it. With an invisible finger we move through the space around us, go out to the distant places where things are found, touch them, catch them, scan their surfaces, trace their borders, explore their texture. Perceiving shapes is an eminently active occupation. . . . If vision is an active grasp, what does it take hold of? . . . If an observer intently examines an object, he finds his eyes well equipped to see minute detail. And yet, visual perception does not operate with the mechanical faithfulness of a camera, which records everything impartially: the whole set of tiny bits of shape and color constituting the eyes and mouth of the person posing for the photograph as well as the corner of the telephone protruding accidentally behind his or her head. . . . Seeing means grasping some outstanding features of objects—the blueness of the sky, the curve of the swan's neck, the rectangularity of the book, the sheen of a piece of metal, the straightness of the cigarette. A few simple lines and dots are readily accepted as "a face," not only by civilized Westerners, who may be suspected of having agreed among one another on such 'sign language,' but also by babies, savages, and animals. Köhler terrified his chimpanzees by showing them "most primitive stuffed toys" with black buttons for eyes. A clever caricaturist can create the speaking likeness of a person through a few well-chosen lines. We identify an acquaintance at long distance by nothing more than the most elementary proportions or motions.[74]

If things are not to merge into mere splotches, we need to make out edges, pick out properties, follow contours. In the 1960s J. Krauskopf had subjects view a red circle surrounded by a green disk. When he stopped the eye from following the inner contour of the surround,

> The astonishing result was that the inner red disk disappeared and was filled in by green to create the perception of a single large green disk! The improbable conclusion from such experiments is that the visual system . . . seems to work by detecting spatial and temporal structure: finding moving contours and other spatio-temporal changes in the stimulation it receives. From this primitive information it apparently fills in and otherwise constructs the visual experiences we have.[75]

Stereopsis

Seeing in depth is a formidable synthetic task, aided by cues of texture, scale, and shading, parallax, and feedback from the ciliary muscles as they adjust the lenses in our eyes. We use the seeming convergence of lines in the distance, of course, and the actual convergence of our eyes as we single out objects. But nothing contributes more to depth perception than our binocular vision. The brain achieves stereopsis by comparing every point where the overlapping images from our two eyes differ. The receptive fields of the bipolar cells are critical here, since some bipolar cells seem to be directionally responsive.

Susan Barry, a neurobiologist who teaches at Mount Holyoke had misaligned eyes from infancy, their competing signals too disparate to resolve: "for each neuron one or the other eye won out." As a result, she lost stereovision at an early age. Her eyes were straightened surgically for cosmetic reasons, but her brain could still not correlate the conflicting images.[76] Through youth and into her adulthood the prevailing medical wisdom was that by about age eight the neurons that might coordinate these images have lost that capacity. Developmental optometrists had for decades been using subtle but simple exercises to overcome the brain's penchant to suppress one discordant image or the other, or oscillate between the two. But disparities in training, culture, and authority between optometry and ophthalmology left this work largely unknown among physicians and typically unreported in medical textbooks.[77] The medical doctrine Barry had learned pronounced that she would never see things in depth.

David Hubel and Torsten Wiesel had discovered the binocular neurons and many other facets of visual processing. They won the Nobel Prize for their work in 1981. Covering an eye in very young animals, they found, induced marked brain preferences for the images from the good eye, even after the blindfold was removed. If the occlusion were switched to the other eye, the preference switched too—but only until a certain age. Severing the medial rectus muscle of one eye in very young kittens, they found in 1965 that hardly any neurons developed binocular capabilities. Many physicians inferred that the loss of stereopsis was fixed early in life.[78]

Fortunately for Dr. Barry, the brain is more flexible than that. Binocular neurons, as Hubel conjectured, are present from birth in the visual cortex. Evidently not all of Barry's had been lost. The animal experiments indicative of a critical period had honed in on neurons with a receptive field of just 5° but overlooked those critical for depth vision, which need far wider receptive fields for their images to overlap. The presence of such neurons was Susan Barry's window of opportunity. Just as an infant with normal eyesight actively experiments with things, essentially training the key neurons, she now had to train her vision as an adult. Guided by a dedicated developmental optometrist, she had to learn to use her eyes in tandem and train herself to stop suppressing the input of one eye or the other.

She had been compensating for her deficit for years, relying on parallax, differences in scale, and other cues to navigate, teach, and even drive. But as her therapy took hold she suddenly discovered how much she'd been missing. Her reports suggest the joy she felt as she realized the richness and depth, literally, brought to visual experience by the brain's active integration of dual images, translating the pictures painted by light on our two retinas into electrical sequences almost out of phase, as if two voices were singing in close harmony. It was a late winter day, and she was "in the early stages of gaining stereopsis," not yet fully trusting in the hope the therapists were holding out—

> I rushed out of the classroom building to grab a quick lunch, and I was startled by my view of falling snow. The large wet flakes were floating about me in a graceful three-dimensional dance. In the past the snowflakes appeared to fall in one plane slightly in front of me. Now I felt myself in the midst of the snowfall, among all the snowflakes. Overcome with happiness, I forgot all about lunch and stood quite still, completely mesmerized by the enveloping snow.[79]

Barry's epiphany showed her firsthand what V. S. Ramachandran and S. Blakeslee had meant in speaking of the irreplaceability of qualia—"the raw feel of sensations such as the subjective quality of 'pain' or 'red' or 'gnocchi with truffles.'"[80] The qualia here were not simple sensations but products of elaborate behind the scenes brainwork.

> When I first learned about stereopsis in college, I wondered if I could imagine this way of seeing. Now I had my answer. I could not. Stereopsis provides a distinctive, subjective sensation, a quale. . . . While I could infer indirectly a sense of depth through cues like perspective and shading, I could not synthesize stereoscopic depth from other visual attributes, such as color, position, form, or brightness. The sensation provided by stereopsis of empty space and things projecting or receding into that space is unique. . . .
>
> . . . I, like most other scientists, assumed that I had always obtained a good sense of depth through motion parallax. Then one day in the fall of 2005, I learned that I was mistaken. I had based this assumption on the erroneous premise that a strabismic sees the world like a person with normal vision who has simply closed one eye.
>
> On that fall day, I was taking my dog for a walk along our usual route. My schnauzer felt compelled to sniff every blade of grass, leaving me bored and impatient, swaying absentmindedly underneath a dense network of tree branches. While gazing up at the trees, I was startled to see the branches in layers of depth. I saw how the outer branches captured and enclosed a palpable volume of space into which the inner branches permeated. I could make sense of the whole intricate network. From that day to the present, I have always walked to work so I can pass under the trees and get this stunning sense of three dimensions.[81]

"I felt like I was immersed in a medium more substantial than air, a medium on which tree branches, flower blossoms, and pine needles floated." Was this the sense of air, she wondered, that Monet was reaching for when he said, "I want the unobtainable. Other artists paint a bridge, a house, a boat. . . . I want to paint the air which surrounds the bridge, the house, the boat"?[82]

Neuroplasticity was the key to Dr. Barry's new world:

> When I learned to see in stereoscopic depth, I realized that wiring must have changed in the visual cortex of my brain. . . . Changes in brain circuitry depend in part upon the growth of new connections, or synapses, between neurons and the elimination of old ones. But the fastest learning may result from changes in the strength of already existing connections.[83]

Depth vision came to Dr. Barry not by a fixed scenario but by her own active, well guided efforts. She would not have attained it had her visual cortex lacked all binocular neurons. Perceptually, as in every other way, we have to work with the bodies and brains we have. Hubel and Wiesel had shared their Nobel Prize with Roger Sperry, whose brilliant fish and frog experiments proved that eye-to-brain connections are hardwired. Neuroplasticity complements that story. With effort, intelligence, knowledge, and commitment, personal and professional, Barry was able to activate her binocular neurons and train them to work in tandem. Here the mind was not passive. Just as we must open our eyes to see the world around us, we can, in some measure, control *how* we see. The soul here—intellect and affect, desire and sociality—was working with the body, not to overcome its limits but to reach them.

Do blind persons have especially sharp hearing? The truth behind that bit of folk wisdom is neuroplasticity: The brain can map audible cues onto the visual cortex, giving hearing the kind of detail and directionality familiar in seeing.[84] Indeed, "Some blind children discover spontaneously how to use echolocation. Hand clapping, stamping the ground audibly with the feet, tapping the long cane produce sounds that blind children can use to detect their own distance from a wall and gaps in it."[85] So blind children can learn fencing, and sighted persons can train in swordsmanship blindfolded, enhancing their coordination and proprioception.

Neuroplasticity helps explain how blind persons can learn to recognize faces by touch, or read braille, skills that the sighted often find daunting. Formerly sighted persons have more trouble learning braille than the early blind, possibly because brain space is already allocated. Braille, researchers find, is often read dot by dot. Only proficient users read its letters as wholes. But when that does happen, it's by repurposing space in the auditory or visual cortex.[86] The cross-connections that help us coordinate signals from our different senses facilitate shifting tasks from one brain region to another, with new connections laid down by new patterns of use. Quite a variety of neuroplastic responses involve such remapping.

To ancient skeptics, refraction was just another sign of perceptual fallibility: The oar in the water looks broken. But to creative minds, refraction would mean a chance to grind glass into lenses that would correct fuzzy vision or allow the no longer naked eye to view microbes or the stars. Learning to hear with a cochlear implant, or overcoming aphasia after a stroke, call upon agency as well as neuroplasticity. Perception is no mere frailty, let alone a demonic deception. The senses do put us in touch with the world, not infallibly but impressively. Perception, active or augmented, belongs to our subjecthood. It empowers capabilities too glibly imagined only to hem in the self—as if the body were the enemy or prison of the soul rather than its vehicle and home.

Gestalten

Like colors, lines and curves are seen relationally. Hence many of the illusions that skeptics decry but artists and architects rely on. Since all animal species are products of evolution, Gestalt researchers reasoned, their neural processes must adapt them to deal with the world, including one another. Unintegrated sensa would be useless. So, "we do not see the world as an assemblage of dots (as in a pointillistic painting), but as extended areas and volumetric bodies."[87] We continually estimate sizes, shapes, positions, and distances. Pointillism, in fact, helps show how, as Hardin explains:

> Whereas the effect of contrast is to intensify large color differences and minimize small ones, the effect of assimilation is to minimize large color differences and intensify small ones. . . . Assimilation effects play a substantial role in the famous vibrant grays of Seurat's divisionist paintings. Adjacent red and green areas that subtend a relatively large angle at the eye vibrate against each other, but if they subtend a sufficiently small angle, they neutralize each other. . . . there is a point before they fuse optically with each other at which the areas of color both neutralize and vibrate against each other. This is the point (in the case of Seurat's *Les Poseuses* it is about six feet from the canvas) at which the lustrous gray—and the spreading effect—appears. Achromatic examples of the spreading effect may be found in any engraving, for example, the portrait of George Washington on a dollar bill. Shadows and variations in gray are rendered by fine black lines, so the darker areas have a higher line density, and the lighter areas a lower density. If Washington's likeness is viewed with some slight magnification the graying effect persists despite the fact that we see that the area consists solely of clearly distinguished black and white areas.[88]

Nature has its patterns, and so does perception. Bringing the two into registry is an achievement of the mind, a heritage of evolution. Perception favors order. The mind, Gestalt researchers found, works to organize the visual field into "effigies." The design principle they called *Prägnanz*, a word suggesting compact elegance, pregnancy with meaning, and, as Susanne Langer wrote, a "tendency to closure."[89] We feel that urge to complete a pattern when we tap our feet in time with the music or clap in syncopated cadence. *Prägnanz* is at play in theory choice as well. The elegance insight-ful theorists seek is not just fashion or familiarity. On the contrary, styles and fashions reflect aesthetic interests, caressing, pursuing (or flouting) per-ceptual biases as well as contextual allusions. For our ideas of order and intelligibility reflect all that life has taught us individually, as members of communities, and as a species.

Viewing an array of dots, Köhler observed, we tend to group them, giving meanings even to random patterns, much as ancient sky watchers grouped the stars in constellations, finding portents in arrays of stars now known to be many light years apart. Sometimes we look for images in the clouds or the flames in the fire, playing with our penchant for shaping what we see. More broadly, we may group items that are close together, or similar in size, shading, color, or trajectory.[90] Perceptually we use multiple cues to locate edges, follow surfaces, complete broken lines. "Straight lines, continuous contours, symmetrical shapes are ubiquitous properties of natural objects," Spillmann writes. "To make up for any stimulus occlusions or distortions, neuronal mechanisms may have evolved that strive to perceptually rectify crooked lines, fill in gaps, and complete patchy surfaces."[91] Vision paints a fuller picture than the images on the retina. "An incompletely drawn circle looks like a complete circle without a gap. . . . In a melody one may 'hear' by induction the regular beat from which a syncopated tone deviates."[92]

Distinguishing figure from ground was always critical for the survival of predators and prey. It's not about whether zebras are white with black stripes or black with white stripes. It's a matter of life and death on the veldt to dis-criminate grasses from lions in the dun-colored scene. It's because percep-tion interprets what we see and resolves ambiguities that we can make out stars in the sky and books on the shelf. We don't just see shifts in color or light. But we can be deceived. Sometimes we miss even what we're looking for, because the brain's rules to distinguish objects override surface appear-ances. The invisibility of an object in plain sight is a price we pay for our alacrity in picking out objects at all. That double-edged effect helps explain why camouflage works well, and where its limits lie.

We are primed to perceive things that make sense or seem natural or incongruous to us, using *Prägnanz* to parse objects and find boundaries.[93] Comparison is critical. Our perception sharpens some edges and dulls others, depending on what's nearby. Brilliant plumage makes a mallard drake easy to spot. Despite striking internal color contrasts in its plum-age, surface continuities, especially as it moves, clearly betray its form. The female blends into the reeds, its irregular tints obscuring the continuities and discontinuities that perception needs.[94] A monkey can track four to seven dots among a hundred, if they move coherently. But once stilled, the subset disappears into the background.[95] Prey and predators co-evolve in an ongoing arms race of forms and colorations. So does their behavior. Deer freeze instinctually on sensing a predator nearby, and the stalker holds still before its final spring.

Brain signals course both in and out, with plenty of feedback and inter-action. We don't see all the ninja work, any more than we see the tiny in-verted image on the retina. But the order and simplicity in what we do see is mind-made. Eyes, nerves, and brain collaborate. There's bottom-up infor-mation flow, from retina to cortex; top-down, from higher to lower cortical levels, all the way back to the movements of the eye itself, constantly scan-ning and readjusting, refreshing and renewing the signal; and lateral flow, within each of the six tiers of cortical cells, reconciling our variant views of the shapes and features of things, allowing us to frame coherent images—a feat that mere associative linkage of sense-data would be powerless to per-form.[96]

Perception, as Wolfgang Metzger explains, is integrated with our general awareness. So we perceive what medievals call the meanings or intentions of things:

> Although the difference between a glow of light and a patch of color cannot be conveyed by rays of light, this is even less possible for such attributes as the cheerfulness and the kindness of a person or the fury of a raging bull. . . . This holds not only for the adult, who has had the opportunity to accumulate expe-riences over many years, but also (and especially so) for the several-week-old neonate, who, when one smiles at it, also starts to smile. It is not helpful to say that it is an innate instinct to reply to a smile with a smile, because even for an instinct, the unsolved riddle remains as to how the smile of the other person ever reaches the baby if light rays do not carry it.[97]

"Smile" is not found in the optic nerve. Nor will it do, Metzer writes, to ap-peal to some mysterious sixth sense. We don't know the bull means business by echoing its emotion, or recognize that it's charging because we've been charged by bulls before. Nor does the bull's growing image in our visual field by itself betoken danger. Metzger's challenge here echoes Avicenna's thoughts of a thousand years before:

> We find in our perceptions meanings that are not sensed, either because such intentions are not such as to be sensed or because they are sensed but not when the judgment is made. Not an object of sensation, for example, are the

mortal danger, hostility, and threat the sheep apprehends in the shape of the wolf, or any threat that might lead it to bolt, and the welcome intention it perceives in the shepherd, or any approach it finds friendly and familiar. Such intentions are apprehended by the animal soul, although the senses bear no hint of them. They must be grasped by some other faculty. Call it presentiment (*wahm*). As for those that are sensory, we see something golden and take it to be honey, and thus sweet. But that's not what the senses tell us immediately. Sweetness can be sensed, but it's not what we're perceiving now. We anticipate sweetness, but we're not tasting it now. We've just made a judgment about it that might actually be mistaken.[98]

The faculty psychology here serves mainly as a tool of analysis, differentiating functions: Intentions are not what the senses apprehend. Sight at its barest, as Metzger stresses, registers only light differences. But animals wouldn't last long if dead to intentions. Infants need to find the breast. Horses must recognize their food as food and distinguish onions from clover. Instinct is relevant, but perception comes first, if only to rouse the instincts. Reasoning is not what's at work here, and sheer sensations aren't up to the task. But patterns perceived by an integrated and active sensibility can be invested with the kind of significance that survival demands.

It took an art historian, Metzger writes, to alert psychologists to the mood or intent a stance might convey. This was no deep mystery. There's a reason, after all, why both emotional and bodily postures are called attitudes. The two are connected: "people who are really angry can, in a sort of feedback loop, pull themselves even more deeply into their anger by roaring and stomping."[99] Method actors know that. Darwin too observed that the gestures and expressions that evince an emotion can elicit or intensify it. Portrait painters exploit that fact to convey something of a sitter's character, and Rembrandt practiced portraying diverse emotions by sketching *tronies*, faces evincing a variety of emotions. Patterns and postures, facial expressions and tones of voice, reveal the linkage of perceptions to meanings. It's not as if smiles or frowns were abstractions gleaned from more elemental data.

Christian von Ehrenfels (1859–1932) was the art historian, a student of the philosophers Franz Brentano and Alexius Meinong. Inspired by ideas from Goethe and Ernst Mach, the utopian Ehrenfels introduced the term *Gestalt* in his 1890 work *Über Gestaltqualitäten* (On pattern qualities). He found a favorite case in our ability to recognize a melody in a new key. Lockean sensations don't help much here. What we recognize is not notes heard before but a pattern. Buildings, bracelets, or cars may look attractive or ugly, the woods may look threatening or inviting. Music may sound joyous, somber, or ominous. Light waves and air oscillations don't explain our responses. But perception is rarely a matter of sensation alone. We link up what we sense with the matter of memory, convention, and yes, even instinct. Context and experience assign meanings to appearances. The face we see, the wall or arch, the earring, the melody heard for the first time, may resonate, Metzger says, with our inmost nature—or, his translators propose, updating his language, as though our responses were "innate or hard-wired."[100]

> Individual points of a seen image, except for their location, exhibit *only three properties: brightness, hue,* and *degree of saturation.* . . . Yet at the same time we admit that the *totality* of these same points may possess *properties of an entirely different kind,* for which there is no counterpart in the properties of light rays, properties such as taut, smooth, slim, cheerful, graceful, stern, or proud. . . . Even physicists unhesitatingly ascribe properties to atoms that they deny to their components. . . . And this is repeated in the relation of the molecule to the individual atoms of which it is composed.[101]

Emergence in this case, the logical counterpart of reduction, is the work of the mind, framing connections, responding to the face of an enemy or friend, a garden, beach, or pool. Few any longer think perception passive. So in stressing perceptual activity we may seem to be beating a dead horse. But action and efficacy are the clearest markers of reality: We see souls at work whenever we confront the unity and coherence of visual perception.

Face recognition is a paradigm of the mind's visual work. As Christopher Mole writes, "One can recognize a large number of faces viewed at various angles and in various lights, and one can recognize them beneath a wide range of hats, spectacles, false noses, and so on." The example calls to mind Peter Sellers's wild and hopeless disguises when Inspector Clouseau tries to work undercover:

> The invariances which one exploits in face recognition are at such a high level of description that if one were trying to work out how it was done given a moment-by-moment mathematical description of the retinal array, it might well appear impossible. There surely is no simple pattern of retinal stimulation that always and only occurs when I see a face as being my brother's. My ability to recognize him is not a matter of my being triggered by some simple property of the array he projects to my retina.[102]

There is no simple signal behind Mole's recognizing his brother. There are confirming and disconfirming signs, of course. But we rarely see each other in just the same light, at just the same angle, with just the same facial expression, etc. And friends typically lack the "attributes" medieval painters used to label the saints and martyrs in their altarpieces. Yet we do recognize faces. The prosopagnosia that some of us (including the brain scientist Oliver Sacks and the portrait artist Chuck Close) suffer from suggest how much integrative work facial recognition demands. It can't be done by simply matching "stimuli." Experience, after all, doesn't offer neatly ordered stimuli. The constants we count on to make sense of what we see and with whom we're having the pleasure are products of our own minds—not sheer figments of imagination, but not untouched by its paintbox. Mole compares the sense of touch:

> A well trained boy scout can recognize granny knots, reef knots, and sheet bends by touch alone, but the features that he uses when making these discriminations would be extremely hard to recover from a moment-by-moment presentation of the pressure that each knot exerts on his fingertips. There is certainly no profile of finger-tip pressures that is always or only associated with granny knots.[103]

Feeling the differences among standard knots is a far simpler task than recognizing a friend. But, as the tenth-century Brethren of Purity observed, lambs can find their dams just hours after birth: "In a flock of sheep and ewes a great number may give birth in a single night. Then in the morning they're driven out to pasture, not to return until nightfall. Yet when the young, a hundred or more, are released, each is seen to find its dam, without any doubt by the mother or confusion by the young."[104] The lambs probably rely on scent; and the scouts in Mole's example, on touch. But regardless of the sense modality, a high degree of active integration is called for in any act of perceptual recognition. And the capabilities a dog or a horse uses to recognize its master, or a lamb to find its dam, presage the integrative strengths that humans beings use in recognizing one another's faces—or following a conversation in a crowded space.

Hearing

We've spoken of the need to distinguish signal from noise. The metaphor comes from electronics, but its literal sense relates to hearing. Here, as in seeing, we actively search for and construct meaning. Sounds mingle, but the brain labors to keep the world from falling into a muddled roar. The crash of waves or thunder, a child's voice, the crunch of gravel in the driveway—we differentiate thousands of sounds. Hearing pursues events rather than objects. So it's more time-bound than seeing: A sound begins and ends. A similar sound might occur, but no sound recurs. With sight, touch, and taste, we may know what we're sensing as we sense it, or in advance, with help from the other senses. But sounds often reach us ahead of other signals, and are identified only after they have been heard. Roger Scruton writes,

> Our ears are presented at every moment with an enormous perceptual task, which is to group sounds together in such a way as to make sense of them. . . . In certain applications, this search for the good *Gestalt* can be explained as the evolutionary epistemologist would explain it, namely as a first step towards tracing a sound to its cause. However, it differs in a crucial respect. . . . Suppose you are looking at a dot-picture, and unable to make out the figure that the dots compose. And suppose that suddenly the figure "dawns" on you, and there, before you, in the unseen lines that join the dots together, is the outline of a face. . . . The perceptual *Gestalt* shares properties such as shape, size, and color with its object. . . . Auditory scene analysis is quite unlike that. Streams are not described or recognized through properties that could be exhibited by the physical events that produce them. Sounds that succeed each other on the pitch continuum seem to "flow" along the continuum; tones an octave apart are heard as parts of a single tone, as when a congregation sings a hymn in what sounds like unison.[105]

Hearing, like seeing, is an achievement. But rather than edges we follow an auditory thread, a stream, as Scruton calls it. Perceptual psychologists label our ability to pursue a strand of meaning in a welter of sound the "cocktail party effect."[106] We can carry on a conversation in a crowded room or pick out familiar voices in a sea of noise. Like the answering calls of birds in the rain forest, that suggests what the brain does for hearing. Chiefly in the temporal lobe, sound frequencies are broken down and reconstructed. We distinguish voices, hear what our dinner partner is saying, and ignore the couples nearby. The sounds reaching our ears don't come labeled by source. Even prominent "target signals" may be masked by noise. Complexity increases as the crowd grows. Our remarkable ability to tune out distractions rests on our capacity to trace the rhythms and harmonics of one voice, filling in what we can't hear, much as we fill in visual contours. Distinctive speech patterns, phonetic and syntactical, help us keep on track. Our binaural hearing orients us toward one voice. Visual signs help too. So we watch for cues, offering and eliciting gestures and expressions that confirm or correct an impression.[107] Mathematicians, using tensor analysis, have modeled how the brain may meet the challenge, and computer engineers have built multichannel systems that can track a chosen signal in a crowded room. But we don't yet know just how human brains handle the cocktail party problem. Clearly pattern recognition is essential—itself very much a matter of pattern *formation*:

> In hearing speech sounds, we are presented with a continuous sound stream with no gaps indicating the boundaries between words that we find in written language. If there were gaps between words in human speech, it would sound unnatural and hard to follow. . . . In fact, much of what we supposedly "hear" in the speech signal makes no public appearance at all. Word boundaries, non-overlapping syllables, restored phonemes; none of these items is present in the speech signal, and yet all are perceived as being there. Somehow the mind imposes such items on the sound stream presented to us.[108]

Our hearing is attuned to our needs as language users. The brain regions lighting up in functional MRIs at the sound of phonemes are not the ones active when nonsense syllables are heard. We process spoken words swiftly and efficiently and filter out extraneous sounds, much as our vision distinguishes figure from ground. In a language we don't know, the words fly by too fast to seem intelligible, reflecting the brain's privileged handling of familiar language. Foreign streams of speech are barely distinguishable as words at all. Hence the pejorative names—Babel, *barbaros*, *ᶜajam*—mocking inarticulate jabber. We need to know a language even to hear it properly.

The pattern recognition needed for linguistic comprehension relies on top-down constructive work centered in the left cerebral hemisphere, producing phoneme constancy—like the color constancy of visual perception. That's critical in helping us disentangle and disambiguate words. Some of the acoustic signal, Barry Smith explains, is discarded "in the process of chunking, ordering, and reducing." And crucial content is added.[109] Meanings are "read into" sounds, not "read off" from them.[110]

Not long after World War II, efforts were made to build a reading machine to help veterans blinded in the war. The limited technology of the day precluded building an actual reading machine. But it was hoped that a machine could be made that would make some distinctive sound for each letter of the alphabet, or each phoneme. The project failed:

> The listener's ears just couldn't keep up. If one's reading machine was making its sounds at a pace that was anything like the pace at which our mouths make sounds when we speak, then it was making sounds at a rate that was

far too fast for the listener to resolve. If the sounds were given slowly enough for the listener to resolve them, then they came far too slowly to effectively communicate a text.[111]

As Alvin Liberman, one of the project researchers, saw, "Only the sounds of speech are efficient vehicles of phonetic structures; no other sounds, no matter how artfully contrived, will work better than about one tenth as well."[112] Once again, what the experience revealed is that perception clearly does not mean jamming together atomic impressions in the cyclotron of sensory associations. Wherever we find perceptual constancy, we're encountering the mind at work.

We recognize familiar voices with far more sensitivity than Mole's boy scout had in his fingers. Most of us can distinguish thousands of voices—of friends, family, acquaintances, celebrities—often out of context and without supporting cues. And we can tell when a voice expresses anger or disappointment, pleasure or excitement, irony or humor, drama, or mockery of another voice. Like faces seen in different lights, Robert Remez and J. D. Trout explain, every utterance is unique in its acoustic effects and surround.[113] So even familiar voices present a challenge. Teasing out a message, C. F. Hockett says, is like piecing together the images from Easter eggs of all sizes and designs after the raw eggs have been crushed in a wringer and emerged in a stream of broken and whole yolks, smeared whites, and bits of painted shell.[114] We readily hear LINT BRUSH and BUTT KICKER, even when the sounds uttered were LIMP BRUSH and BUCK KICKER.[115] Our brains accommodate to a wide array of voices and idiolects, allowing for accents, interruptions, noises off, swallowed syllables and fading words. Working memory is critical here: "very little of the auditory sensory effect of speech is left 100 ms after a wavefront strikes an eardrum, and nothing is left in 400 ms"[116]—less than half a second.

The sounds that reach our ears can be fed into a computer, but no program, as yet, hears human voices with the nuance that human hearing routinely finds, generating perceptual constancy despite the variations caused by illness, exhaustion, stress, or wind. The hurdles may slow us down, but they don't block comprehension. Idiosyncrasies that might send a computer into a dither become signature notes. Contexts prompt us to the gist of unfamiliar expressions. As clarity wavers, and as accents and intonations shift or speech patterns shuffle and dance, we still make out words and extract meaning. It helps that unlike speech recognition software we can *understand* what we hear and anticipate a friend's next words. Today's voice reading machines rely on spectral analysis and follow up with a pattern-tagging algorithm. So they can manage only preprogrammed sounds. They're slowed by needing to compare numerous stored versions with each word uttered, and stymied by slight variations that human hearing parses effortlessly.

There's a lesson in our experience here beyond the obvious power of our active interpretive capabilities. Reliance on algorithms and magazines of anticipated sound bites makes even cutting edge software somewhat clunky: The larger the armory the more time spent searching and comparing. Even the best algorithms aren't flexible enough. Often they rely on hand-tailored domain-specific glossaries. The software is improving, but the designers are turning increasingly not just to ever nimbler algorithms but to seeking somehow to simulate human hearing, which is not algorithmic at heart but recursive, constantly testing hypotheses against an open, ever expanding repertoire of hints and signals.

The fiction of acoustically invariant phonemes persisted, Remez and Trout explain, long after vocal sense-data were discredited in laboratory experiments and spectrograms of the highly varied forms of natural speech.[117] The demands of a rigid reductionism kept the dogma alive, *expecting* audible sense to coalesce from atomistic elements serially received and mechanically linked, without contextual cues or relational patterns. Against the notion that we hear each other's speech by popping invariant phonemes into the slots experience has drilled for them, Remez and Trout describe how deaf children learn to hear with a cochlear implant: The implant does not replicate sounds as others hear them. The spread of current along the cochlea "creates a kind of frequency blur" sometimes as wide as "the difference between the first two notes of 'Greensleeves' or the 'Star Spangled Banner'"—a minor third musically speaking. Intervals that large are not resolved by the brain's normal rectifying process. If the shifts were ironed out, pitch differences would become indiscernible. Besides, "the electrode does not penetrate to the apex of the cochlea, and is never proximate to the basilar region of lowest frequency sensitivity." Users with prior experience of speech compare the sounds their implants yield to "munchkin speech." But they adjust, as we all do to varied speech patterns. Voices may sound high pitched and reedy, but the words are not hard to follow.[118] Listeners, in fact, can understand speech artificially generated from a few pure tones that no human voice can produce.[119] Even noises of varying amplitude can simulate intelligible (if raspy) speech.[120] Pressing to absurdity the notion of uniform vocalic signals, Remez and Trout add that intelligible speech surrogates can be generated from the sound of a jazz band or a construction site—trumpets, trombones, saxophones, piano, bass, and drums, or saw, cement mixer, bulldozers, backhoes, shovels, loaders, fork lifts, and cranes.[121] The simulation, as Liberman would appreciate, is hardly optimal. But meanings remain intelligible.

> The key is the use of distinctive oppositions. Talker and listener alike share the small set of phonemes, and though these constituents index words, neither production nor perception must be faithful in producing the segments in their canonical form. A talker must merely indicate at any juncture which of the possible phoneme contrasts is intended. . . . This freedom to indicate rather than to replicate the articulatory choreography specific to a word licenses the talker's use of a wide expressive range.[122]

The role of contrasts helps reveal what is distinctive about hearing speech. "The ability to discriminate one pitch from another," Mole explains, "changes smoothly as a function of the initial pitch. The same is true for volume and timbre." There's no sharp division at which one tone is markedly better discriminated. Not so for speech. In distinguishing /pa/ from /ba/, say, what matters is voice onset time (VOT), the moment in the release of air built up between the lips when the vocal chords begin to vibrate. Here there is no smooth curve plotting discernible differences but a sharp discontinuity where hearers sense very slight differences.

> We don't hear a sequence of /ba/s gently sloping off into penumbral cases which gradually become recognizable as /pa/s. Instead, the first half of the spectrum is all heard as more or less the same /ba/ sound, and the second half of the spectrum is all heard as more or less the same /pa/ sound, and there is a narrow band in the middle of the spectrum, when VOT is around 26.8 ms, where subjects differ as to how they hear the sound. At this transition point subjects can recognize very slight variations in VOT. . . . The difference between a syllable with VOT of 26.8 ms and a syllable with VOT of 36.8 ms sounds like a really big difference, whereas a difference of the same objective magnitude, between, say, VOT of 30 ms and of 40 ms sounds like a very slight difference.[123]

With color, Mole notes, "we perceive two reds as more similar than a red and a yellow, even though the objective difference between the wavelengths may be the same."[124] So semaphore flags use reds and yellows and don't count on the differences between two reds. Languages exploit similar natural contrasts, but selectively: Infants hear all the categorical sound differences found in natural languages, but each language uses its own distinctive subset in making semantical distinctions. Sensitivity to the unused contrasts is lost:

"Japanese speakers *don't* hear the shift from /l/ to /r/ categorically," the way English speakers do, where the contrast marks the difference, say, between 'loom' and 'room.'[125]

Bible readers will remember the story in Judges 12 of Jephtah's men testing Ephraimite infiltrators with the word *shibbolet* (sheaf), knowing it was unpronounceable in the dialect of these tribal adversaries, much as American soldiers in World War II used *lollapalooza* as a password, expecting Japanese troops to have trouble with the *l*s in a colloquial word not likely to have been practiced in language classes. But the G.I.s were probably well advised to use caution. Although language use does attune our neurons to our mother tongue, neuroplasticity allows adults to regain their sensitivity to disused phonetic contrasts with as little as an hour's training.

Just as hearing and touch aid our vision when the view is limited or the scene is dark, our eyes help our ears to an auditory Gestalt, as the so called McGurk effect makes clear. Subjects listening to a recorded voice repeatedly saying /ba/ heard the syllable clearly, but if they listened while watching a video of a person saying /ga/ they heard /da/, a phonetic middle between /ba/ and /ga/.[126] With recordings doctored to remove from the sound in the headphone the "initial boost of acoustic energy" that differentiates /ba/ from /ga/, the listeners couldn't tell just which they were hearing. Supplying *to the other headphone* that telltale burst of energy, which by itself sounds like a little non-linguistic chirp, allowed the subjects readily to discriminate the sounds: Their brains had reassembled the phoneme from the severed pieces.[127]

Sounds in general are first addressed cerebrally in the primary auditory cortex (A1) of the temporal lobe, where we assay volume and pitch. Like harp strings or organ pipes, the neurons here form a array, those most sensitive to low frequencies at one end, those best attuned to high frequencies at the other. The brain's pitch map, then, like the color map of the visual cortex, is hardly a tabula rasa.

Musical structure, like language, evokes more integrated attention. We need the frontal cortex, parietal cortex, and cerebellum to follow a simple beat or rhythm; the cerebral cortex, as well, for trickier rhythms. "Rhythmic grouping," Scruton writes, "is a *Gestalt* phenomenon. . . . It relies on an underlying temporal measure which it does not generate. . . . The grouping of sounds is not dictated by their real relations, but is completed by us, in an act that is subject to the will."[128]

In hearing tonal and melodic patterns we use the prefrontal cortex, cerebellum, and multiple areas of the temporal lobes.[129] Music, then, is not as sheerly sensuous as Kant supposed. In listening to it we engage three of the four lobes of the brain—frontal, parietal, and temporal. Some music even arouses the visual cortex in the occipital lobe, as listeners call up visual images responding to what they hear.

The temporal lobes hold the present memory of tonal patterns, letting us hear arpeggios, and melodic phrases and themes. So, like language, we hear music in coherent sequences, not disjointed blasts of sound. Cerebral language centers light up in fMRIs when musically trained persons listen to music. The electrical potentials characteristic of syntax processing look indistinguishable overall when such subjects follow a musical composition or a prose text of comparable complexity. Patients who have lost their syntactical capacity through trauma to the brain lose their ability to follow musical structure as well.[130] We can hear music as music, then, because memory works with imagination, relating the passing moments as though they were laid out before us.[131] Perceptual constancy assists:

> When music is performed, many notes are played out of tune (the wavering voices of singers are particularly inaccurate). But we don't hear varying performances as different pieces, . . . we focus on our own categorization of sounds. This suggests that even our "immediate experience" of music has less to do with the raw sensation of sounds arriving from the external world than with an awareness of our minds at work interpreting those sounds.[132]

Glitches may disappear, but patterns persist. We integrate what we hold in the buffer of working memory with our longer-term memories and anticipations of how patterns might be resolved. Just as we hold a sentence together, using our implicit linguistic knowledge and contextual understanding of a speaker's intent, in music we shape what we hear even as we color it with our own emotional responses.

So, beyond its syntax, music has a semantics, which, like that of speech, bears emotional overtones assigned by memory and convention, or (especially in music) wrought by our somatic and empathic responsiveness. In music, as compared with language, syntax all but changes places with semantics, form taking on the prominence that language more typically assigns to meaning, perspicuity growing more active in the play of forms as ambiguity creates openings for revery and response.

Time is the medium music sculpts and paints. Hence the felt immediacy of music. The rhythms of speech and breathing, walking, running, marching, or dancing connect what we hear to the sensuous footings of emotion, making music expressive and evocative. As with color, personal and shared experience modulate these connections, giving public and private meanings

to musical form and matter. We connect sound with sound to build structures, sometimes quite elaborate, sometimes echoing or adding filigree or
harmony, or even mockery, to what we hear.

Even the most evocative music, as Anthony Storr explains, draws its
power not straight from a composer's emotions but from the encoding of
feelings in a language of timing and tone. Rather than simply pour out a
composer's emotions, music seeks to communicate how a composer makes
sense of those feelings in structures that transform them expressively into
art.[133] That requires a hearer as well as a performer, responding to the patterns of sound in which emotions and ideas are encoded.

In a well loved passage from the finale of the Sibelius Violin Concerto,
Scruton (or the musical adept he imagines as his ideal reader) can hear "the
quavers either trailing from or leading to the crotchets." Perception, feeding
expectations, projects patterns of pitch, intensity, timbre, texture, harmony,
and rhythm. The opening theme of Rachmaninov's Second Piano Concerto,
Scruton writes, is introduced by passages that ready us to be led into "a new
region of the melody." We don't need loudness or timbre to highlight a
motif. A quiet phrase can command attention: "The musical *Gestalt* stands
out in something like the way that a configuration stands out in a drawing
or puzzle picture."[134]

That effect is critical in counterpoint. In the *Musical Offering*, "the or-
chestration compels you to hear Bach's melodic line as *background*." But
in the canon of the Goldberg Variations, "a melody emerges from two or
more voices which interweave." So "the melodic *Gestalt* emerges only for the
person who gives equal weight to the voices which create it and who therefore hears three simultaneous movements in the melodic foreground: the
two upper voices, and their melodic synthesis."[135] That synthesis puts the listener in conversation with the composer, conductor, and performers, mind
to mind and soul to soul.

In their essay on music, the Brethren of Purity speak to the sense of its
immediacy: "Every craft," they write, "takes physical things as its matter and
gives them a new shape."

Music is the exception. Here spiritual substances, the listeners' souls, are the
matter worked up; and the effects too are spiritual. For musical strains—
melodies and tones—affect the soul much as a craftsman's art affects his
materials: Melodies and tones may stir our souls to backbreaking labor or
tedious industry. They may spur us on and strengthen our resolve in arduous
tasks that exhaust the body and drain our spirits and our means. Such are
the martial strains that urge men on in the battle's fray. . . . Other strains and

melodies may soothe the storm of anger, dissolve rancor, foster amity and reconciliation. . . . Still others may shift a soul from mood to mood and turn one's disposition to its opposite. . . . Music, then, can affect the souls of those who hear it in varied ways, much as a craftsman's art can alter the materials he works with. That is why all human nations use it—and even many animals as well. One can see its impact on the soul from its use in times of joy and celebration—parties, feasts, and weddings—and in times of grief and mourning, loss and disaster, in houses of worship, on festal and market days, in households, on the road and in town, in labor and at rest, in royal courts and commoners' homes. Men and women, the young and the old, the learned and the ignorant, artisans, merchants, and folk of every class employ it.[136]

The Brethren know, of course, that we hear with our ears (and our brains, as they stress) They also know that music is made with instruments and that sounds are vibrations spreading like waves through the air in all directions, like a glassblower's glass, they say. Both bodily organs and musical instruments are called tools in Arabic. Neither is the musician's raw material. The chief impact of music, as the Brethren stress, is not on the instrument or the air but on the soul. It comes from patterns resonant with meaning, native or acquired.

Western, tonal music, Leonard Bernstein wrote, in a way epitomizes the natural order—resonating, as it were, to the music of the spheres. But, *pace* Bernstein—and Pythagoras—just as the "sound of the sea" heard in a seashell is actually the echo of our own blood coursing through blood vessels in our ears, the music we love answers more closely to our internal order and the way minds and bodies relate, not just to sound but to time, informing, teasing, soothing, sating, shocking, or surprising the expectations that patterns in sound elicit.

Smelling

"When I am queen of the universe," Tania Sanchez writes, "the epithets 'the most primitive sense' and 'the most mysterious sense' will be banned from all writing on smell." Striking a blow against mystagoguery, she continues: "as with all of the work of evolutionary psychologists, the conclusions that support our desires and reinforce our prejudices are those of which we should be most wary."

Skim the shelves of any bookstore nonfiction section to see a large selection of fiction: pop psychology books assuring us that, since we're no better than the average dog . . . all our behavior is nothing but the basest animal instincts in different dress, that men will always be peacocks in full strut looking to distribute their genetic material as widely as possible, and that women will always be gregarious hens pecking at each other to attract the alpha male. . . . This point of view never cost a psychologist his or her job or interfered with book sales, and offers the irresistible premise that biology releases us from the responsibility to make choices. Pop psychologists love smell. Smell is supposedly about sex and deeply buried memory, a sense that bypasses the rational mind, thwarts all efforts of language to describe it, and reaches sneaky neural wiring directly into regions beyond thought—for example, forcing you to be sexually attracted to or threatened by the perspiration of basketball players or generating forceful hallucinations of childhood triggered by smells of floor wax. It's the fondest hope of every perfume firm that the psychologists should be right, and that human beings should be sniffing each other to say hello and see who's been where and with whom. Psychology is supposed to be a science, and science makes profits predictable.[137]

Insects have olfactory receptors on their antennae, palps, legs, and other organs. But humans smell only with the nose. Mammals average about a thousand types of olfactory receptors, developed at the direction of corresponding genes—some 3 percent of the genome. Mice have about 1,300 of these genes, about 1,100 active. But in humans all but about 350 of the thousand such genes we inherit from our evolutionary ancestors have gone dead. Smell has diminished in importance for us. We rely more on sight, hearing, and inference. Our olfactory epithelium occupies about 1.6 square inches. In some dogs the surface area is seventeen times that and roughly a hundred times as densely innervated. A rabbit has some 100 million olfactory receptors; a dog, 220 million; humans, only 5 or 6 million, in two small patches of yellowish cells high up in the nasal passages.

Clearly we don't smell as well as dogs can. But we aren't poor smellers. In tests of olfactory sensitivity, Gordon Shepherd notes, "humans outperform the most sensitive measuring instruments such as the gas chromatograph."[138] Dogs outsniff humans in detecting aliphatic molecules. But these include fatty compounds important in a canine diet. We humans notice longer chain compounds first, like aromatics with benzene rings. Vanillin is one example, in natural vanilla. Benzene itself is another, first isolated by Michael Faraday in 1825, highly flammable and carcinogenic, but sweet smelling. The resonant double and single bonds of the hydrogen and carbon atoms in the benzene ring are thought to produce the aromatic qualities in the many compounds that contain it.

We humans may not need the olfactory quiver that other animals have, Shepherd speculates, since ground dwelling animals have convoluted respiratory membranes that clean, warm, and humidify the air they breathe, guarding against infection, but perhaps masking odors. Our ancestors lost such filters long ago. Bipedalism took us off the ground. So we need no long snout; it would only impede our binocular vision.[139] But it seems most likely that other species simply followed their own evolutionary path, one that made olfaction their keenest instrument in trying to solve the mysteries they face—as many a dog or cat owner has noticed.

Besides the main olfactory system, sensitive to volatile odorants, most mammals and reptiles have an accessory system sensitive to fluids like the pheromones that powerfully influence animal behavior. The role of scents as insect sexual attractants was first hypothesized in the 1870s. Adolf Butenandt in 1959 first isolated a pheromone, from female silk moth secretions, winning a Nobel Prize. But, despite many an urban myth, pheromones play a slight role at most in human behavior. The genes that code for the vomeronasal organ responsive to pheromones seems to have been lost to our primate ancestors around the time they gained color vision. With the sight brain as its base, human reasoning advanced as the smell brain lost prominence. When human consciousness begat thought and deliberation and created language and culture, instinct-driven behavior became not just less relevant but downright unhelpful.

Human olfaction takes two directions, orthonasal and retronasal: the former, for sniffing odorants in the air; the latter contributing the critical olfactory component of flavors, activated as we exhale while eating and integrated with tastes proper by the brain. Humans can distinguish some 10,000 odors, some in concentrations as low as a few parts per trillion. That's possible with our limited variety of receptor types since the cells work in tandem, their output refined, integrated, and interpreted in the brain. Each type responds to a specific chemical family, and each chemical type may bind to a variety of receptors. So one odorant can have quite an elaborate odor profile. The indole group, for example, which includes the scents of orange blossoms, jasmine, coal tar, pineapple, mammalian excrement, and dozens of other substances, is handled by several types of receptors, each type specializing in specific radicals. In orange blossoms, say, one smells their distinctive indole along with the citric acid characteristic of oranges— and a hint of polyurethane.

Odorant molecules bind at specific receptor sites like a key in a lock, if perhaps a little loosely, like a skeleton key. Their docking sets off a signal cascade as the receptor depolarizes, triggering action potentials in the olfactory nerve. At its far end, that nerve thickens to form the olfactory bulb, at whose surface some ten million neurons from the two nares converge with neurons called glomeruli. Several thousand neurons at any given moment may be conveying the same or related signals to glomeruli attuned to specific receptors. Grouped, like singers in a choir, by the family of odorants to which their receptors preferentially respond, the glomeruli amplify and modulate the incoming signals, announcing their sequence and affinities to the brain's olfactory cortex by way of the mitral cells.

Sharing parts of the temporal and frontal lobes, the olfactory or piriform cortex connects intimately with the limbic system, which includes the amygdala, hippocampus, and entorhinal cortex. The piriform cortex links parts of the limbic system to the neocortex, allowing much recursive communication between these "primitive" and "higher" brain regions. The limbic system can generate intense, immediate responses of fear and panic, disgust and delight. Here learning can take the form of classical conditioned reflexes like those that Pavlov studied. But the piriform cortex also projects to the thalamus and on to the orbitofrontal lobes. Its workings are not yet fully understood, but its location, close to brain systems that modulate emotional memory, may help explain how odors can establish or revive long-term memories of far greater depth and complexity than any merely mechanical response. Olfaction is the only sense not first mediated by the thalamus—a hint of its high value as a tocsin. Our responses, even to the first whiff of an odor, reflect the potency of limbic circuits, among the oldest cortical pathways to evolve. But even our gut responses to an odor are often learned. And, like auditory sensations, scents are dismantled and reconstructed by the brain, not passively received, let alone cut off from memory and understanding.

Odors are typically complex, so multidirectional information flow is critical. Top-down signals from the cortex edit olfactory messages, helping us identify and source a scent, moderate our responses, and suppress perception of persistent odors. Lucretius tells of scents "dying away in the air" (De Rerum Natura 4.692–93). But it's not there that a scent first dies, but in our awareness. There's "adaptation" in olfaction, as in vision: The brain kills a signal soon after it's noted, making way for rapid response to new cues in the olfactory landscape.

The olfactory cortex compares glomerular signal patterns against a template of known scents. So unfamiliar scents may be hard to make out at first. But new odors are quickly learned and added to the template. Context and experience tellingly influence response. Americans find wintergreen pleasant, perhaps because it reminds them of candy. But many Britishers dislike the scent, which may remind them of arthritis salves. In one experiment students reversed their appraisals of patchouli, menthol, and a mixture of isovaleric and butyric acids after a week's interval, depending on whether they'd been told the scents were "musty basement," "chest medicine," or "vomit," rather than "parmesan cheese," "incense," or "breath mint."[140] Perception here was clearly an integrated experience, fraught with meaning, even if the meanings were rather visceral.

Experience tellingly affects our olfactory preferences. Food poisoning by meat gone bad that was seasoned, say, with coriander may provoke a lifelong loathing for that spice, nausea at its mere aroma. The aversion circuits of the mammalian amygdala are powerfully associative and suppressed, if at all, only partially and with real effort. In societies where the scent of excrement is everpresent, the odor is less likely to trigger immediate revulsion than outsiders might expect. Few smells are universally hated, as military researchers trying to weaponize a stench have found. Even the scent of decaying meat finds favor in some places. In East Asia, especially Japan, many cheeses prized in Europe provoke aversion—as does Asian "stinky tofu" among Europeans.[141] Such odors are perhaps an acquired taste, cultivated by the frisson of teasing one's sensibilities with a mix of irritating and ingratiating messages. Scent, clearly, is an integrated experience, not an isolated and atomic sensation.

The working genes that code for olfactory receptors vary slightly from person to person. So responses to a scent may vary. But there are limits. Odorants, after all, can affect our thermoreceptors, pain receptors, and pH receptors. The burning sensation induced by cardamon and the cooling effects of menthol or tea tree oil are not olfactory at all. They're signals from the trigeminal nerve, which responds to pain and heat as well as contact. Such scents can be enjoyed. But no one is likely to learn to love noxious scents like those that assault the mucus membranes or the more serious burning of turpentine or ammonia fumes.

Uncompounded odorants may be pleasant, writes Saadiah Gaon (882–942), citing camphor, saffron, musk, sandalwood, and amber. But he finds more subtlety in the perfumer's artful blends, underscoring his thesis that a good life, too, wisely blends a diversity of goods. Art seeking to shape olfactory experience is less familiar than perfumery, but it has been tried. Oscar Hammerstein, grandfather of the lyricist, booked a perfume concert by the photographer Sadakichi Hartmann in one of his Broadway showplaces. A special machine gave out lilac and other aromas. The event was a one-night stand, but performances were also held at the avant garde Ferrer Center in New York and in the 1920s in Southern California. Attempts were made in the 1950s to add scent to film, culminating in Mike Todd's use of

Hans Laube's idea of releasing odors at preset intervals in movies. The efforts foundered on the high cost of the equipment and audience complaints about missed cues, faint scents, and the sound of fellow viewers' sniffing. But artists like Koo Jeong A, Haegue Yang, Federico Díaz, and Ernesto Neto have used scent in art, following up on early twentieth-century experiments by artists like Marcel Duchamp, who filled a room with burnt coffee scent at a Surrealist exhibition.[142] In a 1965 April Fool's stunt the BBC pretended to broadcast scents of an onion being cut and coffee brewing. Suggestible viewers called to report the scents. Olfaction, then, is remarkably suggestible, again belying the myth of passive perception. People pretty readily identify an odor as what they're told it is. But attitudes, once an odor is identified, rightly or wrongly, tend to be stubborn.

Tasting

Taste, strictly, is what the taste buds report. The combined experience of taste, scent, mouth feel, etc., is flavor, a mental composite. The subtlety and complexity of flavors affect notions of taste. So, despite the relative invariance of response in the taste buds, words for taste in many languages refer to personal preferences. But taste may also mean connoisseurship. In Arabic the undeniability of tastes makes the corresponding word (*dhawq*) a favored Sufi expression for the certitude pursued in mystical experience. Aristotle remarks that young people of generous inclination are sooner moved by appeals to nobility than are more ordinary folk, who are more swayed by pleasure and fear of pain than the joys of moral excellence, "since they have never tasted it" (*Nicomachean Ethics* 10.9.1179b7–16).

Taste buds lie mainly on the upper surface of the tongue; but some stud the soft palate, epiglottis, and esophagus. They're grouped in papillae of three types: fungiform (mushroom shaped), each bearing just a few taste buds and densest at the tip of the tongue; circumvallate (raised and "moated" like a fort), a dozen or so toward the rear of the tongue; and foliate (ridge-like), toward the rear edges of the tongue. The dense array at the tip of the tongue favors testing of what we taste. The papillae further back may facilitate a gag response, protecting us from harm by what's already in our mouths.

Each taste bud holds fifty to a hundred receptor cells with microvillae (to maximize surface area) that extend into a tiny mucus filled pit where food chemicals dissolved in saliva stimulate the receptors sensitive to specific tastants. Traditionally, tastes were classed in four broad types: sweet, sour, salt, and bitter. But serious cooks have long sought the rich, meaty flavor of prepared stocks. In 1908 Kikunae Ikeda of Tokyo Imperial University identified monosodium glutamate (MSG) as the source of the pungent flavor of seaweed broth, a staple in Japan. Umami, or savory, proved to be a fifth basic taste, produced by the carboxylate ion of the glutamic acid in meat, cheese, and mushrooms. Glutamates, the salts of this acid, bear the same ion and are widely used in cooking. Ikeda, in fact, collaborated with the Ajinomoto company in marketing MSG. But glutamates are found naturally in soy sauce, fish sauce, Parmesan cheese, ripe tomatoes, anchovies, and other seafood. Bacon is said to contain six types of umami.

Our taste receptors respond to sweet, bitter, and umami flavors, but salt and sour have more direct effects: The sodium in table salt enters a cell directly, depolarizing it and setting off an action potential. Sour, technically, is acid. H^+ (acid) ions, too, penetrate cell membranes and trigger a direct response. Various sweet tastes may be detected by a single multitasking receptor type. But perhaps thirty different types respond to bitter tastes, a multiple warning system perhaps evolved to protect against toxicity.[143] The variety of our taste receptors may exceed the basic five. Rodents respond to fatty acids, important also in human nutrition. But the jury is still out on whether we have special receptors for these. Nor do we know if humans have calcium taste receptors, as some animals may. With flavor, as with scent, some of our response is irritation rather than a tuned taste response. As already noted, the menthol in mint provokes a cooling sensation, and capsaicin from chili peppers jangles our heat receptors rather than our taste buds. Carbonation too acts as an irritant, the CO_2 in soft drinks forming carbonic acid on the tongue.

Texture, elasticity, viscosity, hardness, color, and even sound contribute to flavor. But none more so than scent.[144] Fresh bread gives off 296 different volatile chemicals. A banana spreads 225; chicken on the stove, 381; a tomato, 385; white wine, 644; coffee, 790; tea, 541. So if you hold your nose while eating, blocking retronasal olfaction, you lose much of the flavor experience. Of 750 patients reporting trouble with their sense of taste at the University of Pennsylvania Medical Center, nearly 60 percent said they could neither taste nor smell. But tests confirmed that in only 4 percent. For most the problem was olfactory.[145] So here again synthesis is of the essence.

The brain's sensitivity to a vast variety of tastants tracks its work in olfaction. In both cases, combinations typically seem less intense than do the ingredients alone. The brain buffers the effects, yielding subtleties of the sort that Saadiah praised in perfumes. But one needn't take too seriously James Bond style claims from some gourmands about the sensitivity of their palates: There's an upper limit to our ability to tease out distinctive scents or tastes in combination: Subjects with practice could identify individual scents 82 percent of the time, but only 35 percent of the time with binary combinations; 14 percent with ternary trials; only 4 percent with four components; and never with five.[146]

Wine experts do no better than lay wine drinkers in re-identifying a wine they've already tried—although both do better than novices, and the experts outperform the rest in describing and classing wines they've tasted. Discrimination improves with feedback. But wine experts and novices don't differ in the thresholds at which they detect various wine tastants and odorants.[147] Familiarity with established names and types aid the afficionados. But even arbitrary tags help the beginners, confirming the connection of taste to values, experience, knowledge, and emotion: The more we care, the greater the range of flavors we can name.

For humans, foods, like music, have meanings. Our experience in eating collates taste and scent, texture, temperature, color, and sound with setting and situation, memories of family gatherings and personal relationships. Specific tastes and dishes, rituals and occasions give flavors a significance that embraces but far exceeds the sensory presentation.

Touching

Jump into a swimming pool, and the water typically feels cold. The initial shock is brief. We say we're getting used to the water. Our nerves, in fact, register the differential between our new surroundings and skin temperature, but the signals fade as the sensation grows old. Locke made quite a point of the relativity of heat perception. He asked readers to poke a cold finger from one hand and a warm finger from the other into the same glass of water. The water feels cold to the warm hand, warm to the other. Locke's explanation anticipates today's understanding, even as it harks back to Democritean ideas: Warmth, Locke reasons, is not an objective "primary" quality in the water. Certainly the water does not *feel* what we sense. That's *our* response. Locke pleads the distinction to advance his causal realism, as he seeks to explain how "the same Water may at the same time produce the Sensation of Heat in one Hand, and Cold in the other":

> If the Sensation of Heat and Cold, be nothing but the increase or diminution of the motion of the minute Parts of our Bodies, caused by the Corpuscles of any other Body, it is easie to be understood, That if that motion be greater in one Hand, than in the other; if a Body be applied to the two Hands, which has in its minute Particles a greater motion, than in those of the other, it will

increase the motion of the one Hand, and lessen it in the other, and so cause the different Sensations of Heat and Cold.[148]

Locke's aim was to reduce qualitative properties to the quantitative, mechanical properties of the "minute corpuscles" that scientists were again beginning to posit as the realities behind physical change. But there's a further moral: Once again, seemingly elementary sensations are relational. We don't just passively sense the water temperature, we actively assay it.

Oliver Sacks tells the story of Madeleine J., a blind woman whose cerebral palsy had so restrained her that for sixty years she'd been fed, dressed, and cared for by others. She called her hands "useless, godforsaken lumps of dough." Yet Dr. Sacks found normal sensation in her hands and had the nurses tempt her into using them by leaving her food just out of reach, as though they'd forgotten about it. Groping impatiently for her meal, she found a bagel and ate it hungrily. Excited at the discovery of her hands, she began to explore with them and before long asked for clay and began to sculpt. The sense of touch that had lain fallow for a lifetime had come alive.

In a study of "haptic perception," as the tactile sense is called, a hundred blindfolded subjects identified a comb, tea bag, and mitten with 100 percent accuracy in less than two seconds.[149] Touch, as David Katz argued in the 1920s, mentally constructs shapes.[150] Generally more linear than sight, it traces objects literally, whereas our eyes caress them only metaphorically, often snatching holistic impressions as we scan for significant details.

Human skin has receptors sensitive to pressure, stretch, temperature, vibration, and pain. Textures are sensed through the changes in pressure as our skin traverses a surface. The brain assays the variation against a baseline supplied by further pressure receptors deeper down. Contrast is essential. So is integration: Temperature sensations influence our perceptions of texture, and we typically enlist other sense modalities including sight to confirm what we feel. Experimenting with sheets of paper from the thinnest tissue to stout cardboard, Katz found that touch "far surpasses the eye in sensitivity to differences in thickness." Tissue samples were judged by the "veiling effect" as sheets were rubbed between the fingers; ordinary paper, by its flexibility. Only with thick cardboard did subjects try to estimate the gap between thumb and fingers as if with callipers.[151]

Sensory neurons in the skin extend to the spinal cord, where each synapses with a nerve that has its cell body in the brain, often the thalamus. Haptic signals from the skin bearing data about temperature, pressure, pain, and the rest are assayed in the postcentral gyrus of the parietal lobe, much as V1 maps the visual field. This map follows the skin's topography, but not to scale: Large cortical surfaces are dedicated to the hands and lips, given their extensive innervation.

Sensing, as the Epicureans understood, is about change. So touch needs ever new information. Movement here is "a creative force," as Katz writes: "Smoothness and roughness occur not at rest, but really only when the touch organ moves."[152] Our eyes survey a scene, and we sniff the air at a new odor. Active touch, similarly, reveals far more than a momentary brush: We reach for an object and knead or stroke it.[153] Yet pressing hard on a bump or spot, as users new to braille may do, "results in loss of sensation, much as prolonged fixation does in vision."[154] Vision stabilizes the dancing scene before our eyes, but touch turns static objects "cinematic." Atomistic accounts easily miss that dynamic.[155]

If you move your hand across stiff brush bristles, Katz proposes, "you will feel a discontinuous space filled with points, a tactual figure. The points give the impression of a great numerosity, whose estimation might seem a hopeless task. Between the points, there is not 'nothing' in a tactual sense. . . . The space between forms the *tactual ground*." Tactual figure and ground, unlike their optical counterparts, are not reversible. But just as an object "pops out" of the landscape when we distinguish figure from ground, we sense discrete bristles, despite their numbers, by their tactual distinctness from the intervening ground. Edge perception, however, is in some ways harder for touch than for sight. Both sighted and blind people have trouble identifying the shapes of raised line figures by touch alone, since the lines by themselves don't help much in discriminating figure from ground. So memory matters more with touch than with sight: A tactile field can't be taken in at a glance. It has to be built up in stages.[156]

What memory holds onto haptically is the prick, or warmth, or suppleness, the ice cream's chill on our palate. The sensation may loom larger than the object. But we tend to put ourselves in the picture. Subjects asked to describe their tactile sensations, Katz reports, invariably mentioned the organ, typically, their fingertips, feeling the wood or glass, fur, silk, leather, paper, wool, or emery cloth: "I have never succeeded in producing a tactual representation from which the image of the touching organ was completely excluded."[157]

Our penchant for perceptual constancy preserves the tactual shape and texture of things regardless of our feeling them with more or less sensitive organs. And the brain, as with vision, fills in the blanks: We feel a continuous surface even though our finger strokes were broken. And, just as sight registers the reflectance of a surface, touch assays the specific heat and thermal conductivity of materials, registering the heat lost or retained by our fingers when we touch glass or metal or put on gloves, the active haptic sense making our body heat its baseline and finding wool or metal of a given temperature warm or cool by the changes we feel in touching it.[158]

We check our senses against one another—one advantage, Aristotle writes, in having more than one. Sight and touch work notably in tandem:[159] We run our fingers down the oar, knowing it's not broken, despite the optical illusion. We hold a moistened finger to the wind and touch the velvet to feel if it's lush as it looks. Pragmatist philosophers used to equate physical reality itself with confirmation by one sense of another's report. Touch was typically the clincher.[160]

Koinē Aisthesis

Aristotle made colors, sounds, odors, and savors proper domains of sight, hearing, smell, and taste. These are never mistaken for each other. Motion and rest, number and unity, figure and size are perceived by multiple senses, thus, he held, sensed only "incidentally." The question of specificity leads on to issues of interpretation: Vision apprehends, say, something white; we recognize Diares' son (*De Anima* 2.6.418a20–25). What we see coming up the hill doesn't tell us who his father is. Still, as Gestalt psychology and the brain science that follows up on it reveal, it's not always easy to draw strict lines between just seeing and seeing *as*. We do discriminate objects by discerning shapes and sizes, edges and contours—features that can also be felt. But shapes, like colors, *are* seen, not inferred. Faces, voices, and object types, we now know, are perceived directly; and we see motions with greater immediacy than colors.

It matters to Aristotle that we have no special sense organ for "common sensibles" like motion and number. We need a way of coordinating sense modalities, or we wouldn't know that the same liquid (honey, say) is both sweet and golden (*De Anima* 3.1.425a14–425b4; 3.2.426b16–24). "So we must conclude that there is some one faculty in the soul by which it apprehends all its percepts, although it perceives each type through a different organ" (*Sense and Sensibilia* 7.449a8–11). This faculty, Aristotle calls *koinē aisthesis*, the common sense. Avicenna assigned it apprehension of the meanings or intentions in things: The lamb does not need reasoning to perceive the wolf as a threat and the shepherd as a friend. Modern ethologists speak of instinct or imprinting here, but what either of these respond to is an image—neither a syllogism nor a color patch but a categorization vital to survival:

> The common sense is the faculty to which all sensory perceptions are brought. Without a single faculty to apprehend color and texture, we would not be able

to distinguish the two. . . . If love of sweets, say, were not linked by imagination with the figure of the sweet, animals that do not reason would have no inclination to eat it when they see it. Similarly, if we could not relate this white form to the song we hear we could not say if this person were the singer. Life would be all but impossible for animals if they could not correlate their perceptions: Scents would not lead them to foods, nor would sounds. The form of the stick would not remind them of pain so they could balk at it. There has to be some way of connecting these images internally.[161]

The interpretive perceptions that Avicenna posits are what Gestalt psychologists pursue. We've seen how colors and edges are perceived by contrast and coordination, sharpening and softening what's painted on the retina. With all the senses, Katz writes, "differentiation, necessarily must be complemented by integration." We can distinguish the contributions of each sense. But "Functionally, the sensory elements obtained by dissection, are, in the final analysis, artifacts. In the living organism (whose expressions, after all, are what we wish to understand), large coalitions of sensory elements will always work together."[162]

Proprioception and Kinesthesia

Painters and art lovers know how brush strokes can give expressive value to a work. Movement might be conveyed by a line, and intensity by impasto, the artist's hand still present in a gesture. In dance, the performer is the medium. Our sense of our own movements, kinesthesia in common usage, was first noted in 1557 by Julius Scaliger (1484–1558), a multi-talented scholar who had studied art under Dürer. He called it our sense of locomotion. The vestibular sense is a key component, its signals reaching the brain even faster than those of sight, to be integrated with complementary or conflicting cues.

In the labyrinth structure of the inner ear, fluid-filled canals loop at right angles to one another in all three dimensions, working like a carpenter's spirit level. At the base of each canal, in a bulblike structure, a teardrop of gel shifts with the nodding, turning, or shaking of the head, disturbing tiny hairlike fibers linked to an array of receptors lining the canals. The brain coordinates their reports, tracking the head's motion. Between the cochlea and these canals another component of the vestibular system operates: the otolithic organs, two fluid-filled sacs, again containing hairlike cells that reach nerve receptors in a gel. Here tiny grains of calcium carbonate roll like balls on shipboard, imparting a sense of the horizontal and of the head's acceleration and orientation relative to the ground: Are we standing or sitting, leaning back or lying down? Sufferers from Ménière's disease, a change of fluid volume in the inner ear, know how critical the vestibular sense is in keeping one's balance.

Susan Barry tells of her husband Dan's experience on returning from his first space mission as an astronaut. Their ten-year-old daughter, working on a science fair project, found her dad unable, when he closed his eyes, to judge how to raise his arm to plumb vertical, or to stand on one foot without falling, or even walk from bedroom to bathroom without crashing into a bookcase. In the microgravity of the orbiting space capsule, Dan had ceased relying on his vestibular sense. He had counted on his eyes (characteristically privileged in the primate brain) and on feedback from his bodily movements to keep his balance. It took him three days to readjust to terra firma and stop unconsciously discounting his vestibular cues. After his third space mission, he could shift modes quite spontaneously.[163] We learn and adjust, consciously or unselfconsciously. Neuroplasticity lets us compensate for changed circumstances.

Proprioception, awareness of the movements and relations of our limbs, is tightly intertwined with our tactile perceptions but quite distinct from our awareness of external objects. First described by Charles Bell in 1826, proprioception was among the earliest cases of feedback to be noted in the human nervous system: The muscles, Bell saw, must report back to the brain on their performance. Charles Sherrington developed the idea, proposing that "interoceptors" signal the movements of muscles, joints, and tendons. Among the receptors are the Pacinian capsules discovered by Filipo Pacini (1812–1883) in 1831, the same scientist who identified the cholera bacillus in 1854. Others include the Merkel receptors, thought to respond to pressure on the skin and, unlike other sensory receptors, not swiftly adaptive; the Meissner corpuscles, rapidly adapting tactile receptors sensitive to fine sensations in small skin areas; and the Ruffini cylinders, sensitive to the stretching of the skin. All of these receptors are active in every tactile sensation. Their input is coordinated in the brain with signals from the muscles, joints, and tendons and integrated further with the messages of the external senses. Without the constant feedback from these systems we would be unable to move freely or handle objects. As athletes, pianists, watchmakers, and ballerinas know, proprioception can improve with training, shortening response time and enhancing precision—neuroplasticity again allowing us in some measure to govern the performance of our brains.

Proprioception itself is hardly passive. There are significant top-down components when children learn to walk or talk and when anyone learns new skills like driving, fencing, flying a plane, or playing the cello. Millions of receptors in the muscles provide the feedback needed to coordinate our gait. As each new skill is learned, conscious control drops into the background: A writer can concentrate on content rather than the keyboard, a violinist can focus on the music, not the tablature. The pattern, one might say, is now in the fingers. Signals are issued there. But governance, like a dancer's body image or an archer's visualization of the target, is worked out in the brain and dynamically adjusted as feedback arrives.

Phantom Sensations

It's been known since antiquity that amputees may have sensations seemingly from the lost limb. Descartes, a veteran of the Thirty Years' War, takes such reports as one good reason to distrust even internal sensations. Feelings from a lost foot, he reasons, may originate anywhere along a nerve's route to the brain, or in the brain itself.[164] The phantom limb phenomenon, as surgeons named it shortly after the American Civil War, was often ascribed to nerve damage at the stump. Some physicians thought it psychosomatic. But the pain is real enough. Its source, in fact, is not the sensory nerves. Descartes' second guess struck closer to home than his "bell pull" explanation. The sensations, sometimes following the contour of a lost limb, a surgically removed organ, or the vanished tissues of some highly inervated region like a nipple, lip, or nose, form up in the brain.

Phantom sensations are felt by more than 95 percent of amputees. At least 60 percent involve pain. The sensations may be faint compared to somatic sensations, and the missing limb may feel shorter or smaller than it was. But its felt presence can be vivid. Many patients still feel a watch or wedding band on their lost hand; some involuntarily move to parry a blow or break a fall with a missing hand, or intentionally if unreflectively reach out for things or clench a phantom fist. Over time the pain recedes, perhaps gradually, retreating from the upper to the lower arm, until only parts of the hand are felt, and finally the sensation is gone. Ramachandran thinks the "telescoping" may track cortical remapping as the brain adjusts to a lack of signals.[165] Brains need time, he reasons, to adjust to radical changes in somatic feedback. That some patients feel facial stimuli as if coming from an amputated or insensate limb confirms that account, and Ramachandran has devised successful therapies for the pain with that idea in mind.

Phantom limbs highlight the interaction between our dynamic body image and afferent signals from the nerves. The interaction rarely demands much close attention. But phantom sensations bring to the fore the more tacit facets of the bodily awareness that help us manage our every move.

Far from being illusory, phantom sensations are outspoken markers of the way the mind knows and governs our bodies. The illusion, Peter Halligan remarks, is not the sense of a missing limb but the notion that such sensations are pathological, reflecting the presumption that our working body image simply registers somatic reports.[166] On the contrary, the body image so critical in our self-awareness and activity, although fed by somatic signals, is constructed by the brain in ongoing conversation with the rest of the body.

As Halligan showed, following up on Ronald Melzack's work with phantom limb patients,[167] the peripheral nervous system does provide inputs to construct a "neural self." But these somatic inputs are neither necessary point-for-point nor sufficient in shaping that image, and their contribution to one's self-concept is too readily exaggerated. Our body image is the work of the mind. Children born without a limb, indeed, may have congenital phantoms. A child born without hands and forearms, reported vivid phantom limbs that gestured freely in conversation. A baseline body image is perhaps innate; and awareness of our bodies, their limits and integrity, develops early. The mental map overlaid on that baseline changes with growth, training, age, or injury. But an established body image may well persist even in the face of traumatic loss. Once again we find, then, that soul and body work together not just at the high points of cognitive or affective experience but in the most basic, seemingly elemental activities of walking, speaking, eating dinner, driving a car, playing the piano, or simply sitting down.

Synesthesia

In synesthetes the familiar sensory modalities are intact but overlapping. That possibility sets in high relief the workings of sensory integration and interdependence.[168] Francis Galton, Darwin's cousin, the sometime adventurer, scientific inquirer, and founder of eugenics, first noted synesthesia in 1880. But it was long before scientists took seriously the idea that, say, colors might be perceived musically. Some dismissed the reports of colors triggering the hearing of specific notes or tones in a certain key. Others blamed the intrusion of memory: Colored road markers or neon signage must have marked the minds of those who saw numbers or letters in distinctive colors. Over the years, however, Ramachandran and his colleagues have shown that synesthesia is perceptual and not an artifact of cognitive associations.

Synesthesia is involuntary, a letter, say, and its color perceived together, although synesthetes readily distinguish the two conceptually, as they must to describe what they perceive. Colors aren't *confused* with musical notes. The two are just perceptually inseparable. Brain scans reveal the patterns typical of perception, spikes far too early in neural processing to depend on language or memory.[169] As in ordinary vision, there's color constancy in synesthesia, as well as adaptation: The colors perceived fade out over time, just as other visual sensations do in the *eigengrau* phenomenon. There is top-down feedback in synesthesia, as in all our senses. But in experiments designed to weed out interference, Ramachandran showed that synesthesia is caused by cross-wiring. The brain's perceptual boundaries, it seems, are functioning more as bridges than as barriers. One sensory modality is arousing another.[170]

There are dozens of synesthesias. But the color-grapheme type is most common: letters and numbers perceived in specific colors. The effect is not surprising, since color and grapheme perception are mediated in adjacent areas of the fusiform gyrus. Given the extensive evidence that synesthesia is hereditary, Ramachandran reasons that the cross-linking is inherited, and activated when a synesthete learns to read.[171] In rare cases, all five basic senses are implicated, and many synesthetes experience multiple links, perhaps because their neural connections have undergone less than the usual "pruning" in the course of development. But synesthesia is not purely developmental. Color-grapheme synesthesia can be hypnotically induced.[172]

Noting the prevalence of synesthesia among artists, poets, and musicians, Ramachandran and Hubbard speculate that artists have a natural penchant for metaphor and other ways of linking seemingly disparate phenomena. Certain metaphors, they note, come naturally: People say that acetone smells "sweet." We say "loud shirt" or "sharp taste," but rarely speak of a "red sound" or a "bitter touch." Natural language might be tracing neural pathways used in integrating perceptions.[173] In every culture non-synesthetes connect sense modalities, associating stronger smells with darker, deeper colors, linking loud music with bright lights. The faster a drumstick strikes a cymbal, say, the louder the expected clash. We readily associate high-pitched bird calls with bright plumage, but not with beak or claw shape.[174]

Synesthesia is stable over time, although specific links may grow and change.[175] But synesthesia is highly individual. One person sees B as purple, another as red, apparently depending on individual history and neural development. Color-grapheme synesthetes see color in black-on-white characters even before identifying the graphemes. Signals about a letter are forwarded to brain areas responsible for interpretation. But feedback to color mapping areas outpaces them.[176] The cross-linkages of synesthesia underscore the holism of perception. Culture and learning, values and preferences assign meanings to all that we perceive. But the mind is actively at work integrating experience from the earliest stages of perception. Souls emerge where our integrated apprehension of the world joins and helps form a sense of self.

THREE

Consciousness

A Mystery in Plain Sight?

Modern physics could not get underway successfully before investigators had developed clear definitions of mass, force, momentum, gravity, inertia, and the like. Work on consciousness today enjoys no such luxury. There is no sharp, generally accepted definition of consciousness. Caregivers use the Glasgow scale of motor, verbal, and eye responses to gauge a patient's recovery after surgery. But such measures say little about what's going on in another's mind.[1] Opinions about consciousness vary widely. Some deny it altogether and expect any discussion of consciousness to sink in a sea of confusions and fairy tales. Others find nothing more certain than our own consciousness. Disputes about consciousness readily run aground in swampy worlds of zombies, Turing machines, vatted brains, and liquids with every property of water that are somehow not H_2O—figments of fantasy that displace fairy tales in philosophy's twilight regions. Even highly disciplined thinkers may seize upon a favorite corner of consciousness, like the blind men in the Hindu fable who disagreed so heartily about the elephant they ran into.

Any definition may confront a countercase. Even things that readily answer to a name may slip out from under its proposed criteria. Consciousness is especially slippery. Traits presumed in one context are contested in another. Formulating definitions can be like threading a needle. Synonyms alone are uninformative: To call consciousness awareness, say, reveals nothing to those who don't already know what consciousness is. But the tempting alternative, reducing consciousness to something else, risks losing hold of what we had hoped to define. So there's some subtlety, doubtless born of experience, in John Searle's deceptively simple, negative account: Consciousness is what makes the difference between waking and, say, dreamless sleep, coma, or death. The homey language gets the ball rolling, but it does lean on familiarity. And there are lots of differences between sleep and waking—pulse rate, for one—that are not consciousness. Responsiveness seems important in consciousness. Yet a person might be conscious but unable to respond. We can't define consciousness, Searle says "in terms of necessary and sufficient conditions," nor in Aristotle's manner, "by way of genus and differentia."[2] Is it better, then, to treat it as a primitive, not definable without circularity? Even then controversy threatens. It's puzzling that something so familiar could become so fraught.

Clearly consciousness takes many forms and has many facets. It can mean wakefulness or self-awareness, focus on an object, or a sense of one's body and surroundings. It may refer to attitudes and beliefs, whether or not they're topmost in mind—as we say we're conscious of a friend's opinions. Numerous nonconscious events contribute to consciousness. So it's unlikely to be pinned down at a single cerebral address. One of its barest roots lies in the brain stem, where harm to certain ganglia immediately induces a coma. But so does damage to the thalamus, and without an intact thalamus a sleeper will not wake.

At times the great issue about consciousness seems to be a poetic one, to find the right metaphor, apt but not misleading. Ancient poets and philosophers sometimes spoke of an inner eye. But the question naturally arises, who sees with that eye? Wouldn't that internal gazer be our real consciousness? Often consciousness is conflated with conscience, which is part of it, sometimes called a voice, one's own or God's, urging uprightness. But so-called inner voices may also be demonic or delusory, whispering seductions, *waswās* in Arabic, sly and insinuating. Or conscience might be made out a little creature snapping at our inwards, as suggested by the word *remorse*, or the fourteenth-century Kentish work of popular morals, the *Ayenbite of Inwit*.[3]

Some today describe consciousness as information processing, or schematize it as an interactive map, a neuronal network, or the traffic on neuronal tracks. But such models prompt questions about what's become of the human subject. Philosophers protective of subjectivity speak of qualia. But others compare consciousness to a demolition derby among neural circuits, or a committee, or a gang of memes shouting for attention—the homunculus of the spectator idea now cloned uncontrollably like the magic brooms in Goethe's Sorcerer's Apprentice, shattering the unity of consciousness. Computer comparisons have become a cliché, and like most clichés misleading. They suggest something more mechanical than thoughtful. But unity, subjectivity, and thought have their champions too, saving a place for the *I* to speak from, softly, perhaps, in the prompter's box when we're on, but not wholly silent even while we sleep.

The idea that consciousness is perspectival exploits images of vision; and Thomas Nagel's saying that what he's getting at in his essay "What Is It Like to Be a Bat?" is that experience has a way of presenting itself *for* or *to* the bat suggests that consciousness is both a picture and a gift. The regular resort to metaphor suggests an elusiveness at odds with the immediacy of consciousness. Is this the purloined letter kind of blindness to what's obvious? Tim Crane suggests as much when he begs off analysis, saying simply that someone "puzzled about what we're talking about here," is unlikely to be illuminated by any definition.[4]

Nagel's brief rests on recognizing that only bats know what it's like to be a bat, and they're not telling. It helps his case that bats can fly under their own power and navigate by echolocation. That puts us at a remove from what it's like to be a bat. The Catholic biophilosopher Pierre Teilhard de Chardin made a similar point to Nagel's, by speaking of the emphasis on "tangential energy" in the sciences, foregrounding the interactive dispositions of things, at the expense of "radial energy," meaning what it *is* for something to be what it is. That inner side of things did interest Keats, who summoned up his "negative capability" to put himself in the place of another person, or even an object. But terms like "negative capability" and "radial energy" don't reveal much by themselves. Consciousness is much more familiar.

Nagel's "what is it like?" and the technical ring of 'qualia' win a certain currency, by targeting something distinctive, highlighting how consciousness resists translation into terms that compromise our subjectivity. In that spirit, philosophers sometimes adopt 'like' as if it held the whole milk of subjectivity. 'Qualia' may settle for something more indivisible, a counterpart to 'sensibilia,' aiming to isolate the subjective feel of an experience. But neither the seeming informality of "what's it like?" nor the gesture toward precision in 'qualia,' says much to anyone not already on board. Nagel's 'like' can fly off in two directions: On the one hand, one can't really convey what an experience *feels* like. On the other, 'like' almost invites saying: "Well, I can't communicate my experience in full. But I can say what it was *like*." It's easy, willfully or naively, to miss the reference to subjectivity: There's something it's like to be a summer's day, but that has little to do with consciousness, and nothing at all to do with Nagel's point.

Within the strictures of (Cartesian or Pyrrhonian) skepticism, it may be reckoned impossible to tell if B-flat on the trumpet sounds the same to others as it does to oneself. Yet language does aim to communicate our experiences, and it doesn't wholly fail. We know that to most people B-flat sounds more like the same note if repeated than it does like F-sharp. Language doesn't merge minds, but it does connect subjectivities. In the end

Nagel turns us back to ordinary experience. As for qualia, the impression of rigor conveyed by dropping into dog-Latin hardly renders subjectivity bulletproof. If qualia really are incommunicable, one riposte goes, don't they fall to Wittgenstein's Private Language Argument? If language, as Wittgenstein taught, is inevitably social, doesn't that prove qualia illusory, since they can't be shared?

That charge fails, first, because language does communicate experiences. 'I have a headache,' gives others some idea how one feels, especially if they've ever had a headache. One needn't share the headache. Besides, what won't go into words is not therefore illusory. That notion just perpetuates a bias, using Wittgenstein's name to dismiss the subjective sheerly for its subjectivity. In other words, it begs the question.

Consciousness can be reflexive: A mind can make an object of itself even when the self is not the cynosure. Yet self-consciousness runs no risk of an infinite regress. Human thought, by nature is (in some measure) potentially self-aware, the *I* in the background, centered on its objects, not lost in itself but always on the move. Flowing is a natural metaphor. Joyce, for one, sought to capture the fluidity, by presenting, say, Bloom's thoughts as they shift and turn and chase memories, hopes, associations. But, as Sorabji argues, it's a mistake to reduce consciousness to its flow, as if the self—or soul—were a mere stream of events. Memory, interest, continuity, associations, and our embodiment, give consciousness a unity, despite its movement, much as a Heraclitean flux gains unity from the constancy of its flow. Ownership, Sorabji writes, unites the experiential stream. Without a subject, he argues, echoing an argument of Aristotle's, there would be no difference between my perceiving something white and sweet and your seeing it was white while someone else tasted its sweetness.[5]

Continuity and subjectivity allow consciousness to build an identity. Memory and a sense of engagement collaborate with agency, affect, and interest. So one needn't *equate* the soul with consciousness. Much that minds do is unconscious. And dreams, although our own, compromise the sense of agency and continuity that order waking experience. But the work below decks that finds the words we want just as we need them or links scents to memories long out of mind promotes the claims of consciousness to selfhood. If consciousness is not the soul, it's the flagship. Clearly, if souls are constructs, they are not just social constructs or figments of convention, but realities made possible by concerted work within the body—the brain in particular—and by the articulate, reflexive awareness of consciousness itself.

Varieties of Consciousness

One way of anatomizing consciousness is to distinguish levels of awareness. Wakefulness is the base metaphor. Barbiturates suppress consciousness by binding to a site on the GABA-α receptors of the brain's neurons, replicating the normal calming effect of GABA inhibition, inducing deep sleep. Strong doses can depress the system dangerously, even blocking arousal. When we wake, normal consciousness resumes. We know who and where we are, connecting present awareness with a wider context and restoring the sustained continuity that's lacking in dreaming and vulnerable to disruption by drugs or madness.

Dreaming and hallucinations, then, might count as semi-conscious: Continuity is uncertain and active engagement limited. Mystics place special mental states on a plane beyond that of ordinary consciousness. Eleanor Rosch, a cross-cultural psychologist, finds much to enrich our understanding of the mind in Eastern meditative traditions. Meditation can isolate and stabilize consciousness, casting a light different from that of experimental psychology with its controlled studies of tasks like visual tracking or list memorization.[6] Buddhism, at its core, rejects substantial selves, not for the reasons that troubled Hume or today's physicalists but in reaction to Hindu concerns with karma and rebirth. Nevertheless, James Austin argues, Buddhist meditation, by relaxing goal-directed activity and clearing away social and egoistic distractions, can enhance consciousness and promote a cleaner, purer, core identity.[7] Substantiality is not the focus here. But the Zen aesthetic of negative space, reflecting Buddhist ideals of emptiness, opens another window on identity. Deacon invokes such thoughts in defining what he calls "entention." Purpose and direction, he argues, reflect not a presence but an absence: The still emptiness at its center is what allows a wheel to turn.[8]

Monists of the Advaita vedantin school distinguish ordinary waking from dream consciousness, and both of these from unifying consciousness, rising to a plane where only the divine Mind is known. Meditative techniques often pursue contact with a higher reality. The disciplines practiced in that quest can prove valuable in worldly terms, in coping with anxiety, firming resolve, sharpening one's martial, athletic, or aesthetic mettle—in effect, perhaps paradoxically, strengthening the sense of self.[9] Mystical explorations typically have social settings, aspirants guided and guarded against the risks of the terrain as they move ever further from the comforts of the familiar. The experience remains ultimately personal. So its often intense social milieu may be slighted in mystical theory. But worldly consciousness, for its part, is typically overtly interpersonal, as its traditional linkage with conscience suggests.

Perceptual awareness, as we've seen, recruits a suite of capabilities, integrating information about an object's size, shape, distance, motion, and the like, and assaying relevance and risks. But perception is just one facet of consciousness. Singing, hoping, dreaming—literal and figurative—are others. Consciousness, like perception, is integrative, but it reaches far beyond perception. As we wake from sleep we may often be aware that we've been dreaming. But the dream that seemed so vivid scatters and a more orderly form of consciousness takes charge, as if the mind could no longer afford to dwell on the dream scenario, being now more fully occupied with waking experience.

Gilbert Ryle, impressed by Wittgenstein's attention to language and keen to treat minds behaviorally, described consciousness at its most cognitive as a kind of inner monologue.[10] And it's true that we articulate factual judgments sententially. But facts are often recognized before they're stated. Judgments, attitudes, biases, and opinions, we suspect, cohabit in the mind with sentential fragments and uncompleted propositions, all babbling or gesticulating like old friends, some garrulous, others quieter or dreamy. Many a painter or composer knows that verbal, graphic, and musical expression have distinctive strengths and deficiencies. And any artist, by default or design, may have much more in mind than a work expresses.

Theorists and researchers debated for years whether thinking amounts to images or sentences. Was it descriptive or depictive?[11] The pictorial model presses consciousness toward perception. The linguistic, toward speech—as though language were ever fully separate from thought. But it's pretty obvious that most of us use both images and phrases to help us frame our thoughts, some being more adept with words and some with images. And the imaginative need hardly be confined to visual images. It's doubtful that composers, in orchestrating a work, say, confine their thoughts to visual images *or* to words. Much of their recourse, undoubtedly, is to thoughts of tones, timbres, and harmonies. Many of our thoughts, indeed, are not especially verbal or pictorial but have their own nature, affective, perhaps, or somatic, or conceptual, or mathematical. We all know how it feels to be in a bad mood, or to admire or dislike someone. Sometimes we can put a name on our mood or trace our attitude to some experience, but even then we might think the name inadequate or confess that the irritant we've fingered doesn't capture how we feel. Evidently there's more to consciousness than images *or* words.

Psychologists find it useful to distinguish consciousness from attention. As Plotinus says, "We are always thinking, but we do not always apprehend it" (*Enneads* 4.3.30)—not self-consciously, that is: "The person reading need not be aware that he is reading" (*Enneads* 1.4.10). Still, absorption in a task doesn't mean the task absorbs us. It won't normally swallow up our identity or subsume all that we know, think, and feel. There are "hyperattentive" states, but they're rarely sustained. Even with advanced meditative states, a sense of self generally returns in short order. More typically, as we concentrate we can stand back and see ourselves as subjects distinct from the objects or issues that engage us.

William James located many thoughts and feelings at the fringes of consciousness. He mentioned our sense of familiarity with a scent or scene before we fully place it.[12] Psychologists pursuing that thought today describe attention partly in negative terms, as a filter against sensory or cognitive overload. Vision alone takes in perhaps a megabyte per second of raw data from the million optic nerve fibers. We triage the input both unreflectively (bottom-up) and purposefully (top-down), perhaps ignoring even salient cues as we focus on a task or interest. So, many actions—typing, running, driving, reaching, tying our shoes—need little direct attention and remain at or near the fringe. We background one task to concentrate on another. Musical and athletic virtuosi focus on selected aspects of a performance, but not the elementary mechanics, which are well ingrained and need little attentive scrutiny.

Consciousness acts as the administrator, highlighting anomalies, choosing gestures, making evaluative judgments and self-critiques, plotting a course. The Berkeley neuroscientist Bruce Mangan stresses the interactions of focal and fringe consciousness. Lurking in the fringe, as James noted, are words and names that seem elusive, just on the tip of one's tongue. We know them all right, Mangan argues. But not everything we know can be focal at once.[13] That thought is not inconsistent with Freudian ideas of a mental block, an emotive, perhaps inchoate distraction.

Mangan sees in James's metaphor of a stream of consciousness clear recognition "that consciousness is saturated with fringe experiences." Our conscious thoughts and feelings open onto vast reservoirs of detail, a host of background assumptions—object permanence and other paradigms that frame the *Prägnanz* of Gestalt psychology. Much of the continuity of consciousness comes from constantly checking what is focal against expectations in the fringe.[14] Arrays of topic-specific patterns crowd the wings—implicit memories that prompt anticipation that a tottering tower will fall, or that make a sentence sound ungrammatical, presumptions about others' feelings or intentions, moral, aesthetic, or sensuous norms, provoking queasy feelings, say, about a dubious business proposition or a sketchy restaurant, all asking implicitly, "What's wrong (or right) with this picture?" Much of this mental furniture is portable and mutable, but not always easily. Mangan cites Archimedes' conceptualization of specific gravity: Intuitively a body's displacement might be expected to match its size. The eureka moment came when seeming common sense was hauled before the critical tribunal and Archimedes in his tub suddenly realized that an object would displace water with a *mass* equal to its own—any less and it would float!

For James, consciousness was "a selecting agency," an image consonant with his pragmatist philosophy. For the first great selection behind the rise of consciousness, he argued, is between self and world: "Every actually existing consciousness seems to itself at any rate to be a *fighter for ends*, of which many, but for its presence, would not be ends at all. Its powers of cognition are mainly subservient to these ends, discerning which facts further them and which do not."[15] Consciousness here becomes more than a chooser of ends. In a way it creates them. Such themes are elaborated by Evan Thompson, following up on Francisco Varela and Humberto Maturana's work: "An autonomous system, such as a cell or a multicellular organism," Thompson writes, "is not merely self-maintaining, like a candle flame; it is also self-producing and thus produces its own self-maintaining processes, including an active topological boundary that demarcates inside from outside and actively regulates interaction with the environment."[16]

Sorting the varieties of sentience, we can track the emergence of consciousness in evolutionary terms. Planaria, as high school biology students learn, will migrate toward sugar and avoid vinegar. The reflective awareness of self and others on which we humans pride ourselves stands at the far end of the spectrum, grounding the subjectivity that affirms itself as a personality. Self-awareness, primitively, answers to a creature's need to deal with its surroundings. Supplementing a sense of potential harm or benefit, animals with well integrated nervous systems rely on a sense of their own bodies. Birds and mammals learn to gauge the impact of their movements and volitions. Kittens tussle playfully, testing how far a spring will take them and where it's safe to jump. "Implicit knowledge of one's body," Steve Giambrone and Daniel Povinelli write, "must be widespread among animals and would have evolved early on—possibly as early as the evolution of full-blown sense organs."[17] Awareness of others' awareness is adaptive too, assaying threats and opportunities—predators or prey, potential mates or rivals. Many species, especially social primates, practice deception. They know and care what others know. Chimps and orangutans can recognize themselves in the mirror. And only they, unlike other primates, will use a mirror to explore unseen parts of their own bodies. Seeing lipstick on their ears or eyebrows, only these will touch the spot and not the mirror.

Human awareness often dwells on what we think others are thinking. In a classic article David Premack and Peter Woodruff called such thoughts a theory of mind.[18] Their experiments parsing such capabilities launched a debate about the mammalian precursors of higher order thoughts in humans. Darwin set the stage, by distinguishing human from animal intelligence only in degree.[19] And efforts persist to smooth the transition from our animal ancestors to the human case. Evolutionary psychologists often treat consciousness as a quiver of heritable modules, bundling human dispositions with their presumptive precursors and eliding much that is unique: Logical reasoning, moral choice, language use and generation become instinctual. What's fluid or dynamically interactive becomes a mechanism, erasing rational control. As a corrective, Premack and his colleagues singled out some distinctively human facets of consciousness: "When a child is shown a dog that sees a bone in a box he expects the dog to get the bone."[20] Suppose the child, but not the dog, sees someone hide the bone. A two-and-a-half-year-old will expect the dog to hunt where the bone was first seen, knowing the dog was tricked. A chimp will fail that test, expecting, if anything at all, the dog to look where the chimp knows the bone is hidden now. The toddler distinguishes its own knowledge from the dog's. A chimp cannot.[21]

Is it language that makes the difference? Not always. In a classroom setting a child watches another watching a third, who pays attention to a teacher. There's a thought here about another thought, about yet another: "Nothing comparable is found in animals," Premack and Woodruff write.[22] Animals do assess each other's intentions. But they tend to rely on what's visible. Chimps follow another's gaze but do not readily distinguish what they see from what the other is seen to see. Children, from infancy on, make judgments about unseen relations in their social world. No other species has a comparably articulated body of expectations, or capacity to acquire it. Human consciousness, then, is not just advanced ape intelligence. It is different in kind. Darwin acknowledged that in a way: An ape, he wrote, might "form an artful plan to plunder a garden," but "the thought of fashioning a stone tool was quite beyond his scope."[23]

Chimps do share and cooperate, adopt orphaned young, and reconcile after a quarrel with members of their troop. Similar behaviors are found in other species too. "Dogs and cats have no trouble reading our moods and we have no trouble reading theirs."[24] The cat knows we want her off the counter and waits to try her luck until we've left the room. Non-human animals anticipate threats and weaknesses in others. But they are hardly aware of thoughts as thoughts. Social learning and stepwise problem solving are distinctively human. We break down complex problems into subproblems and knit them up again, invoking seemingly unrelated resources in the effort—as Darwin himself did in framing the theory of evolution, and as every creative mind and every human being must do day by day.

Dolphins, like primates, mimic human behavior. Herd and pack animals are clearly attuned to one another's sensibilities. The parallels with human behavior are close enough, Frans de Waal argues, to warrant applying some common terms.[25] But human beings, as Premack shows, make distinctive uses of consciousness. We make elaborate plans, trying to anticipate future options. The general knowledge we use in dealing with novel circumstances is distinctively human. Human consciousness allows us to contemplate and draw inferences, forge new ideas, and wrestle with problems, pragmatic, conceptual, moral, spiritual, or aesthetic. Humans show a far wider range of talents and varieties of intelligence than other animals. "Notice how interesting we find it that crows make tools in the wild," Premack writes. "Why? because most animals do NOT make tools in the wild."

> We are struck by the finding that cats and meerkats teach for the same reason—they are virtually the only animal species that teach. Planning in the scrub jays, too, is noteworthy because other species do not plan. . . . The flexibility of human intelligence is, at one level, hardly a mystery: humans command all cognitive abilities, and all of them are domain-general; animals, by contrast, command very few abilities, and all of them are adaptations restricted to a single goal or activity.[26]

Animal sagacity is not topic neutral. It tends to center on food, mates, young, and hierarchy—although interests do grow more flexible and diverse as consciousness emerges phylogenetically.[27] Ariadne's thread, as Teilhard calls the line tracing the course of evolution, leads not just to the emergence of intelligence, but, along with it, the emergence of disinterest—which is to say, diversity of interest, and the capacity to choose interests and in the process to define the kind of self distinctive to human personhood.

The Mind's Eye

Parmenides freely describes consciousness in visual terms: "Gaze on things remote, firmly present to the mind, which will not sever being from being."[28] Bodily eyes are sightless, the goddess tells him, alongside reason, as unqualified to judge as tongues are to rule.[29] Pindar (ca. 522–443 B.C.E.), similarly speaks of a "blind heart";[30] Aeschylus (ca. 525–456 B.C.E.), of the eyes of understanding.[31] Epicharmus (fl. 485–467 B.C.E.) writes: "Mind sees, mind hears; all else is deaf and blind" (frg. 12). Without consciousness eyes are use-less. Gorgias (later fifth century B.C.E.), fancifully defending Helen of Troy, declares how swiftly thought shifts images before the mind's eye. He pic-tures soldiers routed by the thoughts aroused by seeing enemy arms and armor.[32]

Plato presses the advantage of inner over outer sight when Socrates compares his own moral and intellectual beauty to Alcibiades' good looks, archly charging the younger man with offering false coin for true, "the sem-blance of beauty for the thing itself"—like Diomede in the *Iliad* exchanging his bronze armor for Glaucus's golden arms. "The mind's eye," Socrates says, "begins to see clearly when the outer eyes grow dim" (*Symposium* 219a). In-struction, he insists, cannot give sight to blind eyes: Knowledge must mean turning the soul's eye away from "becoming" toward timeless Ideas, which we know innately, since souls too are eternal:

> Our reasoning shows this power to capture the truth to be in every soul al-ready. But just as one might have to turn one's body about to see light rather than darkness, the whole soul must turn away from this changing world, like a scene shift in the theater, for its eye to contemplate reality and the supernal splendor that we call the Good.[33]

Aristotle takes light as a natural metaphor for the conditions of under-standing and echoes Plato when he calls practical wisdom (*phronesis*) an "eye of the soul" (*Nicomachean Ethics* 6.12.1144a28; *De Anima* 3.5). Cicero preserves that practical outlook when he speaks of envisioning future troubles.[34] Galen (ca. 129–ca. 216/17) reverses Plato's preferences: Dissec-tion is "an eye witness" (*autoptēs*)—autopsy, as we say—far trustier than speculation (*On the Natural Faculties* 1.6).

Aristotle ascribes self-awareness to the senses (*De Anima* 3.2.425b12–19). Commentators, uneasy with that thought, seek some abler faculty. Alexander of Aphrodisias chooses *koinē aisthesis* since it relates perceptions: "We surely don't see that we're seeing or hear that we're hearing; seeing and hearing aren't visible or audible. Self-perception belongs to the overarching perceptual power that we call the common sense."[35] But self-awareness is not just per-ceptual. Plotinus assigns the godlike power to an intellectually oriented side of imagination, but the more distracting sort of self-consciousness to a lesser side (*Enneads* 1.4.10, 4.3.30–31). Plutarch makes self-awareness the work of judgment. Proclus gives it to reason.[36] Philoponus (ca. 490–570)—or a text ascribed to him—finds reflexivity in all experience and assigns it to the uni-fied and unifying mind, acting through a dedicated faculty of attentiveness:

Modern commentators do not tremble at Alexander's frown or pay heed to Plutarch. Spurning even Aristotle, they have devised a new account: that it's the task of the attentive (*prosektikon*) part of the rational soul to capture sense activity. In effect they say the rational soul has not just five faculties—conceptual and discursive thinking, judgment, will, and choice—but add a sixth, "the attentive," that oversees what goes on within and says, I've had a thought, worked out something, formed an opinion, or gotten angry, or desirous. It keeps track of all the faculties—rational, non-rational, and vegetative. So it might as well include the senses and say, I've seen, I've heard.

If attention says such things, it must be what apprehends perceptions. What follows everything must be one, since a person is one. For if one part of the soul caught *this* and another *that*, it would be like your perceiving this and my perceiving that, as Aristotle says elsewhere [*De Anima* 3.2.426b17–21]. Attention, then, must be *one*, ranging over all the faculties, cognitive and vital. It is called attention when it regards the cognitive. So if we want to chide someone who is woolgathering we say: 'Pay attention!' But when it oversees life functions it is called consciousness. Thus, in the tragedy: "Conscience (*synesis*)! For I am conscious (*syneidenai*) of the dreadful deeds I've done." [Euripides, *Orestes*, 396] Attention, then, is what marks the doings of the senses.[37]

Koinē aisthesis, Philoponus argues, stops at sense objects. Only reason (*logos*) can track all experiences. Aristotle, he complains, did not "earn his pay" when he called the senses self-aware.[38] He failed, Fazlur Rahman charges, "to formulate the idea of an individual central ego." Consciousness, for Philoponus, being intellectual, needs no sensory object. It may intend physical things, or turn, inward, as Plato put it, or toward ideas.[39]

Sorabji cheers the ancients' idea that self-awareness must be unified, but he's disappointed by their vying to locate it in a single faculty—"a wrong question, because there is no single answer to it." Rather, "what needs to be unitary is not the faculty but the owner of the faculties." A unified self would be an evolutionary imperative: "The particular mechanism, on this view, becomes a less urgent question"—obviating the call for recruits from faculty psychology, or any one part of the brain. Encouraged by Philoponus, Sorabji turns the tables on the moderns: The unity of self is not the question but the answer: Consciousness gets its unity from the self—or, as we might say, the soul.[40]

Escapes from Embodiment

In antiquity self-awareness was assigned to reason partly on the basis of the belief that only the nonphysical and immortal could "turn back upon" itself.[41]

That line of argument anticipates Descartes' thought-extension dichotomy. It makes reason our true identity, building on Plato's claim that access to eternal ideas proves the dealthlessness of the rational soul. Plato's *Alcibiades I*, long the gateway to philosophy in the Academy, imagines Socrates inverting the sense of the Delphic maxim KNOW THYSELF. To pilgrims at Apollo's shrine those words were an admonishment: Recognize your mortality![42] But to Socrates God is the best mirror for the inner eye, since consciousness is divine. In the later Academy, as in the Platonizing Stoic Posidonius, and in Cicero, Philo, and many a Christian and Muslim thinker, self-knowledge becomes the route to God. The monotheists skirt Plato's claim to the soul's divinity. But since man and woman were made in God's image, they don't disclaim the kinship.[43]

Augustine retraces Plato's steps: The mind "has its own eyes, the senses of the soul"; "entering my inner self, . . . I saw with my soul's eye." What he saw was nothing physical. For the surest truths were those made visible by God's sunlight (*Soliloquy* 1.6.12):[44] "Is Truth nothing because it is not extended through space?" "He who knows the Truth, knows what that Light is—and knows eternity." Then, apostrophizing his God: "Love Who art Truth! Eternity Who art Love. . . . I should sooner doubt that I live than that Truth is not" (*Confessions* 7.10.16).

> When we read one precept, *Love thy neighbor as thyself* (Leviticus 19:18), three kinds of vision occur: With our eyes we see the letters; we conceive the neighbor even in his absence by our human spirit; but through the mind we see and understand love itself. (*De Genesi ad Litteram* 12.6.15)[45]

Trusting his inner vision, Augustine encounters God as if a lover: "You stroked my head, unseen and closed my eyes to vanity. I stood back a little from myself and my madness and was lulled to sleep. I woke in You and saw you differently, as infinite, with a sight not taken from the flesh" (*Confessions* 7.14.20).[46] Thoughts of God, like thoughts of the self, demand the introspective eye. And either of these opens a doorway to the other.

Avicenna, like his Platonizing predecessors, splits awareness from embodiment. In a celebrated thought experiment that anticipates Descartes' *cogito*, he asks one to imagine oneself without sensation—"floating in the air or space, not buffeted by any perceptible current of the air that supports him, limbs not in contact with one another, so as not to feel each other." One would still know one's existence, he urges, without "affirming that of any of his limbs or inner organs, his bowels, or heart or brain, or any external thing."[47] If positing the self presupposes nothing physical, Avicenna reasons, the self depends on nothing physical. Like Philoponus, he has his eye on immortality: If consciousness is self-sufficient, won't it survive the body? Despite its ingenuity, the argument does not go through. It no more proves souls self-sufficient than geometry makes its figures real.

But more is at stake here than yearning for deathlessness. Our own quarry is not disembodiment. Our question is whether consciousness must be the dependent variable, a function of our bodily states. That leads us to ask: Can we intend only bodies? Or is awareness never more than the reflex of bodily states? Are human choices mere ripples on the surface of the pond, stirred by unseen movements from below? Kant argued powerfully against the disconnected mind, aiming squarely at Cartesian "Problematic Idealism."[48] Consciousness, he held, is *not* conceivable apart from bodies. For even if Cartesian doubt or Avicenna's flying man brackets all sensory objects, awareness remains temporal and thus presumes some physical process—one's heartbeat, precession of the equinoxes, some ongoing change marking the time that consciousness traverses.

Kant's argument recasts in psychological terms Aristotle's brief for the eternity of the cosmos. The very anatomy of time, Aristotle argued—a before and after for every moment—demands that time have no end and no beginning. But since time is the measure of motion, the cosmos too must be eternal, if only to mark time's passage. If temporality is inextricable from our consciousness, Kant reasons, and time is still the measure of motion, consciousness entails process and thus, bodies in motion. It is not conceivable without them. *Noumena* might transcend space and time, the "forms of sensibility." But empiric selves need time.

Yet one needn't fly quite so high as Avicenna or pound quite so hard at heaven's gate to recognize that human minds can intend nonphysical objects—as we do in mathematics. That doesn't make those objects real. But it does mean that awareness need not be of the physical, even though the body is its ground and time is unavoidable for us. Nature does anchor our gaze in our embodiment. But minds see what bodies cannot, although our vehicle is bodily.

It was against enchantment by the siren song of mathematics that Kant warned:

> The light dove, cleaving the air in her free flight, and feeling its resistance, might imagine that its flight would be still easier in empty space. It was thus that Plato left the world of the senses, as setting too narrow limits to the understanding, and ventured out beyond it on the wings of the ideas, in the empty space of the pure understanding.[49]

Jet flight beyond the realm where air resists and gives support was not yet known—although Hero's engine was propelled by jets; and Newton, Kant's paragon of scientific thinking, had framed the theory behind jet propulsion in his Third Law of Motion, marshaling mathematically the force familiar to anyone who skates or throws a ball, as palpable as wind in a dove's wings. One needn't try to build a world of mathematicals, as Plato or Pythagoras did, or ontologize them, as Quine did, to keep them safe for science. It's enough to know that consciousness flies free, not by escaping the body (any more than rockets fly without fuel) but by intending things other than the sensual, including its own nature. Souls need bodies as their base. But brains, at work as minds, do project ideas. Just as physicists need mathematics to state a law of nature, minds need thoughts of their own devising, hinted by sensory experience, but not confined there.

The Flight of the Alone

Plotinus saw souls as embarked on a journey home from exile. He called our trajectory "the flight of the alone to the Alone" (*Enneads* 6.9.11).[50] The soul's charge, as Plato put it, is to escape. He pictures Socrates, not long before his execution, interrupting an inquiry about knowledge to counsel a mathematician who voices a certain disappointment with the world:

> Ills can never be eliminated, Theodorus, for the good must always have its contrary. Having no place in the divine world, they inevitably haunt this earthly realm and our mortal nature. That is why we must fly from this world to the other as swiftly as we can. That means becoming as like to the divine as possible—which means becoming holy, just and wise.[51]

As Socrates faces execution, Plato imagines his response to a question about how he should be buried: "Any way you like, if you can catch me!" (*Phaedo* 115c). The Alone of Plotinus, where the soul finds rest and its true counterpart, is God. Reducing Plato's prescription to the barest ascetic simplicity, Plotinus urges: "Cut away everything!"

Ibn Ṭufayl (d. 1185), an Andalusian philosopher, seeking to reconcile the Sufi mysticism of the theologian al-Ghazālī with the philosophical mysticism of Avicenna, recasts Avicenna's thought experiment and his allegory of the flight of the soul in a "thinly veiled" tale meant to suggest a way of living in the world but not of it.[52] That problem held special poignancy for a court physician and philosopher in the eye of the storm created by the violent extremists of the Almohad dynasty. Ibn Ṭufayl pictures an infant,

Ḥayy Ibn Yaqẓān, cast away on an equatorial island, or generated there by the infusion of divine spirit into vesicles formed in the island's fecund clay. Growing up alone, without language or instruction, Ḥayy must retrace the steps of human development, discovering for himself the truth about the cosmos and his own being. Isolation is a challenge, but also a boon: Native curiosity and intelligence (his allegorical name means the Living son of the Aware) allow Ḥayy to search unimpeded by dogma. Tradition, at its best, he learns, only cloaks the truth. Symbols may point toward it, but often they obscure it, mistaken for what they represent—shadow, in Plato's candid image, taken for substance.

Ḥayy finds a friend and follower in Absāl, an eremite, who had hoped at their first encounter to win favor from his God by inducting the self-taught philosopher/mystic into his own faith. But Absāl's scriptural religion, true enough as far as it went, proves a mere tintype of the wisdom Ḥayy has discovered on his own. The two men pursue their quest in perfect fellowship. But they cannot raise the mass of humanity to their level. Even the most dedicated of ordinary humans shun the higher plane of thought and self-demand that Ḥayy and Absāl seek. Socially the two remain what Ibn Ṭufayl's predecessor Ibn Bājjah called "weeds," persons out of place.[53]

The isolated soul has a checkered history, from Odysseus, sole survivor of the Ithacans he led to Troy, to Melville's Ishmael, who echoes the words of the messengers of disaster to Job's household: *And I only am escaped alone to tell thee.* The sense of isolation deepens as modernity takes hold. Don Quixote grows from a figure of fun, an anachronism tetched with delusions of chivalry, to a new man, decent and honest, but mocked and out of place, tossed in a blanket, deluded yes, but not so lost as the inquisitors, swindlers, and ruffians around him. In *Robinson Crusoe*, a work influenced by Ibn Ṭufayl's tale,[54] the protagonist, like Ḥayy, must struggle to survive in isolation and then find his higher, spiritual vocation.

In many a Renaissance and Enlightenment work, the social innocent becomes a model of humane and independent exploration and discovery, celebrated by Moses Narboni, Hasdai Crescas, Pico della Mirandola, Thomas More, Robert Boyle, the interlocking circles of Spinoza and Locke, and new thought experiments in Rousseau's *Emile* and Voltaire's *Candide*.[55] But the shadows deepen as alienation grows and worldweariness shifts from Plotinus's yearning for a home beyond "this blood-drenched life" to the desolation that existentialists will call forlornness. Formulaic thrillers set the isolated individual at sea, shorn of friendly surroundings and often of memory, struggling to regain a lost identity, much like an exiled orphan prince in folk tales that play on the fascination of dreamlike loss and waking recovery.

Artfully adapting the image of the isolated soul, Descartes, in the *Meditations*, painted himself reflecting alone in epistemic borderlands. Hyperbolic doubt replaces a more picaresque paranoia. Dreams and the spectre of delusion replace the wizards of chivalric romance and the hags and ogres of folk tales. The treasure Descartes must retrieve, diving deep below his doubts, is no golden fleece or firebird but his own nature. Consciousness becomes the prize that will return him safe to the world of objects and other persons. Methodical doubt falls to a rival method, reasoning favored with the colors of the new science. Freed from doubt by the very self-containedness of thought, Descartes regains his footing only when he dispels his self-induced anxieties about an omnipotent deceiver, allowing the senses a qualified trust, at least in the life tasks for which they are best suited.

Cartesian doubt, as Spinoza saw, was theater in good part. The real anchor of Descartes' recovery was not the *cogito* but divine perfection. Recognizing the incoherence of the notion of a perfect deceiver freed science for its rightful role: Method, if systematic, could penetrate any merely finite ruse.[56] What, then, becomes of consciousness? Spinoza develops Descartes' thought that perception begins in bodily awareness. But he presses further, making consciousness "the idea of the body." Where Descartes had snarled himself trying to link body to mind, Spinoza boldly cuts the knot: Mind is the body made conscious. That doesn't make consciousness simply *about* the body. Just as the eye does not see itself, the brain does not perceive itself. It could hardly give one awareness if it did. Our consciousness is reflexive, but only rarely is it its own main object. Its regular work is to objectify, remaining present tacitly within our thoughts. Ideas, Spinoza said, are not like pictures on a pad[57]—not passive and static but active and subjective. Aristotle had identified the thought, the thinker, and the act of thinking (*De Anima* 3.4.430a). That unity grows livelier in Spinoza's reasoning, without Plato's expectation that being must be static—and without the hoary idea that ideas must be uninterested.

Stoic philosophers, focused on the moral dimensions of belief, distinguished what today would be called a propositional content from one's attitude toward it—commitment, say, or its alternatives. The Skeptics exploited the distinction, to press for detachment from beliefs they deemed problematic. Cicero adopted the Stoic division of the cognitive from the volitional, and Augustine learned it from him. So when Descartes sought to explain the possibility of error (paradigmatically, for Christians, a failure of faith), volition was at hand to take the blame: Error meant will outrunning understanding, leapfrogging the evidence. The bifurcation of the volitional from the cognitive persists in Frege and many another analyst, who found it useful to distinguish a propositional content from the "assertoric" sign marking affirmation.

Spinoza, with a deep distaste for the hypostatized will—making a cause out of a mere satchel of effects—rejected the Cartesian bifurcation. Our responses to an idea belong to the idea: To understand a thought is to see its truth if it is sound, to see through it if it's not. But we're interested beings. (Indeed, interest is the unique essence of every being for Spinoza.) So we relate emotionally to every thought we encounter. Adequate ideas, well grounded in a grasp of causal contexts, make us more adequate causes of our actions. Inadequate ideas are fragmentary—"mutilated," Spinoza says, since they're ripped out of context. Such ideas, underlying many a prejudice, fail to situate things fairly in their causal settings. So they weaken us, make us more the butt of circumstance than active, coping subjects.

Spinoza's account will prove helpful in thinking about agency. But it also insightfully addresses consciousness. Rather than pursue some pseudo-physical hook-up in the pineal gland, Spinoza sees the body as the first object of consciousness. That puts us in touch with the physical world. From here, having gained a sense of its own strengths, consciousness can progress to understanding things in context, not just as they appear. Descartes, like his Platonizing predecessors, assumed that bodies cannot be conscious. But the real question, given nature's demands, is how can living beings not be conscious? The question for science: How do bodies do it? How do brains make consciousness possible?

Consciousness and the Brain

Modern neuroscience took its rise in nineteenth-century Europe, pioneered by French clinicians. Studies of reflexes and the impact of lesions on behavior and motor deficits led to the identification of brain centers dedicated to speech, word recognition, and vision.[58] But consciousness could not be pinned down to a specific brain area. Paul Broca (1824–1880), a founder of physical anthropology, pioneered in linking trouble spots with specific disorders. Jean-Martin Charcot (1825–1893), who established the neurology clinic at the sometime gunpowder factory and later prison and hospital called the Salpêtrière, followed up on Broca's work, focusing on motor disorders, aphasias, and behavioral disturbances. But he avoided speculating on the broader workings of the mind.[59] Classic studies of spinal reflexes, especially by Albrecht von Haller, revealed much about how the brain and spinal cord govern such automatic movements. But voluntary movement remained a puzzle. Scientists focused on more tractable questions like muscle-nerve interactions and tended to bypass the fraught interface of thought with action.

Consciousness could hardly be ignored in studies of the sleep cycle, where awareness is rhythmically shut down, restricted, then restored. Alexander von Humboldt, one of the last great nineteenth-century polymaths, thought oxygen might play a role, since ether and other anesthetics were thought to work by limiting oxygen supply.[60] But the hypothesis did not pan out. Altered states induced by drugs or hypnosis were often seen as possible windows on consciousness. What disrupts a function, it was thought, might point to its cause. Similar reasoning prompted fruitless searching for sleep inducing factors in the brain. Such chemicals have since been isolated, although their mechanisms are not yet clearly understood. The notion was that higher and lower brain centers are uncoupled from each other in sleep or loss of consciousness. But consciousness is more than wakefulness. Jan Purkynje in the 1840s argued that consciousness needs a constant flow of afferent stimuli. But neither he nor his contemporaries could say just why or how consciousness returns when we wake. Here, as with lesion studies, knowing how a function fails reveals little about how it works.

Deeply troubling to William James was the question as to how consciousness can produce any practical effect. Broadly educated in the humanities and sciences in Europe and America, James held an M.D. from Harvard and had studied with European physiologists in Germany, Switzerland, and France. He began his teaching career at Harvard with courses in physiology and anatomy, returning to Europe years later for fuller contact with leading figures in the nascent science of physiological psychology. Returning to Harvard, he founded America's first psychology laboratory in 1874. Even earlier he was immersed in thoughts about the nature of consciousness, challenged by claims for epiphenomenalism when that doctrine was a new idea. Shadworth Hodgson had argued in *The Theory of Practice* (1869), as James later wrote, "that feelings, no matter how intensely they may be present, can have no causal efficacy whatever." Consciousness, Hodgson held, may color the mental mosaic; but neural events are the stones.[61] T. H. Huxley, similarly, classed consciousness in animals as a byproduct of bodily function, "completely without any power of modifying that working, as the steam-whistle which accompanies the work of a locomotive engine is without influence on its machinery." Volition in animals, "if they have any," he wrote, "is an emotion *indicative* of physical changes, not a *cause* of such changes."[62] That thesis, Huxley insisted, applies to humans too—just as he'd pressed to include the human case under Darwin's evolutionary umbrella: Consciousness was a symptom "of the changes which take place automatically in the organism."

So "the feeling we call volition is not the cause of a voluntary act, but the symbol of the state of the brain which is the immediate cause of the act. We are automata."[63]

That thought threw James into a funk. If consciousness was just steam rising from the engine, identity was a wisp of smoke; choice and volition, mere signals of bodily work conducted out of sight with a fatality that belies human freedom. It was a Darwinian thought that lifted James's spirits in late 1872 or early 1873, as a letter from his father to his novelist brother Henry reveals.[64] James tried out his idea in an 1875 book review, having jotted a note about spontaneity the previous year. He developed his alternative in an 1879 article in *Mind*, challenging Huxley's thesis in his title: "Are We Automata?" Later, James expanded the piece into a chapter of his *Principles of Psychology* (1890). The argument: If consciousness evolved to a level beyond, say, the reflexes of an oyster, it must have had adaptive value. So it must have been efficacious.[65] Those epiphenomenalists who say we can't imagine how mere ideas would exert physical effects, James retorts, seem to write as though Hume and Kant had never lived: We have no idea how *any* cause exerts an impact: Science has moved on; it has discarded "Scholastic rubbish" like "forces, attractions, or affinities," content now with simple correlations, "bare space relations."[66]

James's rhetoric faithfully reflects the sea change in much modern thinking about science. But it isn't deeply satisfying. In a way, his squid's ink masks the fact that the epiphenomenalist mystique just restates the old cartesian conundrum about interaction between disparate worlds: Ideas must float far above mere matter, solid, stolid, and inert. Psychologists knew little about how ideas take shape in the brain, let alone become motive causes. But critics wanted a mechanism, and James had none to offer. The problem he finessed persists today. We don't know just how consciousness (in all its protean variety) comes about. But, then again, the mechanists seem to be barking up the wrong tree: Sheer mechanism only denatures consciousness, robbing it of subjectivity, missing something essential about consciousness in its eagerness to find out where consciousness comes from. But despite the still unanswered questions, James was right: Epiphenomenalism is a no go, for good Darwinian reasons that appealed to his robust appreciation of the activism of the mind. A purely passive consciousness would not be adaptive. Small wonder that Freud, James's younger contemporary (1856–1939), saw progress in his own work only when he called a truce between psychology and physiology and began to study consciousness, and the unconscious, in their own terms.

Early in his career Freud, like many interested contemporaries, pursued lesion-based research. He'd worked under Charcot at the Salpêtrière in 1885/86. But as he turned from neuropathology to psychotherapy and his clinical experience grew, his focus shifted toward the experiential. The mind, he held, lives in the natural world, subject to natural causality and clearly constrained by the brain's limits. Psychologists, he was confident, would one day plumb the neural roots of experience. But to understand consciousness and personality one needed to consider more proximal causes and effects. The psyche acts and suffers on social and emotional planes unseen at the neurological level. Freud never doubted that the mind could be anatomized scientifically. But science, to be empirical, must deal with things as it finds them. Sheer physiological reduction only impoverishes our understanding of the psyche.

Freud understandably disliked Behaviorism: Dogmatic rejection of consciousness doesn't fulfill the promises of neurophysiology but only claps the how and why questions into a black box. Freud hoped to open that box and explore its darker corners. But part of what he found was that not all the questions, or answers, were physiological. Seeking language to describe human drives and distractions, he canvassed the rich resources of classical and German philosophy and literature, often finding it soundest to speak of the soul, *Seele* in German, a word infused with meaning by generations of philosophers and poets.[67] In English translations and works seeking to legitimize psychoanalysis in the clinical canon and among a scientistic public, 'mind' (which would be *Geist* in German), was substituted, damping down the humanistic resonance. *Geist* had broader connotations than the English word 'mind'; but 'soul' for Freud was no mere place holder for an unknown that neurology would discard. It named something with a dynamic of its own. Freud's faith in neurobiology never flagged. But souls remained a living presence in therapy, dialogue, and self-awareness, sharply distinguishing Freud's "psychic reductionism" from the prevailing currents of radical, physiological reductionism.

Never abandoning his early interest in brain pathologies, Freud saw a need to distinguish psychic illnesses from those directly rooted in the body. Gross disorders of the brain—that today's psychiatrists might treat with drugs or ascribe to hormonal surges or neural degradation—were not the only problems psychotherapists saw. Some problems had mental or emotional causes. The need, as we like to say, was to treat the whole patient. Souls rose from the biological and were always swept by neural weather. But they were different from those ocean deeps—and riven with depths of their own. Self-knowledge meant plumbing unspoken drives and urges, suppressed traumas and repressed conflicts. Introspection was not enough—

not because the psyche was unreachable but because psychology was stuck at the surface if it confined itself to perceptual consciousness, rationality and rationales, underrating the soul's unconscious side.

Both conscious and unconscious events and forces, Freud argued, reflect a history. Context here, as in Spinoza, entails causation. But philosophers sensitive to Freud's deep naturalism may overstate his determinism. His aim in pursuing causes, physical or psychic, was not to lay bare a fatality but to guide therapy. Like Spinoza and Plato before him, Freud saw self-understanding as the route to freedom. He studied human drives and conflicts, confident that facing our unacknowledged urges could enhance our control of our lives.

Successful approaches to mental illness like object-response therapy have sprung from the psychoanalytic tradition. But many Freudian therapies are clinically discredited, and much of Freudian theory has been discounted conceptually.[68] Powerful drugs now regularly sideline labor-intensive psychoanalytic sessions, masking or swamping the effects that Freudian therapies pursue. Familiarity has numbed us to the once stunning novelty of Freud's proudest discoveries; and new and diverse cultural trends qualify the vaunted universality of the Freudian mythos of oedipal conflict, guilt, and repression. Yet much that was insightful in Freudian psychodynamics remains valuable in understanding human development, family relations, and the interplay of consciousness with the world of dreams and unspoken desires. Not least among Freud's lasting insights was the need to understand consciousness and the unconscious in their own terms. Freud did not discover the unconscious. The drama and dialectic of unconscious desires and drives were favorite topics of medieval pietists like Bahya Ibn Paquda.[69] But Freud's work gave new credence to that drama, where rationalist/egoist varieties of reduction had slighted it.

Wilder Penfield uncovered a quieter dialectic: the conversation among brain regions that discredits attempts to localize consciousness. Penfield began his career as a materialist. Having studied neurophysiology as a Rhodes scholar at Oxford and medicine at Johns Hopkins, he trained with Harvey Cushing, the pioneering inaugurator of modern neurosurgery, and went on to found the Montreal Neurological Institute at McGill, where he pioneered successful surgical treatments for epilepsy. Using local anesthesia, since the brain is without sensation, Penfield probed diverse brain regions and mapped the effects of electrical stimuli on speech and recollection. But his holy grail was consciousness. His search in the late 1930s centered on the brain stem, since the electric storm of neural firing in a seizure begins in a small area of the temporal lobe and spreads to the brain stem, resulting in unconsciousness. Penfield could simulate that effect, leaving patients able to perform complex, if mechanical, motor tasks, but temporarily bereft of many distinctively human traits of personality and emotion.

Stimulating certain parts of the temporal lobe could provoke powerful flashbacks. But patients remained aware that the flashback came from brain stimulation by the electric probe. They were not disoriented but monitored the present even as they vividly relived their past—a kind of "double consciousness." Penfield knew that the brain supports the mind. But he grew chary of calling the mind a product of brain. Clearly seizures powerfully affect consciousness. They can be crippling. Yet the mind, he reasoned, reviewing his decades of studies, is not reducible to the brain if it can stand apart and appraise a situation even when one is largely helpless. Action and sensation are more than mechanical responses to stimuli: "Something else finds its dwelling place between the sensory complex and the motor mechanism. . . . There is a switchboard operator as well as a switchboard."[70]

Penfield's was a voice in the wilderness. Behaviorism remained the dominant psychological school. Consciousness was a no-man's-land. Howard Gardner, as Searle notes, "in his comprehensive summary of cognitive science (1985), does not include a single chapter—indeed not a single index entry—on consciousness."[71] Freudians at midcentury might speculate about subconscious dynamics. But scientists were expected to steer clear of awareness, lest they seem to posit some inner subject rather than an unseen clockwork behind behavior. The positivist maxim ruled: What can't be tested can't be real. Verification meant sensory ratification. But consciousness was private and subjective, not perceptible.

As the twentieth century drew to a close Behaviorism began to lose its glow. Carl Sagan's bestseller, *The Dragons of Eden* (1977) traced human consciousness—and other familiar characteristics—to animal, indeed reptilian roots. The tone was reductive in a debunking sort of way. But Sagan did not expunge his explanandum. Sociobiology was proposing evolutionary origins for altruism. Neuroscience seemed ready to open the black box, and cognitive science was making it respectable to speak of mental events. Consciousness was still approached sidelong and gingerly, through studies of perception, response time, or the old backdoor, lesions and lapses. But even as the fog began to lift, new shoals appeared. Paul and Patricia Churchland elevated caution about consciousness to a metaphysical thesis: Minds were a myth; there are no thoughts or emotions, only brain events. Consciousness, an artifact of folk psychology, was a superstition sure to be silenced as neuroscience grew.

Recovering Consciousness

Searle was something of a maverick in an environment where science was still widely equated with reducing things to their least particles, and philosophy often saw itself not as eliciting meaning from experience but as analyzing language. What caught Searle's eye was the idea of intentionality, where a wrinkle in language seemed to reveal something critical about the nature of things: Our thoughts are typically *about* something. They point to or intend something. Not every mental event does that. Pains and pleasures and other sensations need not have an object beyond the feeling. And sometimes we have nameless fears, or a vague sense of well-being. But beliefs and attitudes clearly do intend something. So do perceptions and dreams. The objects of intentions might be things like that tree, or they might be facts or propositions. When we know, believe, or hope, there's something *that* we know, believe, or hope for. Likewise with expectations—except the vaguest sort. The feeling that someone else is in the house is clearly intentional, even if its object is unspecified. Suspicions, doubts, loves and hates, are intentional. But intention means more than directedness. Digestion has an object too, lunch perhaps. But it's not *about* lunch. It doesn't have an intentional content as a plan or memory about lunch does.

The idea of intentions comes from medieval philosophy, borrowed by scholastics from earlier philosophers who wrote in Arabic. It was taken up by Brentano in 1874 and naturalized in English by Roderick Chisholm in 1957. *Intentio* was a Latin calque on the Arabic *ma'nā*, a word for meaning or intent, itself a calque on Aristotle's word *noēma*, an object of thought. We get a good example of how Arabic philosophers used their term from the Brethren of Purity. Words, they said, are like bodies; without meaning they're like bodies without spirit.

The Brethren were Neoplatonists, comfortable with the idea that words refer to things by way of concepts: Anything real, they reasoned, reflects its source in the world of Forms. But even without that platonic nimbus, the old theory proves instructive. Rather than call meaning a relation between words and things, the Brethren see a three-term relation: There's an expression and an object but also a concept, an idea *in terms of which* the object is characterized. Behind that relation stands a subject who characterizes something this way. That approach is fruitful: We do typically characterize the things we talk about. We don't just point. Even if we coded things by number, our tags would inevitably make reference to our numbering system—thus, indirectly, to the intentions of the system's designer. We can call what's on the table an apple, or something that adds color to the fruit bowl, or a vitamin source.

Thought, like language, is always construing things as this or that, such or other. So the intention of a term might be the object to which it refers. But it's equally natural to understand it as the concept or notion under which that object is conceived.

Words here are assumed to serve purposes. Thus 'meaning' or 'intention' can also mean 'purpose,' as when we say 'What did you mean by that smirk?' Words and gestures have meanings because people intend something by them, typically proposed to be understood. Expressions have meaning because persons have minds. Books and letters don't write themselves, and words don't speak—or understand themselves. A red sunset, people sometimes say, promises fair weather. But if we resolve the metaphor, there's a mind involved—not in the evening sky, of course, but in those who interpret it. There's no weather forecast without a forecaster. Regardless how fine a barometer we buy, there's no reading it without a reader, no theory without a theorist. Talk of evidence or signs or portents always posits some consciousness with an idea of what the signs might mean.

The Arab grammarians captured something important about intentionality when they singled out what they called "verbs of the heart." Such verbs regularly govern two direct objects, as in 'She thought him a fool.'[72] Verbs of the heart signify thinking and related speech acts—promising, appreciating, naming, doubting—'I considered him a friend', 'Call me Ishmael.' The paired direct objects might have been treated as subject and predicate complement; in a sentence differently constructed they sometimes are. But singling out this special class of verbs calls attention to an important fact about predication: In any indicative sentence something is designated and then characterized. Verbs of the heart embed the characterization in someone's mind. So there's a theory of mind at work here. The aboutness that interested Brentano is a distinctive mark of "mental phenomena."[73]

Intentional objects need not be real. If propositional, they need not be true. One can imagine or discuss Pegasus. One can wish for infinite wealth or believe Elvis is still alive. The fact that propositions can be believed even if untrue points, as Brentano saw, to something distinctive about the mind: One can't sit in a chair that isn't there. But one can erroneously assume there's a CD in the slot and hit the PLAY button. Intentionality here reconnects with the idea of intension (with an s). Leibniz coined that term to express the notional meaning of an expression, as distinguished from its *extension*, what's now called its reference class. If the extension of 'invertebrate' is all the animals without backbones, the intension is the concept, 'animal without backbone.' There are lots of ways of describing that group—"creepy crawlies," say. Indeed, Lamarck is said to have coined the term invertebrate because he preferred not to be called Professor of Worms. The idea of an intension corresponds roughly to what Frege meant by the sense of a term as distinguished from its reference, which would be its extension.

Because intensions always involve a construal, they lie in the lee of someone's thinking. That creates an intensional context. Terms embedded that way, whether they represent propositions or things construed a certain way, generate referential opacity: Sentences containing such terms may change their truth values when a (referentially) equivalent term is substituted. So 'Jill knows the Nike is in the Louvre' does not imply her knowing that the Winged Victory of Samothrace is there. She might not know that both descriptions pick out the same sculpture. The truth value of an ordinary complex sentence is determined by the truth value of its clauses. But the truth value of an intensional complex is not. 'Harry believes the moon is made of green cheese' is true or false depending on what Harry believes, regardless of the veracity of Harry's opinion. Referential opacity is a marker of minds at work because it tracks intentions. One's beliefs might be true or false; one's construals, apt or canted; one's attitudes, hopes and fears, memories and aspirations are highly personal. In their detail they're unique. More than markers, then, they're signatures, fingerprints of the soul.

Searle is protective of intentionality. "Nothing," he writes, "could be further from the truth" than the "pervasive" notion of contemporary philosophers "that there is some close connection, perhaps even an identity, between intensionality-with-an-*s* and Intentionality-with-a-*t*." The mistake, he explains, stems from the fact that "Reports of Intentional-with-a-*t* states are characteristically intensional-with-an-*s* reports." We mustn't confuse a thought or propositional content with the report about it.[74] True, of course. But intentions-with-a-*t* are always products of some mind at work. Hence what Searle calls their aspectual shape.[75] Someone has construed or named, described or characterized something in some way; someone has permitted or prohibited some act, affirmed, denied, or doubted some proposition, admired or decried, hoped for, feared, awaited, or acquiesced in some state of affairs.

Modal propositions (those involving notions of possibility, necessity, or impossibility) are sometimes distinguished as intensional with an *s* but not a *t*. The claim is, they need not invoke reference to any mind. But even here minds seem to lurk. Consider the special type of modal proposition involving probability: Notice how probabilities change as we gather information. That suggests some mind keeping tabs on the odds, and the evidence that makes the odds, and the weightings assigned to diverse types of evidence. Similarly, many philosophers believe that notions like necessity apply properly only to propositions, not to things or states of affairs. Again there seems to be implicit reference to a framework of assumptions that situates the modality.

Here the air does get a little thin. It's hard to see why all modal notions must be *de dictu* (artifacts of someone's judgment). Perhaps some apply *de re* (as features of the way things are). There are laws of nature, after all, and things do have properties, regardless what anyone thinks. Still, there does seem to be a framework invoked in notions of necessities and possibilities—even if it's as broad as "the world as it is." Likewise with construals: We can never say all there is to say about anything. But we don't just point and grunt (as Plato laughingly remarked), we *name* things *as* this or that and predicate something of them. We do construe—the apple as a splash of color in the fruit bowl or a source of potassium in the diet. There are infinite ways of relating to any object. So construals are unavoidable, at least for us. Minds do the judging. They specify and tease out features that matter in a given context at a given moment. Even when we reference the world as it is, we tacitly intend the world as our thoughts or theories take it to be. If our information changes, so does our framework, even if the world stays the same.

What drew Chisholm to intentionality and led him to link it with Leibnizian intension was that here, as Brentano promised, lay a decisive marker of the mind. In the teeth of midcentury Behaviorism, Chisholm saw believing, say, as no mere disposition to behave a certain way, as Behaviorists proposed and as philosophers like Ryle and Carl Hempel agreed. If Billy likes candy, Chisholm argued, he'll take some—but only if he has a notion of what it is and thinks taking it is ok. His readiness to take it is *not* explained without reference to further intentional states—bits of knowledge, attitudes, and beliefs. Intentional states, then, are only multiplied, not eliminated, by a dispositional analysis. Mental acts and states are not reducible to purely behavioral terms.[76]

As often happens, one thinker's *modus ponens* is another's *modus tollens*: Quine took the behavioral irreducibility of intentional items as an argument *against* mental acts or states.[77] Yet intentionality remained a tough nut to crack. Referential opacity was the shell that preserved it. How could subjects be rendered down to objects if the very thoughts that make minds fallible shield them from reduction? It's because Jill and Harry's thoughts are personal, not public, that one can't turn minds to mere behavior.

In the heyday of Analytic philosophy, when many philosophers expected logic to dissolve perennial disputes for good, by exposing underlying—ultimately linguistic—confusions, Ryle could treat soultalk as a category mistake: People who think minds real are turning verbs and adverbs into nouns.

In reality, soul is to body as kick is to leg. But if consciousness is not a be-havioral disposition, minds are not so readily dismissed. The revived idea of intentionality brought the authority of logic to the old debate about souls: A person's thoughts, emotions, and experiences are, in the first instance, that person's alone. One who wants to share them can search for the right words or other signs. But an inventor or poet, mystic or lover, can keep things private. And, if one's words are misunderstood, one can always say, "It's my idea, damn it! That's not what I meant at all!" Consciousness, in other words, is not freely exchanged for common currency. That's a weakness in a way, but also a strength. Privacy makes consciousness irreducible.

For Searle intentionality is a clear marker of consciousness: "no sane person can deny its existence, though many pretend to do so."[78] "If you're tempted to functionalism,"—making minds an input-output mechanism—"I believe you do not need refutation, you need help."[79] Consciousness, for Searle, is a biological process, like respiration, but too basic for proof: How "would one go about refuting the view that consciousness does not exist? Should I pinch its adherents to remind them that they are conscious? Should I pinch myself and report the results in the *Journal of Philosophy*?"[80]

There's more to consciousness than intentionality, of course. It's active and reflexive, labile and spontaneous, unified and unifying in its special way. Beyond or behind intentions, there's the subject who does the intend-ing. Our construals involve (and help solidify) a point of view, aspectual, yes, but also interested in the way James cared most about: Some thoughts or experiences, some facts or possibilities, are welcome, others not. For the cat some things are food, others playthings, or companions to groom or tussle with, or rivals to challenge. There are keepers, friends, to be nuzzled, kneaded, snuggled with. To humans the sea may look beautiful or ugly, skies may threaten snow, neon lights may promise dinner or a warm bed. Human consciousness always has a content, determinate or vague, but never wholly constituted by its object. Consciousness is always, at least tacitly, self-affirming, and often, in some measure, self-directed. It's many things, then. But intentionality vividly shows the resistance of consciousness to terms other than its own.

A book has meaning because someone gave it one; it's understood in-sofar as someone grasps that meaning, or distorts, or deepens it. Having a book is not the same as reading it, and neither is it much like *being* a book. The computers where this book is coming together hold every word of the text, and many other things. But those words and the computer codes that record them are not the book. The computers don't know the book. As we write, only we do. When you, the reader, hold the book in your hands, it will be you, not the book who considers its contents. A stop sign has meaning, but not in itself. That's part of what Wittgenstein meant about language being social. The word STOP is there because someone put it there. The red hexagonal sign is effectual insofar as someone takes its sense and responds. But response alone does not demonstrate understanding. That thought leads Searle to his famous Chinese Room thought experiment, drawing a bright line between consciousness and the input-output functioning of a computer. Searle pictures himself locked in a room receiving slips of paper with Chinese writing on them. Using carefully prepared instructions he writes responses.[81] If the instructions are good enough the responses, he argues, might convince outsiders that he understands the writing. But Searle knows no Chinese. His responses simulate understanding, but he has no idea what they mean. A computer, similarly, can generate responses but isn't conscious. It doesn't know what it's doing. To simulate the functions of a washing machine, Searle says, is not the same as doing the laundry.

Ned Block takes a similar stand. He distinguishes three main approaches to consciousness. "Higher order" theories restrict consciousness to reflective awareness. Block thinks these theories aim too high.[82] Self-awareness is precious. But excluding animal sentience and even our own less reflective moments seems unduly restrictive. Computational models, "global-workspace" theories, as Block calls them, aim too low. They reduce consciousness to prizes won by a neuronal alliance and fail to distinguish brains from machine processors. One can, Block argues, imagine a machine passing a Turing test: Given time and program planning enough, it might spit out seemingly intelligent "responses" to any conversational gambit, although "actually, the machine has the intelligence of a toaster."

Block's "Blockhead" argument (1981), like Searle's Chinese Room (1980), plays on our readily distinguishing thought from mechanism. The answer machine, Block writes, is more like a radio (or a jukebox?) than a conversation partner: "If one is speaking to an intelligent person over a two-way radio, the radio will normally emit sensible replies to whatever one says. But the radio does not do this in virtue of a capacity to make sensible replies that it possesses."[83] Cervantes pictures Don Quixote teased for days with an "enchanted head" that answers all manner of questions. But the seeming oracles come from the piped in voice of a hidden accomplice.[84] The machine Block imagines *conceivably* passing a Turing test, would still be a machine, he writes, with no notion of the pertinence of its "replies." As Deacon says, computer agency "is just the displaced agency of some human designer."[85]

Block's machine might well seem clunky, we suspect, not least when creative thinking is required. But Block is impressed by the powers of programs to deceive. He relates with relish how an early computer, programmed to simulate psychotherapy, led the designer's secretary to request some time "alone" with the machine. But even a machine that passed a Turing test, Block writes, would not be conscious, regardless how apt its comebacks. It seems almost churlish to mention his stipulation that the memory called for to load the machine with every response it needs would exhaust the computing capacity of the universe.

Block finds his middle ground between too high and too low in biology: Consciousness is a brain state. Biology connects physiology with phenomenology. Searle too favors a biological approach, although he bluntly rejects Turing tests and the presumption that we know each other's minds simply from observed behavior. We know computers don't think, he argues, through our background understanding of the way things work—the kind of causes that produce human or animal behavior, and the kind that don't.[86] The arbitrary exclusion of background knowledge from appraisals of the thought experiment harks back to the way Cartesian doubt bars premises not formally ticketed for admission. So Searle's distaste is hardly surprising. He calls post-Cartesian philosophy "sordid" and "bankrupt" and blames methodical doubt not just for dualism but for the physicalist reaction to it.[87]

The fear of consciousness, as Searle diagnoses it, reflects its privacy. Objectivity is often assumed to demand a third-person stance. But consciousness lives in the first person. The third-person bias emboldens eliminativists like the Churchlands, Paul Feyerabend, Richard Rorty, and Stephen Stitch, and spurs on functionalists aiming to reduce consciousness to an input-output algorithm.[88] Introspection, once trusted in psychology, fell on hard times as psychologists sought scientific respectability, eager to burnish an image long marred by anecdotal and armchair accounts. Recent researchers like A. I. Jack and A. Roepstorff have campaigned to restore credence to first-person accounts by using specially trained rapporteurs.[89] But consciousness itself hardly needs testimonials. Even Auguste Comte recognized objective facts about subjective states. He set beliefs at the core of sociology for that reason. Not everything real is "equally accessible to any observer."[90] Granted consciousness is not public. Special pleading, wishful thinking, or intellectual dishonesty may also be called subjective, but in a quite different sense. Theorists dismissive of consciousness, Searle writes, are simply privileging one form of subjectivity (lab reports) over another, firsthand experience. But their intent is to privilege one kind of reality over another.

Searle is not skittish about his ontology: Consciousness, he writes, "falls into place naturally as an evolved phenotypical trait of certain types of organism with highly developed nervous systems." It's "a higher-level or emergent property of the brain in the utterly harmless sense of 'higher-level' or 'emergent' in which solidity is a higher-level emergent property of H_2O molecules when they are in a lattice structure (ice)." But then, "The brain causes certain 'mental' phenomena such as conscious mental states, and these conscious mental states are simply higher-level features of the brain."[91] Does brain dependency wash away the efficacy of consciousness? That's how Jaegwon Kim reads the evidence: Neural events are the causes; consciousness, the effect: "If this be epiphenomenalism, then let us make the most of it."[92] Searle demurs. Acknowledging "that macro mental phenomena are all caused by lower-level micro phenomena," he still insists: "that the mental features are supervenient on neuronal features in no way diminishes their causal efficacy"—any more than the supervenience of solidity on molecular structure somehow robs a piston of causal impact.[93]

We get a hint of higher stakes when Searle, although calling consciousness private, rejects talk of "privileged access": The "metaphor doesn't work," since it separates awareness from its objects—as though thinking were "a private room" where only ego enters.[94] Perhaps the metaphor fails because one's thoughts *are* one's consciousness, as Aristotle and Spinoza suggest. Consciousness, then, would be nothing separate to be "introspected." In great part it would *be* the mind. But if so, in an important sense, it's a substance, not a process.

Both Searle and Block trust biology to distinguish consciousness from computation.[95] Thompson shows how this might work. He rejects the sharp dichotomy that Nagel and others draw between "the internal, subjective, qualitative" life of consciousness and their "external, objective, structural, and functional" view of life itself. Life too has an interior, he argues.[96] Integument is just as critical as sentience in framing and sustaining an identity. If so, perhaps the gap between brain events and subjectivity that so troubles philosophers of mind is not the abyss that's sometimes painted but the artifact of an artificially objectified vision of life processes: Biology bears the seeds of subjectivity.

Zombies, Thompson argues, (bodies behaviorally indistinguishable from humans but without consciousness, so that "all is dark inside") are *not* perfectly conceivable, as Kim imagines—the way a "mile-high unicycle" is, Kim says. Such fantasies play only if we suspend our background knowledge. We know no one could ride Kim's unicycle, just as we know that the comic book "Blob," a multi-ton unicellular organism, is thermodynamically impossible. We know in the same way that we humans can't live as we do without consciousness—any more than we can live without brains. If we hope to understand consciousness, Thompson writes, "We need to start from the lived body"—*Leib* in German, not *Körper*, the passive corpse.[97]

Consciousness and Biology

Francis Crick and Gerald Edelman were among the researchers who restored consciousness to scientific respectability. Both came not from psychology, like the Behaviorists Watson and Skinner, nor from philosophy, like the Churchlands, but from biology. Having won the 1962 Nobel Prize for his part in unraveling the double helix, Crick (1916–2004), saw consciousness as "the major unsolved problem in biology." Unhappy with the Behaviorists' black box and stirred by the unsettled state of earlier investigations, he gathered a team more piqued by the chase than fazed by taboos and spent the last quarter century of his life in search of the physiological foundations of consciousness, convinced by his earlier successes that structure is the key to function. As in his DNA work, Crick favored the theorist's role, well suited to his background in theoretical physics. His key experimental partner was Christof Koch, a biophysicist with a quantitative bent and a doctorate in philosophy. Koch chose primate vision as his experimental model. There was solid data here and resonance with Crick's idea of consciousness as a shifting panorama of the world.

In 1983 Crick published *The Astonishing Hypothesis*, proclaiming the identity of mind and brain, then a commonplace view not yet dismantled by philosophers. Consciousness, Crick announced, results from coordinated neuronal firing. Strictly speaking, an identity theorist should have *equated* neuronal with mental events. To distinguish the two as cause and effect cedes ground to irreducibility. But Crick swept past such niceties. The motives behind his stand were stouter than the reasoning beneath it: The mind, he held, should be understood without recourse to complexity theories, mysticism, quantum physics, or religion. Consciousness is just the play of neurons: "You, your joys and your sorrows, your memories and your ambitions, your sense of personal identity and free will, are in fact no more than the behavior of a vast assembly of nerve cells and their associated molecules."[98]

If consciousness is coordinated neuronal firing, Crick reasoned, specific neural groups must be its seat. Consciousness for him meant attention, modeled on visual perception. We select thoughts from what Koch came to call the pile of possibilities. That presumed some agency to do the picking—despite the intent to erase any subjective, managerial self. The lumber pile was another problem: Did it consist of thoughts, unthought thoughts? Does consciousness need a prior consciousness, inchoate perhaps, to feed it raw material? If so, just how much does the model actually explain?

Edelman, like Crick, turned to consciousness after winning a Nobel Prize, his in 1972, for work on the immune response. Consciousness, as he saw, it relies on integration and differentiation. Integration builds a scene, interweaving strands from perception, memory, and affect, cognition and valuation. Differentiation sorts and sifts the makings of billions of possible scenarios in fractions of a second. Guided by EEGs and functional brain imaging, Edelman found the relevant working groups in functional clusters of neurons. Neither the whole brain is in play, as James surmised, nor just one region, as Crick assumed, but swiftly shifting cohorts, their work coordinated, typically in the relay station of the thalamus. Block might call Edelman's neural network theory a "global workspace" account. But Edelman would dispute that, given his respect for self-awareness. He finds functionalism insensitive to the "reentrant connections" that progressively widen and expand neural pathways.[99]

Like James or Searle, Edelman sees consciousness as a process, not a thing. The notion has its attractions. But it's also unsatisfying. Does the process have a subject? Consciousness is no mere sequence of events. It belongs to someone. We're both active and passive when we worry, care, or plan. These occurrences are ours. Thinking is not like tracking someone else's brainstorms. Still, calling consciousness a process, Edelman hopes, might end the bootless search for its location in the cortical mantle, and quash any notion of "conscious neurons."[100] Following James and Kant, he thinks of self-awareness as a synthesis, "primarily in the remembered present"—a sense of personal history, enriched by our penchant for assigning meanings.[101]

The complexity of the neuronal forest, Edelman argues, its linkages formed and pruned as we mature and experience grows, explains the uniqueness of minds and thoughts. The fluidity of thought, swifter than shoals of fish, is stabilized in patterns of connectivity among our hundred billion neurons. The directedness of functional clusters explains our need to keep distractions in abeyance. We can background two or three non-focal tasks, or as many as seven objects like names, numbers, or phrases. But multitasking is not our forte. The need to marshal our powers around what we want to do well or think through thoroughly helps explain why. At the base of that explanation lies our embodiment: Human thought processes are temporal, although their objects need not be, and there's only so much a mind can do at any given time.

Crick recognized the brain's complexity but scorned emergence. He embraced a physicalism that took on new meanings every few pages in his book. Koch, more disciplined philosophically, judged consciousness real, not an illusion or linguistic artifact, as philosophers like Dennett were urging. The old campaign to reduce consciousness to behavior, he felt, omitted much that psychologists must acknowledge and that biology should explain. The explanations he offered were evolutionary and pallidly emergentist, *malgre lui*. He saw precedents in other mammalian species for many of the operations of human consciousness. The complex that supports language use and self-awareness, for example, he reasoned, was pieced together from neural hookups and routines first useful in plainer tasks. But the richness of human consciousness was hardly predictable from the work of its prosaic precursors. Consciousness was not a spandrel, a mere byproduct of evolution, but adaptive in its own right, indeed a complex of adaptations greatly favoring its bearers, just as James had reasoned. It conforms nicely to evolutionary theory, then, and needs no new physical laws, as Roger Penrose imagined.[102]

Giulio Tononi's work frames a biological account of consciousness using metaphors drawn from computer science—particularly, from information theory: Qualia can be assembled only with information from many parts of the brain. So consciousness clearly is emergent, far surpassing the input of the contributing neuronal groups.[103] Tononi knows why consciousness is lost in seizures: A perfect storm of neuron firings disrupts the integration of information. Indeed, there's evidence that concentration, say on a demanding piece of mathematics, can avert an epileptic seizure, as if channeling the overload and heading off a traffic jam.[104] Noting how some anesthetics block activity and pain but allow dreaming, Tononi sees a layering effect in consciousness rather than a simply steady flow. As his team describes it,

> consciousness is not an all-or-none property . . . It increases in proportion to a system's repertoire of discriminable states. The shrinking or dimming of the field of consciousness during sedation is consistent with this idea. On the other hand, the abrupt loss of consciousness at a critical concentration of anesthetics suggests that the integrated repertoire of neural states underlying consciousness may collapse nonlinearly.[105]

Tononi's aim is to quantify consciousness. Assuming that all thoughts break down into discrete information bits, he expects essentially similar neuronal coding mechanisms in all sentient species. So his efforts to chart awareness in anesthetized and waking patients are of a piece with his attempts to calculate the information content in the nervous system of the roundworm *C. elegans*.[106] Consciousness for Tononi is emergent, "generated by the whole above and beyond its parts." Yet, despite his deference to information theory and complexity theory, he holds out hopes of reducing consciousness ultimately to a single number, *phi*,[107] in effect collapsing the multiple layers of awareness that his theory might have upheld and turning the integrative work of the brain into some final summing up of assets and liabilities rather than reflecting the brain's synthetic work of weaving together a complex, interactive picture of the world and one's position in it.

Koch, like Crick, and Searle, drew on familiar notions in describing consciousness: "Consciousness consists of those states of sentience, or feeling, or awareness, which begin in the morning when we awake from a dreamless sleep and continue throughout the day until we fall into a coma or die or fall asleep again or otherwise become unconscious." Using that sketch for his wanted poster, Koch pursued the "neural correlates of consciousness"—NCCs for short—the minimal set of neuronal events and mechanisms sufficient to produce a given conscious state. NCCs in an organism, he wrote, "summarize the present state of affairs in the world, including its own body."[108] As this "Executive Summary Hypothesis" has it, special NCC neurons project to the regions in the frontal cortex that coordinate planning and action. Competition underlies the process, normally forestalling overload: "Any one conscious percept is associated with a coalition, consisting of multi-focal activity at numerous essential nodes."[109] The principles of selection vary. Some are saliency-based, others involve top-down choice: The eye's reflexive turn toward the apparent source of a sound thus contrasts with purposeful staring.

As sensory signals advance through the cortical hierarchy, the receptive fields for vision and the other senses enlarge, and the affected neuron groups compete in cascades, as if in a tournament. Signals from multiple assemblies drop out at each stage, leaving just one coalition in the end to declare its representational content. But winning coalitions recruit others in a "penumbra" that may invoke past neuronal associations and link up to varied cognitive contents and future plans. Our unique qualia thus reflect the moment-to-moment happenings in parallel networks of the brain, and the penumbra holds room for those fringe areas where thoughts connected to one's present focus seem inevitably to announce themselves from just offstage.

Making visual perception his prototype did lead Koch to see consciousness as an all or nothing affair: Competing percepts must pass a threshold to become objects of awareness. Relatively few cells in the visual cortices change their firing rates when an object is seen. But in the ensuing competition—in binocular rivalry, say—there's much firing of neurons, and most stimuli are suppressed. It was in the selection process that Koch thought he had found the key to consciousness. He posits a substrate in "activating systems" within brainstem nuclei and in the thalamus and basal forebrain, systems that project extensively to the cortex, controlling cycles of sleep and arousal. The "wide input domain" of these systems contrasts tellingly with the narrow and specific input domain and detachment from working memory seen in rapid, reflex-like responses.[110]

Koch's localized model contrasts with Edelman's more global account. Both men are in pursuit of explanations, but Koch is often willing to stop short at correlates, as though these too might count as explanations. The near boundless possibilities for reentrant connections that Edelman prizes seem to Koch "a sobering drawback," given "the inherent difficulty" in tracking holistic processes."[111] Koch, like Edelman, assumes vast behind the scenes connectivity. But he remains convinced that the brain activity that generates consciousness will in time be mapped and quantified, pinned down point for point to brain events. Holism is "defeatist," and that speaks ill of Searle and especially of David Chalmers for raising what Chalmers calls the hard problem of consciousness, the stubborn reality of subjective awareness.[112] Philosophy, by raising questions as to what is and is not knowable about our brain states and their connections to our thoughts, is an enemy of inquiry, willfully seeking to bar the way to a successful reduction of phenomena to physical facts.

Only science, Koch urges, offers certainty. Philosophy can only pretend to set its boundaries: "How could mere words, without the benefit of either a mathematical or physico-empirical framework, establish anything with that degree of certainty?" Reasoning about the limits of reductionism offers only illusions in exchange for the discoveries it forswears. The record of science in predicting physical events assures us that its reductive tools "should also help us to explain the world within us." Higher levels of analysis like those of cognitive psychology, naturalistic observation, evolutionary psychology, or phenomenology, have nothing substantive to contribute: "In the final analysis, psychological methods are too edentate to fully resolve this issue. Without delicately intervening into the underlying brain circuit the distinction between attention and consciousness will not be fully resolved."[113]

Koch's appeal to the record of science is not unmoving, but it does not dissolve the distinction between electrical impulses and awareness. Scientific understanding may advance (and *has* advanced) by both holistic and reductive means. It works best, as Darwinian biology clearly shows, when the two go hand in hand. No lover of science would demean experimentalism. But no experiment can answer questions it was not devised to address, and Koch's drive for experimental validation, while sensible enough, has, in fact, pushed his account of consciousness in the direction of visual awareness— clearly a relevant area, but hardly the full picture. Seen objects often are our mental focus. And perception is selective, as Koch's model proposes. But consciousness is not just perceptual, and the Koch-Crick model does side-line the self. The fact remains, despite the appeal of experimental work, that neither Koch nor Crick—unlike Edelman, say—has framed a model of con-sciousness confirmed in living experience outside the lab. Alive to the thick complexity of consciousness and more welcoming to emergence, Edelman (whom Koch acknowledges and respects) does not expect neural networks to displace selfhood. Nor does he expect a brain-based theory magically "to generate qualia"—any more than meteorological theories about hurricanes would "create the experience of hurricanes."[114]

Visual awareness, Koch's favored paddock, has offered convenient and steady grazing. But perceptual selectivity does not suffice to explain con-sciousness. Emotions like fear and love, as well as abstract thinking, can have visual triggers. But pleasures and pains, moods and attitudes, are not chiefly visual. We dream. We form mental associations without hard thinking about it. Beliefs and skills, memories, hopes, and goals are present even when not uppermost. Given the varieties of liminal awareness and our rapid shifts between foreground and fringe, perception hardly captures the fullness of experience and thought. And reduction will never tell us more than half the story of consciousness unless it remains coupled to an account of what it was that excited so much interest in the prospect of discovering its roots.

Body Image and Phenomenology

It makes sense to distinguish the bodily awareness animals use in finding their way from our awareness of self and others as beings with ideas and intentions. But somatic sensations are a vital part of consciousness, at its core for some. Long fascinated by Spinoza's bodily grounding of conscious-ness and his recognition of valuation in all our thinking, Antonio Damasio came to see consciousness as an extension of the brain's somatic regulation mechanisms. Paring down Spinoza's account, he situated it in an explicit evolutionary narrative: Minds began as gauges tracking bodily states but gradually took on more elaborate functions. Somatic markers, as Damasio called the monitoring signals, are projected to brain regions that mediate the emotions. The limbic system of the medial temporal lobe and midbrain, traditionally thought rather a visceral region, in fact engages with the fron-tal lobe, yielding the emotional impetus critical in all thinking. In making decisions, Damasio argued, we coordinate our emotional markers with the logic of our options. Patients with damage to the ventromedial prefrontal cortices, he noted, lose the input from emotionally freighted bodily sig-nals and have trouble solving everyday problems.[115] Damasio won plaudits for finding neural roots to Spinoza's recognition of the cognitive impact of emotion. But his model pivoted on experiments with just a few tasks studied in the 1980s and '90s. So there were predictable calls for further testing of its scope.[116]

In *The Feeling of What Happens* (1999) Damasio broadened his paradigm: Consciousness proved adaptive because it applies externally modes of response long vital in regulating life processes: "the organism, as represented inside its brain, is a likely biological forerunner for what eventually becomes the elusive sense of self." In a way that story presumes what it aims to explain. Perhaps that was inevitable. For James was surely right that the earliest distinction an organism must make is between self and other. So even an amoeba has a primal sense of self, if it pursues what attracts it and avoids what might be harmful. But it's hard to see how the somatic self can regulate bodily functions without somehow already representing the environment. Self and other are both already implicit here. The emergence of the distinctive human self, moreover, involves a diversification of interests and enlarged flexibility of aims, not just a shift from internal to external reports.

In *Self Comes to Mind* (2010), Damasio further broadens and tempers his views. Surveying a wealth of research on neural networks, integration, and recursivity, he still draws experience at large from somatic awareness. But now there is a self, albeit, once again, a process, not a thing: "My working definition of the material me, the self as object," he writes, " is as follows: a dynamic collection of integrated neural processes, centered on the representation of the living body, that finds expression in a dynamic collection of integrated mental processes."[117] There are many ways, he allows, to explain the disengaging of self from other. But "protofeelings" seem important. That sounds a lot like sentience—in effect pushing back the explanatory question and abandoning the reduction of consciousness to mechanism without subjective remainder. Damasio now lists the functions he deems critical for brains to generate a sense of self. But he does not seek to verify their presence or analyze their workings. He stands by somatic monitoring, acknowledging rival approaches without quite making them his own. Deep fault lines in his new account reflect his efforts to hybridize mechanism with subjecthood. He invokes feedback loops, for example, to generate conscious thoughts. But, as Tallis complains, he does not explain how mere loops can yield consciousness.[118]

Increasingly sensitive to the poverty of mechanism, some recent psychologists, biologists, neuroscientists, and philosophers have looked to the anti-reductionism of phenomenology, a school of thought pioneered by Brentano's student Edmund Husserl (1859–1938), who sought to build on Descartes' focus on consciousness.[119] Aiming to make a place for consciousness in the body, Maurice Merleau-Ponty (1908–1961) highlighted the play of mental patterns and our active engagement with things: Like a soccer player, a living being navigates a world of obstacles and opportunities. Consciousness entails motility and doing. Interests situate everything: The crumbs we notice in the corner are not what the mouse sees.

The approach dovetails with Gestalt findings and with recent research that presents consciousness in perceptual terms. Rodolfo Llinás, for example, treats consciousness as a projection into space of the body image of an organism pursuing food and safety. Shaun Gallagher too highlights movement: Consciousness makes frequent reference to bodily schemas and mental maps projected, often unconsciously, by the brain. Motility here is wedded to intentionality. Merleau-Ponty's dynamic view is a welcome alternative to any freeze-frame analysis. But the stress on kinetic actions and intentions may shortchange the stable and reflective sense of self—as if the I, no longer a bundle of impressions, had become an array of bodily aims: PICK UP THIS SPOON, TURN OFF THAT LIGHT.

Phenomenologists are sensitive to temporality, starting with the now that James and Bergson, using E. R. Clay's term, called the specious present. That moment was often thought measurable, lasting perhaps a few seconds, although, of course, the self typically persists far longer and frames an identity partly by recognition of its own persistence, stitching moments together—as thinkers as diverse as Augustine and Edelman have stressed: The very temporality that may seem to fragment consciousness or even annihilate the self helps it weave an identity, transforming the stream of consciousness from a process to a person. The linking of moments by our subjectivity is what Kant called the transcendental unity of apperception. Without it, he argues, there would be nothing we could recognize as experience.

Thompson, accordingly, prizes synthesis: "experience itself is temporal, and particular experiences are temporally related to each other." Husserl and James, Thompson writes, rightly saw the present not as a "knife-edge," vanishingly small, but as a duration, with "a bow and a stern," as James put it. When we hear a melody, besides what Husserl called the "primal impression," there is also retention, "directed to the just-elapsed phase of the just-heard melody, the just-heard note, which though no longer actual, is still being heard in the mode of just-past." There's "protention," too, "directed in a more indefinite way toward the immediate future . . . unfilled or indeterminate." Despite its openness, protention "does involve a sense of anticipation, for were a melody to stop abruptly or were a wrong note to sound we would be surprised." Composers play to that sense of anticipation, from the crudest musical gagline, musical pratfall, or sour note to the subtlest symphonies. "It is always possible in principle for us to be surprised . . . our consciousness always involves an open and forward-looking horizon."[120]

Augustine anticipates that thought. He knows the rupture time can bring: "I have flown apart into moments whose order I know not; and my thoughts, the deepest workings of my soul, are shredded by the havoc of change" (*Confessions* 11.29). Yet consciousness can spin a transient unity: "The presence of things past is memory; the presence of present things, attention; the presence of future things, expectation" (*Confessions* 11.20; cf. 11.11).[121] *Continuitas* is Augustine's name for the temporal unity that consciousness gathers, in which to unfurl itself. Reflexivity permits the continuity that renders consciousness coherent. So we are conscious not only *in* time but *of* time. By constant cross checking of present moments against the past in our wake and the openness ahead we orient our identity, consciousness positioning itself between emotion laden *memoria* and value freighted *expectatio*. Fleeting and linear sentience alone would be sterile by comparison, its sheer immediacy divorced from choosing, feeling, coping—the engagements that make consciousness real.

Nyaya Thoughts

The Nyaya school of Indian philosophy, founded by one Gotama (not to be confused with Siddharta, the Buddha) and elaborated in works dating from the sixth century B.C.E. for at least a millennium more, challenged Buddhist denials of an enduring soul or self.[122] The Nyaya were not materialists, although, like Democritus, they held atomistic views of matter.[123] Their teachings stressed predictability in the universe. Understanding was grounded in logic, with grammar at its base: "Grammar is God," one Nyaya thinker said. The self was a central concern of every Indian school. Some equated selves with souls; for others the self was a composite of soul and a body expected to fall away when the soul rejoined its source in Brahman. Nyaya schools offered an array of technical conceptions of the self but concurred in setting the self at the center of experience and activity. Embodied selves exist in time and space, developing as experience unfolds.[124]

Nyaya philosophers sharply divided not body from soul but thinking from nonthinking beings.[125] Situating the self in the world, they did not reject the veracity of appearances, as their Buddhist adversaries did. They acknowledged the power of illusion and the deficits of an imperfect understanding. But they trusted the senses, if guided by sound reasoning, to help us know and navigate the world. In life as we live it, soul depends on body. But no major Nyaya philosopher made souls reducible to bodies, since only souls are conscious. Consciousness, however, is not the self. For selves may lose consciousness. Nor is consciousness the same as cognition, since consciousness needs no object, as cognition generally does. But consciousness does connect with the world: The soul stands at the core of an active self, which appropriates and interprets all feelings, thoughts, and perceptions.

To the Nyaya, C. Ram-Prasad remarks, psychoneural reductionism would be just another delusion. No mere collection of bodily or mental states adds up to a person.[126] Brains, as K. K. Chakrabarti observes, may be the most complex objects in the world, but complexity alone can't make a block of wood or chunk of meat aware. Stars and galaxies are vastly complex, but not in ways that make them conscious. A special kind of complexity fits the brain for its many tasks as the seat of the self. But it is only to the understanding and intending self that desires, pains, and pleasures have meaning.[127]

"Perhaps the most impressive argument in Vâtsyâyana," Sorabji writes of a key Nyaya theorist active around 400 C.E., "is that I touch the very same thing that I see"—a counterblast to Buddhist efforts to partition the self into discrete moments or dissolve it into the flow of events. Sorabji sees an affinity here with Aristotle's plea for perceptual integration: isolating sense modalities from each other is no better than assigning perception to separate persons (*De Anima* 3.2.426b17–21). Sorabji presses the point against Derek Parfit: Why dissociate the self into a bundle of impressions and such while preserving unity for things like blocks and brains?[128]

Self-knowledge, the Nyaya claim, is won by turning inward. Reason and reflection lift consciousness above the transitory fray. A mere stream can't anchor an identity. That demands memory, which is inexplicable, Ram-Prasad argues, "if all cognitions are momentary and there is no permanent self."[129] Nyaya thinking shows more confidence in agency, understanding, and awareness than reductionists typically countenance. But their denials bend not to the evidence but to a passionate rejection of its impact.

The ritual denunciations of Descartes by reductionists voice deep suspicions of religion as an implacable foe of science, if not Epicurean worries that souls mean immortality and subvert moral naturalism. Why else would facts as manifest as consciousness, and the related facts of agency, be denied, and sophisticated thinkers step into Humean or Hobbesian boots to quash the very thought that subjectivity subtends a self? Or why would defenders of intentionality and careful students of neuropsychology and phenomenology insist on calling selves processes rather than realities resident in nature—even as they affirm that consciousness is self-organizing, self-maintaining, and self-affirming?

Enactive Dynamicism

Pace the Behaviorists, organisms are not merely reactive. They can't afford to be. "No animal," Thompson writes, "is a mere passive respondent; every animal meets the environment on its own sensorimotor terms."[130] Still, the old stimulus-response model is often retooled computationally, making the mind a computer running algorithms. "Computationalists," Thompson writes, "focus primarily on discrete states and treat change as what happens when a system shifts from one discrete state to another." Fixated "on the internal formal or syntactic structure," patterns "laid out statically (like snapshots)," they see cognition as the rule-governed transformation of one such static structure into another." The lockstep progression is "sense→perceive→think→act"—input undergoes a sequence of operations yielding an output. Then the system halts.[131]

In reality, Thompson argues, thought, like any life process, is always *in medias res*: "cognition unfolds as the continuous coevolution of acting, perceiving, imagining, feeling, and thinking."[132] Consciousness is dynamic: "the dynamicist does not depict the brain as a processing hierarchy that starts at the sensory end. Strictly speaking, brain processes are always ongoing and do not start or stop anywhere . . . preparation, expectation, emotional tone, and attention . . . are necessarily active at the same time as the sensory inflow."[133] Augustine's *continuitas*, Kant's unity of apperception, and Bergson's duration come together in that description of neural and sensory flow. The self rides *in* and *above* the flux it seeks to marshal.

Thompson sees both top-down and bottom-up aspects in life and thought: The parts produce and sustain a global order even as "global behaviors . . . constrain or govern the behavior of the individual components."[134] This reciprocal action—"circular causality"—divides organisms from machines. It renders "rigorous" the Aristotelian understanding of organisms as complexes whose components are defined by their contributions to the whole.[135] Even in bacteria, "cells tumble about until they hit upon an orientation that increases their exposure to sugar, at which point they swim forward, up-gradient, toward the zone of greatest sugar concentration. These bacteria . . . embody a dynamic sensorimotor loop: the way they move (tumbling or swimming forward) depends on what they sense, and what they sense depends on how they move."[136] Comparable up- and down- escalators are at work in every organism, all the way to our own capacity to choose goals and purposes: Neuronal inputs are integrated to achieve cognition, emotion, action. Understanding such patterns might help answer Tallis's question about Damasio's loops. Organisms, Thompson argues, are operationally closed systems—not in that they need nothing from the outside but in defining and maintaining a boundary between self and other. Such "operational closure," Thompson holds, is critical in any nervous system, recapitulating neurologically the "autopoiesis" that sustains an organism's identity.[137]

"The organism cannot properly be compared to a keyboard" played by external stimuli, Merleau-Ponty argued, since an organism inevitably contributes to shaping its experience.[138] "Stimuli" matter, of course, but just *how* depends on the organism. Nothing is a "signal" by itself; and neurons, by themselves, do not interpret sensations. Edges, lines, and movements matter, as we've seen. But it takes assemblies of neurons to discriminate such features, laying the groundwork for construction of their meanings. What the brain builds, Thompson explains, quoting W. J. Freeman, "is not a representation of the stimulus" but a dynamic pattern fraught with contextual meaning: As "brain stem nuclei bathe the forebrain in neuromodulatory chemicals," vast synaptic networks link past experience, present attitude, and future aims to shape a response.[139] If a reflex sounds a note, consciousness performs a symphony.

'Enactive' is Thompson's epithet for the dynamic of consciousness: An organism does not process information in the abstract, as if without a context, "Rather it brings forth or enacts meaning in structural coupling with its environment."[140] Consciousness constructs its environment, not in the shallow sense that wishful idealists may imagine, by dreaming it into being, but also not in the mechanist's sense, by simply changing it as a beaver builds a dam. Organisms construct their environment by *construing* it: Life itself introduces norms and meanings. That makes living beings "a new order of nature," not well described in the terms apt for describing a flame or a soap bubble: An animal is "an individual in a sense that begins to be worthy of the term *self*."[141]

Humans pursue that trend into yet another order of nature by using symbols, signs relating not just to an object but to other symbols and thus to a symbol system. But for symbol use to reach the level we take for granted, not just manipulative skill is needed but an awareness of other subjects, and a culture that allows individuals to answer and anticipate one another's intentions and needs—a society of intensively intersubjective persons.[142]

The Social Self

Healthy persons think about others. They relate to family, neighbors, and a larger society, often in terms of roles and expectations. Even when thoughts aren't especially ethically attuned, they're colored by concerns with others' feelings, words, and actions. Ethologists, sociobiologists, and evolutionary psychologists, viewing consciousness as an adaptive trait, have searched for its evolutionary roots. Some, seeking the origins of human aggression, stress the negative traits observed in primates and slight the nobler traits, de Waal complains. Chimps do have marauding "gangs" and conflicts. But they also show an interest in fairness and reciprocity: "A chimpanzee stroking a victim of attack or sharing her food with a hungry companion shows attitudes that are hard to distinguish from those of a person picking up a crying child, or doing volunteer work in a soup kitchen. To classify the chimpanzee's behavior as based on instinct and the person's behavior as proof of moral decency is misleading, and probably incorrect."[143]

It's hard to test animal intentions, but de Waal finds clear evidence of other-directedness in primates. Injured rhesus monkeys may get special treatment from all but the most difficult group members.[144] Responding to critiques by Peter Singer and Philip Kitcher, de Waal charges evolutionary psychologists with neglecting primate empathy, perhaps assuming that "natural selection is a cruel, pitiless process of elimination," that can only have produced "cruel and pitiless creatures."[145] Convinced by his own observations that "apes take one another's perspective," de Waal traces human morality to the empathic tendencies of the great apes.[146] Darwin laid the foundations here, deriving morality from herd instinct and pack behavior. Properly moral thinking emerged as self-awareness, memory, and abstract thinking evolved, laying a groundwork for anticipating outcomes and experiencing regret.[147] For de Waal, theory of mind is central: Awareness of others' needs and wants transforms choice making by extending personal interests beyond the self. The philosopher Emanuel Levinas finds the core of ethics in the human face. 'Face' for Levinas is a richly laden term, redolent of the inestimable claims of personhood. But elementally face means the look in another person's eyes.

De Waal lays heavy weight on empathy, an almost visceral sense of fellow feeling. He finds rich evidence of its power in our primate cousins. There's more to morality, of course, than a twinge on witnessing another's pain. Humans are pretty good at quelling such feelings. Surgeons and soldiers may need to do that.[148] And squelching pity may foster cruelty. So, beyond empathy, moralities invoke rules, principles, and intangible values. They praise personal and social virtues and blame misbehavior. Levinas finds a window on transcendence in the appeal of a human face. But de Waal begins with empathy, rooted deep in the evolutionary past.

"Most of the apes," he writes, "want to be the first to put their hands on food, such as watermelons, because once they have it it's rarely taken away by others. There actually exists respect of ownership, so that even the lowest-ranking female is allowed to keep her food by the most dominant male."[149] Rank is not a false anthropomorphism here. One could hardly study ethology without the notion. Ownership is more metaphorical, perhaps. But respect by powerful males toward others' food can't fail to count as deference.

The worries about anthropomorphism that de Waal and other primatologists often face echo the impact of Behaviorism and its denial of consciousness in *any* animal. Behaviorism, de Waal writes, "has wreaked more havoc" than any other psychological school—not just on the academic discipline but on the lives of individuals such as children in orphanages. Given the doctrine "that behavior is all that science can see and know and therefore all it should care about," emotions became "largely irrelevant," and the "inner life of animals" became "taboo." "Animals were to be described as machines."[150]

Watson, in the 1920s, confident that conditioning could manufacture any sort of human being, campaigned against the "over-kissed child." Convinced that maternal fussing instills weaknesses and fears, he established a "baby farm," where maternal contact was minimal: Parents were to touch their child "only if it has behaved incredibly well, and not with a hug or kiss, but rather with a little pat on the head." The effects, de Waal writes, "were deadly." Orphans kept in cribs, separated by white sheets, without social stimulation or body contact, never cooed to, held, or tickled, "looked like zombies, with immobile faces and wide-open, expressionless eyes." Harry Harlow's experiments with maternal deprivation of monkeys had similar devastating effects. Monkeys reared in isolation proved unable to interact socially: "As adults, they couldn't even copulate or nurse offspring."[151]

An ironic byproduct of the mechanistic bias was the term 'bonding,' originally coined to deaden anthropomorphic overtones. Life itself was the corrective. The mechanistic connotations of the word gave way in time to the warmer tone familiar today. Describing a shared eureka moment, de Waal relates how the Yerkes staff labored through the summer to build a new climbing structure for the center's chimps, keeping them confined during construction. The team wondered which chimps would first touch the big wooden poles, and which would first climb to the top. But "we had forgotten that the apes had been locked up for days in separate cages. The first minutes following the release were all about social connections. Some chimps literally jumped into each other's arms, embracing and kissing."[152]

Noting the thread of sociality that unites groups in many species, de

Waal sees security as "the first and foremost reason for social life." That theme has varied meanings in schooling fish, flocking starlings, geese flying in V-formation, migrating wildebeests, and pack hunting wolves. De Waal compares the single-file march of chimps to the way humans fall into step with one another. The moral he draws is neither romantic nor reductive. He knows that chimps make war and can be vicious. "There exists, in fact, no obligatory connection between empathy and kindness, and no animal can afford treating everyone nicely all the time: Every animal faces competition over food, mates, and territory. A society based on empathy is no more free of conflict than a marriage based on love."[153] Nonetheless, he sees in animal bonding traits critical to all sociality and foundational in human caring.

Apes laugh, de Waal notes, "their hoarse, panting laughs . . . often in response to incongruity—such as when a tiny ape infant chases the group's top male, who runs away 'scared,' laughing all the while."[154] Primates laugh together and yawn together, as people do, "but children with autism are immune to the yawns of others." Chimps teach each other new skills. An experienced mother modeled the cupped hand in which her friend could catch her newborn. Others gathered to watch the birth and then embraced each other. The "separation calls" mammalian mothers use to round up their lost young are no surprise. But de Waal can also cite Russell Church's finding that rats will forgo pressing a lever for a food reward if they see it causes pain to another. "This work was subsequently ignored, due partly to the taboo on animal emotions, and partly to the traditional emphasis on the nasty side of nature." But fashions change. So there's a "growing consensus that emotional linkage between individuals has the same biological basis in humans and in other animals."[155]

> It's obviously not the imaginative kind of empathy that makes us truly understand how someone else feels, even someone we don't see, for example, when we read about the fate of a character in *War and Peace*. . . . Imagining can be a cold affair, not unlike the way we understand how an airplane flies. Empathy requires first of all emotional engagement. The mice show us how things may have gotten started. Seeing another person's emotions arouses our own emotions, and from there we go on constructing a more advanced understanding of the other's situation. Bodily connections come first—understanding follows.[156]

The affective expressions of animals, de Waal writes, are "most parsimoniously explained in the same way we explain our own behavior—as the result of a complex, and familiar, inner life."[157] Reductionism flattens the

connection, pushing humans toward the animal pole. Reflecting on his encounters with Richard Dawkins, de Waal writes: "The selfish/unselfish divide
may be a red herring. Why try to extract the self from the other, or the other
from the self, if the merging of the two is the secret behind our cooperative
nature?" Empathy need not be kindness, de Waal concedes. But empathy, he
adds, as if echoing Levinas, "needs a face."[158]

A macaque, as Giacomo Rizzolatti and his colleagues discovered, has neurons that respond to the motions of companions with essentially the same
signals as those that fire in the actual production of a corresponding gesture.
Here motor and sensory functions meet and seem not just to track but mentally to emulate another's movements.[159] In these "mirror neurons," which
somehow seem to double at performing the conventionally discrete sensory
and motor functions, we can see, at the neuronal level, a physiological but
also *social* counterpart to intentionality. Marco Iacoboni and his colleagues
suggest that mirror neurons can detect quite subtle differences of pattern, allowing human subjects to distinguish, for example, whether someone picking up a teacup meant to drink from it or just to clear the table. Empathy, too,
Iacoboni reasoned, has roots in mirror neurons. De Waal is inclined to agree.

Mirror neurons may help explain how sports fans share vicariously in
the actions they observe on the court or in the field, and become so engaged in a game or match they're watching: In a sense they're not just watching but mentally taking part. For Ramachandran, mirror neurons lie at the
critical interface between self-awareness and social awareness. For the two
are clearly intertwined, at least in origin. Human infants will return a smile
in two months or less; within a year most learn to wave. Far more than
modeling is at stake in such a response. Our responses to one another as
we mature and our interactions proliferate don't just *reflect* one another's
movements or intentions but grow truly interactive: Displays of anger might
elicit matching anger—or, fear, perhaps, or conciliatory words. Consciousness here, with all its privacy, is also social—social because it is personal, but
personal because it is social.

Connecting self-awareness and consciousness of others, Ulric Neisser
(1928–2012), a founder of cognitive psychology, distinguishes five ways in
which we know ourselves:

The ecological self is the self as perceived with respect to the physical environment: I am the person here in this place, engaged in this particular activity. The
interpersonal self, which appears from earliest infancy just as the ecological
self does, is specified by species-specific signals of emotional rapport and communication: I am the person who is engaged, here, in this particular human

interchange. The extended self is based primarily on our personal memories and anticipations: I am the person who had certain specific experiences, who regularly engages in certain specific and familiar routines. The private self appears when children first notice that some of their experiences are not directly shared with other people: I am, in principle, the only person who can feel this unique and particular pain. The conceptual self or 'self-concept' draws its meaning from the network of assumptions and theories in which it is embedded, just as all other concepts do. Some of those theories concern social roles (husband, professor, American), some postulate more or less hypothetical internal entities (the soul, the unconscious mind, mental energy, the brain, the liver), and some establish socially significant dimensions of difference (intelligence, attractiveness, wealth). There is a remarkable variety in what people believe about themselves, and not all of it is true.[160]

Neisser sees the "ecological" and "interpersonal" selves as complements, not alternatives, one situated in the natural environment, the other in a society of selves.

> Human beings have access to many forms of knowing about self and world—ecological perception, social perception, memory, verbal instruction, conception, reflection, introspective awareness. But philosophers concerned with the self have not treated all those forms with equal respect or given them equal time. From Descartes and Hume through James and Mead to modern cognitive science, theorists of the self have usually looked inward, trying to find the self inside the head. The results have been disturbing: the harder they look, the less self they find.[161]

Neisser quotes Dennett, "one of the most articulate of the current crop of mentalists":

> Searching for the self can be somewhat like [this], You enter the brain through the eye, march up the optic nerve, round and round in the cortex, looking behind every neuron, and then, before you know it, you emerge into daylight on the spike of a motor nerve impulse, scratching your head and wondering where the self is.[162]

Neisser comments:

> Dennett eventually concludes that the self simply does not exist; it is only a 'narrative fiction.' This outcome is hardly surprising: David Hume reached

more or less the same position two hundred years ago on the basis of a similar argument. I think that such conclusions are inevitable as long as the search for the self is confined to the inside of the head. Fortunately, there is another place to look. Each of us is an active agent in a real environment, and we can directly see that this is the case. Thus we are and know that we are ecological selves.[163]

Borrowing the phrase 'ecological self' from his longtime Cornell colleague James Gibson, Neisser enriches the idea of self-knowledge, underscoring the multifaceted character of consciousness. Granted some psychologists equate self-awareness with the ability to recognize oneself in the mirror. But, as any teenager working out an identity surely knows, self-knowledge can mean much more than that. And even a child's ability to distinguish self from other builds upon a core sense of self already in place. Once again we find that searching for the smallest parts of a thing is not always the surest path to understanding. Context can give understanding more scope.

Broadening Gibson's concept of "optic flows," visual cues that we use in plotting bodily movements, Neisser describes how we assemble information about the world, relating it to a sense of self that we construct in counterpoint with a growing sense of our surroundings. Physically this self may include clothing, shoes, prostheses—any extension of the body "responsive to intentions and coordinated with shifts of viewpoint."[164] It may also take in property and one's personal space and reputation. We do distinguish ourselves from external things. But a rider or driver readily treats a mount or vehicle as an extension of the body—just as an instrumentalist might with a flute or violin.

Ecological consciousness relies on perception, but it is hardly a bundle of sensa. Perception already presumes a perspective and a sense of self, even if inchoate. We naturally measure the world against ourselves, scaling things to our gaze. So childhood settings look smaller when we revisit them as adults. Bjorn van den Hoort and Henrik Ehrsson of the Karolinska Institute in Sweden supplied volunteers with video feed from the perspective of dolls much smaller or larger than they. Simultaneous tapping of a subject's body and the doll's induced impressions of inhabiting the doll's body. The surroundings were judged accordingly: The room seemed larger when viewed from the miniature doll's standpoint.[165] Hobbyists flying remote controlled aircraft have the sense of maneuvering as if in the cockpit. Architects use human and inhuman scale to make settings feel homey or intimidating. As we learn to navigate our world, even in infancy, our reliance on self-reference grooms our self-awareness. Our sense of agency, similarly, develops as we take in others' responses.

The ecological self is a perceiver, but it is also a doer. . . . As we act in and on the environment, we are aware of our actions and know them for our own. . . . I grasp a glass of water: the visual and auditory and tactile feedback thus produced coincides appropriately with the intention that drove the movement. . . . I know what I am doing as well as where I am going.[166]

The interpersonal, like the ecological self, acts in a world of meaning, oriented not by eye height but by interactions with others, who are often less predictable than objects. As we adapt, we enlarge our self-knowledge.

Although the notions of *encounter* and *between* may be unfamiliar to psychologists, they are well-known in the philosophy of dialogue. An especially powerful formulation is that of the Hasidic theologian Martin Buber, presented seventy years ago in his book *I and Thou* (Buber, 1923/1955). Buber distinguished two primary relations in human life, which he called *I-It* and *I-Thou*. The more familiar of these, *I-It*, is the relation between ourselves and some other person or object that we try to manipulate for purposes of our own. All of us relate to most of the world, most of the time, as *It*. Something very different happens on the rare occasions when we encounter another person directly, meeting them as a *Thou*. The relation *I-Thou* is one of immediate engagement, free of intellectual forethought or manipulation. It cannot be forced. The essential component of the encounter with *Thou* occurs between the participants; it is not to be found in either of them taken alone. There is at least a superficial parallel between Buber's dichotomy and my distinction between ecological and interpersonal perception. The *I* of *I-It* is something like an ecological self, while the *I* of *I-Thou* is an acutely interpersonal one.[167]

Neisser is rather courtly in saying that psychologists may be unfamiliar with notions of encounter. By now many have come across such ideas. But neither Behaviorists nor midcentury philosophers, troubled about our knowledge of other minds, made much of the interpersonal self—although Levinas clearly did. For Buber the *I-Thou* ontologically precedes either *I* or *Thou* alone. The Hegelian basis of that thought is spelled out by the structural linguist Émile Benveniste:

Consciousness of self is only possible if it is experienced by contrast. I use *I* only when I am speaking with someone who will be a *you* in my address. It is this condition of dialogue that is constitutive of *person*, for it implies that reciprocally *I* becomes *you* in the address of the one who in his turn designates himself as *I*.[168]

Sorabji makes a similar point: Descartes was wrong to suggest that we see others only as hats and coats and must *infer* the reality of anything more. Infants, in fact, "become aware of themselves as conscious beings only as they become aware of their carers as conscious beings." As a frontispiece Sorabji chooses a Mary Cassatt drawing of a mother and baby studying the child's image in a mirror, a classic moment in the emergence of personality, as shared attention holds and gently releases an independent awareness, much as a parent might model words and sounds or help an infant test leg and arm muscles.[169] A robust sense of self emerges gradually as infants detach their thoughts to follow interests of their own. Sorabji tells of a grandchild's response to a funny sound: "he looked at me first to see my reaction before feeling able to indulge in pleasure at it." This "alignment by the infant of its action or emotion with the *approval* if a carer" is part of the social referencing that marks the tandem emergence of a sense of self and other.[170] Just as body and soul are complements, not rivals, so are parent and child partners as an identity takes shape, the social self shaping and shaped by the inner, private self.

Adapting Buber's *I-Thou* idea, Neisser sees a ubiquity belied by the rarity of authentic encounter. But the special connection that Buber hallowed persists. For even in our most mundane relations we rarely confront one another as mere things.

> The sense of mystery and unpredictability that characterizes genuine encounters with other persons begins in the first weeks of life. It may be some dim memory of that primary experience that allows us to resonate to Buber's categories—to feel, as he did, that there is something especially powerful about the encounter with Thou. After all, we can affirm the ecological self whenever we want to, just by looking around and moving about. The interpersonal self comes into being only by the grace and response of another human being.[171]

Neisser preserves the primacy of perception. But he takes perception broadly. For, as the Gestalt psychologists saw, we perceive persons as persons and objects as things. In both cases we're anchored in self-knowledge, not subjectless impressions or passive associations but a motile self-awareness. For, whether in an *I-It* or an *I-Thou* mode, we engage the world as agents, our actions affecting our surroundings and mirrored in one another's eyes.

Consciousness and Souls

Intensive study of brain systems has begun to track the processes and support staff behind consciousness. Experimental psychology, behavioral neurology, and rapidly advancing research on visual awareness are opening the black box that long seemed so dark inside that some declared it devoid of content of its own, let alone substantiality. If immediate experience leaves any doubt that consciousness is real, a flood of new evidence swamps the old taboos. Complexity theory shows how self-organizing, self-referential systems can arise and flourish, emergent from simpler parts and procedures. We don't yet have a full picture. Our understanding is itself emergent. Pieces of the puzzle lie scattered on the table. But the facts and facets to be acknowledged are ever clearer. Brain imaging, experimental psychology, and clinical neurology reveal consciousness not as a jerky silent film viewed through a single cyclopean lens but as an active and reflexive subjectivity drawing upon a host of neural events integrated by the very subjecthood that its own awareness helps to constitute.

The idea of souls that science supports rests not on gaps in our knowledge but on the evidence for an emergent reality. Failure to find specific neural correlates of some phase of consciousness is no way to make room for souls. And finding such correlates does not diminish the soul. Substance, as we see it, is a matter of agency. So as long as subjects act, think, and choose, souls are undeniable. Understanding the workings of the brain does not unsettle that claim, any more than the fact that baseball pitchers need an arm discredits the fact that pitchers, not arms, play ball. Pitchers, it's true, are bodies. So are brains. But pitchers are also persons, and it's not as bodies but as living, thinking beings that pitchers play. Brains support consciousness, much as a good arm (working with many other body parts, including brains) makes pitching possible. Brains are not subjects, but they make subjecthood possible, not by housing some ethereal stuff but by fostering the emergence of a subject who can say 'I' and 'it' and 'you.'

Futurists entranced by knowing that the same content can be coded in quite a variety of systems, project visions of downloading human minds into self-repairing, even immortal machines. Such fantasies, we think, miss the message of our embodiment: The uniqueness of individual brains is as critical to our identities as the (related) uniqueness of our histories. Consciousness, unlike computer code, is subjective and interested. Our interests are anchored in our bodies; subjectivity sharply distinguishes consciousness from an algorithm.

Consciousness is not the whole person or even the whole mind, let alone the whole human soul. But much of the soul's distinctiveness is visible in consciousness. Emergent developmentally and phylogenetically, consciousness is rooted in the multiple layers of chemical and biological activity that enable the brain to do things no other living tissue can, coordinating the vast neurological array that puts our minds in touch with the body and the world as we turn from one thought or object or person to another, wake or dream, focus or meditate, zone, eat, walk, run, or ride.

Thermodynamics, Thompson observes, demands that any autonomous system "actively regulate its external boundary conditions." But, for that reason, "we can no longer regard life as a mechanism in the classical sense (an arrangement of parts externally related to each other through efficient causal relations)." Rather, we must see nature "as having a kind of inner life, for which the classical notion of mechanism is completely inadequate." Having exorcized the ghost in the machine, we move back "toward Aristotle, for whom mind and life belonged together under the heading of soul or psyche."[172]

FOUR

Memory

In antiquity memory and learning were sometimes described as markings on a tablet. Events and experiences, it was said, left an image, much as a signet seal shapes soft wax or clay. But if concepts came from repeated similar impressions, and general ideas resulted from multiple impressions, wouldn't the marks blur? And how do related impressions find and stamp just the right spot? Appealing as it was, the signet metaphor was misleading. Concepts are often crisper than sensations. And some memories match no actual image. We remember chores, appointments, skills, numbers like the square root of two. We may have images in mind when we think of such things, but the image is not the same as what we remember. Memories can be mistaken,[1] and memory has volitional and emotive aspects. Some things are hard to remember; some memories, hard to dredge up. Others come unbidden. We never fully, firmly control memory; but we do make conscious, often successful, efforts to recall specific ideas and experiences. And we can run down others, tracing one thought to another that seems related. Clearly memory is no mere imprint—the mind, once again, is no passive medium.

The oldest Greek texts distinguish *mnēmē*, a memory, from *anamnēsis*, the act of remembering—literally, "unforgetting." *Mnēmē*, the object of memory, might be a sign or memorial. Anamnesis brings it to life by making it conscious. In Sappho's poetry the mind is "shaken" into remembering. Diogenes of Apollonia (mid-fifth century B.C.E.) ascribed thought, emotion, and memory to air movements in the brain. Air was physical, but also divine, stirring differently in each of us. So memory, like inspirations or revelations to a poet or seer, was a divine presence or gift. Working out the genealogies of the gods, Hesiod made memory, Mnemosyne, mother of the Muses fathered by Zeus on nine successive nights (*Theogony* 53, 915).[2]

The arts dear to the Muses—dance, music, epic and lyric poetry, tragedy, choric song, comedy, astronomy, even history—were performative. Painting and sculpture were not included, their images, perhaps, too present to need a Muse. But astronomy was a daughter of Memory, reliant as she was on tradition, not mere fashioning. The name, like the parentage of the Muses, reflects the idea of mentation. So the Muses naturally became patrons of every intellectual pursuit—especially the seven liberal arts of the free man—the verbal arts of the trivium: grammar, rhetoric, and logic; and the formal arts of the quadrivium: arithmetic, geometry, music, and astronomy. Memory here connoted lore, but not slavish imitation, being self-directed and vital to creativity. As Plutarch wrote:

> Above all children's memory should be exercised and trained. For it is, as it were, the treasury of learning. That is why the myth makers made memory the Muses' mother, to hint that nothing in the world is like it in nurturing and creating. (*Moralia* 9e)[3]

The idea of transmigration gives memory special weight for Pythagoras. He could remember twenty past lives, his disciples boasted.[4] The uninitiated, they said, dwell in forgetfulness. Strenuous purifications could free the soul to recover its forgotten wisdom and escape the cycles of rebirth. In an Olympian ode for a Pythagorean patron, Pindar pictures the soul's requital in the afterlife (2.56–77). So cosmic justice too remembers. In his "Nemean Ode" (7.12), the Muses, knowing all, keep memory alive. Only they preserve great deeds, otherwise lost to "a sorry grave in deep darkness" (Paean 6).[5]

Plato moves artfully between a mythlike idiom and the image of memory as an impression—or, as he playfully suggests, given the elusiveness of memories, perhaps an aviary, where birds alight or flit just out of reach (*Theaetetus* 191c–196c). *Anamnesis*, as in Pythagoras, surpasses ordinary thought. It captures the pure Forms presumed in all real knowledge. Our access to such ideas proves the soul eternal—divine, in fact, awaiting only the cleansing bath of doubt and the vigorous rubdown of dialectic to scrub away vulgar prejudice and bring us home, aligned with every fulfilled intellect, in contemplation of the Forms, which the mind's unsleeping inner eye knew all along—timelessly. The images of things are cues at best, prompting recall of the realities that share some measure of their truth with the objects we perceive.

Aristotle keeps the signet metaphor (*De Memoria et Reminiscentia* 449b31, 450a25–31; *De Anima* 431a16–19). But Plato's point survives, even without the disembodied Forms, in the sharp insistence that although memories spring from sense perception they're more than images. For, as Anthony

Kenny says, "when we think in images it is thought that confers meaning on the images and not vice versa."[6]

Memory, the mainstay of tradition, partnered early with literacy. So the Muses were natural patrons of libraries and the places Greeks called museums, collections meant to stimulate memory and inspire creative pursuits. Plato, to whom memory meant so much, made a shrine to the Muses at the school he founded, the Academy at Athens—the first museum (Diogenes Laertius 4.1.1).

It's natural to think of memory in terms of storage, items pigeonholed until the proper hook retrieves and sets them on stage, like puppets in a show. The spectator account of consciousness resurfaces here: Memories wait offstage until hailed into the spotlight by the right cue. An anonymous handbook of rhetoric from the first century B.C.E., labeled with Cicero's name, vividly elaborates: Memories, like texts inscribed on wax or papyrus tablets, are stored in "the treasury of ideas supplied by invention, memory, the guardian of every part of rhetoric." An orator should read from these, picturing his mental tablets at some thirty feet, against a backdrop, in a niche, perhaps. Anticipating the complaint that such techniques are just tricks of training, the handbook responds that natural memory follows the same pattern. Training only enhances its work. A professional will arrange his points in order, selecting what to use and deleting all distracting thoughts before rising to speak (*Rhetorica ad Herennium* 3.16–24).[7]

The techniques prescribed in that Roman handbook and in a work actually by Cicero, *De Oratore* (2.353–60), like many things Roman, have much older Greek roots. The focus on technique shows how highly memory was valued by professionals. Plato tells of an orator's boast that he could reel off fifty names on just one hearing (*Hippias Major* 285e). Seneca's father claimed he had once repeated two thousand after a single hearing. He bragged that he could recite two thousand lines of verse shouted out by an audience, and even reverse the order. Naturally some talent was in play, if the stories are believable (and modern counterparts confirm their possibility). But technique backed up the talent. A favorite device was to learn a sequence, say of the houses on a familiar street, and link them mentally with each item to be recalled. The background image, once learned, was reusable, wiped clean, as it were, and re-inscribed like an actual wax tablet.

The technique, ascribed to the Greek poet Simonides (late sixth to early fifth century) was useful in debate and recommended by Aristotle,[8] whose early work in Plato's Academy was teaching students to parry the ploys of Sophists, who, of course, had their own bag of tricks.[9] The modes of argument Aristotle taught were thus called places, *topoi* in Greek, suggesting the mnemonic array. The usage survives in the title of Aristotle's early work the *Topics*, and the way we tick off arguments (perhaps on our fingers): 'In the first place. . . . In the second place . . .'[10]

Places were not the only mnemonic framework. There are alphabetical acrostics in the Psalms and the book of Proverbs. Students still use mnemonics like *On Old Olympus' Flowering Tops a Finn and German Brewed Some Hops* to memorize the twelve cranial nerves, just as music beginners learn *Every Good Boy Deserves Fudge*. These hardy techniques highlight the value of linking what we hope to retain to a structure or storyline, an alphabetical, numerical, or topological sequence, a rhyme scheme, or an association— like remembering Chrysippus's name by thinking of a golden horse in connection with his hair color, or reminding oneself of Mr. Short's name by recalling how tall his wife is. Bare lists are dull, hard work. But parts of a system, storyline, or argument come easily. Hence the force of *anamimnēskesthai* in Aristotle's title *On Memory and Reminiscence*: reminiscence here is not nostalgia but *being reminded*, as Sorabji notes: One thing is *reminiscent* of another, which leads to others still. Memory pursues connections. Hence the famous flood of memory loosed by the taste of a madeleine in Proust's novel celebrating the work of memory, which for him, as art so often is, was cast in a redemptive role.

Is Memory Just about the Past?

Always ready to find a physical substrate for mental functions, medieval faculty psychology, drawing on Galen's physiology, segmented the brain into functional regions for reason, memory, volition and emotion, sensation and imagination. Some philosophers put volition in charge, loosing or reining in the rest. So prominent was the recording imagery in the Latin West that some authors even equated memory and text: Both were inscriptions.[11] Didactic sources constantly admonish the reader: Fix this in your mind.[12] But modern cognitive psychology and neurobiology undermine the notion that memory is static, or even fixated on the past. Some ancient writers anticipate more fluid, modern models. Vergil, for one, aiming to celebrate the imperium of Augustus and define Rome's mission, pictures Aeneas, the Trojan refugee and fictive founder of Rome's future greatness, encountering his father's shade in Elysium and hearing from his lips words that bespeak Rome's destiny:

> *Tu regere imperio populos, Romane, memento*
> (*hae tibi erunt artes*), *pacisque imponere morem,*
> *parcere subiectis et debellare superbos.* (*Aeneid* 6.851–53)

> Roman, ever bear in mind the art that shall be yours:
> To rule nations and lay down ways of peace,
> Sparing the vanquished but battling down the proud.

Anchises wants Aeneas not just to recall past promises of his destiny but to live ever mindful of the role that it prescribes. He hails his son portentously, as "Roman," obliquely charging Vergil's readers to remember that Rome must rule—nobly, the poet hopes, in the cause of peace, clemency, and justice. Those who inherit Aeneas's mission must bear in mind, in their every deed, no mere text but a pattern of rule, Rome's destined art, contrasted here with the "softer," Greek arts of sculpture, rhetoric, or astronomy (*Aeneid* 6.847–50). What needs to be remembered, as Vergil projects it far into the future, is a way of life. Hence the force of *morem*, placed strongly at the end of the line proclaiming Rome's ultimate triumph, conflict past and sword sheathed, but ready to enforce the peace. Memory here, enlivened in the abode of the dead, is not just about the past. It points toward a future to be won, issuing a commanding message to be lived by and lived up to.[13]

Biblically, too, the claims of memory scan the future, inscribing a sense of mission onto a divinely mandated ethos—not dominion won in battle, but peace and well-being preserved by active remembrance of God's laws of justice and mercy.[14] Biblical memory too, then, links ancient visions with present commitments and future aspirations. In Islam the word that nominally means memory (*dhikr*) makes God the cynosure, a presence pursued in the whirling dance of dervishes, ecstatic loss of ego promising souls a taste of immortality. As Yadin Dudai remarks, "Human language commonly associates memory with the past. But memories are made mostly for the sake of present and future."[15]

Jurists and statesmen have long tied peace to forgetting—from the Law of Oblivion in Socrates' time, meant to blot out memories of civil betrayal and terror and quash endless rounds of prosecution and revenge, down to the legal barriers drawn today in South America or South Africa by Peace and Reconciliation commissions. Here again, memory is seen not as a static record but as a motive force in need of legislative or juridical control. Freud and other psychoanalysts see another active arm of memory, when they speak of "concealing memories," false recollections masking trauma. Memories, indeed, can change. Roger Pitman of Harvard and Alain Brunet of McGill used the anti-hypertension drug propranolol to ease clinical phobias in the victim of a violent robbery. With anxiety diminished by the drug, the patient's memories were refashioned, in hopes of making them no longer paralyzing.[16] We all know that memories fade, but this therapy showed that they can be altered. Tyrants and propagandists have long known that and tirelessly try to erase or revise public memories, which greatly depend on steady confirmation. Memory, like all of the mind, it seems, is labile.

Memory and the Self

In keeping with his role as a champion (and arbiter) of common sense, Locke follows the warehouse tradition, calling memory, "as it were, the Store-house of our Ideas." Its function: "to revive again in our Minds those Ideas, which after imprinting have disappeared, or have been as it were laid aside out of Sight."[17] As in the signet metaphor, memory here seems rather passive. The privileging of sensations leaves little room for the actual work of, say, committing things to memory. Activity comes to life when ideas are recalled, for "secondary Perception":

> the Mind very often sets itself on work in search of some hidden Idea, and turns, as it were, the Eye of the Soul upon it; though sometimes too they start up in our Minds of their own accord . . . rouzed and tumbled out of their dark Cells, into open Day-light, by some turbulent and tempestuous Passion.[18]

The storm imagery deflects attention from a deeper point. Even with unbidden memories, the mind is active, not intentionally perhaps, but through its own liveliness. The constructive activity of the mind in forming memories has long been known and was first formally described in the 1920s after a young Russian psychology student, Bluma Zeigarnik, and her mentor Kurt Lewin observed the striking difference between a waiter's prodigious recall of a long series of restaurant orders and his utter forgetfulness of the list once the orders had been served to customers. The Zeigarnick Effect, named in the student's honor, reflects our penchant to hold onto the memory of unfinished tasks, one aspect of the mind's propensity to complete a pattern, to build *Prägnanz*, one could say. Roy Baumeister ascribes to the same tendency what he calls "ear worms," the little tunes one can't seem to get out of one's head. It's not the melody that lingers but the mind that won't let a pattern go, least of all one that seems to need completion.[19] We see memory playing a similar active role when we tacitly supply answers to a rhetorical question or make the connections needed to get a joke or solve a riddle. But facts like these don't readily fit the storehouse model. Hence the evocation of stormy passions that stir up latent images. Empiricist theory wants atomized images as raw material. It readily slights the inherently referential, constructive, and often judgmental character of our thoughts. Even at their seemingly simplest, as we've seen, perceptions are synthetic and subjective, linked to one another and often to an object and to varied values and anticipations. Memories, naturally enough, are as well.

Locke knows that memory may be active or passive, retentive or spotty, quick or halting in accessing what's "laid up" within, weak or strong in connecting thoughts to form a picture or narrative.[20] But the warehouse model pays little heed to our penchant for forgetting, or just not registering past experiences. A host of sensations go unrecorded. Locke knows we can't be constantly aware of all that we encounter or keep before us all that we have learned. But he doesn't see how vital the filtering is that distinguishes a healthy intelligence from that of a savant who might recall long lists of random numbers but has trouble sorting out contextually relevant ideas.

Memory is critical for Locke in grounding one's identity. Indeed, his use of the term identity (which originally meant just self-sameness) reflects his construal of the self in terms of continuity.[21] Having anchored consciousness in sensations, he sees that without the power to connect and relate impressions there would be no self. Impatient with claims about spiritual or material souls, he locates selfhood not in matter or spirit but in the connectedness of our experiences, "the identity of consciousness, wherein, if Socrates and the present mayor of Quinborough agree, they are the same person: If the same Socrates waking and sleeping do not partake of the same consciousness, Socrates waking and sleeping is not the same person."[22]

Pressing Locke's empiricism to the point of deconstruction, Hume asks where one could find the impression to warrant any claim to reality for the self:

'Tis certain there is no question in philosophy more abstruse than that concerning identity, and the nature of the uniting principle, which constitutes a person. So far from being able by our senses merely to determine this question, we must have recourse to the most profound metaphysics to give a satisfactory answer to it; and in common life 'tis evident these ideas of self and person are never very fix'd nor determinate. 'Tis absurd, therefore, to imagine the senses can ever distinguish betwixt ourselves and external objects.[23]

Later Hume adds:

There are some philosophers who imagine we are every moment intimately conscious of what we call our self; that we feel its existence and its continuance in existence; and are certain, beyond the evidence of a demonstration, both of its perfect identity and simplicity. . . .

Unluckily all these positive assertions are contrary to that very experience, which is pleaded for them. . . . If any impression gives rise to the idea of self, that impression must continue invariably the same, through the whole course of our lives; since self is supposed to exist after that manner. But there is no impression constant and invariable. . . . When I enter most intimately into what I call myself, I always stumble on some particular perception or other, of heat or cold, light or shade, love or hatred, pain or pleasure. I never can catch myself at any time without a perception, and never can observe any thing but the perception. . . . If any one, upon serious and unprejudiced reflection thinks he has a different notion of himself, I must confess I can reason no longer with him. . . . I may venture to affirm of the rest of mankind, that they are nothing but a bundle or collection of different perceptions, which succeed each other with an inconceivable rapidity, and are in a perpetual flux and movement.[24]

In what follows Hume compares consciousness to a theater.[25] But by admitting to the realm of appearances only experiences that leave a distinct and distinctive impression—a trumpet note, say, or a hunger pang—Hume renders his empiricism highly atomistic. By demanding invariance he erects a hurdle he's confident no candidate will clear—recapping the demand Plato used to dismiss the sensory world in favor of ideal Forms. Locke had pursued continuity of awareness, often of pleasure or pain, happiness or misery—tacitly positing an interested perspective underlying our sense of personal history. Others, like Spinoza, had seen the self in terms of agency as well as interests. But Hume renders memory even more critical than Locke had. For how, if not by memory, will the flux of sensory impressions be tied up in a bundle? And bundling is as far as Hume allows memory to advance in unifying experience.

Kant, the most penetrating philosopher to answer Hume's challenge, accordingly invoked memory to forge a sense of object permanence, much as Locke had called on memory and the association of ideas to generate universal concepts, and as Hume himself had asked the same pair to prompt our sense of causal necessity. But Kant went further. The transcendental unity of apperception uses memory to connect fleeting sensations, lest experience melt away entirely. The natural question: How is this done? Kant's answer looked suspiciously like faculty psychology reborn. It readily fell victim to the same critique Renaissance masters had used in castigating the scholastics, for purveying pseudo-explanations that merely rename what they offer to explain: We're nourished by a nutritive faculty or aroused by an irritable faculty. Nietzsche lampooned Kant for discovering that minds work "by virtue of a virtue."[26]

How, indeed, are Hume's "impressions" bundled? By some inner affinity? And are bundled impressions mere neutral facts? If so, what makes them *ours*? We remember what happened on Sally's birthday, how the canoe tipped over and we all nearly drowned. That's different from remembering, say, that Bogota is the capital of Colombia or that δ is a rate of change. But even such memories are not utterly impersonal. Jim knows what Bill does not, and every memory is pregnant with personal associations. Are there memories without a self?

The Anatomy of Memory

What recent brain science and cognitive psychology have shown is that memory is better viewed as an activity than as markings on a medium or even an active filing system. The brain is responsible for memory, of course. But multiple, highly interactive regions take part. There is no storage bin. The anatomy of a memory, then, is best pursued not via dissection, but by distinguishing its types and following the work of memory formation and retrieval.

In a classic nineteenth-century study Edouard Claparéde wrote of a woman now known to have suffered from Korsakoff syndrome, a result of alcohol poisoning caused by a metabolic deficiency. Her memory of facts learned long ago was intact, but she could not remember recent events. When Claparéde pricked her finger, she could not remember his doing it. She flinched when he reached for her hand again but could not say why. Evidently, memory had distinct implicit and explicit moieties.

Researchers today distinguish several types of memory—most basically, perhaps, procedural and declarative. The first involves skills like cycling or playing piano, skills rarely called to mind in practice—and least explicit, we've noted, once habitual or when deployed by experts and virtuosi, despite the keen focus on their elements while the skills are mastered. Much of what we do in speaking or walking involves procedural memory. Declarative memory, by contrast, is referential, overtly intentional—*knowing that* as distinct from *knowing how*.[27]

Among declarative memories, psychologists and cognitive scientists broadly distinguish the episodic from the semantic: Semantic memory, despite the name, need not be verbal. It might include our memory of a face or voice, a car model or dress design, the savor of a wine or scent of a perfume.[28] It covers concepts and categories ('Is a wrench a tool or a pet?'), facts and the properties of things. Semantic memories are objective, not in that they are always accurate but in the sense that they have communicable content, albeit emotionally or attitudinally freighted. Episodic memory represents one's personal history from the standpoint of the present. Since even general facts are seen from a personal perspective, William James saw subjectivity alive and at work in every memory:

> Remembrance is like direct feeling; its object is suffused with a warmth and intimacy to which no object of mere conception ever attains. . . . Whatever past feelings appear with those qualities must be admitted to receive the greeting of the present mental state, to be owned by it, and accepted as belonging together with it in a common self. This community of self is what the time-gap cannot break in twain, and is why a present thought, although not ignorant of the time-gap, can still regard itself as continuous with certain chosen portions of the past.[29]

James speaks of a "mere conception" here to highlight, by the contrast, what is personal in memory. But, as his own pragmatist philosophy stressed, and as Spinoza saw clearly, no idea is strictly neutral. We affirm what we understand, reject what we deny, bracket what we doubt. Even a logical law like *modus ponens*, as pragmatists rightly insist, is fraught with value commitments. The warmth and intimacy that James cites caution us, in effect, that Locke put the cart before the horse: The sense of self is not a product of memory. Subjectivity is present and active in the framing of memories, which they enrich in turn. For if a bundle of impressions won't yield a self, still less can a mass of facts: "Memory requires more than mere dating of a fact in the past. It must be . . . 'appropriated' by the thinker as his own."[30]

Studies of amnesia confirm the point. Episodic memory can be lost without a corresponding loss of factual knowledge—but not without deficit. In 1953 a patient later given the code name HM suffered grave brain injuries in surgery intended to alleviate his epilepsy.[31] He became an anterograde amnesic, unable to form fresh memories. His childhood memories were largely intact. So were his working memory and short-term memory: He could recall what he'd just done or seen and did not lose the thread of a thought in mid-sentence. He could remember the events of, say, the past half hour or hour, or even, at times, a full day. But after a day the memory was gone. He had no long-term memory of events in his life post-surgery.

HM did learn new motor skills; his procedural memory was largely unaffected. As for semantic memory, his factual knowledge survived, although he learned new words and facts at best with difficulty. He was good at crosswords and could draw a detailed map of his new home but had trouble with spatial memories of his larger environment. Extensive studies of his case helped clarify the types of memory and showed our need to "consolidate" fresh memories if they're to be retained long term and not be swept aside, as it were, by new experiences.[32]

HM had a moral sense. In broad terms he had a personality too. But his emotions were impaired. The amygdala, the seat of fear and pain responses in the brain, had been lost to his devastating surgery, and his sense of self was so diminished that he didn't know his own age or recognize himself in old photographs. He did not think of his hair as having grayed but said, on looking in the mirror, "I am not a boy." He could no longer make memories his own—appropriate them, as James might have put it. Gradually HM's declarative memory eroded as well: After thirty-one postoperative years he still did not know where he lived, who cared for him, or what he had eaten for his last meal. In trying to estimate his own age he missed by ten to twenty-six years, and his guesses about what year it was were off by as much as forty-three years. By 1980 he said a hippie was a dancer, Howard Cosell a newscaster, and Raymond Burr an actor who played a television detective – although almost every American his age at the time knew Cosell as a sportscaster and Burr as the actor who played Perry Mason, the Erle Stanley Gardner defense attorney, on a popular TV program. At his thirty-fifth high school reunion, HM was remembered by many classmates, and one woman even kissed him, but he seemed to recall none of them by face or by name.[33] His surgery impaired both his memory and his emotional responses. But the dual losses seemed to aggravate each other: It's hard to remember what one can't care about, and hard to care about what doesn't resonate as part of one's personal story. In building and sustaining a healthy sense of self, memory and affect seem clearly to go hand in hand.

In another classic case, a motorcycle accident at age thirty left KC with bilateral lesions to the hippocampus, the brain region associated with spatial memory and the forming of long-term declarative memories.[34] Like HM, he suffered severe, lifelong anterograde amnesia. But he proved far better at making new uses of his earlier knowledge. He remembered the events of his past life. But the memories were "semanticized": He could not place himself in the recalled situations. They were now like facts about anyone else. Often he knew what had occurred to him. But he could not recall it as his own experience. He could name his classmates and the school he'd attended but could not remember being there.

KC's moral judgments too were depersonalized. He had definite likes and dislikes but could not relate them his own personality or character. He had a sense of humor and did respond to tragic and joyous events, but without strong emotion. He reported as a mere fact his family's evacuation from their home after a spill of toxic chemicals when a train derailed nearby. He recalled the September 11, 2001, terrorist attack as a fact, but his emotional responses were like those of someone hearing of the horrors of that day for the first time, no matter how often the events were recounted to him. KC volunteers weekly at a local library and learned the Dewey decimal system, but he could not say why or how he had learned it.

These and other striking cases reveal the vital nexus of episodic memory to identity. In normal life, we experience the past as our own. Our episodic memories, as Endel Tulving put it, are "accompanied by a special kind of (autonoetic) conscious awareness."[35] Such memories both support and presume a sense of self: Whether we embrace our experiences or recoil from them, or respond in any of countless other ways, our sense of ownership relies on and helps build our identity. For, as any good novelist knows, a character without a backstory is no character at all. Our growing, changing sense of self provides the glue and twine that bind up our achievements, losses and discoveries, joys and pains, fears and hopes, allowing us, pushing us, to flesh out our individuality, so that we can call this life *my life*.

Tulving calls episodic memory a kind of "mental time travel"—not that we relive the past as if it were present: "When you remember an event, however vaguely, you are aware that the present experience is related to the past experience in a way that no other kind of experience is."[36] Episodic memories, Tulving argues are impossible without self-presentness. They are unique to humans:

> episodic memory differs from other kinds of memory in that its operations require a self. It is the self that engages in the mental activity that is referred to as mental time travel: There can be no travel with a traveler. . . . "Self" and "self-awareness" are among those terms that are indispensable for discussing phenomena of the mind. . . .
>
> Some thinkers prefer a philosophical framework for the scientific approach to mental life in which the phenomena to be explained are expressions of processes, but in which the entities that do the processing (agents) are not permitted. Thus, thinking occurs without thinkers, knowing without knowers, and consciousness without anyone being conscious. . . . Eventually, self may turn out to be like phlogiston or ether, a convenient, temporary prop. But the problem today is that the story of the mind is incompleted and awkward to tell if a concept like "self" is omitted from it.[37]

Knowing that science progresses, Tulving concedes that selves may vanish like phlogiston or the ether. But he also challenges that expectation: If thinking demands a thinker, the admission that selves might one day vanish breathes less deference than defiance. The triumphalist expectation is that the more we know about the brain the less philosophy or science will care about souls, leaving only the word as a relic in poetry and other supposedly fringe domains—old line or new age churches. But Tulving's findings about episodic memory don't wash away so easily. The underlying processes, well anchored in the brain, are not mysterious and not likely to disappear as brain science advances.[38]

Memory, then, like consciousness, is not more aptly described neurophysiologically than in the terms the mind itself supplies. Molecular and cellular neurobiology study the same events that psychology and minds themselves survey. But they use differing standpoints. Expectations that either will collapse into the other only obscure their complementarity. Attempts to dissolve mental into molecular events will rarely yield a richer, fuller account than pursuit of the synergies of psyche and brain.

Location, Location, Location!

Modern efforts to localize memory took root with the vogue for the phrenology of Franz Gall (1758–1828). But anatomists since Vesalius had pursued the ancient idea that every faculty has its place. Steno, Malpighi, and Willis in the seventeenth century, von Haller and Morgagni in the eighteenth, Broca and Ferrier in the nineteenth, probed cadaver brains in search of the seat of brain functions.[39] Clinical experience complemented their speculative probing. As antiseptics and small bore ammunition allowed many more war casualties and victims of industrial and mining accidents to survive, physicians in charity and military hospitals increasingly saw patients whose injuries to specific brain regions could be matched up with specific mental or emotional disabilities and memory deficits.[40]

Eager to link brain to behavior, researchers soon turned from clinical gleanings to animal experiments, hoping that purpose-made lesions would uncover the home of memory. One stimulus was the discovery by Charles Bell (1774–1842) and the vivisectionist François Magendie (1783–1855) that the ventral roots of the spinal cord carry motor signals; the dorsal roots, only sensory messages. That finding discredited the notion that nerve impulses might readily course in any direction, or even both ways at once, as many had presumed.

Three lines of research converged, all three still pursued today: (1) studies of memory loss and the underlying brain lesions and pathologies, (2) studies of the brain's fine anatomy, opened up by the discovery of the neuron and synapse, and (3) studies of the electrophysiology of nerve signals. Connecting cellular and molecular physiology to the findings of psychology, it was widely hoped, would transform accounts of human thinking, feeling, perceiving, acting, choosing, and, of course, remembering, into a story about brain events. Using autopsies of patients who had suffered from various disabilities Broca identified brain regions for motor and verbal functions and singled out areas devoted to verbal memory.

Théodule-Armand Ribot (1839–1916), who had trained in philosophy and later inaugurated the first Sorbonne course in experimental psychology, worked with living patients affected by various dementias. He saw a clear progression of memory loss: First lost were episodic memories, as they're now called, fading in sequence from the more proximate to the more remote. Next affected was semantic memory. Then the memories lapsed that seemed most emotionally freighted, particularly those involving affectionate attachments. Finally affected were procedural memories, skills like horseback riding. Well acquainted with the findings of the neuroanatomists who had been among his teachers, Ribot reasoned that memory losses must reflect disruptions in specific brain regions: "Higher memory," the personal and factual content that he classed as intellectual, must reside in the cerebral cortex; "lower memory," the affections and other emotions, and one's repertoire of daily skills, lay in the brain's "inferior regions."

Carl Wernicke (1848–1905), treating psychiatric patients in Berlin and Halle, proposed the anterior temporal lobe as the site of verbal comprehension, since aphasia followed injuries there. Wernicke was no enthusiast of strict localization. He anticipated the finding that memory coordinates activity in a variety of brain regions. But his contemporaries and immediate successors were thrilled at the prospect of finding specific street addresses for speech comprehension and the memories that support it.

The Catalan neurologist Santiago Ramon y Cajal (1852–1934), following up on the work of cellular anatomists like Theodore Schwann, Rudolf Virchow, and Matthias Schleiden, and the crucial staining techniques of Camillo Golgi (1843–1926), discovered that brain tissue consists not of continuous nerves but of the microscopic cells later named neurons. He numbered them in the millions, although his estimates proved low by several orders of magnitude. Struggling with staining techniques, Cajal made out faint extensions at the fringes of the neurons. Did these, he wondered, allow neurons to interact? Here, in "the garden of gray matter" he saw "cells with delicate and elegant forms, the mysterious butterflies of the soul." Here, perhaps, were the roots of memory, elaborated as experience forges new connections among the neurons. Cajal shared the Nobel Prize with Golgi in 1906.

Committed to his cells, Cajal balked at Golgi's vision, of brains functioning as networks of fibers. His model encouraged the idea that memories are sited molecularly in specific cell groups. The findings of the psychiatrist Alois Alzheimer (1864–1915) seemed to confirm that thought. Following up on pathology reports, where histological stains had exposed many a disease condition, Alzheimer linked the memory loss characteristic of the syndrome later named for him with the plaques and other intrusions he saw in the autopsied brains of patients who had suffered from severe dementia and memory losses that left a patient confused and at a loss in mid-sentence. Confidence grew that memories would find their place in brain cells.

Electrical studies of neurophysiology date from the earliest experiments with electricity. But it was long after Galvani found that electric charges can make even detached muscles twitch before scientists sought electrical explanations of memory. Hermann von Helmholtz (1821–1894), the German physicist/physician who invented the ophthalmoscope, a versatile investigator of sight and hearing, whose thoughts on color vision we've already encountered, championed mechanistic accounts of life in general and perception specifically. Rejecting Galvani's vitalistic ideas about animal electricity, Helmholtz showed that the axon, the threadlike extension of a neuron, transmits sensory signals or motor commands down its length, as electrical impulses actively propagated from neuron to neuron.

In 1902 Julius Bernstein (1839–1917), a former assistant of Helmholtz's, hypothesized (correctly) that the "resting potential" of a neuron results from the differing concentrations of potassium ions inside and outside the cell membrane, laying a chemical basis for the action potentials that nerves transmit. Some scientists saw these pulses as a sort of telegraphic code and wondered if they might also store information. But, as Edgar Adrian (1889–1977) showed, all action potentials are alike. So they seemed ill-suited to archival use.

Alan Hodgkin (1914–1998), for whom Hodgkin disease is named, and Andrew Huxley (1917–), of the distinguished literary and biological family, traced the ion movements in an action potential and modeled the process mathematically. The firing of an axon is a release of current caused by a change in polarity: Sodium ions rush into the cell through tiny channels in the cell membrane; potassium ions stream out. Huxley and Hodgkin shared the 1963 Nobel Prize for their work, foundational to later work on ion channels. But their findings clinched Adrian's case: Not only do neural impulses have no nuances. They are are too transitory for storage. The quarry, then, would be some cellular structure or specialized tissue marked by experience—or so it seemed.

The Search for the Engram

Working in Berlin and later Breslau, Hermann Ebbinghaus (1850–1909) devised a variety of tests of verbal memory, aiming to quantify memory and memory loss.[41] Charting the speed and fluency of recall for lists of words and nonsense syllables, he plotted a general rate of human forgetting: Memory, he found, declines swiftly in the first twenty minutes, then less sharply within the hour. Losses level off within a day. The exponential decline mimics the learning curve Ebbinghaus also discovered. Both curves resemble charts of bacterial or organ growth and decline, inviting physiological explanations, much as Mendel's numbers fired dreams of access to the fine anatomy of inheritance, leading to the discovery of genes and the dance of the chromosomes. Inspired by Ebbinghaus's work many investigators set out to find the elements of memory: Knowledge would resolve to quanta, memory granules registering the sensa of which thought was made. The question was, Where?

Ebbinghaus's tests framed the paradigm of the "engram," a palpable memory trace.[42] The treasure map was drawn by animal experiments correlating brain lesions with lapses in learned behaviors—themselves atomized on the Behaviorist model. Ethologists could train rats to find and remember the path through a maze to a reward. Karl Lashley, a leader in the hunt, lanced or ablated parts of trained rats' cortex and retested the rats, seeking to single out the site where the memories were stored. The results were troubling: No specific laceration or removal produced the expected deficits. Massive damage had predictable outcomes, and bilateral lesions impaired memory more severely than damage to just one hemisphere. But no precise address was found. Brain scientists in the 1920s were stunned. Grimly Lashley wrote:

> This series of experiments has yielded a good bit of information about what and where the memory trace is not. It has discovered nothing directly of the real nature of the engram. I sometimes feel . . . the necessary conclusion is that learning just is not possible. It is difficult to conceive of a mechanism which can satisfy the conditions set for it. Nevertheless, in spite of such evidence against it, learning does sometimes occur.[43]

Lashley did not give up. He rationalized his disappointing results with a new theory, of mass action: Memories were still markings, but broadly preserved across the cortex; impairments reflect the extent of the damage. The metaphor of storage was preserved, as was the engram, since learning, as Lashley wrote wistfully, does sometimes occur. How could traces persist without places in the brain?

Even today some neuroscientists hold fast to Lashley's faith: He was right in principle but just gave up too soon. Some think he missed areas still out of sight. Or perhaps the lesions he inflicted were too gross. Lashley was John Watson's student, but like many a neurophysiologist he had discounted the black box idea, committed to exposing the neural substrates of behavior. His negative findings led him to extend Watson's policy: Psychology must bracket not just motives, intentions, or thoughts but any reference to physiological underpinnings. Watson himself continued to affirm only what could be observed. So, although he admired Lashley's work he gradually gave up calling neural mechanisms difficult or impossible to pin down and declared them simply irrelevant to psychology, in effect, off limits.

Refining the Search

The roadblock Lashley faced marked a fork in the road for later brain research. Some still sought the engram, emboldened by the work of Wilder Penfield and others, who correlated memory deficits with brain lesions.[44] But Lashley's doubts about the prospects of rummaging through the bureau drawers of memory prompted others to take a different tack. Spurred by the birth of cybernetics in the wake of World War II, they began to picture memory not as a nest of pigeonholes in a Victorian desk but as a network of processes. Philosophers, increasingly dubious about matching up thoughts with things, were also turning away from mental objects toward mental processes. But the hope of localizing such processes remained. Donald Hebb (1904–1985), a student of Lashley's, theorized in 1949 that the quarry must be a network of synapses that grows or strengthens with repeated or insistent stimulation. Friedrich Hayek, the author of *The Road to Serfdom* (1944) and winner of the 1974 Nobel Prize in economics, independently elaborated similar views in his 1952 book *The Sensory Order*.

The key figure in uncovering the workings of Hebbian plasticity, as it was called, was Eric Kandel (1929–). Disappointed with the Freudian psychoanalytic tradition, in which he had been trained, Kandel turned to brain physiology in search of the mechanisms behind the brain's adaptability. Ever hopeful that new techniques would shed light on memory and learning, he explored and exploited every breakthrough in molecular and cellular biology as it arose. His work on memory, recognized with a Nobel Prize in 2000, vividly reveals the strengths and weaknesses of the reductionist approach.

Seeking a lab animal with the simplest nervous system that still showed learning functions, Kandel chose the sea slug *Aplysia*, which has only about a thousand neurons. Egg laying, respiration, and the slug's complex sexual behavior, he found, all involve multiple ganglia. But the gill withdrawal reflex of the excretory siphon employs just one ganglion. This tiny knot of neurons became Kandel's favored research target. Even the creature's defensive inking response, also centered in a single ganglion, involved more than twice the neurons. Here was memory at its simplest.

In efforts to reinforce or inhibit the withdrawal response, Kandel found that multiple light touches to the siphon produced habituation, attenuating the reflex. The stimulus, in effect, became trivial. Harsh stimulation, as by an electric shock, produced sensitization, exaggerating the response even to mild stimuli. Kandel correlated specific neurochemical changes in the ganglion with each phase of the learning process. A sharp stimulus provoked an immediate action potential and withdrawal. Repetition enhanced the emission of a neurotrasmittor by the presynaptic cell and enhanced receptivity in the corresponding dendrite. Feedback to the presynaptic cell augmented its production of neurotransmitter.[45] Habituation meant diminished neurotransmitter production and an inhibition of response. For short-term memory these chemical effects seemed to suffice. But in longer-term sensitization Kandel observed the *formation* of synapses: New active sites grew on the presynaptic cell; new receptors, on the postsynaptic cell. Long-term habituation brought diminution of active sites and receptors. The anatomical changes, Kandel found, are gene induced.

To simplify their work yet further, Kandel's team isolated a circuit of just three neurons: one sensory, one motor, one specialized in releasing neurotransmitter. A key choke point, they found, was cyclic adenosine monophosphate (cAMP), operating as a second messenger, that is, relaying to the interior of the motor neuron the state of the receptor surface. At a single stimulus, the neurotransmitter serotonin was released, the motor neuron fired, and a transient sensitization followed. But once the circuit was sensitized by repeated or strong stimulation, serotonin production increased, augmenting cAMP production in the motor cell. A cascade of further signaling followed, activating cAMP Response Element-binding protein or CREB. That switched on genes in the cell nucleus that promote the growth of new synapses.

Here, surely, were the roots of memory. Flush with new Howard Hughes Foundation funding, Kandel zeroed in on the serotonin-cAMP-CREB sequence. Others had found such cycles in the neurons of *Drosophila* and other invertebrates. What about mammals? Tim Bliss and Terje Lømo in

Oslo had shown that electrical stimuli to hippocampal neurons taken from rabbits could strengthen synaptic connections for as long as several days. They named the effect long-term potentiation, LTP.[46] The hippocampus was known to be critical to memory, especially spatial memory. Were strengthened synaptic connections in the hippocampus the key to memory?

Activation of some of the pertinent hippocampal neurons is modulated by NMDAr, the NMDA receptor. Glutamate, the main excitatory neurotransmitter, will trigger these receptors, but only if the other hippocampal glutamate receptors, the AMPA receptors, are already firing. That requires a certain threshold of stimulation. With both sets of receptors firing, the NMDAr calcium channels were found to open and calcium flowed into the neuron, triggering a biochemical cascade that activated cAMP and CREB. The mice showed LTP: Long-term memories were being inscribed. The double key effect ensured that casual or transitory stimuli had no long-term effect.

But if memories are formed by synapse activation, how is it that, say, three hundred synapses of the hundreds on a given axon become active at a given stimulus? Are synapses somehow scored by repeated activation, letting protein messengers find the right site when a renewed stimulus promotes LTP? When chemical tags sensitive to serotonin and thus able to do the job were identified by a team member, Kandel had his answer.[47]

Using mice genetically modified with deficits in the expression of genes that code for key messengers, researchers were able to subvert long-term memory: Fears induced by training disappeared. When an inhibitory sequence was genetically disrupted, mice were bred fearful of any stimulus that had previously provoked fear: Learned fears were now uncontrolled.

Capping his decades of work, Kandel was ready to generalize: "The fact that the switch for converting short term memory to long term memory is the same in a variety of simple animals was heartening, confirming our belief that the core mechanisms of memory storage are conserved across different species."[48] Kandel and many others believed they had cracked the code of memory, much as Watson and Crick had broken the genetic code common to all living beings:

The mutually reinforcing results in *Aplysia* and *Drosophila*—two very different experimental animals, examined for different types of learning using different approaches—were vastly reassuring. Together, they suggested that the cellular mechanisms underlying simple forms of implicit memory might be the same in many species, including humans, and might be at work in many different forms of learning. For the mechanisms, it could be argued, had been conserved by evolution.[49]

Kandel had a point. Indeed, the pathway is not unique to memory. As Earl Sutherland (1915–1974) showed after he and Theodore Rall first isolated cyclic AMP in 1956, its biochemical effects are pervasive—in the gut, kidney, and liver.[50] Among known second messengers, in fact, the cAMP system is probably the most primitive. It is the crucial and sometimes the only second messenger system in single celled organisms. In *E. coli* it signals hunger. So the biochemistry here did not arise specifically to support memory. Neurons seem to have recruited an efficient signaling system already in use and put it to work to produce the changes in synaptic strength that memory requires.[51]

For Kandel, the ubiquity of the system was a strength. But applying the same explanatory model to conditioned reflexes in a rat, *Drosophila*, or *Aplysia* and, say, an actor's recall of her lines and motivations in a play, a conductor's memory of the nuances in a score, or a painter's recollection of a scene in the woods reconstructed in the studio, masks the differences in kind between memories laden with meaning and mere recoil at once-painful stimuli. Glossing over such distinctions risks ignoring critical differences among species. It's one thing to find what evolution has retained; quite another to suggest that evolution, over eons, has made no differences. But to sustain the reach of his hypothesis, Kandel ellides those distinctions:

> Repeated shocks to the tail are a significant learning experience for an *Aplysia*, just as practicing the piano or conjugating French verbs are to us: Practice makes perfect, repetition is necessary for long term memory. In principle, however, a highly emotional state such as that brought about by a car crash could bypass the normal restraints on long- term memory. . . . Similarly, the exceptionally good memory exhibited by some people may stem from genetic differences in CREB-2 that limit the activity of this repressor protein in relation to CREB-1. Although long-term memory typically requires repeated, spaced training with intervals of rest, it occasionally occurs following a single exposure that is not emotionally charged. . . . Some Talmudic memorists from Poland can recall, from visual memory, every word on every page of the twelve volumes of the Babylonian Talmud, as if that one page (out of several thousand) were in front of their eyes. . . . The same CREB switch is important for many forms of implicit memory in a variety of other species, from bees to mice to people.[52]

Gliding smoothly from explicit to implicit memory Kandel here papers over the divide between content and habit. His Talmudist, moreover, is not remembering mere marks on a page. He remembers their meaning. The feat would be difficult, to put it mildly, even for someone with a "photographic memory," who knew no Hebrew or Aramaic. But breaking down the distinction between explicit and implicit memory was part of Kandel's intent: "By combining behavioral analysis first with cellular neural science and then with molecular biology, we were able, collectively to help lay the foundation of a molecular biology of elementary mental processes."[53]

The work was foundational. But a foundation is not an edifice. Results with *Aplysia* or even rats or rabbits don't cover every sort of memory in every animal species. And even the *Aplysia* withdrawal reflex proves far more complex than first appeared. Kurt Danziger issues a sapient note of caution:

> the localized pattern of brain activity would constitute only a necessary, not a sufficient condition for the performance of a particular human action. These actions, remembering among them, are always part of a human situation, a social, cultural setting, from which they derive their meaning. Certainly they are necessarily *enabled* by brain activity, but they are neither identical with that activity nor mechanically caused by it.[54]

Necessary steps are not the same as sufficient causes or achieved results, and synapse changes are not thoughts. Brute memory of the sort needed to memorize, say, a hundred digits of π, are not the same as the rich connections that might help in memorizing French conjugations. Nor are those the same as the memory a French child uses in speaking her native language grammatically. Visual memories like that of Kandel's Talmudist are very different from, say, the memory of a traumatic experience, or the words of a song or movements in a dance, or steps in a proof or recipe, or the route to a familiar or unfamiliar address. Reflexes and episodic memories differ hugely, even if they do use some of the same physiological processes. The active side of memory is more obscured than explained by talk of reflex arcs. Memory is no more reducible to reflex action than it is to kidney function.

Kandel knew his model was only a beginning. But his vision of what it lacked reflects the limitations inherent in the research program that built it, the eager expectation that a single key to memory must lie in some critical neurological link. When a member of the team identified another element-binding protein, CPEB, that is activated only by repeated bursts of serotonin but then persists and indeed self-perpetuates, Kandel was elated: "Most proteins are degraded and destroyed in a period of hours. What maintains growth over longer periods of time," he reasoned, could preserve, say, childhood memories. That made CPEB "ideally designed for memory storage"—since it allows "information to be stored selectively and in perpetuity at one synapse."[55] But finding permanent changes at specific synapses does not explain how such changes might bear content. The reductive model is far too static and generic to answer that question. In a way it has not moved far beyond the signet ring idea—and, in a way, of course, it's less specific.

The Dynamic of Memory

Molecular and cellular neuroscientists often target a protein critical to some complex function in search of a crucial link. But, valuable as they are, break-throughs of that kind lack the comprehensiveness that would foster real understanding. One admirer, speaking at a seminar, we recall, called Kandel "the man who found the engram." That encomium far exceeds Kandel's claims. He anticipates the tracing of many a biochemical byway before the engram is snared. But engrams are more like unicorns than like viruses or genes. Memory is no mere marking system but an activity, integrative and synthetic. And the synaptic changes that make memories possible can no more be called memories than can the changes in behavior that memories may prompt.

Finding that the American aircraft used in the Berlin Airlift, the C-47 Skytrain, and its civilian counterpart, the DC-3, both used high-test aviation fuel does not show that high octane fuel caused the airlift, or that all goods reaching Berlin before and since came in DC-3s or Skytrains. Even during the airlift the British used a variety of planes to ferry their support. And we know nothing about other traffic from identifying these historic transports. Nor does scrutiny of the fuels reveal much about the cargo—any more than the original mission plans could anticipate the ex tempore candy drops that evolved into Operation Little Vittles.

The flaw in the reductionist models of memory reflects the question they began with: What are the simplest mechanisms of memory? The assumption was that every complex operation is explained by—or even eliminated in favor of—its elemental components. But, as Aristotle says apropos body and soul, a physicalist might say a house is bricks, but others might want to mention its use in giving shelter; a physiologist might call anger boiling of the blood "or some such thing," but it could also help to mention the urge to answer injury with injury (*De Anima* 1.1.403a30–403b10).

The search for the engram continues. Bruno Bontempi and Thomas Durkin speak of memory traces stabilized and consolidated at the cellular level.[56] B. J. Wiltgen, Alcino Silva, and their colleagues expect neuro-anatomical and pharmacological studies of the mouse neocortex to "open the door to a systematic and comprehensive study" of the molecular, cellular, and cognitive dimensions of long-term memory.[57] Memories, they allow, may lodge widely across the cortex. But they still see memory as a grand filing system, and many of their experiments seek traces of remote memories in the same region of the neocortex where an initial sense impression was processed. Relying on the idea of working memory, they blur the distinction between memories and sense images. But memories, unlike such images, typically reference the past as past. And, as Hume stressed, memories can be rather vague compared to perceptions. Indeed, Wiltgen and his colleagues acknowledge, "more often than not memory has a tentative, imperfect and fuzzy character that is hardly captured in molecular, cellular and systems studies."[58] Yet, despite the difficulties, the idea of a memory code persists.

Given the appeal of computer metaphors, notions of a memory code are not likely soon to disappear. As the dynamic character of memory grows ever clearer, the storage model has begun to look as faded as an ancient tapestry. But, even as the evidence mounts, those committed to cracking the code of memory have intensified the search and proliferated new experimental snares. Much as allegorists toward the close of the Middle Ages invested ever more imaginative energy in the symbolism of the hunt for the unicorn, today's engram hunters seem too entranced by information theory to conceive that the very idea neural coding is a false scent.

Joe Tsien, a former collaborator of Kandel's, writes: "real-time patterns" of memory traces have been "mathematically described, directly visualized, and dynamically deciphered."[59] He sees the activity of neuronal circuits, recorded in aggregate and analyzed mathematically, as "the basic mechanism the brain uses to draw vital information from experiences and turn that information into memories."[60] Recording neural firing patterns in a mouse brain, using large scale "ensemble recording" to capture the neural cacophony as a mouse undergoes "robust episodic experiences" like free fall or cage rattling, Tsien grouped the firings in "cliques," and with an elaborate pattern classification algorithm extracted strings of code representing high and low amplitude firings. The interventions mimicked events of presumed evolutionary significance—an earthquake, say, or a fall from a tree or cliff. An air-puff simulated an owl's silent stoop. Tsien's conclusion: A universal binary code "can provide a potentially unifying framework for the study of high cognition, even across animal species. For example, should a mouse, dog, and human all experience a sudden free-fall in a plunging elevator, the activation patterns of the general startle neural clique, drop-specific clique, air-puff clique, and earthquake clique in their brains would produce the identical real-time activation code (1,1,0,0)."[61] Further specifics may vary, but the initial firings will be constant.

Experience, however, is never invariant. Memory, as Edelman explains, is "a dynamic, recategorical system property, not a fixed storage of all the variants of a scene."[62] The memory "code" is degenerate, in information theory parlance: Many pathways yield comparable results. Redundancy, Edelman argues, fires darwinian competition among synaptic linkages, strengthening some, weakening others. It's in each individual's unique forest of linkages that memories arise. But the self is active here, not passive, constantly sorting and reclassifying content. Waking and sleeping, we link thought with thought and interweave memories with emotions, attitudes, values, and other memories, magnifying and multiplying the uniqueness of experience in the kaleidoscope of our subjecthood.

So there is no uniform memory code or common mental language. Minds read themselves, but they will not be read by machines, electrical or chemical, or remote, as some have fantasized. There will be no "cerebroscope"— not just because brains are too complex: "even if we could accurately record and analyze the activity of millions of brain neurons as an individual formulates a sentence, we could not precisely specify the contents of that sentence by reference to neural recording alone."[63] The unique and dynamic pathways opened up as we respond to experience render memory pathways literally incalculable—and explode the topographical myth of memory. Yet mechanism, the root myth, lives on.[64]

The Price of Reduction

Dudai imagines three types of Martian cyclops, each able to perceive, analyze, and understand all life processes but fixated on a single level of organization: One knows only behaviors; one, only neural circuits; one, only molecular mechanisms. Serious investigators, of course, might learn to shift levels and translate from one diction to another. But in much work on memory, Dudai writes, researchers tend to keep to the technical realm they know best—although a respectable reductionist agenda at its best would relate and connect the molecular, cellular, tissue, organ, and organismic levels. None of Dudai's cyclopes pays much heed to introspection. Yet it too might offer some helpful hints. Dudai unfurls a reductionist banner, but his preference is not to press to the molecular level. The "molecular and cellular findings are fascinating," he writes. But the simplest memories must lie in neural circuits.

> The molecular devices unveiled by LTP, e.g. the NMDA receptor and its associated metabolic pathways, appear very important in plasticity, therefore the chances are good that they are intimately involved in the elementary syntax

of learning. But it would not be surprising to discover that some other molecules, initially implicated in plasticity, when searching for molecular correlates, in the absence of circuit contexts, turn out to be, as far as memory is concerned, incidental.[65]

In the few years since Dudai wrote these words, LTP has been shown to be *syntactically* significant, as he suspected. Studies of addiction, pleasure, reflex formation, and the like have enriched our understanding. But there's been little about how memories become thoughts. Despite the enthusiasm for models based on the idea of coding, it remains unclear how LTP or any other mechanism of synaptic plasticity *bears* rather than enables content.[66] The *semantical* story remains to be told.

Psychologists, Dudai writes, were long prone to define memory as an "experience dependent adaptive change in behavior." But the reference to adaptation, he explains, packed the proposed definition with "Panglossian" assumptions as to the beneficial impact of all that might be learned. Beyond that, the reference to experience risked confounding memory with other changes—injury or disease, for example. And, perhaps most misleadingly, the reference to behavior, even when qualified with the assumption that the "change" might be latent, delayed, or dispositional rather than immediate, bypassed the *representational* character of memory: Behaviorists and others under their spell had conscientiously ignored the constitutive role of knowledge in memory. Partly as a result, they had negated the cumulative character of memory, the fact well known, at least since Plato (*Theaetetus* 153b), that knowledge grows from knowledge. So eager had they been to shun any suggestion of an inner life of the mind, that they had erased from their account the experiential intentionalities of remembering, recalling, and forgetting that brain science strives to match up with neuronal events.[67]

Learning, as Dudai argues, is about representations. Representations have intentionality. Memory is their retention. It originates in the world it seeks to chart and shows its impact in behavior and disposition. Its locus is neural circuits. So following these will help us see how memory works. But an isolated external account won't say much about the subject who owns these representations or that subject's perspective, the memories one just can't seem to shake, or the efforts one might make consciously to commit a fact, a name, a story or a song, to memory.

Undaunted by Dudai's cautions, reductionists like John Bickle expect psychology ultimately to yield to ever deeper reductions: first to neural networks, then to synapses, then to biochemical processes. Neuroscientists today, he writes, track mechanisms that will reduce complexity to simplicity and replace even biochemical findings with quantum formulae. Today, "the entire psychophysical reductionist project is at the earlier stage of development. . . . But the result is a step toward a biophysical reduction of mind. Except for heuristic and pragmatic purposes we will no longer need to speak of membrane potentials interacting with voltage-gated receptor proteins as a mechanism. The known biochemistry and biophysics (which I have only gestured toward here) will supersede the explanatory need to talk that way."[68] Learning how cellular and molecular changes underwrite LTP is not enough. We need to wade upstream to the tributaries and rills, to track the genetic determinants of our basic dispositions and portage back to the motor neurons and muscles, and ultimately to atoms and subatomic particles, dissolving everything human, biological, or even chemical in the end—as though only physics held understanding or could offer well formed explanations.

Fragments of a perfectly legitimate research program are here pumped up to omnicompetence, ultimately displacing the mental phenomena to be explained: Memory becomes a mechanism, and the actions and intentions that aroused interest in such mechanisms are erased. Where Behaviorists invoked black boxes to avoid explaining how sensory stimuli become motor responses, placing the putative mechanisms out of reach, Bickle announces the grand opening of the box and exposure of its workings, but all that can be seen, as Leibniz might have predicted, is the linkage of one mechanism to the next:

> Heuristically, higher level investigation and explanations are essential to neuroscience's development. But once they have isolated the relevant neuroanatomy and the candidate cellular and molecular mechanisms, the explanatory investigation shifts to the "intervene cellularly-molecularly and track behaviorally" approach. Once these heuristic tasks are complete there is nothing left for higher level investigations to explain.[69]

But explanation can take more than one direction. If we could complete the Democritean task of explaining all material things in terms of their atomic or subatomic composition, how would we understand the *relevance* of atoms—unless by reference to the complexes they compose? Some explanations are inevitably holistic or contextual; some are historical, as in studies of evolution; some are functional, without which there would be no physiology or medicine, and no concept of adaptation to anchor evolutionary theory.

Bickle finds all that's needed to frame a plausible theory of memory consolidation in *Aplysia* and *Drosophila*.[70] But can a conditioned reflex in an invertebrate ganglion or a trio of cells in vitro even be called a memory? The fairest way to adjudicate such semantical disputes is probably to tease out the senses of a term. But one needs to watch out for slippage from one sense to another in an argument or explanatory narrative. Clearly plasticity is involved when any memory is formed, and the biochemistry learned from work with *Aplysia* and *Drosophila* does shed light (heuristically!) on memory's evolution. But it's hard to say much about a sea slug or fruit fly's experience, and awkward to ascribe subjectivity to the electrochemical dynamics of excised neurons.

The familiar response of mechanists to the limitations of reductive models, is to punt downfield toward complexity, the immemorial mystique of reductionism—but an odd refuge here. Shouldn't reductionists be seeking ultimate answers in simplicity? The notion, evidently: Simplicity explains; complexity is what remains to be explained. But patterns too can make things clear. Without some pattern to frame the elements, even the finest atomism would not make things much simpler.

What, Then, Is Memory?

The memory a bee or ant relies on to relocate a food source is not the same as the conditioned reflex of withdrawal at a painful stimulus. Neither of these is the same as, say, Augustine's recollection of his youthful passions. Human memory is an active function of an active mind. It constructs contexts using the materials of experience. It is aggregative, each memory building on others and forging connections with others. Like consciousness, memory is emergent developmentally and over the course of evolution. Like other brain systems, it gives new uses to well established biological tools. Emergence is evident in the co-opting of cAMP but also more broadly, in memory's defiance of reduction to the mechanisms that support it. Reductionism, here as elsewhere, is confining, ultimately self-defeating, since it looks in just one direction, whereas explanation, in a living system and in mental systems par excellence, is multifactorial and demands a variety of explanatory modes.

Human memory, like human experience in general, relies on synaptic connectivity and the strengthening or inhibition of synaptic pathways. But our memories draw richness from the linkages established by active thinking as well as tacit associations. When we detect the scent of a familiar wine or cheese, or smell smoke, or urine, odorant molecules bind to nasal sensory neurons linked to the brain by the olfactory (first cranial) nerve. The olfactory bulb and the somato-sensory cortex create a unified sensation. Action potentials and second messenger pathways register the scent cortically. Just how is not yet fully understood. Our affective response is clearly centered in the amygdala, which is linked in a circuit with the olfactory bulb. We may feel fear, disgust, pleasure, or desire, even before the scent is specifically identified, the amygdala triggering a brainstem response resulting in immediate changes in heart rate, blood pressure, and epinephrine secretion, without direct cerebral involvement. Conscious memory blossoms in a variety of associations as signals pass to the thalamus and hippocampus.

Lively memories may hark back to our childhood. They resemble conditioned reflexes in that way, and reductionists like to ascribe their vividness to the close proximity of the amygdala to the hippocampus. But smell familiarity differs strikingly in neural profile from scent recognition. We know how odorant molecules affect the nasal tissues and how the signals they spark reach the cortex. But we still know little about odor recognition. The experience, as we relate a scent to other times and places, give it a name, seek a description, far outruns the conditioned reflex arc. Functional MRIs show wide regions of the brain lighting up. A holistic account explains more than reduction here. It's no longer enough just to follow action potentials from neuron to neuron. Knowing how olfaction works does not explain our experience of scents.

We experience our memories *as* memories. We don't just view them like old videotapes, unless, perhaps, in dreams. We experience memories *as* ours and *as* about the past. The freighting with associations is typical. In recognizing faces, or remembering places, flavors, or scents, we recollect related moods and attitudes. Old emotions may return, but when they do, our memories are layered with new meanings overlaid by later experience, perhaps even reversing our former attitudes, or coloring them with a sense of loss or gratitude, resentment or affection. Memories of this kind lodge in no simple circuit. They course actively, recursively through networks of millions of neurons that reconstruct the import a past experience might have for one.

Research on memory, as Danziger observes, is often skewed by the methods deployed. More than one researcher cites the old joke about the man hunting for his wallet under a street lamp. "Is that where you lost it?" someone asks. "No. But that's where the light is." Early studies of memory losses and lapses pushed thoughts about memory into clinical categories: The real subject matter was forgetting. The clinical work was revealing, but the focus on lesions fostered a "subtractive logic," as Danziger calls it, necessary links often treated as sufficient—as if finding some sine qua non meant capturing memory itself.

To Ebbinghaus and other experimentalists of his day, memory appeared most manageable if broken down to bite sized behavioral tasks, which Ebbinghaus conceived on the model of memorization. But our memories, say, of what we had for lunch, aren't so labor intensive.[71] We may admire feats of memory and delight in mnemonics. But neither is characteristic of memory's everyday uses. Learning the notes of a scale, a list of monarchs, the magnitudes of the stars in Orion, Danziger argues, is more like habit formation than like the memory of lived experience. He finds the elaborate taxonomies that some psychologists favor too deeply invested in "subtractive logic." Even the distinction of emotional from semantic memory, he notes, would have made little sense to medieval theorists, "because it was generally taken for granted that all sensory experience is affective in character."[72] We know now, and probably should not so readily have forgotten, that skills and knowledge are not unrelated.

Part of the appeal of the taxonomies elaborated in the 1930s to '50s lay in the hope of pinning each memory type to a specific brain region and settling each memory in its own synaptic niche. Cognitive psychologists, evolutionary biologists and ethologists, neural network theorists, and some geneticists and philosophers have criticized the notion. But its reductive appeal keeps it alive in the work of influential researchers like Kandel, Larry Squire, and Gary Lynch. Memories here become switching patterns. That means ignoring context as well as content and dropping purpose from the picture. But the breach between fact and value in HM and KC's lives poignantly reveals the centrality of their union when human experience is intact.

Just as tasks foregrounded in clinical and lab research promoted subtractive thinking, the machine analogies given eclat in the computer age distort the image of memory. Early on, when minds were compared to computers, serial processing was typically presumed. But if we must use computing imagery, human thinking is more like parallel processing, where multiple tasks are coordinated.[73] Linear models make memory too plodding. The rise of complexity theory and massive systems like the World Wide Web suggest the recursive, associative, interactive features that enliven our memories. To make room for procedural memory, critical not just in experiments with rats in mazes but also, say, in human speech, we need to consider the conscious and less than fully conscious engagement of the brain's subcortical regions.

Still, even the richer computer model is misleading, as Edelman observes: The human brain, as we've had good reason to understand, does not work by running algorithms. They would be of little use in meeting the challenges of a dynamic environment: "brains operate prima facie not by logic but rather by pattern recognition. This process is *not* precise, as is logic and mathematics. Instead, it trades off specificity and precision, if necessary, to increase its range."[74] Machines, in a word, are too mechanical. Real life demands continuous recalibrating and reorganizing of our thinking. Memory is critical in this give and take. But the agency here, especially in our most dramatic changes of course and redefinitions of priorities, is our own.

Toward a More Holistic Approach

A wealth of recent work reflects the rich complexity of memory in our daily lives. That was Neisser's hope when he urged broader approaches to memory in a 1978 broadside. Neisser had coined the term cognitive psychology in the 1960s. By the mid-'70s he was voicing broad criticisms of the methods long familiar among experimentalists. An underlying issue was the use of operational definitions to reduce memory (and other psychic work) to observable tasks. Operationalism drew its authority from the positivist equation of a proposition's meaning with its means of verification. Rich and complex realities became testing techniques. As Behaviorism faded and logical positivism lost favor, psychology proved ready to move on, partly in response to Neisser's critiques. But the old assumptions survive in molecular and cellular neuroscience: Memory is still not identical with tasks or lab observations. Conditioning may train Roquefort to navigate a maze. But the performance is not the experience.

Neuroscientists do reap results with rats, correlating brain changes with phases in the learning process. But changes are not memories. Cocaine-addicted mice, some neuroscientists claim, tell us all we need know about addiction—defined, operationally, as just another form of learning.[75] Human learning would be just a scaling up of the mouse's simpler circuitry. Wasn't that what Kandel showed? Not at all. To label a process generically, as "adjustment," say, or "problem solving," says nothing about how it's done, or what (in Nagel's terms) it "is like." Such labels fall back on the old device of renaming an effect and expecting the tag somehow to impart explanatory power.

'Plasticity,' can work that way, sliding from its technical use, denoting changes in synaptic strength, to a generic description of every lasting brain transformation, but expecting the word to hold its explanatory force. 'Plasticity,' John Bruer complains, is at heart a descriptive term often assigned explanatory work. The concept works well enough if we keep the word honest and avoid equivocation—assuming, of course, that mechanisms are what we're after. But often, as Anthony Kenny suggests, "mentalistic descriptions"—'he was trying to open the door,' 'he was threatening her'—

outshine "precise reports of physical movements."[76] 'Plasticity,' used generically, can be too general to explain much. Used technically, it may leave motivations quite opaque, partly by ignoring background and context[77]—as if we humans could not size up a situation, decide what we need to learn, think things over, and, quite literally, change our minds.

Neisser's focus is on human memories. Why, one might ask, do some people have trouble remembering appointments? Why do some know dozens of songs by heart but have trouble navigating the mall? Why do some have virtual street maps in their heads but balk at a punch line or movie plot? Are different brain systems in play? Neisser wouldn't disagree. But it galled him to see cellular and molecular biologists ignoring every line of inquiry but their own. He was interested, inter alia, in the nexus of memory with values. Strictly cellular studies looked blinkered: "shouldn't memory have something to do with the past?" What some experimentalists study, he complained, is not memory at all. That shoe fits many a current research program. On questions he thought critical Neisser heard only "thundering silence." The mechanists "were not uneducated or incompetent people." They slighted basic questions about memory because they thought they were "doing something more important."[78]

Mahzarin Banaji and Robert Crowder typified the trend Neisser rebelled against. They branded efforts to study memory in context through interviews and observations, primitive, prescientific, like doing astronomy with the naked eye, or chemistry by watching the dough rise.[79] But one needn't choose between controlled experiments and open observation. The question is whether studies of rabbits or zebra fish are examining the same thing as human memory. Knowing the simplest parts and processes, the experimentalists assume, should yield a general theory that needs only scale, and the bells and whistles that make human memory special. The possibility that memory differs in different species was excluded from the start.

Theorists, Neisser writes, were slow to recognize that learning as such does not exist. It might be many things, even in a single species. Familiar terms of art like conditioning and reinforcement need constant reinterpretation if applied in different domains. Ultimately, such terms lose their purchase since they name no single class of things. A good ethologist will guard against anthropomorphism. But reductionists sometimes miss the corresponding risk, of treating human minds by reference to a favored animal model. Rats and songbirds integrate past experiences into their lives in strikingly different ways. Just so, Neisser writes, generic memory "does not exist." The notion is a residuum of faculty psychology. What psychologists should be seeking out are the varieties of memory. This naturalistic approach, as Neisser called it (because it approaches nature with an open mind rather than a set of preconcerted concepts and presumpitons) has been yielding troves of meaty data,[80] vindicating Neisser's confidence that studies of *Aplysia* or lab rats are not the only avenues to a more perspicuous understanding.[81]

Much of what matters to human beings in memory, as Augustine, Locke, James, Tulving, Edelman, Neisser, and others have seen, is personal narrative. We recall little of our early childhood and nothing of our infancy. Freud called this nescience childhood amnesia. But Katherine Nelson, applying Neisser's holistic approach, judged the term a misnomer. Young children, she found, have pretty good memories, evident almost as soon as they can speak. Their little monologues, she found, serve mainly to rehash recent events. As language increasingly becomes a vehicle of shared experience, the children's priorities about what's memorable change. A child remembers getting a new doll, but to her parents the big event was a family move or the birth of another child. Quotidian memories of routine events, which to innocent eyes are filled with wonder, may be sidelined by memories deemed more significant by grownups.

Analyzing children's narratives for the content of memory, Nelson found that small things which had loomed large in childish experience may be forgotten once isolated from shared family narratives. The extent to which parents engage their children in dialogue about the child's experience has a powerful impact on the range and vividness of childhood memories. But so does each child's level of interest and facility in contextualizing past events.[82] Jerome Bruner writes of one child's reports, "we were struck by the *constitutive* function of her monologic narrative. She was not simply reporting; she was trying to make sense of her everyday life. She seemed to be in search of an integral structure that could encompass what she had *done* with what she *felt* with what she *believed*." Memory, it seems, emerges pari passu with language use. Both are critical in building a sense of personal identity, and that in turn is critical in constructing and integrating a sense of personal history.[83]

Nelson's work shows how misleading it is to think of memory in general and autobiographical memories specifically as mere data sets stored in neural networks. Synaptic plasticity is critical. But what we remember is no summation or resultant of synaptic changes. Even in a rat, memory is highly integrated, engaging multiple cortical and subcortical regions, including the amygdala and hippocampus. The simplest maze task calls upon a kind of subjectivity, the rat's subjectivity as it experiences discomfort, fear, appetite, pleasure, efforts at orientation, using what a rat can learn from its senses of sight and balance, proprioception, and, not least, olfaction. A simple task, then, is not so simple.

Many a reductionist would grant that memory does not resolve to some simple synaptic tattoo. Hence the stress on scaled up complexity. Tens of millions of neurons are excited or inhibited in any human act of memory. But more than complexity is at stake. Emergence is a better description. Remembering, like other mental acts, won't boil down to its presumptive elements or underlying mechanisms. When you bake a cake, or a dozen danish of different flavors, you can't just dismantle what comes out of the oven and put the ingredients back in their canisters. The brain collates memories and can, in some measure, manage them, helping us set our course by relating present with past experience. So, to function fully, memory must be subjective and intentional, focused on the past, with a view to the present and future, and typically aware of that. This intelligence gathering and reflexivity give dimension and depth to our sense of self. The work depends on feedback loops typical in living systems. But memory, like consciousness, does not reduce to the electrochemical events behind it.

A striking finding of cognitive science is the inadequacy of familiar notions of consolidation, which rest on the old storage model. Recall does not just hail discrete data from its garage. In using our memories we relate them to an array of cognitive, affective, attitudinal, and appetitive dimensions of experience. Each time a memory is recalled its contents are revised in light of present circumstances, past experiences, and future expectations. These linkages make revision inevitable. Memories decay or shift, suffer misattribution or misinterpretation, and are assigned new meanings. Strictly speaking, Lynn Nadel argues, the classic concept of consolidation stands or falls with the engram. And that idea, given memory's dynamism, "sinks under its own weight."[84] Science is a better analogue of memory than the old storage or marking metaphors: Science changes constantly as received ideas are revised, discarded, given new or diminished import, related to new, familiar, or forgotten findings. Science does retain an identity, but through continuity, not invariance. Memories, as Edelman showed, developing Hebb's insight, arise through multilevel competition among neural circuits in diverse brain regions. But competition alone does not explain the freshness of memories. Our memory of a familiar room is not a picture pressed in some album but active engagement with a plethora of patterns. By its constant reinscribing of experience the brain makes our personhood dynamic. Memory is inherently creative.[85] The life of the soul, then, is found not just in the connectedness of memories but in their liveliness.

Molecular and cellular neurobiologists, when they campaign to reduce memory to neural terms, capture not the substance but the substrate of memory. Evolutionary psychologists make a similar mistake when they

package putatively elemental functions in heritable neural modules, preprogrammed by natural selection: modules for memory and perception—not
to mention sharing, bullying, sexual aggression, infidelity, even language
and geography. Ramachandran lampooned the approach, proposing that
"Gentlemen Prefer Blondes" because ancestral males benefitted from an
inherited sensitivity: Fair-skinned mates afforded an edge in detecting parasites, anemia, even lying—since blushing betrays infidelity! For some time
the hoax paper was cited proudly by true believers, who imagined Ramachandran had abandoned his skepticism about such modules. Evidently
they missed the irony in his final sentence, calling his dummy hypothesis
"at least as viable as many other theories of mate choice that are currently
in vogue."[86]

Any evolutionary just-so story must posit some vital impact on the reproductive fortunes of those favored with a given heritable trait. So memory
becomes trait, a function reified, not a congeries of activities, processes,
thoughts, emotions, reflexes, cues, and values. We revert to faculty psychology, much as the cult of localization returns with finer tools to the failed
project of phrenology. Once again reductivism is running hard down the up
escalator. Atomic ricochets can't explain the work of memory. Only the active
work of the mind or soul can do that. Yet no breach of thermodynamic laws
need be posited. Plenty of energy is on hand to fuel the brain's micro-voltage
power needs. The activism of memory reflects the recursiveness—and inter-
estedness—of thought. As Edelman writes: "memory, imaging, and thought
itself all depend on the brain 'speaking to itself' by reentry."[87] The speaking
here need not be verbal. "Nothing is said, there are no words, their voice
is all unheard," as the psalmist has it (Psalm 19:4). Reentry here is simply
Edelman's term for the recursiveness that lets us think about our thoughts.

Beyond the Brain

Memory, we've noted, has a social as well as a personal side. It's not pent
within the brain or in a single mind. We make to-do lists, tie a string around
a finger, remind one another of things. Family and communal memories,
as Neisser and Nelson's work shows, can shape, focus, correct, or distort
personal memories. We use flags and insignia to evoke large complexes of
values with varying meanings for diverse individuals. Monuments and me-
morials preserve and give social definition to events and assign significance
to the lives and doings of individuals. Rituals enshrine social memories and
can also create, flatten, or re-color them. Texts and now the internet open
vast resources of social memory, much as tradition has long used song and

story. Literacy is a powerful tool of social memory, bridging barriers of time and geography, culture and confession.

The invention and spread of writing allowed civilizations increasingly to rely on texts, prompting persistent worries that memories would pale or fade. But the reality was more complex. Oral traditions, after all, are notoriously fragile. In classical civilizations like the Chinese, or traditional Islamic culture, or the Talmudic ambience, memory was a vehicle, but textual traditions were the precious cargo. Writing changed the way words were used and remembered, and literacy, as David Olson wrote, brought with it a need "to compensate for what was lost in the act of transcription."[88] Details gain momentum as personal recollections can be cross checked against more public perspectives. Broader contexts and greater explicitness are called on to resolve the ambiguities opened up when communication reaches beyond face-to-face encounter and the cues of tone and gesture, vocal inflection and facial expression disappear. As orality receded, documents were memorized, their sources still notionally oral in whole or part. A textual canon grew, pages laid out like a garden, text and commentary, orthography and calligraphy, inscribed graphically in memory, even their stresses and cantillations recorded, the written phrase echoing the stylized tones of the rostrum or lectern or the sing-song dialectic of study partners. The riffs and molten repertoires of bards and tale sellers, with their prodigious and creative memories, fed concerns for accuracy and detail. The gist romance gave way to Chinese and Arab literati who prized literary classics and honored verbatim recall. Far from freeing the mind from rote, literacy heightened the memory burden. Spontaneity retreated to the well schooled brush stroke and calligraphic line, and then the carefully edited printed book—and then, the electronic text, open, in principle, to anyone's correction or revision or dismissal. Texts and received traditions do not banish memory. Emblems, symbols, social cues, the repertoires and repositories of language, externalize the precipitates of thought. Memories were always both personal and social, but they swim in an ever wider cultural sea.

Memories are at times most tightly shared in families, but they also help form broader communities, which, in turn, keep them alive. A sense of shared identity is sustained by memories referential to a common history, powerfully linked with a sense of common interests and destiny. Written records can help shared or overlapping memories gain coherence and stability. Authorship breeds authority as a shared literature fosters communal sensibilities, actively preserved in the fluid memory of songs, sayings, and stories. Unique experiences become canonical, even celebrated, not just moments in the flux but festivals. Group norms and values are honed into concepts and arguments, theories and laws, tested in conversation, deliberation, and debate, and projected as seemingly abstract ideas and lifeways. Literacy extends (and potentially fragments) communal identity as publication expands the practical and intellectual franchise and links individuals in a broader transgenerational society. Personal insights and perspectives join the common stock. So shared memories, fed from fresh sources, can avoid stagnation—not least when the sources are exotic. But personal consciousness too is fed, as dialogue helps frame identities that are autonomous but not isolated.

Civilizational memories reach wider still—but spottier—bursting the vagaries of orality or the nostrums of community but insistent on expertise.[89] We like to say we know things about nuclear chemistry or astrophysics. But most of that knowledge belongs piecemeal to specialists. Much of it, in its most advanced form, including much of the working know-how of our way of life, is shared memory only in a very special sense: inoperative without collaboration. That was true even in the stone age cultures of the Oldowan, Acheulean, and Mousterian cultures. But it's far truer today. As Andre Leroi-Gourhan wrote,

> tradition is just as biologically indispensable for the human species as genetic conditioning is to insect societies: ethnic survival depends on routine, and the dialogue that is established brings about the equilibrium between routine and progress, routine symbolizing capital necessary to the group's survival, and progress the intervention of individual innovation that produces a better survival.[90]

FIVE

Agency

Our discussion of consciousness left questions about agency hanging like the heroine in an old time movie serial. James cleared the fog appreciably with his Darwinian reasoning, that consciousness would never have evolved had it lacked adaptive value—and thus efficacy. He left to future neuroscience questions about just how agency might work. We've now learned much along those lines. But many still see a murky no-man's-land between thought and action, thinking science incomplete until purposes are reduced to physiology—denatured, in effect. Unreconstructed dualists hail the "gap" between internal and external perspectives, as the moat preserving subjectivity, guarding the irreducibility of plans and purposes to mere causes. The alternative they hope to guard against is to treat our intentions as if they were mere occurrences that might just as well have happened anywhere—as if we were not the authors of our own acts and choices. But the impotence of neurophysiology to transform purposes into something they are not is no failure of science. It simply marks the differences between subjects and objects, treating human beings as physiological specimens and treating them as actors with souls and motives of their own.

Effectiveness

Great physicists long upheld the conservation of matter and of energy—as bastions of the ancient law *ex nihilo nihil fit,* nothing comes from nothing. Only in the twentieth century did those parallel principles converge: Matter and energy *together* are conserved. Exchange between them proves not to be impossible but a powerful and dangerous practicality. The regent formula of Einstein's new alchemy, $e=mc^2$, displays the terms in which the seeming incommensurates take each other's measure, linked by the squared speed of light. Fission and fusion are real—and, within limits, even manageable. Shifts of matter to energy, first hypothesized by Sir Arthur Eddington, prove as promiscuous as sunlight. The energy economy of voluntary actions is hardly as recherché. We know there's profit or loss in information. That thought is implicit when we conceive of entropy as loss of the ability to do work. For work requires energy differentials—and purposes to be won by shifting one energy modality for another. We can't get work done at no cost, by simply segregating higher from lower energy particles. It takes work to separate the particles, and even if we let them migrate on their own, energy is needed to assay their energy levels. That's an information cost of work.

The Biosphere 2 experiment, begun in the late 1980s, aimed to create a "closed," "self-sufficient" environment for research purposes. Built near Tucson at a cost of some $200 million, the facility was shut down by 1994, after facing numerous social and fiscal issues. But self-sufficiency was illusory from the start, belied by the heavy reliance on solar energy, not to mention the large start-up investment. The need of one participant to exit for medical attention, bringing back supplies (including tampons, it was said), brought media attention. But the reliance of the eight inside crew members on knowledge they'd brought with them, and their access to outside expertise, made the denizens of the three-acre terrarium no more self-sustaining in reality than the ancient stylites who used to sit on pillars in the desert awaiting food from their supporters, who also carted off the bodily wastes. The illusion of self-sufficiency lay in large part in discounting the energy value of information—including the information coded in capital. Thoughts don't weigh much, but they do matter.

Human agency is never wholly isolated from the body—or the social environment. Lesions, hormonal imbalances, drugs, and trauma can limit our control. Yet the notion that free choices demand a physical or social vacuum stirs the claim (or fosters the fear) that thoughts move nothing. Many fail to see (short of ghostly bumps in the night) how ideas could have an impact on our bodies or the world. They fall back into the very Cartesian trap that many proudly disavow, not seeing that the "gap" that excites their vertigo yawns before them only because they don't see that mental events have both an objective, physical and an internal, subjective side.

Some voluntarists welcome "spooky" modes of action. Nothing natural, they imagine, can render thoughts effectual. Nature, after all, must obey physical laws: determinate causes for determinate effects. But the assumption that causal determinism bars human freedom is, in our view, misguided. What starts out as an appeal to causality, in the end undercuts it by pressing for *immediate* determinations, denying causes the time or space they need. The demand for immediate results, cash on the barrelhead, in effect collapses time and compresses nature into what James called a block universe. It makes all necessities logical necessities. Natural causes, originally paraded as icons of determinism, now prove merely decorative.

The necessity of the past and determinacy of the present, understood in dynamic, causal terms and not crystalized as necessities of logic, do not extrude fatality. What is so need not always have been so. The assumption that no past cause could ever have been other than it was belies nature's fluidity and excludes all new and emergent causes. But in nature no event becomes inevitable until its causes have done their work. *Given* those causes, things must pan out as they will: Causes make the present what it is and make the past unalterable. But causes can be headed off by other causes. Causation is not a wall but a progressively closing door. So Yogi Berra was right: It ain't over 'til it's over.

Critics may hint at paradoxes in the very idea of agency, asking whether we might act otherwise than we do, as if to conjure up worries about identity: Surely one wouldn't suggest that things might be anything other than they are. Yet things do change. Time, if only for that reason, cannot be neglected: Causes coalesce; options narrow. *Up to a point*, we may do otherwise than we might have. As we act, the die is cast.

To uphold human agency, one need only recognize that we too are causes, not aberrations but players who naturally influence natural events. We are not sheer butts of circumstance. So if all events are causally determined, there's still room for agency. Our choices are not outside the panoply of causes, because we're part of it. Yet somehow this line of response to denials of human freedom, natural contingency, real possibility, and the open future, seems underutilized. Underrating the work of feedback, memory, planning, reflection, and judgment—perhaps presuming only third-person perspectives to be objective—many seem to think of all causation as *external* and overlook what we contribute when we act.[1]

Those who deny inboard agency stake the farm on nature's "closure," calling rival views unscientific.[2] But if closure means no energy from "outside" nature, voluntarists need not worry. Organisms harvest plenty of energy, including what they need to make their way. The question is not how they find the energy they need but how they exercise volitions—make choices in the human case. James's short answer was that evolution has graded the road. A longer answer, tapping the brain science James awaited, needs nothing spooky, or indeterministic, even if we do see something miraculous at each evolutionary and developmental stage as autonomy emerges.

The reality of souls stands or falls with agency. If persons influence the future, persons are real—soul being the name for what makes a person distinctively a person and not a zombie or a machine. If our actions reflect our choices and not just the play of past events, human agency bespeaks a subject irreducible to the conditions that surround it or the composite that grounds it. In any chemical reaction the reagents play both active and passive roles. Human doings too have an active and a passive side. But the test of personal reality is whether things might have gone differently without one's active engagement. Souls affirm themselves insofar as things might have gone otherwise without some person's active choice.

All events, we're told, are determined by the basic properties of physical things—atoms, molecules, and their subassemblies interacting under the core laws of physics; human choices are no exception. If brains and other complex bodies play a role, their behavior too must result from the disposition of their elements: Physics governs all events, its uniformities fixed eons before anyone was born, making every outcome determinate. Free will and personal choice are illusions.

But notice the glissando when a philosopher like Kim reads his resolution, "never go outside the physical domain" as demanding a supervenience which "guarantees" that *the mind cannot vary independently of the body.*"[3] Does 'independently' here mean without some corresponding bodily change? Or does it mean 'without a causally prior change'—leaving us hamstrung? In the name of naturalism, bodily events are set ahead of mental ones, lest souls be dreamed to act alone—as if body and soul were competing for control and body were presumed the victor, leaving no room for the emergent self to take direction of one's body.

Does the sovereignty of natural causes make the broadest natural laws sufficient to explain all events in nature? Or does naturalism mean simply keeping nature's laws inviolate? It's one thing to say that no body literally defies gravity, quite another to pretend that principles as broad and bald as gravitation can explain why marsupials have pouches. That's the core problem with reductionism: confusing generality with comprehensiveness— taking scope won at the cost of vast abstraction as if it offered a universal touchstone of explanation, privileging the primitive and ignoring the special capabilities that arise within nature's parameters at each order of complexity, capabilities (in the case at hand) that allow the kind of reflexivity that nurtures an emergent autonomy.

Democritean and Epicurean Freedom

Mechanism is an ancient corollary of atomism. Each Democritean atom was a physical miniature of Parmenides' universe. In each, in deference to

Eleatic logic, there was no multiplicity or change. But atoms themselves were many and moving. All visible changes reflected their presence or absence, aggregation or dispersal, as they fell or ricocheted in the void. There was a kind of emergence here, a colorful world arising from simpler natures. But the thrust of the scheme was reductive, deriving all qualities from the quantitative: shape, speed, and configuration.[4]

Strict determinism seems naturally to follow from the atoms' absolute solidity, every event the reflex of their collisions—a pinball world. Apparent chance was in fact mere randomness, the result of interactions too intricate to track. Everything must happen as it does. Still, Democritus seems unworried about free action. He freely dispenses worldly advice: "Don't try to understand everything, lest you end up ignorant of everything" (frg. 169), "Magnanimity means bearing tactlessness unperturbed" (46), "One must be good—or imitate someone who is" (39), "Immoderate desire marks the child, not the man" (70), "The envious torments himself like an enemy" (88), "The slave of wealth can never be honest" (50). Souls, like everything else, were arrays of atoms. For no primary reality could generate something wholly unlike it.[5] Each person, was a little world (*microcosmos*)—an enduring metaphor perhaps grounded in visions of the steady working of our parts and our sense of self-containedness.

"Virtue," Democritus said, "consists not in avoiding wrongdoing but in having no desire for it" (frg. 62). Character is not mere tepidness but nurtured by self-cultivation. Democritus does not blame poor life choices on bad influences but on those who choose bad models and fail to seek better (79). He rejects the relativistic apologetics of permissivism: "Pleasures may differ from one person to the next, but the good and true are alike for all" (69). He counsels choosing wholesome pleasures (74). Only fools, he says, make advantage and not reason their teacher (76). He warns against procrastination (81), calls it shameful to be more interested in others' business than knowledgeable about one's own (80), and even pictures the body suing the soul for abuse through lust and drink, mishandling a precious but delicate instrument (159; cf. 21). Evidently the atoms' dance left one free enough to chart a course—obey the law, the ruler, and the wise (47), seek moderation (285), and favor the soul's interests over the body's (37).

In the Hellenistic age, with personal choice a cynosure, determinism seemed a threat. Drawn to atomism by the Democritean promise that death means only dissolution (frg. 297), Epicurus resolved on a repair. He adds an uncaused swerve, the *clinamen*, to the motions of the atoms. If solidity grounds determinism, couldn't vacuity leave an opening for spontaneity? Thus Lucretius writes of the clash of atoms: *durissima quae sint / ponderibus solidis neque quicquam a tergo ibus obstet*—"atoms being so hard and solid— and nothing behind to bar the way" (*De Rerum Natura* 2.87–88).

The swerve was not mere randomness, near equipoise of rival causes, but genuine chance. It allowed Epicureans to explain the fruitful interaction of atoms, lest they just rain endlessly through space (*De Rerum Natura* 2.216–24). And it exempted volition from iron causality. "Better," Epicurus had said, "to accept the myths of the gods than be enslaved by the determinism of the physicists: Myth at least holds out some hope of grace through honors paid the gods, but the necessity of determinism is implacable" (*To Menoeceus*, 134).

Several modern thinkers, similarly, have thought chance the final refuge of free will. Eddington, for one, saw promise in Heisenberg's Indeterminacy principle.[6] But a freedom worth having, in Dennett's phrase, is not indeterminate. For indeterminism surrenders volitional control. A free electron, Susan Stebbing wrote, has nothing to do with human freedom.[7] Eddington had hoped to reserve "in a human being some portion of the brain, perhaps a mere speck of brain-matter, perhaps an extensive region, in which the physical effects of his volitions begin." But soon he saw the dead end and retreated: "There is no halfway house. . . . Either the behavior is a matter of chance, in which case the precise behavior . . . depends on chance and not volition. Or it is not wholly a matter of chance, in which case the Heisenberg limits are . . . irrelevant."[8]

Some voluntarists still invoke indeterminacy, but Eddington's quandary persists. Robert Kane, favoring a quantum approach, cites the Nobel laureates Arthur Holly Compton and Sir John Eccles as kindred spirits. But he's keenly aware that to surrender choice to chance undermines freedom rather than preserving it. Chance twitches and tremors would only disrupt our actions. Brain flickers might turn volitions into dithering and indecision. What would keep our feet from just walking away with us unbidden, as Schopenhauer once suggested?[9] What freedom needs is *self*-determination.

Self-awareness can reopen the terrain, as Aristotle saw: Rationality (*logos*) makes us responsible for our choices. We know something of our options, and the agency is our own when we consider the possibilities and choose reflectively among them. Are irrational choices unfree, then? Are we free when we heed reason but not when we make appetites or passions our "teacher"— reason "dragged about," by its inferiors, as Plato put it (*Protagoras* 352)? Are actions free only when wisely chosen, leaving us not responsible for our misdeeds? That question troubles Kant's account, where freedom hews so close to reason that selfish choices are branded "heteronomous." Kant denies that immoral acts are *eo ipso* unfree, as if to rob agents of the dignity of personhood: We blame the thief because he *chose* to steal. But the nexus of Kantian morals to explanation remains tender and delicate. Autonomy, Kant's counterpart to Aristotle's ideal of self-sufficiency, retreats to the ghostly noumenal world, called to testify in matters of praise or blame, punishment or reward, but unreachable when explanation is the goal. Kant preserves the moral realm, with its implicit reference to freedom, but only by setting fire doors between morality and science.

Aristotle, by contrast, recognizing how our choices help shape our character, finds freedom rooted all our activities, even where appetite or passion crowds or pushes reason. We might have chosen better counselors, as Democritus urged. Habit and custom do shape our actions. But there are thoughtful as well as thoughtless habits. Virtue, here, in fact, is a habit of choosing as reason would advise. Vice mindlessly follows lesser motives, insensitive to circumstances. Cowards shun risk, regardless of the stakes; the rash pursue it, as if it were precious in itself. But the courageous weigh risks and stakes, and every relevant parameter in choosing. Habit and training lend spontaneity to their choices and enhance the work of choice with flexibility and its execution with enjoyment. So, even when there's little time for deliberation, the dispositions we've acquired enable us to act. But our dispositions are formed, in great measure, by our past choices. Our actions, at bottom, remain our own. Nature and nurture do not preempt the existential contributions of the self. Our upbringing and surroundings may have been deficient, but as social animals we've seen a plethora of models. And even when the genetic lottery has predisposed us in a given direction, reason will still see a variety of courses that it might choose. Circumstances, in other words, incline, but rarely necessitate.

Epicureans have their own ideas about spontaneity, less wedded to reason than attuned to chance. Lucretius finds his paradigm in an animal model, sketching the face of freedom in a vivid description of the start of a horse race:

> You can see, when the gates fly open,
> No horse breaks quite as swiftly
> As a mind might wish.
> A moment's delay checks the eager force
> Of all that flesh aroused to motion,
> The great body stirring
> At the mind's incitement.
> See for yourself —
> It's in the heart the motion starts,
> Surging from the spirit's willing,

Spreading through the flesh and limbs,
Quite unlike the movement when we're pushed,
The body shoved along,
As we stumble to keep our balance,
And collect our members by an act of will.
(*De Rerum Natura* 2.263–76)[10]

In human actions, Lucretius reasons, "it is plainly our own will that sets our limbs in motion," spurred by atomic swerves, "at no fixed time, to no set destination," but where pleasure pleases, "wresting freedom clear of fate" (2.257–60). Action is not impulsion from a boundless past. It stems from willing, at the call of pleasure. Pairing *voluntas* with *voluptas* and linking freedom with fecundity, Lucretius opens his epic by invoking Venus, as patroness of peace and spontaneity, fictive mother of the Roman race—and patroness of the generative coalescence of the atoms (1.1–40). The poet's own creativity with words and styles is of a piece with the thrill that sends cattle bounding over fields to find mates.[11] Pleasure is the engine. But pleasure is not choice, still a primitive in Epicurean philosophy. The swerve, nature's alternative to necessity, might underlie spontaneity of a certain sort, were it real. But it cannot explain free choice.

In a way freedom resists explanation, if explanation means specifying necessary and sufficient external determinants. Choice, if free, pursues internal preferences. It's not undetermined but *self*-determined. Our freedom, in that sense, is what or who we are. It expresses and creates an identity. Kane's concerns center on that moment of self-formation. At a moral crux, he argues (although not only then), we may act in ways that strengthen our "moral or prudential characters," or reinforce our "selfish or imprudent instincts." One could, he recognizes, hold persons responsible, on just those grounds, for the tenor of their choices. But he balks: "A familiar and potentially infinite regress" looms.[12] For even our inmost wishes might hark back to causes well beyond our control.

It's in hopes of blocking that regress that Kane invokes indeterminacy, not to make our choices for us but to table an agenda with no preset outcome, allowing rational choice its own determination. It's not the choice but the balanced options that Kane ascribes to quantum differentials, amplified, perhaps, by nonlinear effects of the sort described in chaos theory—giving neural micro-phenomena, potentially, a macro-level impact, experienced as a conflict of motives. The ingenuity invested in that tottering stack of hypotheses hardly seems necessary to explain conflicting motives, however— unless one finds moral conflict odd and imagines psyches powerless to hold rival options in abeyance (as skeptics urge one to do with rival theories). If rational choice is possible, it doesn't need indeterminacy to present a menu of possibilities. We face many a choice that does not seem obvious. And if rational choices are excluded an open menu hardly helps. Kane's gambit does block boundless regress to the past. So it does scotch claims that real choice presupposes magic.[13] But it does not explain how such choice is possible. Like Lucretius, Kane presupposes that.

We probably must enter the woods Kane skirts. But real forests don't have endless pathways: Not every motive trails infinite trains of causes. Chaos theory, at least in its more popular recensions, too readily overlooks destructive interference: A tsunami may build as it crosses the Pacific. But its waves can also lapse, when troughs fall into phase with peaks. The flap of a butterfly's wing in Chile will far sooner fade than trigger earthquakes in Armenia. But, contrary to Kim's charges, souls don't need magic powers to initiate actions and originate choices. Reflection is the critical tool.

We need not balk, then, at the edges of the forest. The tangled roots of motivation raise fascinating moral, juridical, psychological, and neurological questions. But voluntarism need only recognize that both personal and external factors orient our values. Plato saw that clearly. Aristotle spelled it out, treating virtue and vice as habits of choosing that we've made our own. Nature, which in Stoic thinking was also fate or destiny or deity, starts us off with appetite and aversion, as Chrysippus argued. But as we mature and souls emerge, our values grow more discriminating.[14] The Muʿtazilite theologians of Islam, pursuing Stoic themes, saw freedom as a variable, enhanced as we choose wisely, narrowed by foolish moves. As their Jewish predecessors put it in Talmudic times, the reward of one good deed is the privilege and power to perform another (Mishnah Avot 4.2). So Maimonides glossed God's hardening of Pharaoh's heart (Exodus 14:4, etc.), not as divine interference, but as the progressive constriction of that monarch's degrees of freedom as his policy became entrenched, leaving him ever less room to alter the course he'd chosen.

The Megarian determinists in Aristotle's day saw a necessity inherent in the very determinacy of truth or falsity. Applying that view to every future event, Aristotle argued, would obviate all effort and planning. The Muslim philosopher al-Fārābī carried Aristotle's reasoning a step further.[15] He granted that a state of affairs is implied necessarily by the truth of the proposition that predicts it. But that, he pointed out, does not entail the necessity of the state of affairs itself. The necessity of an implication is not transitive to the facts it addresses. Similarly, the necessity of the disjunction between truth and falsity is not distributive: It does not entail necessity in either disjunct. If there is a fact about what Zayd will choose to do, even God's knowing it does not obviate or necessitate his choice. It's the choice that determines the outcome, like any other cause, and it's the choice, *per hypothesi*, that God knows. As Ryle put it, "Events can be effects, but they cannot be implications. Truths can be consequences of other truths, but they cannot be causes of effects or effects of causes."[16]

Spinoza is especially helpful in showing how liberty jibes with determinism. Assimilating logical and theological determinism to the causal type, he sees all things as determined, internally or externally. Freedom is self-determination. God is not "undetermined," but maximally self-determined. Human freedom is relative—real insofar as our doings are explicable by our individual natures. Many things are beyond our control. We can't always avoid catching cold and should not be too sure about not dying. But in our emotional lives we can shift the balance between liberty and bondage—between being active causes and passive pawns.

Passive emotions, in which we are diminished, more victims than active causes, Spinoza holds, amount to inadequate ideas, thoughts ripped from their causal contexts. Adequate ideas, being causally contextualized, make us more effective—more free. Phobias and prejudices, spawned in the giddy thoughtlessness of casual experience (*experientia vaga*) are typically inadequate ideas. Clear, causal thinking dissolves them, allowing the kind of moral take-off that the Stoics envisioned. We dispel passive emotions by seeing through the fragmentary, ill-founded ideas that constitute them. Causality, then, is not the jailer that Epicurus feared. One need not reject the idea that things act in keeping with their natures to keep the door open to freedom. One need only recognize that not all causes are external. We too play roles in forming our own character and motives.

Voluntary Movement

It's tempting to defend free will by raising an arm or a finger. Physicians and loved ones at a patient's bedside may ask for a blink to signal responsiveness and some measure of bodily control. Galen mounts a similar argument, exasperated with the mechanists of his day:

> On some subjects a liar would go undetected by most people. But if he denies broad daylight and says it isn't daytime when everyone can see the sun in the sky, he'll be thought mad. What, then, of the man who says that when we walk we use our legs alternately not in deference to our will but automatically and naturally? To me this man will seem no less insane. We can take faster or

slower, longer or shorter strides, or stop altogether and start up again. So how is one not an idiot who says the action is natural and not controlled by the will? (*De Usu Partium* 10.9, tr. after May, 2.484–85)

Galen may fume, but not every theorist has found his reasoning convincing. Behaviorists treated observable movements like those he cites not as a window on the soul but as the only proper objects of scientific study by psychologists. Less doctrinaire thinkers do see voluntary movement as an expression of unseen mental acts. Others go further. Sir John Eccles regards overt behavior as a portal to the nexus of body and soul.[17] Yet Descartes' speculations about the pineal gland sound a warning that notions of such a nexus can be misleading. Efforts to substitute mechanisms for volition err in a different way, dismissing out of hand the evidence for volition and presuming rather than proving the emptiness of all notions of responsibility and intent—rejecting even the distinction, say, between causes and grounds that underlies their own claims to rational scientific procedure.

The right question, we think, is not how molecules can prompt actions but how persons, using the subtle machinery of the brain, can frame an identity capable of thoughtful acts and reflective choices rather than just reflexive responses to stimuli. Tracing the neural correlates of bodily movements has opened many a doorway to discovery. Synapses and the workings of neurotransmitters, for example, were first understood through studies of voluntary and autonomic neuromuscular control. But the notion of tracing the nerves back to an ultimate locus of the will is a little like the illusion that tracking the Nile, say, to Lake Victoria will tell us all there is to know about where its water comes from—no need to mention rain clouds or admit that water can undergo changes of state.

Muscles, Galen argued, take direction from the nerves, and ultimately the brain.[18] Voluntary movements, he observed, require opposing muscles to flex or extend a limb: "no muscle can do both."[19] He traced the action back to the "animal spirits," a Stoicizing will-o'-the-wisp with a long afterlife in the backlots of science, dispelled only after Galvani saw his frog leg twitch when his steel scalpel touched the brass hook that held it. It was Alessandro Volta (1745–1847) at the University of Pavia who realized that the electrical impulse came not from the severed leg but from the electrical differential between the metals, today measured in units named in Volta's honor.

Medieval theorists, following Aristotle and Galen, saw volition as a given in all animals.[20] But choice, morally and spiritually fraught, was linked with reason and uniquely human. Guglielmo da Saliceto (1210–1277) at the

University of Bologna, the pioneering surgeon whose introduction of the scalpel obviated the use of cautery, and whose practice of washing newborns saved many a life, traced bodily movements to the cerebellum if "natural"; to the cerebral cortex if voluntary.[21]

Descartes set off brush fires of materialism when his *Treatise on Man* described the human body as "nothing but a statue or machine." But he remained in the dark about nerve action. Citing "the grottoes and fountains in the royal gardens" he offered a hydraulic account: "water pressure is enough to set various machines in motion and even make them play instruments or utter words, depending on the arrangement of the pipes."[22] Despite his principled commitment to the union of body and soul, he needed to keep the two separate—to preserve immortality and to spare the nascent sciences the tender mercies of the Sorbonne theologians. So he labored both to naturalize and spiritualize: "parts of the blood," he wrote, "without any preparation or alteration except their separation from the coarser parts and retention of the great speed that the heart's heat has given them, no longer have the form of blood but are called the 'animal spirits.'" Having ridden his mechanist horse as far as it could travel, he's mounted a rather tired scholastic nag:

> Once the animal spirits enter the cavities of the brain, they advance into its pores and from there into the nerves. Depending on which nerves they enter (or even tend to enter) and to what extent, these spirits can change the shape of the muscles in which the nerves end and so move all parts of the body.[23]

Animal spirits, "extremely subtle,"[24] can still do the work of mechanism, but their change of "form" betrays their lineage: They are still substantial forms. Galen had warned that it's not the hand's shape alone but its motion that makes it useful. A motionless hand, he wrote, "would be no different from one dead or made of stone."[25] But animated statuary, not flesh and blood, is Descartes' model. His mechanist mount refreshed by his fanciful hydraulics, he rides freely home: "one may compare the nerves of the machine I am describing with the pipes in the works of these fountains, its muscles and tendons with the various devices and springs that set them in motion, the animal spirits with the water that drives them, the heart with the water source, and the cavities in the brain with the storage tanks."[26] So much for voluntary action. But "natural" processes like breathing depend simply on the flow of animal spirits, steady as a clock or mill.[27]

Eighteenth-century physiologists probed for the link of nerves to muscles, some still invoking the animal spirits. One theory chased those wispy vapors from the cortex through the basal ganglia and cerebellum and on to the muscles through the spinal cord. Galvani's frog legs shifted the focus to electricity. But electricity, like magnetism, was long thought not merely physical (it was not a body in any Cartesian sense). Only in the 1850s was the corticospinal tract traced, fiber bundles from the cerebral hemispheres crossing in the pyramids of the medulla and extending to the spinal cord. Here was the trunk route for motor commands to the skeletal muscles. But knowing that did not explain how thoughts can generate nerve impulses.

Jean Pierre Flourens (1794–1867), a pioneering neurophysiologist, drew on his extensive clinical experience to devise experiments in search of the seat of the will. In one extreme experiment he removed the cerebral hemispheres of pigeons, carefully preserving the brain stem. The decorticated birds perched as if asleep and would neither take flight nor feed. But they did swallow food placed in their beaks, and if tossed in the air would fly. Similar results with rabbits and other animals convinced Flourens that the medulla controls the heart and lungs but that willing lies in the cortex.

Jean Baptiste Bouillaud (1796–1881), the physician who first linked rheumatism with heart disease, pressed on in search of regions controlling specific body parts like the fingers and toes.[28] John Hughlings Jackson (1835–1911) proposed a motor "map" of the brain, aiming to chart control of every muscle. Some epileptic symptoms, he observed, "marched" across the body on the side opposite an afflicted cerebral hemisphere, as if an electrical storm were sweeping the brain. Jackson knew that cortical damage can severely degrade a patient's voluntary movements yet leave some muscle control. The brain, he reasoned, must have dual motor systems: fine, intentional movements managed from the cortex; more automatic movements, by more primitive centers in the corpus striatum and cerebellum, much older in evolutionary terms.

In 1870, Gustav Fritsch and Eduard Hitzig prompted muscle contractions in a dog's leg by electrically stimulating its exposed cerebrum. Hitzig had seen similar responses among battle wounded soldiers. The canine experiments (performed on a dressing table in Fritsch's home, since the University of Berlin banned such work in its laboratories) marked out the "motor strip" behind the frontal lobe of the cerebrum. Aiming to enhance his friend Jackson's brain maps, David Ferrier (1843–1928), applied steady (Faradic) currents to the brains of rhesus monkeys. Stimulating different spots on the cortex induced grabbing, scratching, reaching, and other coordinated movements quite unlike the spasms induced by brief Galvanic shocks. Similar brain areas were found in other mammals. But cortical lesions devastating to apes or injured humans had far less impact on lower animals, where the cortex is less prominent, confirming the evolutionary emergence of voluntary cortical control.

Eye Movement

In tracking objects, primates typically use both continuous visual pursuit and the discrete leaps of the saccades that can instantly shift an image from the retinal periphery to the fovea. Both modes involve active attention—choices in a sense. That thought made eye movements a favored model in studies of volition.[29] Indeed, since the 1970s much experimental work on the neurophysiology of volition has centered on vision or visually guided movement.

Early modern investigators had often treated the eyes as optical instruments, their performance variously enhanced by lenses. The muscular control of vision seemed relatively unimportant. But Enlightenment fascination with afterimages spawned ingenious methods of tracking eye movement and opened an inviting portal on volition.[30] In 1737 William Porterfield (1696–1771), an Edinburgh physician prominent in the Scottish Enlightenment, wrote: "to view any object, and thence to receive the strongest and most lively impressions, it is always necessary we turn our eyes directly towards it, that its picture may fall precisely upon this most delicate and sensible part of the organ."[31] By the nineteenth century, researchers understood that image stability is a dynamic product of eye movement, not of fixation on a single spot. Javal's discovery of saccades meshed with Porterfield's insight when twentieth-century scientists worked out just how saccades construct a visual scene from the array of rapidly scanned foci of attention.

Hitzig had traced eye movements to a region of the frontal cortex. Refining on this work, Ferrier in 1889 found that stimulating an area in the prefrontal gyrus in one hemisphere of an animal's brain caused movement of the eye on the opposite side. In the 1920s, the effect was confirmed in humans, linking the frontal lobes and parietal sensory cortices to voluntary movement.[32] Electric brain probes in the 1880s had located regions that generate saccades. About a century later the parietal and "supplemental" eye fields were linked to saccade control. Much of the control apparently comes from the frontal eye fields. But it's plotted out in the supplemental eye fields and the two superior colliculi, the regions that help orient the head to visible objects. These colliculi receive input from the optic nerves and cortex and encode visual targets in complementary maps, each representing half the visual field. Neurons here are active when the eyes move, those closest to the fovea apparently locking on to an object and directing the saccades to their next target.

In search of volition at its most elemental, neurophysiologists homed in on such targeting. Saccades are not consciously directed and are unstoppable once initiated. Yet they became a kind of paradigm of muscular control. They do scan the field for objects of potential interest and follow-up. But they shed little light on volition. Even our intentional gaze reveals little about our broader purposes. We humans read books, watch movies, stand sentry duty, stalk game. Few of our more complex routines are replicated in other species. But eye movement does correlate with brain activity as recorded in brain imaging studies.[33] There's not much room for movement during an MRI, of course, and only certain activities are amenable to study by matching eye movements with data from scalp electrodes. But eye movements do feature in many a complex routine and often reflect conscious and unconscious mental activity. Researchers, moreover, like the fact that the nerves to the six eye muscles connect directly to the brain without passing through the spinal cord, and that the eyes receive direct feedback from the brain.

Such considerations made vision a favored portal for studies of volition. Psychologists use visual signals, for example, in the Stroop test, to study an elementary form of choice, asking subjects to identify the colors named in letters of a different hue. That does call for a decision process. When EEGs and fMRIs show activation of the cingulate cortex, a collection of neurons between the corpus callosum and the cingulate sulcus, as subjects decide just what to say, researchers can sense that they're looking in on a basic step in human willing—although the elemental task hardly captures the full range and scope of human agency.

Startled eyes turn swiftly toward a novel object. Averted eyes may show distaste. Eager eyes betray our appetites. In a classic Russian study, Alfred Yarbus in the 1950s tracked eye movements as subjects viewed *The Unexpected Visitor*, a genre painting by Ilya Repin. Eye movements differed strikingly when subjects were told simply to study the painting or, alternatively, to speculate about the fortunes of the family it portrayed—their ages, garments, places in the room, what they'd just been doing, or how long the surprise guest had been away.[34] Many later studies confirmed Yarbus's finding: that seeing is "inextricably linked to the observer's cognitive goals."[35] For some, Yarbus had shown simply that perception is not as objective as one might presume. For others, his work held a Gestalt lesson: that seeing is active, not passive or static. But if the work reveals anything about volition, it's that vision as an observable correlate of agency is just one tip of a rather large iceberg. Memory and motive, emotion and intention—all sorts of cognitive and affective agendas—lurk less visibly. Glances are revealing, but they hardly bare all that's going on inside another's mind.

Libet's Hypothesis

Beginning in the early 1980s, Benjamin Libet performed a series of tests seeking a scientific answer to the question: 'Do we have free will?' Researchers in Freiburg in 1964 had identified an electrical event, the "readiness potential" (RP), preceding voluntary movements. Libet sought to correlate RP with conscious choices by having subjects perform various tasks—flexing a wrist, say, or finger, at will—while monitored with scalp EEGs. The whole exercise might sound a bit like trying to calibrate the old case for free will by raising a hand or wagging a finger. But Libet's findings proved striking and controversial. Multiple trials revealed a time lag up to 550 ms (over half a second) between RP and actual flexing.

> The brain was evidently beginning the volitional process in this voluntary act well before the activation. My question then became: when does the conscious wish or intention (to perform the act) appear? . . . If conscious will were to follow the onset of RP, that would have a fundamental impact on how we could view free will.[36]

Subjects clocked their first awareness of an intent to act using the sweep of a dot on a rotating disk. Intervals between RP and that awareness averaged some 150 ms. Libet's striking inference: The brain "decides to initiate" an act before there is "subjective awareness that such a decision has taken place."[37] A storm of comments ensued, as philosophers, psychologists, and neuroscientists probed the evidence. Three well known psychologists called Libet's report "one of the most philosophically challenging papers in modern scientific psychology."[38] It seemed to to confirm long-standing denials of free will.

There were voluntarist interpretations of Libet's data, but many feared his findings would prove demoralizing. He too was concerned and sought to reconcile his results with human freedom, reasoning that conscious choice can still veto an act. But, unlike RP, no veto event was recorded. Subjects do affirm it, but reliance on introspection seemed retrograde scientifically, Libet's qualms were of little avail. Increasingly the understanding was that his work had caught the brain committing to a choice before any conscious decision had been made.

Daniel Wegner, for one, pressed the point, branding free will illusory. Intentions, he argued are not causes of what we (perhaps nostalgically) call "our" actions. A sense of willing is no real evidence that willing produced an action; conscious volitions may be mere concomitants or aftereffects—loose ends, not causes at all.[39] We may *seem* to ourselves to have free will, Mark

Hallett argues, but most of our movements are largely automatic.[40] Even when we suppose we're acting voluntarily we often do things we hadn't meant to or blurt out answers we didn't think we knew. Hallett mingles his examples with accounts of movements provoked by electrical charges to the hand and with details of the engagement of the whole brain in a typical (voluntary) act. There is no person distinct from the brain, he argues. So questions like 'Why did he do that?' may in time give way to the less dualistic: 'Why did this brain generate that behavior?'

That prediction seems shaky for several reasons. No one since Galvani's day can doubt that electrodes induce twitches. But such movements do not discredit voluntary action but confirm it in a way, since the brain events are quite different in movements spurred by galvanic shocks from those initiated intentionally. As for the engagement of wide areas of the brain, that kind of evidence would discourage only voluntarists who are unaware of the integrated work of the brain. It would hardly faze an emergentist who sees body and soul as active partners.

The prominence of habit and other (semi-)automatic sequences does not diminish the role of volition: The violinist *chooses* this encore. She need not agonize over each move she makes in her fingering and bowing. In many a motor performance, as we've seen, backgrounding frees the mind to focus on areas that demand close attention. Hallett shows his hand when he brands talk of persons a throwback to dualism. Is that a scientific finding or a brickbat?

As to Libet's findings, the plot thickened in 2008 when John-Dylan Haynes of the Bernstein Center for Computational Neuroscience in Berlin used fMRIs to track brain activity while subjects pressed a button with their choice of left or right index finger as letters flashed on a screen (establishing the timing): Conscious decisions about which finger to use were reported at about one second in advance. But a pattern of brain activity preceding that decision by as much as seven seconds let researchers predict with 60 percent accuracy *which* index finger was used—not a strong correlation but better than random.[41] Patrick Haggard of University College London made the inference: "We feel we choose, but we don't." "How can I call a will 'mine', if I don't even know when it occurred and what it has decided to do."[42]

Clearly wrist flexing, button pushing, and like tasks, chosen to pare down the complexity of human action don't fairly represent the gamut of our choices. But even internally there are problems with the Libet/Haynes results. Alfred Mele, a philosopher, opens his critique by quoting Haggard's suggestion that in untangling knotty volitional questions, a bit of "conceptual analysis could help."[43] For openers, one could say it's unwise to brand volition illusory categorically. If *no* actions are our own, determinism swiftly turns vapid: If signing on as a sailor is no freer than being sandbagged and shanghaied, what force is left in the distinction of freedom from constraint that gives claims of (external) determination the impact they're typically expected to have?

Mele takes a different tack, laying out some key distinctions of his own, for one, contrasting "occurrent" with "standing" intentions—broad aims and concrete plans:

> Jan says . . . "Ken wants to bowl tonight" . . . knowing full well that what he wants or intends is to bowl with her at MegaLanes tonight for $20 a game until the place closes, as is their normal practice.[44]

We can act intentionally without overtly and explicitly running through each element of what our choices involve. Tennis players routinely cover the court without parsing every move they make—although opponents can sometimes read their intentions from their body language.[45] Attempting to scrutinize every element of one's every voluntary act would swiftly bring one to a standstill. Backgrounding is a useful (and adaptive) function of the fringe. So, as Mele says, "it is implausible that all proximal intentions are conscious." In eating, walking, running, speaking, and many another sequence, even unlocking the kitchen door, detailed consciousness is elided. Otherwise we'd miss much that matters—and probably bore ourselves to death. Many familiar choices involve neurally scripted routines. Typing, driving, and biking are painstaking in the learning phase. Practice makes them matters of habit but not involuntary.[46]

Mele quotes James's sensible evolutionary explanation: "consciousness deserts all processes where it can no longer be of use." Thought, James argues, seeks "a minimum of complication"—a guideline in pattern recognition— "and in the acquisition of every art." James anticipates the *Prägnanz* principle here, linking procedural memory with the more overtly cognitive and thus connecting learning broadly with training at its most bodily. Giving his point a characteristic practical filip, James adds: "We grow unconscious of every feeling which is useless as a sign to lead us to our ends, and where one sign will suffice others drop out"[47]—one more difference between thinking and computer operations.

Given the broad range of intentional but unselfconscious activities, Mele writes: "Wegner's account of intentions is unacceptable."[48] Just as skeptics dismiss knowledge claims by raising the bar, accepting little short of certainty as meeting their epistemic demands, Wegner asks for rare and untoward levels of self-oversight and then declares free agency illusory when such self-scrutiny proves lacking. There's a counterpart here to the demand for too constant and comprehensive a form of self-awareness that Block found so objectionable. Consciousness is at work in voluntary action, especially when we make decisions. But to expect awareness in every phase of every voluntary act slides from commonsense to the outlandish notion that an act cannot be voluntary unless continually leashed to an all but subvocalized 'I'm doing it . . . I'm doing the next step . . .'[49]

It's hardly clear, Mele argues, that RPs preempt decisions. Libet asked subjects to report their first conscious "intention," "urge," "decision," "will," etc., to flex their finger. The RP came some 150 ms sooner; the muscle moved 200 ms later. But wouldn't someone meaning soon to flex prepare mentally to do so? Quoting the vivid biblical description of war-horses sniffing the scents of battle (Job 39:19–25), Deborah Cantrell writes: "the war-horse strove to *explode* onto the battle-scene, much as the racehorse seeks to burst from the gate." Ancient texts like that of Job or Lucretius often notice the "anticipatory excitement," that palpably displays the equine instinct to excel and dominate: "The battle horse shivers, trembles, leaps, stomps, snorts, tosses its head, and sometimes rears up and paws the air. . . . The exhilaration of the moment creates a sensory overload, causing the horse to dance, prance, and quiver from head to hoof as it tries to break loose."[50] Readiness. But not decision making.

Was the RP, then, no mysterious pre-decision but a preparedness event? Taking part as a subject in trials based on Libet's, Mele found he was giving himself mental commands (*now!*) each time he flexed, keen to pinpoint the moment of decision. Perhaps, he writes, that was "my way of forming proximal intentions."[51] Were RPs more the "On-your-mark!" than the starter's gun? Racers do sometimes jump the gun. So they practice separating readiness from action, to avoid false starts. Nothing, Mele concludes, warrants the claim that what one becomes aware of when reporting awareness of an intent to flex is a *decision* already made: Libet and his colleagues "certainly have not shown" that our brains decide on actions "before there is any reportable subjective awareness that such a decision has taken place."[52]

Beyond that, we need to stress how atypical button pressing options are of the range of human choices. Arbitrary choices may well have unconscious (indeed, involuntary) neural determinants. They may involve mentally turning over decisions to randomizing mechanisms or to motives that are random relative to a given choice. Philosophers and theologians, we know, worried for generations over Buridan's ass and the question of whether a choice could be made without a determining cause. Would a human being, it was asked, starve to death if given two equally appealing and equally accessible morsels, two dates, say. Surely that would not happen. The choice in such a case, as advocates of determinism argued, was not between indiscriminable alternatives but between living and dying. But in order to make *that* choice, the Muslim philosopher al-Ghazālī argued, one would still have to choose between two items that were, by hypothesis, equally desirable: The will, he argued, does not just follow determinants; it *makes* determinations.[53]

Here there may be room if not for the play of quantum perturbations then for Lucretius's thoughts about spontaneity—although pure chance is not needed to dissolve the conundrum. Delegation of the outcome to some random determinant would do perfectly well. But in our daily deliberations, the role of free choice seems rather subtler: We decide not just which avenue to take but also to which criteria to give the greatest weight—and, in our more momentous choices, which principles or values should matter most to us—a facet of human decision making that Harry Frankfurt spotlighted.[54]

Even in our simplest choices arbitrariness is rarely uppermost. Merely choosing between coffee and tea, Adina Roskies argues, is far more complex than choosing, say, which hand to use to push a button.[55] Libet's work provoked flurries of interest among attorneys on the hunt for avenues of exoneration, and among theorists excited by the thesis that "most choices are made by the unconscious brain." But the evidence is thin. In many a routine, it's true, we don't puzzle out each step we take. It's true again that multiple factors influence our choices. But the case against free choices (and voluntary action in general) has not been made.

Folk Beliefs?

Libet's efforts to walk back strong readings of his findings met with little success. Yet few of us live our lives on the assumption that our choices and those of others are illusory. We tend to operate on the assumption that we and others exercise free choice. Just as we develop a "theory of mind," we seem to adopt a voluntarist bias, try as some might to vanquish it. Critics describe free will as a relic of folk psychology. That claim has led some researchers to ask just what folk beliefs about free will might be—who holds or uses them, and when?

Eddy Nahmias and his students probed the topic, seeking to pin down "commonsense" thinking about agency. In one study, subjects were asked to imagine a supercomputer that could accurately predict future actions and that had correctly predicted that one Jeremy would rob a bank. Asked if Jeremy had exercised free will, 76 percent said he had. In other scenarios

Jeremy saves a child from a fire or just goes jogging. Participants, again over-whelmingly, said he had. Some 83 percent held him blameworthy in the robbery; 88 percent judged him praiseworthy in the rescue. Few, evidently, thought the predictions precluded personal responsibility.[56]

In another study Nahmias asked lay subjects to imagine a world where all of an individual's beliefs and values were determined by genetics and environment. Suppose a pair of identical twins in that world were raised by foster parents, one family selfish, the other kindly, and in adulthood each found a wallet containing $1000 and an ID. Told that the twin raised by self-ish parents kept the wallet and the other returned it, again 76 percent called both choices free. Despite the premises of the scenario, they affirmed that either twin could have done otherwise.

Evidently, statements for or against free will don't readily dislodge all attitudes about it. But beliefs about determinism do seem to have a moral impact, as Libet and others feared. Katherine Vohs, Jonathan Schooler, Roy Baumeister, and others have correlated exposure to denials of human free-dom with lesser likelihood to render aid and greater likelihood of aggression and willingness to cheat.[57] Deterministic thinking may narrow perceptions about one's options—or offer ready avenues of rationalization. The open-ing lines of Crick's *Astonishing Hypothesis*, "You, your joys and your sorrows, your memories and your ambitions, your sense of personal identity and free will, are in fact no more than the behavior of a vast assembly of nerve cells and their associated molecules," had a similar impact. Punitive attitudes, on the other hand, recede as belief in free will is shaken.[58] Few are prepared (as Spinoza was) to sunder accountability from responsibility. And some adamant adversaries of free will—Pat Churchland, for one—fudge, calling free will a fantasy but urging us to go on living (at least in some respects) *as if* we knew freedom to be real.

Over 90 percent of Nahmias's subjects thought normal adults decide many things freely, and individuals tended to be thought responsible for their actions unless excused by infancy, insanity, brainwashing, ignorance, coercion, or the like. Moral concerns clearly promote voluntarism: Signifi-cantly more subjects ascribed freedom and moral responsibility to those (*others!*) who did wrong than to those whose doings bore neutral or abstract descriptions. Decisions ascribed to thoughts, desires, or plans were gener-ally labeled free. But electrodes and such were exculpatory, even where a blanket determinism was not. Technology, evidently, has mythic power, and thoughts of remote control are concrete in ways that deterministic theories seem abstract. But fantasy science too is rather remote from the practical immediacy of our everyday social world.[59]

How people think about agency depends in part on how they think about God and nature, fate, chance, and luck. In Arabic grammar the passive voice is called *majhūl*, anonymous, as if to soften or qualify attributions of responsibility. People whose languages favor passive constructions are said to be more reticent in assigning individual responsibility than are those whose languages stress active verbs. Language here may be shaping cultural attitudes, as the Sapir-Whorf hypothesis suggests; or linguistic conventions may reflect cultural outlooks. Most likely, culture and language are mutually reinforcing. But individuals within a given culture or language group can differ widely on such matters, and the postures they adopt toward volition may vary sharply with time and circumstance. For, as Nahmias's work suggests, thoughts about freedom and responsibility seem to shift in changing contexts.

Kant proposed reserving causal explanations for science and understanding, and retaining praise and blame, punishment and reward in moral and juridical realms. Yet it's the same person whose acts are explained or blamed. Despite Kane's worries about endless wandering in a trackless explanatory forest, we see no principled reason for throwing up one's hands at the challenge of teasing out an individual's contributions to a given outcome. Finding the points at which personal choices might have made a difference may be difficult at times, but that does not make such efforts impossible or irrelevant. Human life is filled with moments that allow or even demand the judgment that the buck *starts* here.

Social Agency

Agency is ubiquitous in our experience, but mechanism privileges the externalist perspective Searle chafed at, be it Behaviorist or neurophysiological in appeal. Denials of freedom are seconded by an appetite for excuses and a natural desire to forgive. Forgiveness can be generous, even divine. But it seems more fittingly extended to agents who own their actions and own up to them, than to pawns of fate, robots, or marionettes. Pawns may deserve pity. But it's hard to see how it's coherent to offer them forgiveness. How could they accept it, let alone merit it? Kantian thoughts matter here: To medicalize a human action, even out of sympathy, diminishes human dignity by bracketing personhood and erasing agency. To condone is not to forgive.

Often when determinism is made a plea for excuses, blame is laid not just on one's hormones or one's stars but on parents or peers, strict or lax teachers, or cultural trends. There's no dearth of suspects. The tensions bred when responsibilities are offloaded in this way are the focus of Goodman's "point zero argument": Laying one's weaknesses at others' feet both presumes and denies personal agency. It negates the very causes that it blames.[60] The ready counterclaim: Persons are mere conduits of causes long since vanished. That account, again, brackets personhood, prompting the question *cui bono?* What interests are served by negating the self that rationalizations struggle to protect? If the goal was to ease or erase moral judgment and suspend or expunge the claims of taste, truth, and tact by retiring notions of agency, it's hard to say to whom such appeals are addressed, and why they should be heeded—in whose behalf—if selves are nonexistent.

We certainly *seem* to have agency, and use it—some more aptly than others—as we strive to manage our lives and to create and sustain our social and material environment. Historically, we can trace the rise of agency in agriculture, craft, and industry, animal husbandry, technology, the varied efforts of individuals and communities to establish laws and institutions, and the distinctively human semiotic enterprise of building an intellectual, moral, and spiritual milieu that finds expression in religious and moral codes, the sciences and the arts.

Reduction is alluring, not least when it promises to explain all things. The seductive claim: Human motives are not primitive enough to count as primal causes. Scientists are as prone as other mortals to hope that understanding means forgiveness. So a story proffering a moral free pass has its charms. If character comes from moral luck—a gift of the gods—the crevice or crevasse narrows between virtue and vice, and cynics win plaudits for realism by collapsing the distinction altogether. Once again we're being told how good it would be if everyone stopped using words like 'good.'

Euphemisms like 'stability,' or 'adjustment' are about as effective in masking value judgments as fig leafs on a nude. In the long run they only obscure things, lumping subtle decisions and hard choices together with mere technical challenges, blurring the differences between thoughtfulness and, say, conformity. Medicalization hardly helps by turning virtues and vices into traits and symptoms. For human agency continually rears its head regardless, in clinical, ecological, social, and cognitive contexts, leading many now, refreshingly, to acknowledge individual agency in development, education, therapy, and daily life.

Bandura finds agency undeniable. Trained in the heyday of Behaviorism, he came to see externalist accounts of learning and action as simplistic—unhelpful in his early research on aggression; inadequate, even irrelevant, in explaining the modeling he saw in young children. The language of stimulus and response, positive and negative reinforcement, lifted from studies of conditioned reflexes, did not capture adolescents' strategies in planning, making choices, pursuing goals, and acquiring skills. Fitting his tools to his data, Bandura devised a theory of learning that took seriously biological and social constraints and opportunities but acknowledged personal choices and the critical role of thoughts about others. Human subjects manifest a sense of agency from the earliest developmental stages. Candor demanded its acknowledgment. Bandura's approach has since proved fruitful in many clinical, developmental, and educational settings. Social interactions, he found, affect our choices but do not determine them. Indeed, social organization, far from hemming us in, contributes to individual expression by fostering collaboration. Spinoza similarly remarked: "Nothing is more useful to man than man,"[61] an observation, "confirmed by daily experience":

> Let satirists laugh all they like at the human condition, let theologians revile it, and melancholics heap praise on the rude, wild life, scorning humanity and admiring brutes. People learn from experience that it's far easier to secure what they need by helping each other—that only by joining forces can we escape the dangers that beset us—not to mention that it's finer and more befitting our minds to contemplate human than animal doings.[62]

A sense of competence, Bandura found, correlates with personal effectiveness.[63] Self-esteem might turn narcissistic and lapse into failure. But "self-efficacy" builds on real capabilities that grow stronger with success, whether in learning to ride a bike, or read, or swim, or—as Spinoza suggests—winning friends and allies. Confidence in one's ability to marshal one's thoughts and plan one's steps fosters personal growth, modeled, perhaps, in athletic, aesthetic, or intellectual domains and applied in life at large. As we grow more effective we're ever less dependent on past influences, ever more in control of ourselves. Souls, Bandura's work suggests, are not given but grown:

> The sensory, motor, and cerebral systems are tools people use to accomplish the tasks and goals that people use to give meaning to their lives. Through their intentional acts, people shape the functional structure of their neurobiological systems. By regulating their own motivation and the activities they pursue, they produce the experiences that form the neurobiological substrate of symbolic, psycho-motor, and other skills. Should people experience any loss or decline of their bodily systems, they devise alternative ways of engaging and managing the world around them.[64]

Bandura found four components critical in effective action: (1) framing goals and the plans conducive to achieving them, (2) forethought, anticipating future scenarios so as to weigh options before pursuing a course of action (purposive action, then, does not magically reverse the causal order, as if goals somehow drew effects out of the future), (3) "self-reactiveness," active regulation of one's actions (for "one cannot simply sit back and wait for the appropriate performances to appear"), and (4) self-reflectiveness, adjusting plans and even goals to changing circumstances, including new social dynamics.[65]

The anatomy of agency here is commonsensical, but sensible perhaps *because* it's empirically derived. It compares favorably with the narrower models of free choice at a moral crux that some philosophers favor. And it far outstrips romantic confusions of freedom with irrationality. It keenly highlights junctures at which we may exercise our freedom: in choosing goals, devising plans, addressing challenges and changes, appraising results, and recalibrating.

Most human activity is socially situated, Bandura stresses. Like memory and creativity, then, agency is personal but socially situated. Just as texts, monuments, and rituals may help shape and order our memories, and as traditions both goad and assay our creativity, we act in social contexts. Communities and institutions may channel, thwart, or extend our reach, whether in business, education, sports, religion, art, friendship, or love. They modulate but do not efface personal agency.

Freedom, Bandura writes, "not conceived just passively as the absence of constraints . . . but proactively as the exercise of self-influence in the service of selected goals and desired outcomes" is not absolutely requisite for agency. But agency is requisite for freedom. Bandura distinguishes individual, proxy, and collective agency.[66] Individual agency may be as basic as food choices or market transactions. Or it might be exercised in choosing one's friends. Proxy agency is delegated, as in representative democracies, or hiring an attorney. Collective agency may reinforce or curtail personal agency, perhaps in the interest of common goals like road building, pooling individual energies and ideas.[67] "Humans," Bandura writes, "are not like billiard balls propelled solely by forces external to them. . . . Humans can not only think, but, individually and collectively, shape the form those external forces take and even determine whether or not they come into play."[68] Bandura's prose preserves a touch of affront as he contrasts his approach with the soi-disant empiricism he rebelled against:

Psychosocial accounts of human functioning often portray individuals as reactors to environment events impinging upon them. In the neurophysiological quest for the localization and neural circuitry underlying cognitive activities and affective reactions, individuals are transported in a prone position into a neuroimaging device in which they are greeted with stimuli to which they have to react instantly. Such an arrangement allows little leeway for deliberative proactive control of action, much of which must be psycho-socially negotiated and temporally regulated in everyday life.[69]

Which, then, is the illusion, the artificial model built around researchers' convenience and debarring personal experience, or the idea that we are in some measure, individually and socially, authors of our actions?

Gallagher, reacting against a sometimes overweening individualism, stresses the social side of agency yet more strongly. It's because our sense of agency reflects our embodiment, he argues, that it must be social: We don't live in a world of inert objects. Awareness of ourselves as free agents is "inextricably interwoven into and out of our relationships with others." Our actions aim to anticipate theirs.[70] We aren't mere spectators of our behavior but actively shape it in the course of our social engagement: Our sense of self and concomitant sense of agency arise as we relate our history to others.

Agency here, as for Bandura, is not sheer self-sufficiency, an illusion that might hide mere isolation. To quote Spinoza once again, responding to the illusion of what is sometimes called "ragged individualism": "we can never bring it about that we need nothing outside ourselves to preserve our being."[71] But interdependence is not impotence. Agency is as basic in human life as self-awareness. Social engagement is critical to both.

Since social structures both constrain and free us in ways that healthy brains and bodies in isolation cannot, Gallagher argues, free will must be understood in its social milieu. Narrowing the focus to the first-person singular misses freedom just as badly as exclusive reliance on third-person perspectives: "a proper sense of freedom (which comes along with a proper sense of responsibility)—can be found only in the context of social interaction, where our intentions are formed in or out of our interactions with others."[72] Free will, responsibility, and political freedom, then, are inextricably intertwined.

Is Agency Empiric?

Richard Ryan and Edward Deci have conducted a number of studies and cite many more that give experimental and practical application to the claims of human autonomy, by which they mean our capacity to regulate our own actions. Their work is a telling riposte to dismissals of agency as a myth, unobserved, unmeasurable, and unverifiable. Many of the studies gauge the effects of self-determination in Western "individualistic" societies and cross-culturally. The large and growing literature assaying agency developmentally, educationally, and therapeutically, heightens the irony of Bandura's exposure of an a priori bias long spread under the banner of empiricism.

Reductionists favor "lower" explanatory factors. But school reform, say, would probably work better, Ryan and Deci write, by addressing the experience, values, and motives of the actors than their brain cells, cortical regions, and motor outputs. It is always possible, of course, that something in the water is impeding everyone—as lead in the plumbing may have handicapped ancient Romans. Such issues should hardly be neglected. But confining attention to seemingly simpler causes does not enrich explanations or make them more precise. Social and cultural determinism, treating our actions as "scripted" by culture, reduce people to "chameleon-like conformists" with no coherent self to choose, moderate, or influence action—falsifying experience in the name of scientific accuracy.[73]

Autonomy is readily denied if defined over-ambitiously—made absolute, say. Absolute independence belongs to no organism and makes no sense in the give and take of life processes. But Bandura, Ryan and Deci complain, settled for too modest a goal by accepting a mere *sense* of agency.[74] To be fair, Bandura did find much evidence for active self-determination. He stressed the impact of growing recognition of one's own competencies in enhancing agency. Ryan and Deci, too, give weight to self-acceptance. As we see it, the objective and subjective sides of effectiveness would strengthen one another, so long as neither burgeons into hubris. There's no question but that the sense of growing competence is subjective. But it does seem clear that such a sense can augment one's actual competence even beyond the original area. Learning to manage one's body in baseball or swimming may help make one a better public speaker or a more effective leader. But a blanket denial of human efficacy only obscures the question of such spillovers and blurs the scales that might be used to chart them.

Drawing on Harry Frankfurt's philosophical work, Ryan and Deci locate self-determination not in imperviousness to outside influence but in readiness to *own* our actions. One might feel constrained at having to stop behind a school bus. But there's no loss of autonomy in that, as long as one could agree on reflection that it's worthwhile for rules to help keep children safe.[75] Gerald Dworkin, similarly, sees the test of agency in endorsement of one's choices "at the highest level of reflection."[76] One *can* regret freely chosen actions. So ex post facto endorsement is not a necessary condition of agency. Nor is whole hearted endorsement sufficient, since we don't always fully grasp the impact of what we approve. Open eyed authorship still matters.

A tighter test of autonomy than sheer self-acceptance, then, might lie in reflective grasp of one's own motives. Consciousness here once again connects with conscience: We can own our actions insofar as we're capable of knowing who we are. That's one reason why children are not held responsible in the same way as adults are. Their identities are not yet mature and self-possessed. Souls take root in acts of moral appropriation. But we evaluate future as well as past acts, and (like a violinist) must constantly appraise present actions too, as we perform them, or we could hardly make the simplest moves, like picking up a glass of water or waving to a friend. Grave deficits like lack of a sense of personal agency or difficulty in integrating values so as to permit self-acceptance highlight the centrality of self-awareness.[77] It seems specious, against that backdrop, to call agency an illusion, as if there were no difference between free agents and those who have trouble distinguishing what they do from what they suffer. The illusion here is not clarity about what actions are one's own but confusion on that front.

Charting the varieties of self-determination, Ryan and Deci find heteronomy in imposed motives. Closer to home are introjected external standards. More authentically personal are motives that these authors call *identified*, including values well integrated with one's other values and beliefs. Beyond these, they see intrinsic values, wholeheartedly pursued for their own sake, yielding "highly autonomous" action. Using this rough scale, Ryan and Deci can report "literally hundreds of studies" confirming the centrality of autonomy in healthy human living: Integrated or intrinsic motives, for example, are found to foster flexible, heuristic and creative activity. Heteronomy impedes it. Autonomy in relationships, not surprisingly, promotes mutual satisfaction and stability. Far from conflicting with trust or interdependence, it supports mutual reliance—as wise partners and friends have always known.[78]

Many studies find that contingent rewards, long a staple in Behaviorist experimentation, can undermine autonomy by sapping intrinsic motivation, as external rewards eclipse intrinsic values or those one might have internalized. Withheld praise and shame, punitive or invidious treatment, conditional or contingent regard don't just cause pain and shake self-esteem, they undermine autonomy and subvert relationships.[79] The studies vividly highlight the psychosocial basis for the moral imperative to treat others (including children!) with the dignity of subjects rather than try to manipulate them as objects. Selves or souls, once again, are achieved, not given. Their emergence requires support. Without it identities can be stunted or destroyed.

Much of Ryan and Deci's evidence remains in the subjective realm, since many of the studies they cite gauge the impact of perceived autonomy and

perceived supports or threats to it. But real variables were measured and correlated in the studies they cite, variables that point to subjects who act, not
to free floating behaviors. Central among the correlations these studies chart
is a nexus rather willfully neglected by the Behaviorists, the impact of a sense
of agency on individuals' mental health and happiness and the stability
of their relationships. Neuroscience strikingly underscores the psychosocial
evidence. For neural mechanisms differ when we're doing what we're told
or see ourselves as acting of our own volition.[80]

The brain takes up just 2 percent of an adult's body weight. But it uses
over 20 percent of one's energy—much of it in decision making. Numerous
studies have found that demanding efforts at self-control impede or slow
subsequent elemental choices like those called for in the Stroop test. In one
Toronto study EEGs matched the subjects' more hesitant and error prone
performance in naming the color in which characters are displayed, confirming Baumeister's view that the energy needed in making even simple choices
can run low, sometimes dangerously so.[81] Ordinary and clinical experience
with hypoglycemia and diabetes, with accident rates among persons suffering from a bad cold, with simple financial decisions and impulse buying,
with crime rates, juvenile delinquency and recidivism, and with school performance and comportment, show that the brain draws significantly on our
energy supply in making any choice.[82]

A milkshake, in one study, was found to enhance performance at subsequent tasks demanding self-control. But so did a tasteless dairy drink. Self-
governance, here, it seemed, depended not only on gratification but, more
elementally, on food. Researchers enamored of computer models of cerebral
logic, Baumeister writes, "had neglected one mundane but essential part
of the machine: the power cord." Circuitry is "useless without a source of
energy."[83] The findings speak eloquently to our twin themes of embodiment
and emergence. Court records that Baumeister cites show substantial differences in parole decisions depending on the time of day when appeals were
heard—and whether decisions were made before or after a meal. Fortunately,
these were not the capital cases of a more cavalier age. But evidently there
was truth in Alexander Pope's mordant observation: "The hungry judges
soon the sentence sign, and wretches hang that jurymen may dine."

Baumeister calls the downslope of agency 'ego depletion,'[84] somewhat
apologetically, since he's recycling the word ego from Freud. But the studies he cites do point unmistakably to a deliberative subject. By charting our
finite, if renewable, stores of perseverance and self-control and revealing
energy supply as a limiting factor, they mark out key parameters of our ability to act and choose, sketching the boundaries of an active self that doctri-

naire exponents of the external determination of all behavior shroud in a uniformly gray blanket of metaphysical or psychological denial. There's no mysterious source of energy here, of the sort that Kim proposes that free choices would somehow need, nor are choices made without energy to fuel the work. The sources of that energy are much the same as those required by our cells for any of the work they do. But that, of course, does not show that choices are made at the cellular level.

The nominal basis for Behaviorist objections to human agency was that purposes and intentions cannot be measured or observed. But clinical experience and experimental evidence, even EEGs, won't satisfy committed reductionists: "each of us feels that there is a single 'I' in control," Steven Pinker, writes, "But this is an illusion that the brain works hard to produce." Pinker acknowledges "supervisory" brain functions that "can push the buttons of behavior and override habits and urges." But he calls these, "gadgets with specific quirks and limitations," not expressions of "the rational free agent traditionally identified with the soul or the self."[85] It does seem curious, however, that our agency might have limits but no definable shape or detectable reality. The rhetoric, once again, suggests an agenda, not to explain human decision making but to displace it. Pinker, Ryan and Deci reply, "eviscerates the 'I'," only to replace it "with a new intentional subject, the brain, that pushes buttons, controls urges, and spins illusions of self."[86]

One can't help recalling the humanist's response to the Behaviorist: "So what you're saying is that we're anthropomorphizing people?" Intentions arise not in genes or memes or modules but in persons. What activates brain "gadgets" are thoughts, values, construals of events. Thoughts do depend on brain processes. As Ryan and Deci urge: "autonomy requires coordination among prefrontal cortical regions that oversee and integrate regulation, subcortical striatal-thalamic areas that promote or inhibit motivation, and inputs from the hippocampus and amygdala that provide contextual and affective information."[87] Turning James's "blooming buzzing confusion" into coherent experience is an integrative project. A fortiori is hands-on, purposive action a project demanding the kind of integration that only a living self can oversee. Button pushing isn't up to the task. Still less do buttons activate themselves. There needs to be a subject, not the passive impress of past impacts on the brain but a self emergent in the very act of constituting experience, collating memories, assaying meanings, taking a stand, and laying claim to it. To dissolve that self into a panel of mechanisms is not a scientific advance—unless good science means denying what we see. Mechanism turns procrustean here, collapsing the multilevel work of agency into sequences of response incapable of dealing with our dynamic surroundings.

Over-reading the evidence and overriding our experience of thought and action, reductionists expect neuroscience to "crowd out antiquated and ephemeral ideas of freedom and will," Ryan and Deci write.[88] But the targets that mechanists single out are phantoms. So it's hard to keep from asking just who it is who is afraid of ghosts. No serious researcher chases disembodied wraiths. The question we face is not whether persons are ghosts or gadgets but whether agency is real. There's ample evidence that we humans play our part in plotting our own course and don't just think we can. That fact counts in favor of the human soul.

Agency and Emergence

Issues about agency are often presented as a pretty stark dichotomy: Either all events, including human actions, are causally determined under strict physical laws, or some ghostly force makes choices by unseen, physically inexplicable means. So it's understandable that defenders of freedom seek alternatives like those proposed by Epicurus, Eddington, or Kane. But indeterminism, as we've seen, is unhelpful. Chance can't replace deliberation, and even if indeterminacy could somehow level the pool table and equalize the pockets a choice might fall into, it still won't explain how we do the choosing. The same is true of Frankfurt's appeal to endorsement. It's relevant and interesting to explore how deep one's endorsements run. But the Frankfurt model only pushes the active subject further back into the shadows. Freedom in the sense that matters is either presupposed in talk of endorsement (and regret) or elided in efforts to shift the discussion to such questions. As for the naturalist challenge, however, we say again, what freedom needs is not indeterminacy but self-determination. Naturalism is not an enemy but an ally: We act and choose by natural, not supernatural means. Emergence is the critical alternative—not to determinism but to reductionism: Selves are more than products of the past; so choices are not the mere resultants of external forces.

Kim is the imposing challenger here—although his stance was anticipated by Laplace. Kim's argument that top-down causality would violate causal closure restates in subtler terms the charge that human agents amount to ghosts. It's easy enough to make souls seem silly, when discomfort with reductionism provokes extravagant claims about table rapping and conversations with the dead. The idea that souls are real is readily enough confused with attempts to picture nonphysical realities as spectres that appear capriciously if the light is right. But the real alternatives to materialism should not be hidden behind a straw man. Numbers too are not physical things.

Nor is organization, or information. Yet they do matter, not apart from the bodies they inform, but in the way they order them. Numbers don't rattle chains or pass through walls. Nor do they make choices or play piano. But every general knows that organization and information are just as critical as ordnance. If you asked a commander which matters more, numbers or communications, you'd probably earn a pretty blank stare. What emergentists see is not a ghost in the bodily machine but a weakness in the machine metaphor: Brainwork is not sufficiently described electrochemically. The actions of the whole here far exceed the powers of its parts. That's why persons show life and sensibility, consciousness and agency when an atom cannot.

Kim's argument against downward causation in an organism, Thompson writes, "is tantamount to denying that the system's organization exerts any influence on the system's components. The thought seems to be that what we call the macrolevel and emergent causation really happens at the microlevel . . . an effect of lower level causal transactions with no significant causal status of its own."[89]

Perhaps chastened by responses to the severity of his stance, Kim does consider emergentist objections, "but he goes through contortions to deal with them"—acknowledging "microstructural" properties in a complex but still holding them "completely decomposable" into the properties and relations of the components. That "decomposable" is emblematic of the reductive drive. But the counterpoised mention of relations seems in a way to leave room for more than elemental properties. Thompson's appraisal: "Kim gives away many of the issues at stake in the debate about emergence without ever acknowledging that he has done so."[90] For Kim "admits that 'macroproperties can, and in general do, have their own causal powers, powers that go beyond the causal powers of their microconstituents.'"[91] Yet at the same time, "it would seem that Kim simply assumes that the microlevel does not include holistic relations."[92]

Laplace is the éminence grise here, with freedom widely seen as a chief casualty of the naturalism his approach inspires. But Bergson framed a powerful response, noting that a key premise of the Laplacean line of argument is a linear view of time, every moment ended before the next begins. Time, in our experience, Bergson observed, links past and future—as we've observed in discussing Augustine, Kant, and others. Minds stitch moments together to make experience possible. So, the present, as we experience it, the specious present, is no vanishingly thin knife edge or ever diminishing infinitesimal but a span or duration, the worktable, as it were, of choice.[93]

Hume atomized time, quietly presuming each moment to be discrete and isolated from the rest (since there's no logical necessity in any instant that there be another). That gambit left no room for action—or causes of any sort: Every event, being logically discrete, was isolated from the rest. But natural events, not just mental processes, as Goodman has argued, have their own duration.[94] They too take time and connect past with future. So causality is not tipped in awkwardly between passing moments. It spans them. And human choices, like other causes, link events—in this case, intentions with outcomes, purposes with actions, using the worktable consciousness creates, relying on the integrative work of the brain.

Kim prides himself on rigorous thinking. But he comes a crupper when his reductionism parries his good sense. No one expects a glass of milk to have the same nutritional impact as its elements in isolation. Thompson's studies of living systems—brains specifically—allow him to conceptualize how embodiment enables a mind to emerge from the work of a brain—and thus enables human beings to act.

To illustrate just how intimate the nexus is between life and thought and how ill fitting the machine metaphor is, Thompson introduces the analogy of a clock or gauge set to track a process. A digital clock, he notes, marks the passage of time in steady steps, readily charted in an equation that yields a value reflecting a system's state at any moment, given only the starting conditions and the system's working rule. But that assumes the rules don't change. In some systems, however, rules do change as the system functions and Laplacean projections break down. A more qualitative approach is needed, like those Henri Poincaré devised for treating the less tractable sorts of differential equations:

> One thinks of the space of all possible states of the system . . . and the way the system changes or behaves over time as curves or trajectories in this space. Instead of seeking a formula for each solution as a function of time, one studies the collection of all solutions . . . for all times and initial conditions at once.[95]

This kind of model fits living systems better than the clock model. Here new patterns are constantly created and destroyed, modified and repurposed. Dynamic complexity, Thompson argues, recurs throughout nature, from the molecular and organismic levels to the ecological and evolutionary—and, of course, the neural and behavioral. The message here: Dynamics of this sort are not just typical but necessary when self-regulating, self-constructing, or autonomous systems emerge.[96] Life is not mechanical; agency is not algorithmic.

Acknowledging that our bodies are not isolated from their milieu, Thompson pulls in his horns a bit, calling autonomy and heteronomy "heuristic notions," embedded in the interpretive and explanatory stance of an observer or community: "What counts as the system . . . whether it is autonomous or heteronomous, is context-dependent and interest-relative. For any system it is always possible to adopt a heteronomy or external-control perspective, and this can be useful for many purposes."[97] The concession, like the terms it's couched in, derives from Kant. But the perspectivalism here risks compartmentalization, making persons autonomous for moral or legal purposes but heteronomous, say, in clinical or explanatory contexts.

To preserve a robust distinction between what we undertake and what we undergo (subtle as it can be to tease out the causal strands), one might profitably turn to Spinoza—an ally simpatico to Thompson's holistic bent. So we find it reassuring to see Thompson tacking back to the objective differences his argument supports: Models of external control are useful for many purposes, but "this stance does not illuminate—and can, indeed obscure" self-generated patterns of action.[98] The key question about freedom is not whether all events, being physical processes, are externally determined but the extent to which we (or any living beings) make a difference in choosing a path or taking a course of action.

Top-Down / Bottom-Up

It has long been known that nerves in the central nervous system (the brain and spinal cord) rarely heal by themselves, and only with great difficulty. But neuroplasticity, we now know, can compensate in some measure for brain damage resulting, say, from injury or stroke, as cortical tasks are reassigned and the brain opens up new synaptic pathways. Pioneering studies have tracked such work-arounds in monkeys. Unaffected regions take over for damaged areas, and healthy nerves construct new brain maps of the hands or other body parts. New techniques are learned for the tasks of daily living. Right-handed persons may rely more on the left hand, areas in the right cerebral hemisphere taking over for counterparts on the left—although hemisphere-local work like speech and language processing are not so readily shifted. Cerebral shifts may overstress healthy areas or free a damaged limb from exercise critical to recovery (since muscles atrophy with disuse). Shifts in governance may reduce the traffic flow that might promote neural rebuilding in damaged brain regions. So gradual, if spontaneous, neuroplastic compensation may be less helpful than well guided purposive efforts to help injured brains reboot through exercise and training, harnessing plasticity to promote a reconstructive workout.[99] Rehabilitation of any sort takes concerted effort and resolve, but conscious, volitional, culturally mediated work can help rebuild synaptic connections. Healing of this kind is not well described as an *effect* of brain activity. What we're seeing is top-down rehabilitation working the brain and working with it, to rebuild. The neurophysiology is no different from the spontaneous rebuilding of synaptic connections. But the distinctive active cause here is intentional effort.

Mental exercise, sometimes as accessible as crosswords, can slow the cognitive losses of aging. And, at the younger end of the life cycle, researchers find significant changes in brain circuitry when children learn to read.[100] Brain maturation is clearly necessary for reading, and neural losses underlie senile dementia. But it's hardly accurate to lump together retraining with the spontaneous rebuilding of neural connections. Choice and resolve are critical in a demanding mental regimen, just as they are in maintaining muscle tone, flexibility, and agility. One marker of the difference: Cognitive tasks prove far more effective therapeutically when their content genuinely interests patients. Random memorization and trivial problem-solving don't help nearly as much as goal-directed activities. Meditation can enhance resistance to pain, but it does so as a result of conscious decisions and active mindfulness.[101] There's a person at work here, not just a brain.

Our power to make choices, to make, say, dietary and other fitness related changes, like our power to help our brains develop or make repairs, points to the role of agency in making us who we are. Programs of training and education that stimulate and guide our neuroplastic capabilities—whether in learning to read or learning to speak—are striking cases of the mind's ability to attune the brain. That will not mean wishing away cancer. But there is solid evidence that meditative practice, seriously pursued, can affect blood pressure and other bodily parameters. The effectiveness of such efforts is limited by their very nature. Discipline and commitment are never all-sufficing. But with agency, as with consciousness, memory, and perception, the evidence stacks up against reductionism: The mind is choosing a goal. The brain is its tool and substrate, not identical to it. The brain of an athlete or performer, or of a child learning to walk or read, is not *spontaneously* rewiring itself. Neuroplasticity is prominent in all these cases. But practice, be it meditative or musical, military or industrial, intellectual or athletic, involves active engagement of the mind reaching out for control and guidance of the body. The possibility of success speaks to the reality of agency, which speaks in turn to the reality of the soul.

SIX

Creativity

Inspiration, Imitation, Accident

There are three ready ways of dismissing human creativity: reducing it to the play of chance, declaring seemingly new ideas mere copies of old ones, or calling them products of inspiration. A mild schadenfreude heightens the charm of the accident narrative, portraying artists, poets, or inventors as lucky bumblers. Charles Lamb treats his readers to an ironic pleasure by picturing the swine-herd Ho-ti learning the joys of roast pig by accidentally burning down his cottage. Lamb redoubles the delight by proposing it was some time before the neighbors learned to replicate the feat without burning down their own homes. It's fun to think of Fleming stumbling onto penicillin when his bacteria just wouldn't grow in blue-green mold, or Nobel learning how to stabilize nitroglycerine (and stop blowing up his explosives factories) by accidentally dropping a phial of nitro in the sawdust on the floor—and so inventing dynamite. Accidental discovery fits nicely with mechanism: Only random collocations need be assumed, and no troublesome brainwork. Logicists are fond of thoughts of chance and play for similar reasons when seeking the roots of novel hypotheses in science. Explanations, they know, are not deducible from data. If theories won't spring full armed from the phenomena, hypotheses, they reason, must crop up by chance. There's a similar charm in setting play at the base of artistic invention: Thinking is too rule bound to be creative.

Imitation preserves the appeal of chance, since instructive exemplars often come unsought. But both inspiration and imitation permit natural and supernatural readings. Naturalism favors imitation: There's no real originality, we're told—just copying. Or, if that claim seems extreme, context and the flow of history are credited: Had X not thought of this someone else surely would have. History gets the credit or the blame, crimping the style of naturalism a bit—almost as though fate or progress were credited. In tales of inspiration, insight is alienated less impersonally: Divine visitations explain the salience and seeming suddenness of new ideas. The strangers bearing arts and customs linking culture to nature are recalled as demigods, in deference to their bridging role. But the sense persists that they appeared unbidden.

All three paradigms—chance, inspiration, and imitation—externalize creativity and flatter the romantic fascination with irrationality, the same impulse that links genius with insanity and divinity with injury. All three models are in play in Democritus—alongside of reason. Closest to the bone for Democritus is the random play of atoms: Language arose by chance (frg. 26); music, youngest of the arts, flowed from "a superfluity"—from play, then, "not necessity" (144). There's no poetry without madness, Democritus declares (17), Plato repeats that, and the canard echoes for centuries. So does the chance pedagogy of beasts: "We learned spinning and mending from the spider, building from the swallow, singing from songbirds, swans, and nightingales" (154). Morals, the Talmud suggests, needed no divine teacher: We could have learned modesty from the cat, property from the ant, chastity from the dove, uxoriousness from the cock (Eruvin 100b). The Qur'an (5:31) has Cain learning of funerary obsequies from a raven, albeit sent by God.[1] But note the role of persons giving relevance to what's observed. Cain, in the Qur'anic tale, learns penitence by watching the raven and not just how to bury his dead brother's corpse. Likewise, in the Talmud: We don't learn modesty from the cock, generosity from the cat, or flair and individuality from the ant. Even accident and example, it seems, can teach only a prepared mind.

Didn't humans, Democritus asks, learn mule breeding by seeing what became of a mare raped by an ass?[2] The story helps him with his own bridge from nature to culture—a larger theme for him than mere reduction of either to the other. For he sees them not as opposites, in the Sophist manner, but as complements: "Nature and teaching are similar: Teaching shapes the man, and the shaping forms his nature."[3] Democritus avoids making chance our only teacher, as he might have done, exploiting his thoughts about natural affinities: "doves consort with doves, cranes with cranes, and so all animals, and inanimate things too, as one can see with seeds in a sieve or pebbles on the beach: As the sieve is swirled, lentils assort with lentils, barley with barley, wheat with wheat; or on the beach, the waves drive oblong pebbles to the same place as other oblongs, and round ones to the same place as the round, as if they were drawn to each other" (164).[4] Still, chance is not the best teacher: It's "generous but unreliable" (176). Only fools let it shape them (197). Luck may lay a rich table, but wisdom sets an ample one (210). Besides, chance is too often an excuse for stupidity (119). Despite connecting poetry with madness, then, Democritus values the order minds can produce. He sees marks of divinity in Homer's poetic design (21), and inspiration in the beauty of poetry, "inhaled" from the spirit of the gods (18). Still, inspiration demands concerted, learned effort. Thoughtless, mechanical work is ugly. Only discipline and training yield beauty (182). Intelligence, not age, imparts wisdom (183). For experience must be absorbed. Minds, at their best, think divine thoughts (129). They're always at work on something fine and noble (112)—always thinking something new (158).

Creative Endeavor

Creativity, as we understand it, means fruitful originality. It's not bare novelty. What's striking might be merely unfamiliar, reflecting limited experience more than genuine originality. Fruitfulness may be practical, say in an invention; or intellectual, in a theory that opens new conceptual doors; or aesthetic, in artistic departures, or encounters with nature. Defining imagination in classic terms as a reworking of sensory images and memories, Mark Runco distinguishes it from creativity. Creativity may use the materials and methods of imagination, but originality and fruitfulness make it rarer.

Imagination, taken broadly, is a human universal. But it varies in quality, boldness, and interests. One might readily picture a sunset, or anticipate possibilities, or fall asleep and dream. But some people, both children and adults, build elaborate "paracosms" with distinctive geographies, organisms, peoples, possibilities, languages, and cultures.[5] Such worldplay differs from casual daydreaming in its level of detail, organization, and internal consistency. Fantasy worlds may be documented with written scenarios or maps. Children's imaginary companions may be assigned consistent personalities. For adult paracosms, alternative natural laws and histories are sometimes invoked. Such world building differs from madness in being voluntary, its products not confused with pragmatic reality. That helps relate such dreaming to creativity: Those who build fantasy worlds but enter and leave them freely may devise ways of relating them to the common world. So some creative individuals may use paracosms to solve problems, flesh out hypotheses, envision processes, or construct algorithms.[6]

Originality is constitutive in creativity, but human originality always connects novelty with tradition. The balance varies: Devising a new technology or literary genre is quite different from finding innovative uses for a hoary literary trope or poetic meter, or seeing new applications for a familiar machine or pharmaceutical. Phrases, tunes, characters, settings, meters, and countless other bits of cultural patrimony can be combined or reworked to build an original product from well worn components. That's the tinkering of cultural bricolage. Radical departures are rarer, and not always fruitful. But both everyday and extraordinary creativity link rules with fantasies to construct scenarios and weigh strategies. Perhaps because it does so more systematically, worldplay crops up in studies of individuals deemed exceptionally creative: Significant creativity outstrips simple fantasy partly through the rigor it imposes, fleshing out scenarios and confronting real world problems, whether in deference to the laws of nature or in dialogue with traditions in the arts, mediating between the suggestions of a fertile imagination and the demands of workability and intelligibility.

In creativity, as in consciousness and memory, social milieux are critical. Recognition, appreciation, or use may lag, and popular judgment is not inerrant. Many a discovery of real value may be lost, even permanently. But much is preserved, insights and discoveries taken up in the commerce and conversation of human life and civilization. There is intrinsic value in thinking a thought, experiencing a moment of beauty, or solving a puzzle. But scholarship is retrospective, and discovery is integrative. So much that is lost is, in time, rediscovered and registered in the manuals of utility or the scrapbooks and chapbooks of human understanding and delight. History in a broad sense indexes creativity (as well as judging conduct), even if it can never offer an absolute criterion.

By distinguishing creativity from mere novelty we mean to set the bar fairly high. Novelty for novelty's sake rarely has the value or the interest that would give it much staying power, unless perhaps as the record of a fad, documenting human curiosity and the appetite for novelty itself. We're dubious about the notion that we humans can invent our own reality, and the related notion (sometimes cultivated as a convention in the arts or artistic criticism) that seeks to blur the boundaries between reality and, say, theater or fiction. Notions of worldmaking that take the mind's constructive work to mean much more than its ongoing engagement with experience rapidly render mental work impossibly ambitious—as if the recognition that we make what sense we can of things somehow implied that nothing would exist or be what it is unless our thinking made it so. Human creativity, as we see it, works with existing materials, found or received. It's the question of added value that makes the social jury relevant, for its witness to momentary or enduring worth.

Value is of many kinds—and often unexpected, especially when creativity breaks set and does not trundle along in well marked ruts. If there were a formula or algorithm, a recipe or mechanism for creativity, it would not be creative. It's not that unpredictability means creativity. On the contrary, it's creativity that makes what's original unexpected. What's routine—thoughtless, as Democritus put it—is not creative. So if thinking were purely computational, creativity would be impossible—and so would learning anything new.

Creativity is not confined to works of genius. Not everyone is a Mozart or Beethoven, a Newton, Einstein, or Picasso. But everyone uses creativity, in learning to speak and frame sentences we've never heard before, in thinking through the ordinary problems of daily life, in devising answers to the questions we confront. Every bank teller, office clerk, steel worker, backhoe operator, tree trimmer, subsistence farmer, college dean, or civil servant regularly faces problems that demand more than rote responses. Strictly mechanical reactions, executed out of boredom or alienation, or cautious hiding behind a rule, are not just noticeable, they can be devastating.

Since creativity involves values, it can have a dark side, when perversity or nescience puts creative means to ill chosen ends.[7] Advances in transportation, from chariots to rockets, have made warfare deadlier. The Manhattan project mobilized vast intellectual and industrial resources for war. Hitler's Axis was evil. But the devastation wreaked and the dangers unleashed by the bomb did not single out the guilty alone. Military research has bred many a peacetime bounty, not least in medicine and surgery. Great ingenuity, clearly, has augmented the capacity for violence—in the design of weapons and implements of torture like those used by the Inquisition and many a Renaissance court. There are parallels in the cruelties of everyday life and in the exploitative devices of commerce and industry and the expressive realms of literature and the arts. Since 'creative' connotes *fruitfulness*, an Aristotelian caveat is in order. Aristotle distinguished *phronesis*, practical wisdom, in its instrumental sense (knowing effective means to one's ends) from the richer sense that demands knowing what ends are worth pursuing (lest one call mere cunning wisdom and commit to calling wise someone who seeks negative or nugatory ends). Similarly, it's worth distinguishing instrumental creativity from the sort that genuinely augments human flourishing. Weapon design can be creative; and weapons can protect human welfare. As with any modality, the first question is intent: To what end? And then: To what effect? Devices designed with innocent intent can be used viciously; others, intended viciously, can be turned to noble and ennobling uses. Hence the imagery of swords into plowshares and spears into pruning hooks—creative reappropriations pursued when conditions make them feasible.

Studying Creativity

Francis Galton inaugurated modern studies of creativity with his works *Hereditary Genius* (1869) and *Human Faculty* (1883). In time a large literature developed, classified by Mel Rhodes under four rubrics: Person, Process, Press, and Product.[8] Studies of persons might survey the lives of key figures. Work on Product examined the achievements, say, of inventors. Process traced the steps leading to innovations. The idea of Press put forward by the Harvard psychoanalyst Henry Murray (1893–1988) situated creativity amid familial and social pressures.[9] It came, in time, to include any contextual influence—educational, attitudinal, or hygienic. The focus on eminent figures, paralleling the great man approach in historiography, contributed little to penetrating the workings of creativity, in part because it neglected everyday creativity. Persistent hero worship, especially in popular accounts, provokes inevitable debunking reactions, seeking to minimize individual or communal achievements by reducing them to the play of circumstance or by luridly contrasting achievement with decadence or debility in creative people, whether out of prurience, romantic fascination, or tacit permission giving anchored in the confusion of genius with eccentricity.

Some individuals are remarkably creative. But no one knows if what makes a great painter, say, are traits like those of a great theorist or inventor.[10] So it's hard to say if creativity as such has a specific nature. Exceptionally creative individuals may prove to share certain attributes common to talented people. But talent is not the same as creativity, and neither guarantees success or recognition. Many important creators don't stand out from the crowd beyond the impact of their work itself. Surveying a range of studies, Frank Barron and David Harrington found that creative people often share a "high valuation of aesthetic qualities in experience, broad interests, attraction to complexity, high energy, independence of judgment, autonomy, intuition, self-confidence, ability to resolve antinomies or to accommodate apparently opposite or conflicting traits in one's self concept, and finally, a firm sense of self as 'creative.'"[11] How far do those traits exceed what was assumed in identifying creative persons to be studied?

Biographies can shed light on the personalities and circumstances of eminent creators. But following the life of a Galileo or Milton can't plumb the depths of creativity even in an individual, let alone anchor any generalizations. Given the differences between useful and useless inventions, or great and poor art, some of the same qualities of mind may be at work even in kitsch, dime novels, and B-movies. Again, there's not much eminence in the myriad efforts people make to yield smoother commutes, safer streets, better communication—or nicer gardens at home. The steady impact of such efforts attests to the depth and breadth of creativity in the psyche. But it's hard to say just where or how everyday creativity parts company from genius.

Democritus, we think, was right to avoid sundering creativity from learning. He sidestepped the trench Sophists dug between *nomos* and *physis*. A great poet, he reasons, is both learned and inspired—not merely echoing ancient tropes but ringing the changes on them. Great poetry, like great science, springs from tradition. But it doesn't stop there. A scientist typically needs the achievements of predecessors, whether to raise a question or construct a method, or perhaps to give meaning to a discovery. Great music resonates against the echoes of past works. To ignore such backgrounds is to miss the impact of novelty and the richness of synthesis.

Consider how John Harrison (1693–1776) solved the longitude problem: Navigators had long counted knots in a line fastened to a "chip log," cast overboard and timed with a sand glass, to estimate a ship's position and speed. The method was as crude as it sounds, leaving mariners in the dark about the landmasses or hazards earlier sailors had seen. Harrison, a clockmaker, knew that dead reckoning was crude. But astronomical positioning was arduous and not practicable in all weathers. Harrison knew the elegantly simple suggestion of the cosmographer Regnier Gemma Frisius (1508–1555), the teacher of Mercator and Vesalius: that keeping track of the time at home would allow ready calculation of one's east or west position, by sighting the sun and comparing solar time with clock time.

What was needed was a clock that would stay accurate through a long voyage, despite humidity, temperature changes, and the corrosive effects of salt air. With help from other master clockmakers, Harrison built and tested chronometers, improved and redesigned them, waited out the War of Austrian Succession, and redesigned a special steel watch with diamond escapement parts and an internal bimetal strip to compensate for temperature changes. His design passed its gravest test when Captain Cook confirmed its accuracy on his second voyage. But it took a threat from George III, who had tested the timepiece himself, that he would come to Parliament and berate the members, before Harrison, at eighty, was allotted a portion of the £20,000 promised to whoever solved the longitude problem. He was never awarded the official prize, for which he'd labored since he was a young man. Harrison's solution had not come by accident. He had learned from Frisius's insight in connecting time with distance, measured not in miles or knots but in degrees of the earth's circumference. And he had doggedly pursued that thought, surmounting one technical, conceptual, collaborative, and even political and economic obstacle after another for over four decades, before finally winning at least partial vindication.

Aristotle defines intelligence as alacrity in recognizing the middle term that connects seemingly unrelated items: How do we know that all men are mortal? The key term linking 'man' and 'mortal' is 'animal.' Understanding what it means for a creature to be alive explains why all men will die. Not that anyone has observed every human death but because the Second Law of Thermodynamics, as we now know, bars the way to unlimited biological survival. Earlier thinkers voiced their intuitions about entropy, as we now call it, in terms of the inevitable decay of everything that grows. Seeing 'animal' as the missing term connecting 'man' with 'mortal' is one way of articulating that thought. Aristotle's broad point was that intelligence sees kinships behind differences and distinguishes things that seem alike. To work creatively intelligence uses both synthesis and analysis to build connections and make distinctions that are neither trivial nor obvious. That's where the originality comes in.

Generically, creativity involves ampliative reasoning, relating things in ways not evident on the surface—connecting energy with mass say, as Einstein did in 1905. It's never simply a matter of "unpacking" what's implicit in the given. That's why creative thinking is sometimes called lateral or nonlinear. It doesn't color inside the lines but draws lines of its own—yet not arbitrarily. When the U.S. Supreme Court in *Brown v. Board of Education* ruled separate schools for Blacks and Whites unconstitutional in 1954, the Justices stepped beyond the given. Overturning the "separate but equal" precedent of *Plessy v. Ferguson,* they judged racial segregation intrinsically unjust, thus a violation of the Equal Protection Clause of the Fourteenth Amendment—although that amendment did not overtly announce its relevance, which segregationists vehemently denied. The Court disagreed. Even on the dubious assumption that school programs and facilities proved equivalent across racial lines, the Justices found segregated schools "inherently unequal," given the implicit affront to human dignity and the evidence of studies by Kenneth Clark and June Shagaloff of social and psychological harm to Black children resulting from the very fact of segregation. In ways not previously customary, new information was brought to bear, along with a very basic understanding of human nature that allowed a more expansive reading of the idea of equal protection, a hitherto sacred standard that had not yet been invoked in matters of education—or public accommodation.

We've seen creativity in the integrative, pattern making and pattern completing work of perception, consciousness, and memory, and in human agency, which is not confined to mechanical responses to stimuli. Creativity, we think, is found in every human undertaking, although it's natural to single out the more striking instances, just as we call a person tall or resourceful who seems more so than most. Notions of creativity commonly used today owe much to the writings of Polydore Vergil (ca. 1470–1555), whose widely read volumes *De Inventoribus Rerum* saw a common theme in the invention of devices and institutions and the discovery of things and ideas. Very much a man of the Renaissance, Polydore highly valued innovation over static satisfaction with tradition. There were others like him in antiquity and in the Middle Ages for that matter. The medieval writer Hamadhani, for example, called *himself* an innovation. But in his tradition-oriented society innovation was more often a matter for concern than a quality to be boasted of or celebrated. With the coming of the Renaissance the ideal of creativity, long and widely credited to God, caught on as a trait that humans too might pursue.

Human creativity may be radical or organic. But even radical creativity can't start from nothing. Rather, it draws on unexpected sources. Poets capture kinships among seemingly unrelated things, making freshly seen connections a quarry for their imagery. But languages in general grow by similar devices, giving old words new uses and growing meanings out of metaphors. Scientific discovery, similarly, finds pertinent analogies in seemingly unrelated phenomena. Technology puts materials to new uses. Framing a question or seeing a need comes first. That too calls for insight. But each breakthrough involves making connections. The rush of recognition may make discovery seem sudden, even passive. But it's rarely just a matter stumbling onto something.

The mind is always at work, even as we sleep. So it's not surprising that dreams may help, or that we may see how to tackle a question when we're not confronting it head on and letting eagerness or anxiety obscure some unanticipated angle. But John Joly and Darwin's son George didn't just *guess* that radioactive decay within the earth might warm its crust enough to refute Lord Kelvin's low estimate of its age and help vindicate evolution. They *learned* of Pierre Curie's measures of the heat output of radium and of Julius Elster and Hans Geitel's discovery of radiation in the soil. Putting the pieces together, they saw relevance to a seemingly separate biological question: Was the earth was old enough for natural selection to do its work? Accident was not their guide. "Chance," as Louis Pasteur put it, "favors only the prepared mind."[12]

Between Critique and Mystique

Plato aids our understanding of creativity, by exposing some weaknesses in a stringent empiricism. If thinking needs robust generalities that reach beyond direct observation, and science needs truths that hold universally, a strict empiricism can't provide them. Laws like the law of gravity cannot be reached by just chalking up sightings of falling objects. Despite the old story of Newton's apple tree, noticing that objects fall conveys no inkling that all bodies attract each other with a force directly proportional to their masses and inversely to the square of the distance between them. Pure reason can't do that either. There might be some intuitive appeal in the idea that a force extending in all directions would diminish in an inverse square sort of way, if one imagined gravity as a kind of net thinning as it spreads. But first one would need to find and refine some suitable notions of force and mass and bring to bear thoughts of nets and networks. And that wouldn't prove the analogies adequate or apt. Only experience could test them. But sense experience, no matter how extensive, would never yield thoughts of an inverse square function, let alone license its application to unseen cases.

Yet it was only by applying Newton's laws to all bodies, celestial and terrestrial, bodies that had never been weighed, that Urbain Le Verrrier could reason, in 1846, that slight perturbations in the orbit of Uranus are signs of another body in the neighborhood—and thus predict the presence of Neptune. Neptune had, in fact, been spotted earlier. But the Newtonian calculations *explained* the sightings. It's the necessity of causal laws that lifts them above casual sensation and makes them explanatory tools. So apologetically calling such theses "lawlike generalizations" only papers over their power, as principles outreaching experience. The euphemisms only spotlight the problem of induction: Finite experience can't yield truths of universal scope. Perception can't even tell us that our homes exist when we're away, or that nearby bodies have insides. As for core concepts like 'like' or 'one,' calling them higher order abstractions, as we've noted, overlooks our presupposing very general notions like these even in our most elemental comparisons.

Learning from Plato to spot the glitches in a doctrinaire empiricism, Leibniz, in *New Essays Concerning Human Understanding*, defended innate ideas against Locke's empiricism. Kant, roused by Hume's use of skepticism against rationalist pretensions but also guided by that dialogue of Leibniz's, saw that sense experience unaided cannot validate our reliance on concepts like causal necessity or object permanence. Kant called such concepts a priori rather than innate, aiming to disentangle questions of their genesis from those about their warrant. The mind, he reasoned, exercises creativity at a far more basic level than Lockeans had suspected: It gives structure to human experience and form to our understanding.

The weakness in Plato's account of the roots of our ideas lies in his appropriation of the imagery of inspiration, building on the antique suspicion that all great ideas must have some supernal source. For Plato it was not just poetic or artistic or religious inspiration, or legislation or prognostication, that descends from on high, but all real knowledge: If understanding cannot arise from the sweep of the senses, since clear concepts and the universal truths that would amount to real knowledge are not found in the flickering images of changeable things, knowledge must descend to us from the Forms. It does no good to say that what we know, when we really know, was learned in a prior life (as the myths employed by Plato's Pythagorean friends suggested). Inveterate paradoxes and countercases block that path: How could we recognize a concept we did not already have? Knowledge, Plato reasoned, must be by acquaintance. Hence his playful remarks about philosophers and dogs: friendly to the familiar but unfriendly to strangers. And, if knowledge was not acquired through some temporal process it must, in fact, link us with eternity. In our ability to *know*, to teach, explain, and understand, Plato saw proof of the ultimate timelessness, deathlessness, even divinity—of the rational soul. Whether we sense it or not, we are in constant touch with the Forms, the universal archetypes of all things in this shadow world of ours. Once dialectic has cleared away the rime of prejudice and convention, the false conceit of wisdom, the timeless knowledge that is reason's birthright shines through.

But that account leaves behind a problem unsolved by Plato: If intellectual exploration means simply clearing away confusions and all knowledge is by acquaintance, modeled poetically on recollection, minds knowing ideas as one might recognize a familiar face, no room is left for discovery: Knowledge comes from analysis. Nothing is newly known; what we take for learning is just the dredging up into the light what was implicitly known eternally. Troubled by by that issue, Aristotle rejects Plato's imagery of anamnesis and the related notion that analysis is the ultimate source of knowledge. Discovery goes further. It is not just unpacking the treasures hidden in our most universal concepts. We won't know the natures of things unless we study them. Distinguishing his own methods from Plato's, Aristotle proudly calls the syllogism a method of discovery, as contrasted with Plato's method of division, which can yield nothing new but at best reveals only what was implicit in what we knew tacitly already.

If Aristotle's claim for the syllogism seems strange, it may be because we typically read syllogisms backwards, from premises to conclusion, missing the backhand stroke that marks Aristotle's commitment to innovation. The key to the syllogism, we've noted, lies in the middle term linking the extremes but mentioned only in the premises, not the conclusion. If we look at syllogisms as Aristotle's way of charting the adventure of discovery—telling the hunt, as it were—the conclusion stands out as a thesis to be validated. Discovery means finding fit premises, hinging on a middle term that might link up the extremes in the conclusion. Laid out with their conclusions at the end, syllogisms are not ampliative at all. They *demonstrate* only in the sense of showing how a piece of knowledge is assured. Discovery came earlier, in finding a workable middle term, letting insight underwrite knowledge.

Building a syllogism is constructive work, not just uncovering what was present all along, but finding linkages. So, while Aristotle preserves Plato's recognition that perception alone can't yield universal concepts, let alone universal truths, he also sees that thinking, to get anywhere at all, must move, creatively, beyond the given. It needs novelty. Concept formation is not just openness to the effulgence of eternal Ideas. Analysis is one side of the picture. But we need synthesis to connect images and experiences, memories and motives, forming a picture and generating a judgment, predicating *this* about *that*, detecting relations, including causal relations among things in the natural world, dependencies that allow one to judge a connection necessary and not just happenstance.

Aristotle models discovery in a Homeric simile, introduced as he brings his discussion of the syllogism to a close in the *Posterior Analytics*: Concept building is like the regrouping of a cavalry squadron that's been put to flight. A banner is raised, fighting order is regained, perhaps not in a pre-set pattern (as though Plato had been right all along). Sensory images, preserved in memory, are organized, and the patterns they suggest completed. Concepts are built on the skeletons laid down by those schematics.

Like Democritus, Aristotle retains the idea of inspration: The mind can't just kickstart itself, he reasons. It gets a boost toward universal concepts. Admirers of Aristotle have disputed for centuries whether the Active Intellect, which provides that push, was Aristotle's name for an inner faculty (for he does say, as he wraps up his Homeric simile, that the mind is *able* to do these things) or whether it is a divine reality, as the *Eudemian Ethics* proposes. But the question may rest on a false dichotomy. For Aristotle does not sharply divide immanence from transcendence. Like Plato he holds the rational soul to be what is most divine in humans. If asked whether discovery is an act of ours or the work of the divine within us, he might well reply, "yes!"

The difficulty remains that Aristotle does not anatomize the process of discovery. Intuiting the middle term is clearly of the essence, and it helps to understand intelligence as alacrity in making connections and distinctions. But Aristotle does not say how that gets done. A host of philosophers follow up with tales (and disputes) about the Active Intellect, identifying it as what's really meant by talk of revelation, and seeking to connect its interventions with the inboard work of reason. Al-Fārābī will identify it with the cosmic Intellect that moves the lowest of the spheres, the Giver of Forms, responsible not only for our access to concepts but for the order of the cosmos—and the insights of prophets. Avicenna has his own story of rational intuition. But the cosmic Active Intellect only makes it seem that creativity has been externalized again—hypostatized, and mystified. Discovery seems once again beyond time and off limits to inquiry.

Secularized or semi-secularized by Romantics, the ideas of intuition and inspiration collapse into myths of genius. Kant dismisses rational intuition, unready to accept the claim that it transcends time. Poets like Coleridge, imbued with Kantian ideas, shift creativity to the imagination: Once the go-between mediating sensation to rationality, imagination is now charged with generating innovation for artists, inventors, scientists, and performers. Yet the stories persist linking genius with madness—and thus, possession, as the word genius once cautioned: Powerful passions, deficiencies and excesses, thought the price of brilliance, rouse fears and fascination with imagined ecstasies and excursions that defy explanatory—let alone moral—bounds.

As secularity sets in, intuition becomes an epithet applied patronizingly to women (or native peoples), now deemed closer to nature or more in touch with themselves than their tightly wound mates or citified visitors. The stereotypes fly freely, sometimes appropriated in the name of those to whom they've stuck—as Leopold Senghor, say, sought to forge positive attributes from them. Blacks or Asiatics, Native Americans, or tribal folk, so the notion runs, do not clearly distinguish self from other, individual from group, cause from effect, or word from object. In a disenchanted world, words like *intuition, inspiration,* and *genius* lose their charge. The energies seep away that once made them sound like explanations. They become mere labels, the stuff of cocktail party banter, along with other casualties of secularity, words like *sublime* and *divine,* preserving no more real impact or purchase than the costume jewelry and tie clips of the chatterers who use them.

For strict Behaviorists there is no creativity, only chance or imitation—recycling old plots, recopying old poses. Novelty springs from randomness, often equated with play. Accident displaces genius: Innovators do not think through a problem and discover a solution. They fall upon an answer. Not surprisingly, as Behaviorism hits its peak, art forms appear that make accident a virtue. Chance shoulders fate aside. But the old portentous claims persist. So, as chance becomes both a subject and a method, innovators are still hailed as geniuses. Romanticism is not so easily euthanized. Joining hands with its old enemy, the sense of disenchantment that goads it, romanticism revives a still more ancient myth: If reason is mechanism, creativity must be irrational. The éclat of originality eclipses the effort, promoting the illusion that creativity must be radical, rule-breaking (rather than rule-discovering or -enlarging), inexplicable (being foreign to familiar categories), and unanswerable to tradition and its norms.

Sharon Bailin disarms the Romantic view, noting how continuity and discontinuity interact in creative work. She faults Thomas Kuhn for calling what is original "unprecedented" and discontinuous with its past, and cites Herbert Read and Susanne Langer for pointing to the role of traditions in opening up the expressive powers of art and for discrediting the illusion that changing fashions preclude objective standards in art. Artistic taste, of course, cannot mean mere fondness for the familiar (the so-called iconic). But neither can it be mere excitement over seeming innovation. Openness to discovery is critical. But at its best that means an educated capacity to value the new not just for its novelty and the exotic not just for its strangeness but for values perhaps not fully explored in more familiar artistic ventures. Against Paul Feyerabend's subjectivism about scientific achievement, Bailin invokes Karl Popper's vision of scientific progress. She cools Arthur Koestler's breathlessness about rule breaking, observing that no one can break *all* rules. Innovation is meaningful only against a backdrop of relative constancy.[13]

Romantics and mechanists feed off one another's excesses, each proud of the distance traveled from the shunned extreme. But neither approach withstands scrutiny: Innovation need not be radical, and creativity is not irrational. Creative workers in art or science, technology or philosophy, answer questions and address problems posed by a tradition. They use methods, language, media, and tools bequeathed by others. Where they jettison old thoughts they often preserve what was most precious or most viable in them.[14] They do so by the active, critical, and synthetic use of their intelligence. To reject a hidebound rule or critique an unexamined premise is not to annihilate a world. Indeed, to understand an innovation is to see what it alters, what it demolishes, and what it preserves.

Gestalt Discontents

Gestalt psychologists rejected both Behaviorist dismissals and Romantic mystiques, viewing creativity as problem solving, not just in works of genius but in children's discoveries, and animal cleverness too. Anyone may have an Aha! moment like Archimedes' *eureka!* experience: The mists clear, and we see what had seemed obscure.

Loyal to Locke, Watson relied on association. Abstraction, for Locke, was an associative mechanism, bundling like impressions—"as doves consort with doves, and cranes with cranes," in Democritean terms. Hume had linked causes to effects in the same Lockean way, invoking not induction but contiguity. Empiricists were trusted to ignore the embarrassing complexity of comparing and generalizing and the differences between causal reasoning and brute, Pavlovian association. If juxtaposition can manage what others called concept formation, Behaviorists reasoned, why couldn't imitation explain how new behaviors are acquired? The upshot was more a denial of novelty than an explanation of creativity.

Since Locke had tucked analogy under the capacious skirts of his associative rule, strict empiricists could ask analogy to do the work familiarly assigned to creativity. But just how do our minds *find* new and instructive analogies? Mechanists leave it to chance to present phenomena with striking similarities. Often they think of trial and error or picture inventors and other innovators randomly tinkering with things or images until some happy accident yields a mix that works: Poets must play with words, artists with paints, until they happen on success. But what makes a resemblance striking, or a combination click? And what can be said about highly abstract structural affinities? Do we model them in concrete images? Perhaps at times. But how do we discriminate a model or image that is apt from one that is irrelevant or inept? Can mimicry explain the thinking of a diplomat or a general probing the thoughts of an ally or adversary? If random play were to suggest hypotheses, or color options, word choices, or tactical ploys, an alert and critical mind would still be needed, to note *which* ones were worth pursuing. Karl Popper allowed guesswork to frame hypotheses but counted on experimentation to weed out sterile choices. But guesswork does not design experiments. Besides, there are infinite ways of explaining anything; and (*pace* Popper) falsification is never absolutely final, since even the flimsiest hypothesis can be repaired ad hoc to keep it standing. So even assiduous weeding won't diminish the candidate class of hypotheses to workable scale. Likewise with color schemes, word sequences, or strategies.

Some innovators do call play critical in their work. But there's no more randomness in play of this kind than there is in children's play. Asking subjects to verbalize their thought processes, Adriaan de Groot found that chess masters don't systematically review the vast array of moves available at a given juncture. They consider just a few—much as amateurs might do. But the moves that masters consider are typically the best. Years of study and experience let them swiftly size up the board.[15] Painters and poets, similarly, don't just dab at the palette or riffle the thesaurus. Nor do most of us randomly survey the options we face. We look for patterns—or invent them.

Experimenting with primate behavior in Tenerife during World War I, Wolfgang Köhler watched chimps learn quickly to use a stick to reach bananas set outside their cage. They didn't just thrash about or randomly experiment but seemed to ponder for a while, puzzled at first, and then, light up as they saw what to do. Joining two short sticks to reach the fruit, and stacking boxes to climb to reach bananas overhead were further tricks the chimps discovered—although not if the props were out of sight. Did the prominence of perception here vindicate Kant's decision to write off rational intuition? The apparent flash of recognition restored some of the credibility intuition had once enjoyed. But intuition now was housed in the imagination. Was insight, then, essentially a duck-rabbit shift, a perceptual switch like seeing now one corner of a sketched Necker cube, now another, as protuberant? As researchers found means of slowing down creative processes enough to track them, the commonalities of brilliant originality with daily creativity came more clearly into view. The work of creativity was not just perceptual.

Max Wertheimer confirmed the prominence of pattern shifts in his experiments with children's problem solving in the 1920s and '30s. But in a way his work fleshed out much older thoughts about rational intuition. Spinoza had called knowledge gleaned from signs (e.g., via tradition or instruction) or from the senses, "knowledge of the first kind." Sense knowledge, inevitably decontextualized, he branded fragmentary, as we've noted in chapter 3. Communicated knowledge, reliant on the quality of sources, reception, and transmission, is little better than hearsay. "Knowledge of the second kind," reasoning in its familiar discursive form, is solid enough, but dependent on sound general ideas as starting points.

Intuition is critical here, as Aristotle saw. He credits Socrates for his creative use of intuition in induction, which worked not by piling up cases but by grasping relations and connections. Socratic induction did not work to a pattern; it built one. And useful patterns are not always visual. The ones that mattered most to Spinoza were causal, recontextualizing what perception may miss or analysis may abstract from as we focus on one thing and background another. Our third kind of knowledge, then, arises not from rote, or brute association, or even deduction. To advance beyond what we already think we know, Spinoza reasoned, we must understand things causally, seeing nature holistically, as a system.[16] As Gestalt inquiries into creativity advanced, they too moved from analysis to synthesis.

Keenly aware of the Behaviorist penchant for associative psychology, Wertheimer was also sensitive to the old traditions of rote learning and rule dependence that Behaviorism actively encouraged—striking flinty sparks against his more liberal pedagogical ideas. Traditional logic, he complained, might promote rigor (syllogisms read in their familiar deductive form)— but not creativity. Too often its yield is "dull, insipid, lifeless . . . boring, empty," evaporating anything vital, forceful, or creative.[17] Inductive logic as doctrinaire empiricism envisioned it encouraged careful collation of facts but shed little light on relevance. Diligence might amass quite an array of data and even frame a rule. But totting up cases without asking *why* correlations appear leaves it unclear whether one's rule holds in new cases with the kind of necessity that's paydirt for science and critical in daily living, teaching, and explaining. For only generalizations that support a counterfactual yield reliable predictions or scientific laws—the kind of generalizations that philosophers, chary of their strict empiricism and loyal to its skeptical heritage, call lawlike.[18]

Associative psychology has its strengths. But how can animal association of the sort Hume made canonical[19] distinguish causality from coincidence—or trace the etiology of concomitant effects of a common cause, or even distinguish causes from effects? If innovations are forged of linked ideas, Wertheimer asked, and imagination only compiles impressions, how can we distinguish sensible combinations—insight from daydreaming? And if drill is expected to hammer home normative linkages (as Hume's talk of horse training suggests), why should the links riveted by repetition be called thinking at all? Could mental travel on these rails (or in these ruts) ever be creative—productive, as Wertheimer put it, capable of progressing beyond what already seems acceptable?

Visiting a class where pupils had just learned to calculate the area of a rectangle, Wertheimer gave a twist to the lesson plan. The students knew area as a sort of sum of the little squares that might make up a rectangle. Puckishly, he challenged them to find the area of a parallelogram. He seems to smile as one youngster mechanically multiplies base by side. He's less amused at the teacher's response: announcing, then proving, that a parallelogram's area is base times altitude. The pupils dutifully apply the rule. But are they learning how to think or experiencing the joy of discovery: "observing the class," Wertheimer writes, "I feel uneasy. . . . Have they done any thinking at all?"[20]

Probing further, he draws a parallelogram whose altitude falls outside the base. The students seem flummoxed, uncertain how to use their new rule in this odd case. Even those who dutifully recite the rule seem unsure if it applies. Some brighten up and flip the skewed figure on its side to show the rule still works. The teacher is annoyed: You've just confused the class and got them out of step with one another. But working with other children, some as young as six, who'd had no geometry at all (like the slave-boy in Plato's *Meno*), Wertheimer elicits some pretty keen responses about odd figures—and disappointing mouthings of memorized rules, or petu-lant remarks: How should we know? We haven't learned how to do those figures.[21]

If a teacher shows, in a parallelogram, that an altitude can cut off a tri-angle on one side that looks (and demonstrably is) equal to one protruding on the other, children readily start reconstructing these (and other) figures into well mannered rectangles. Given a paper parallelogram, one snips off the "troublesome" part and adds it at the other end, forming a rectangle. The child is a genius, a colleague says. But that's a label, not an explanation. The formulaic Behaviorist appeal to "generalization" Wertheimer finds equally opaque: True, the kids now happily solving his problems are treating rect-angles as a special case of parallelograms. But that's not how they reached their insights. If anything they're treating parallelograms as disobedient rectangles. Notions of generalization only mask the progression of the chil-dren's ideas. And "generalization" still won't make clear why a familiar rule applies, or distinguish where it fails.[22]

Wertheimer comes closer to conceptual intuitions in relating a story about the young Carl Gauss (1777–1823). Gauss was six, we're told, when a teacher challenged him to find the sum of 1+2+3+4+5+6+7+8+9+10 . . . (in some versions, the series runs to 100). It would be tedious just to add the numbers. But for every unit increase at one end of the sequence, Gauss saw an equal decrease at the other. So the sums of the largest and smallest number and of the next largest and next smallest, remained equal. The two sets of pairs met at the midpoint. So that number was significant. Multiply-ing it by the number of pairs gave the answer.

Gauss, it seems, soon generalized the rule—not by piling up impressions but by recognizing the parallels in any like series. Wertheimer helps those of us who are less intuitive with numbers by asking us to visualize the series as a numberline. Many of Gauss's more advanced mathematical discover-ies (and their applications in astronomy, magnetism, optics, electricity, and probability) can be represented graphically. But visualization does not suf-fice in explaining how Gauss reached them—let alone illuminate his paths to the proofs that made them solid mathematics, not mere conjectures. We can see the mind relying more on its own resources than on visualization, perhaps, in a problem Gauss pondered for decades before his friend János Bolyai solved it: conceiving a consistent geometry without Euclid's parallels postulate. It's not hard to call Gauss a genius. Numerous prodigy stories and the well documented discoveries of his maturity confirm it: He was a

Mozart in mathematics. But the title 'genius' refers to outcomes, not to Gauss's means of reaching them.

Tracking the Flash

New ideas often seem to crop up unexpectedly. We don't always know where they came from, just as we often can't explain how we suddenly recall some fact we've struggled to remember. The unpredictability of insight keeps alive the notion of the passive mind and of journeys, in fact or fancy, to another realm, daimonic perhaps, or Platonic, where the time slips away and we're touched by higher truths. The parallels with sudden remembering give color to Plato's image of discovery as a kind of recall—not of the past but of eternity.

Demystifying creativity need not strip it of wonder. What Aristotle saw was that discovery is a process, adding value by connecting thoughts in new ways. Hence his Homeric simile: Memory marshals fleeting perceptions, organizing history into experience, and projecting concepts by completing the patterns that experience can only suggest. Experience permits the framing of plans of action, or of architecture, and the kind of scenarios we might admire as a surgeon, playwright, or strategist gets to work. Beyond experience (which can't always explain itself and remains uncertain of its own scope and workability), human intelligence frames concepts and the general rules that good concepts permit (without which science is mere anecdote). Aristotle can't pretend to know just how we how we press on from experience to full-bodied understanding. He knows the soul is active in discovery but cannot say just how its intellectual work is accomplished. He simply says: "The soul is such that it is capable of this" (*Posterior Analytics* 2.19.100a14).

Philoponus likes the reference to the soul. Its nonrational parts, spirit and appetite, as he names them, help out.[23] But he too is unable to break down the work of discovery into steps. Nor does Spinoza help much here. He does offer an example highlighting the contrast of sensory and learned knowledge with reasoned and intuitive knowledge: Given three numbers and asked to find a fourth "that is to the third as the second is to the first," tradesmen unhesitatingly multiply the second by the third and divide by the first, remembering their teacher's rule: The product of the means equals the product of the extremes. Perhaps they've tried out "cross-multiplying" in sample cases. Reasoners can replicate Euclid's proof about proportions—especially when prompted with a geometrical sketch. But with simple numbers, Spinoza writes, "no one fails to see" what the proportional number must be.[24] That's hard with fancier numbers. But great mathematicians may intuit subtle relationships without prompts. They *devise* the proofs and don't just follow them. That still does not say how.

Robert Weisberg is as happy to explode myths about creativity as a child popping balloons. He likes de Groot's finding about chess masters: It shows they don't randomly attack or laboriously survey each possible option but work methodically with just a few, much as ordinary mortals do—except with expertise. Contrary to romantic myths of rustic genius, experience counts. Recent research, he writes, "has blurred the distinction between performance based on knowledge and performance based on problem solving."[25] Rightly so. Sharply dichotomizing the two obscures the need to integrate insight with experience if one is to accomplish anything requiring much thought. The studies show that experts in a variety of fields tackle complex problems in much the same way and using much the same skills that most people use in handling everyday problems. Clearly creativity is not the same as expertise. Learning won't turn a plodder into a virtuoso. But major creators typically draw on treasuries of practice and experience, intimate familiarity with the matter and the methods of their metier that allow them to deal with its givens freely, sometimes radically.[26]

Creative thinking, Weisberg argues, does not just well up from the unconscious. Coleridge's tale relating that his poem *Kubla Khan* flowed from his pen after an opium dream (although transcription was aborted when the poet was interrupted) is belied by an apparent early draft of the work.[27] Nor is it true, as surviving manuscripts attest, that Mozart never revised his compositions. The story that the structure of the benzene ring came to Kekulé in a dream was retailed by chemist himself at an 1890 celebration honoring his foundational discovery over a quarter century after the fact. Kekulé spoke of a reverie or daydream, not a literal dream. And he told two versions of his inspiration: In one he pictured a snake biting its tail; in the other, there were dancing molecules, pictured as he rode a horse-drawn omnibus years earlier. No one knows how seriously Kekulé meant his stories to be taken. But neither snakes nor dancing atoms would have revealed much about organic chemistry to someone who hadn't spent years laboring to square established evidence about benzene with an account of its molecular structure.

The key to the discovery was not an image at all, but Kekulé's recognition of the import of there being only one isomer of every monoderivative of benzene. That meant that benzene's six carbon atoms were equivalent, allowing only one product for any attachment to a carbon atom. When a student argued that double and single bonds allowed for *two* derivatives, Kekulé revised his model: the double and single bonds connecting the six carbon atoms oscillate! In 1928 Linus Pauling replaced mechanical oscillation with quantum resonance, the now accepted model. Kekulé's breakthrough came not from daydreaming but from careful conceptual work, building on others' discoveries (e.g. about the benzene derivatives), honed by criticism, and enlarged by new discoveries (in quantum mechanics) beyond Kekulé's ken. Kekulé's insight was personal, but the context that made it meaningful was a social enterprise extending before, around, and after his work. Little was passive or automatic in the journey or its outcome. The dancing molecules made a good story, but the real connection was made not by atoms joining hands but by a conceptual synthesis as one mind and then others caught the significance of the limited variety of isomer derivatives of benzene and recognized that its carbon atoms would not yield chemical equivalents unless their placement was also somehow equivalent—like the knights of the table round.

Graham Wallas and other theorists schematized creative work in four stages: preparation (conscious wrestling with a problem), incubation (setting the problem aside, although perhaps still chewing it over unconsciously), illumination (sudden insight, seemingly out of the blue), and verification (testing, revising, correcting, often invoking aesthetic standards alongside more prosaic tests of fit). Studies by Jan Eindhoven and Edgar Vinacke, Weisberg argues, show that it's not always easy to identify a discrete incubation period. Creative workers may carry an issue around with them and worry it incessantly. Breaking off may prove useful, whether because it's restful or because it allows a change of tack. But it's not always necessary. And it can be distracting. Chess players given a break from pondering a problem did no better than others who simply beavered away at it.[28]

Weisberg is suspicious of the Aha! idea, partly because it suggests passivity: Good ideas don't just well up. He blames Gestalt psychology, in part: The Gestalt switch looks too perceptual, too sudden, vulnerable to romantic discounting of prior knowledge, in reaction to the Behaviorists' overvaluing of repetition, association, analogy, and "generalization." Gestalt scenarios of things' just clicking into place, he argues, undervalue experience. Köhler's apes may not previously have used sticks like those he supplied, but surely they had improvised comparable implements while still in the wild. Herbert Birch got no such results as Köhler's with apes raised in captivity.[29]

Tests of creativity, Weisberg argues, often track our ability to restructure a problem and set aside familiar parallels. Such tests, in effect, discount experience and analogy.[30] Granted, experience can be misleading or distracting. It can also be instructive. Weisberg finds talk of divergent or lateral thinking somewhat mythic in character. We see some real value in these notions, especially in their original setting, as antidotes to rigidity and conformity. But when popularized by self-help hucksterism and mechanized in brainstorming rituals, the notions lose touch with their evidentiary base and can lose their relevance and effectiveness as well.

The parallels between sudden recall and sudden insight confirm thoughts of a mental block: We say "I should have seen that!" Something must have blocked our view—fatigue, distraction, sticking to a false path, even a hidden death wish or fear of success. Brainstorming, blockbusting, and other creativity training and stimulating techniques take aim at such obstacles. Some professionals try to gauge creativity by asking people swiftly to name everything they can that's white and edible, or to list the consequences of everyone's having six fingers—or, more practically, to name all the ways a common item might be improved.[31] It's assumed here that thinking is mere "processing." So creativity must mean freeing ideas by removing blockages or skirting them. Creative persons must be eccentric; custom and tradition, rules and frameworks only inhibit childlike creativity. Habits can be hidebound, of course, and rules can be too rigid, especially when enforced by conformist norms. But stereotypes need cautious handling, even when they embed a grain of truth: Not *all* rules are stifling. Creativity is not the same as eccentricity, and fluency is not fecundity.

The brainstorming methods popularized by Robert Olson were motivated and perpetuated by perceptions of a sharp dichotomy between creative and "judicial" thinking. The aim was to prune back the judgmental briars that Olson thought spread as we mature, to restore the copious, unfettered ideation of youth. Wild ideas are to be encouraged in brainstorming; criticism is verboten. Desired is a plethora of possibilities. But piggybacking on another's thoughts is encouraged. Warmth and receptivity are asked to overcome the insecurities that may squelch a great idea.[32] Brainstorming became hugely popular in the later 1950s as corporations and government agencies sought to meet the Sputnik challenge and break away from the postwar "button-down" mentality. It remained a mantra long afterwards, when rigidity, mental or otherwise, was hardly the salient problem. Romantic notions of spontaneity and mutual acceptance help explain its persistence, a lingering sense that wildness must be creative since it's unconstrained. But empiric studies early on undercut the brainstorming mythology.

In controlled experiments seeking to gauge the creativity of scientists and advertizing people working alone or in groups, psychologists found that nominal groups (individuals working alone) averaged 30–40 percent more solutions to assigned problems of varying difficulty than comparable working groups. Independent judges consistently found higher quality in the individuals' ideas.[33] The trends were confirmed by others with groups of varying sizes. Indeed, the advantages of individuals increased with the size of the groups.[34] Team members can complement one another's strengths. But groupthink, as such, does not add value.

As for judgment's inhibiting of creativity, experiments at Purdue disconfirmed the notion. Students were asked to invent brand names, one team using brainstorming, the other encouraged to offer many ideas but make sure they were practical and good. The brainstormers proved more prolific. But the critical group had as many good ideas (as rated by 150 other students)—thus, a higher proportion of good ideas. In another study, some groups worked with brainstorming instructions, some did brainstorming but after setting criteria (reversing the usual brainstorming rule of reserving judgment until ideas had been hatched), and some groups did no brainstorming but were given more analytic instructions: Define your problem, weigh its seriousness, plan a method of attack, compare proposed solutions, and reach conclusions about which seemed best. The two brainstorming groups were most prolific, in quantity and quality. But in *proportion* of good ideas the analytic group far outperformed the others.[35] The use of judgment, even critical judgment, did not cripple creative teamwork but made it more efficient. Applied to individual thinking, these findings suggest something more, that everyone's experience can confirm: Brooding and hatching an idea, if it's to be fruitful, is at its best when it goes hand in hand with judgment. Critical thinking does not stunt creativity but refines it.

Weisberg's chief target are myths about genius. He doesn't contest variations in human intelligence but cites empiric work that discredits the notion that exceptionally creative persons differ from others in key personality traits. Donald Mackinnon studied forty architects nominated by a panel of architecture professors as America's most creative, comparing them with two control groups: their associates, and others randomly selected from the *Directory of Architects* and matched with the recognized group by age and location. On tests designed to assess personal values, the group seen as creative registered much lower in economic and much higher in aesthetic interests than the random controls. They were judged less social, more sensitive, and less self-controlled. But when compared with their associates, the architects deemed especially creative scored almost identically. What Weisberg said "may be the most well-designed" study on the subject" showed that "essentially no unique personality characteristics are related to genius in architecture." The notion of a special type of creative genius was gravely to be doubted.[36]

That conclusion does not imply the nonexistence of remarkable or sustained creativity. But popular stereotypes of genius, like most popular stereotypes, are misguided, prompted, in this case, perhaps, more by mixed fear, envy, and admiration. To this we add a word of methodological caution: Instruments of the type that Mackinnon and other social psychologists use in plotting values and personality traits often entrench or canonize stereotypes. Devised by clustering specific responses to specific questions, they tend to single out or isolate atypical individuals. So the instruments themselves can be procrustean. The take home message from Mackinnon's work remains: Romantic notions of creativity are as unfounded as mechanistic ones. Both images express awe, albeit in different ways. Neither amounts to an explanation.

Creativity and Discipline

Johannes Kepler (1571–1630), the story goes, came suddenly to his planetary theory and seemed stunned when it dawned on him. The emotion is not surprising. Kepler felt he'd pierced God's plan; the inspiration, he was sure, came from God himself. But, if so, it was through the mind God gave him. Of course there's inspiration, as Aristotle too was convinced. But its workings are internal. It's not from someone whispering in one else's ear.

Kepler's elegant model was hardly stumbled upon. He had pondered the planets for decades, laboring to fit their motions into regular figures, spurred on by religious zeal and a Platonic certitude that the heavens form a system that mathematics can disrobe. Yet his quest was not a priori. He had to win the trust of Tycho Brahe, who held his data close to his vest. Then he had to collate his own observations and battle Tycho's heirs for rights to publish the data. His three planetary laws confirmed his faith in the rational structure of the cosmos. But circular orbits had to be sacrificed to ellipses, and geocentricity to heliocentrism. Confirmation came in 1631, when Mercury, traversing the sun, appeared just where Kepler's laws predicted. But full vindication awaited Newton's derivation of the ellipses as the resultants of gravitational and inertial forces.

Creativity is not passive or automatic. It springs not from chance or idle play but from freedom and discipline working together, as they do in a healthy civil society—not as opposites but as allies—criticism and independence strengthened by training and tradition. Picasso knew exactly what he was doing when he painted his proto-cubist *Les Demoiselles d'Avignon* (1907, which he preferred to call *Le Bordel d'Avignon,* recalling a brothel on Avinyó Street in Barcelona). He spent a year on hundreds of preparatory sketches and studies before painting the work and experimented sculpturally with reducing facial forms to their barest expressive outlines, in the end modeling

two faces on African and Pacific Island masks and three on Spanish paint-
erly conventions. The size of the canvas made assertive claims as the artist
abandoned the gentler tones of his Blue and Rose periods. It challenged the
already vibrant traditions of Western art, as if answering the Old Masters,
and El Greco, Ingres, Gauguin, and the Fauves. Ironically saluting Cézanne's
Les Grandes Baigneuses, Picasso borrowed iconography from ancient Egypt
and Greece while throwing down a gauntlet to Matisse. Revolutionary in aim
but traditional in reference (as revolutionary work must be), the painting is
highly disciplined in method but shocking by design. Its savage imagery and
the aggressive postures of the prostitutes echo, in effect, Picasso's combative
rejection of vanishing point perspective.

Comparable things are seen in many path breaking artworks. Picasso
worked assiduously on *Guernica*. It was not casually or randomly that it
achieved its consummately modern evocation of violence. Completed in
1937, just months after the bombing of Guernica by Hitler and Mussolini
in support of Franco's Fascist revolution, *Guernica* was shown that summer
at the Paris World's Fair and later in San Francisco and New York. Outraged
at Franco's treachery, Picasso did not show piles of skulls, as photographers
have done in mutely documenting the horrors of Cambodia's self-genocide.
He focused in on one Basque town—a screaming horse, a lost bull, death
throes of a few schematic victims. The power of the work rests on Picasso's
discipline, recasting ancient and elemental images of suffering in a vocabulary as old as evolution but as immediate as the newspapers and newsreels
that projected the horrors of the day.

Creativity and Emergence

Creativity, like mind and soul themselves, is emergent. It marshals a host of
assets. Psychological instruments, designed to tease out separate factors, can
chart only one or a few strands of mental activity or capacity at a time. But
creativity takes many forms. Its study demands data and techniques from
numerous disciplines—from developmental psychology to complexity theory.
Systems theorists see creativity in the lively encounters of individuals with
their society and culture. Applying his idea of "flow," a broad mindfulness
one may bring to pursuits that absorb one's interest, Mihaly Csikszentmihalyi, views creative thinking not as a set method of attack but in dynamic,
interactive terms: Creativity takes place, he argues, when a person makes a
change "in a domain," that is transmitted through time. Some will more
readily accomplish such changes, either because of personal qualities or because they are well positioned with respect to the domain—have better ac-

cess to it, or social circumstances that allow them free time to experiment.[37] When motivation, attention, innovation, expertise, and talent converge, creative results are possible.

Domains here connect everyday and extraordinary creators. Howard Gruber (1922–2005) focuses on the dynamic interactions of individual creativity in the broader context of society, work, religion—culture at large.[38] Contextualists see economic, social, and cultural constraints that open or close doors: Caste barriers or economic requirements may impede creative work. Market trends or patronage, public or private, may open pathways. Art in the Italian Renaissance, physics and economics in much of the twentieth-century West, information technology today, all draw creative minds, some winning eminence. Some creators will pursue their interests regardless of support or censure. But the likelihood of high levels of success is always limited. Multi-talented people face choices about where to channel their strengths. But their success will hinge not solely on their perspicacity or even the depth of their talents and commitments but also on the rockiness and steepness of the avenues they choose.

What we see in creativity at large shows up perhaps most clearly in its absence. Stolid, witless, mechanical responses to a smile or a remark, a question, or a joke reveal, by their contrast with wit and insight, what we treasure in one another and prize in ourselves: clear evidence of a mind at work, expressing and seeking to realize the desires of a soul.

God and the Soul

The innuendo when reductionists urge that all events need natural causes is pointed: Anyone who doubts mechanism is suspect of commerce with ghosts and betrayal of science. But privileging the very small and seemingly simple masks the emergent properties of compounds and complexes. Mechanism sweeps under the carpet the holism and feedback relations distinctive in all living systems. The most strident reductionists deny purposes and interests in living beings—a fortiori, the distinctive aims and undertakings of human beings, falsifying biology lest mechanism be sullied by any thought of purpose. Causality here is made to carry water for positivism. Yet the suggestion that theists are superstitious if they see a role for God in nature can't push beyond tautology the claim that natural events need natural causes. Today's new atheism, like the old, hides behind a blanket reductionism, now decked out in the language of genes and neurons but still building "smallism" and materialism into the premises of its method and epistemology while presenting them as though they were the latest findings of science.

Our brief for the soul has invoked no supernatural agency. We claim no special access beyond the world we live in. Giving the soul an otherworldly genealogy would cut no ice scientifically. But it would also argue in the wrong direction. We should start from what we know. Informally and introspectively we know a bit about souls, our own and those of our fellow humans. In some ways there's nothing we know better. Scientifically we have an ever-broadening knowledge base in psychology, neuroscience, and the ethology of our own species and its kin. If there's a nexus between souls and the divine, the way to find it, we believe, is to reason from what we know best, not from realms beyond our practical or intellectual control.

Our argument, as we've stressed, is not about immortality. That needed to be said, given the agendas so often motivating soultalk. It's not rare in a culture shot through with Christian traditions for religion generically to come down to matters of sin and salvation. This is not the place to survey the broad sweep of other religious pathways. But it should be said that notions of immortality press human hopes and fears toward an incautious transformation of selves, or kin, or loved ones, into gods. Dreams of immortality, not all of them pleasant, can also seize the reins of metaphysics, pressed on by fantasies of eternal recurrence or a goading sense of boundless psychic debts. The road we've taken, guided by today's first steps toward understanding the biology of the brain, leads in a different direction. The intimate linkage of souls with brains argues against equating substantiality with separability—not least because substantiality for the soul stands or falls with agency. Separability would hamstring agency.

Religious traditions that fuse souls with God or with each other are hardly rare. Vedantin monism is one example. There's a striking family resemblance in Neoplatonic monopsychism. Rival traditions like those of early Buddhism seek to liberate souls from the trammels of transcendence by dissolving them into the phenomena they experience. Hence the kinship a contemporary Buddhist thinker like David Kalupahana sees between early Buddhist thought and Hume. Other traditions, like the Nyaya and much of Theravada Buddhism, separate questions about the soul from those about the divine, probing the ontology of souls in moral, epistemic, logical or soteriological terms. Our own aim is neither to dissolve nor to amalgamate souls but to argue their reality: The soul, as we see it, is emergent from the teeming, self-affirming richness of life—emergent phylogenetically as selves and purposes evolve, and developmentally as we lay claim to our experience and win agency among the supportive, challenging, or indifferent agencies around us. Subjecthood argues for discrete identities and against submersion of souls in one another or in the Godhead.

The reality of souls, like many another fact about the world—the beauty and order of the cosmos, the rise of purposes and possibility of their fulfillment, the miracle of love and caring, the stability of truth and objectivity of justice—argues, in concert with all these facts, for the reality of transcendent value. To spell out that thought: Athens joins hands with Jerusalem when Plato affirms the reality of what is most true, good, and beautiful and Judaeo-Christian scripture, correspondingly, affirms the supreme goodness of the most real and personifies God as creator and judge, a lover of beauty, truth, justice, charity, and mercy, who invites his creatures to find and cultivate those possibilities in themselves, in one another, and in nature.

A penchant for transcendence is attested in the conatus of all things— implicitly in the claims of living beings to life, overtly in the purposes we humans manifest, and often pointedly in the arts and in our moral, social, scientific, and political endeavors. What theists thematize—or theorize—when they find meaning in natural appetites for boundlessness is a common source and goal for all strivings. The groping toward perfection seen in all things bears witness to the ultimacy of the Good they seek. Souls are the clearest voices in that chorus of testimony to the Transcendent: If souls are an achievement of nature, it's not untoward for theists to celebrate them as cuttings from God's tree. But, like any other natural fact, the reality of human souls need not be understood religiously. Inference to an explanation never has the lock on certitude claimed by deductive reasoning.

The thesis argued in this book is humanistic. But not every humanist is a theist. Raymond Tallis, a committed secular humanist, argues vigorously against neural reductionism.[1] Contrary to popular rumor, he explains, neuroscience has not discovered that we are our brains. Granted, selves depend on brains. That says little about what selves are. The brain activity that correlates with consciousness, Tallis urges, turning the tables on his adversaries, is known to science only because conscious persons study it. Only subjects pursue scientific understanding, make observations, or devise experiments. The New Atheists, Tallis argues, too eagerly swallow the claim that neural evidence will disclose all we need to know about our humanity. That's more a matter of faith than science on their part. And faith, in this case, is misguided and misplaced. Linking souls with the theism they fear, mechanist reductionists systematically misconstrue personhood, placing elemental matter where they should have saved room for human subjects. The issue is not that neuroscience only awaits more data. Doctrinaire reductionists fix their gaze in just one direction, breaking down brain activity into minute processes in subassemblies but slighting the holistic and ecological features of the brain's work, the integrative work that fosters the emergence of persons.

Reductionists, Tallis charges, routinely confound thought with its substrate, bolstering their faith in the disappearance of selves with promissory notes—vague allusions to expected evidence and "a strangely triumphant declaration" that whatever escapes the net of neuroscience cannot be real.[2] Their zeal, we might add, smacks of the activism and volition, not to mention conscious reasoning (no mere reflexive reaction) that their theories discount or decry. Not least in what lends an air of strangeness to their triumphalism is a penchant to couple confidence in the progress of neuroscience with an a priori exclusion of counterevidence to reductionism accrued from brain science itself. They know *this* horse isn't coming home because they've barred the door.

The reduction of minds to brain processes, Tallis argues, is no scientific

finding but a diehard dogma made willful by the conviction that materialism is the sole alternative to religion. The reductionists betray their bias
when they speak lovingly of the nerve impulses that guide our muscles but
stay much quieter about those other avenues of top-down causality that we
use in making sense of our world and finding personal meaning in external events. Yet the thoughtful gaze and reflective consideration that precede
action or accompany it are no less real than the pathway from the retina to
the visual cortex.

Thomas Nagel, like Tallis, outspokenly rejects psychoneural reductionism. His most recent book, *Mind and Cosmos*, is one more witness to the fact
that one need not be a theist to be aggrieved at what is lost with the denial
of souls and selves. Nagel has returned here to the concerns that led him
to champion the subjective side of living reality in "What Is It Like to Be a
Bat?" But his short new book strikes a glancing blow. Rather than address
cellular and molecular bottom-up dogmatism, he targets the more extreme
reductionism that fantasizes about dissolving subjecthood and subjectivity
in the flux of particle physics. Naturalism itself is seen by Nagel as a clear
and present danger, for the troubling penchant of its scientistic champions
to project a reductive materialism as the bottom line of science.

Disappointingly, Nagel articulates no solid alternative. So his discontents
only lend credence to the spurious claim that reductionism is the scientific
path and romantic irrationalism the only alternative. Freely conflating Darwinian explanations with the naturalism of which they are so often made the
pennant (whether the accounts are well grounded in evidence or propped by
mythic appeal as just-so stories), Nagel links evolutionary theory at large to
reductionism in neuroscience. The effect is to paint Darwin as the ideologi-
cal destroyer that Dennett and others, friends and foes, have imagined. But
that caricature grossly distorts the achievement of a pioneering scientist who
(despite the hopes and fears of admirers and detractors) did not eliminate
the ideas of species, adaptation, and purpose but gave each of those concepts
a new and dynamic foundation in science.

By making darwinism the foe, Nagel tilts at windmills and bypasses the
challenge of reductionism in psychology and the need and opportunity
to build a scientifically fruitful, non-reductionist account of personhood,
grounded in the phenomena of consciousness that were his early focus. The
real threat to a fair portrait of humanity comes not from Darwin or from
particle physics but from the privileging of parts over wholes and the resultant erasure or displacement of the subject as an author of actions and ideas
and owner of memories and experiences. The elephant in the room here is
the soul and its intimate embrace with the body.

The circumstantial specificity that Tallis offers is a brisk and refreshing contrast. Harking back to the idea of intentionality, he writes, no material object, "is *about* any other." But by collapsing experience into neural activity, psychological reductionism "fastens us into the material world" with "an unbroken causal chain passing from sensory inputs to motor outputs." Some links in that chain, evidently, were forged by the Behaviorists. Echoing Searle (himself no theist) and answering Kim, Tallis finds more play in the causal manacles than might appear: Intentionality "opens up the otherwise causally closed physical world," allowing us to *act*. Subjectivity, in turn, (as Sorabji, Neisser, and others explain) goes hand in hand with intersubjectivity. As Tallis puts it poetically, "the weaving together of individual intentional spaces creates the human world—that shared, public, temporally deep sphere of possibilities, that outside-of-nature which makes our individual and collective human lives possible." Without intentionality, Tallis concludes, "there is no point in the arrival of perceptions, no point of departure for actions, no input and output, no person located in a world."[3]

For our own part, we doubt that freedom needs causal chinks and breaches rather than simple recognition that persons too are causes. But Tallis's *tu quoque* is telling: Mechanists make frequent, active use of just the features of the mind and soul that they most actively deny. We'd like to hear more about how intentionality opens doorways to freedom. But Tallis, Searle, and others make it very clear that one needn't be a theist to recognize the reality of selves—or to see more scientism than science in the one-way glass of physicalist reductionism.

Much of the resistance to the reality of souls does spring from antipathy to religion and not from the scientific findings in which reductive testimonies are draped. Religious traditions, after all, have long nourished ideas about souls, whether as bearers of moral accountability or as go-betweens shuttling from earth to a heaven that objectors have found too high, or an underworld that they've found too dire. If souls are gods or messengers from the gods, many who are restive with religion are as unhappy with souls as they are with deities. And if moral freedom entails responsibility, then those uncomfortable with thoughts of any binding imperative may deny the soul, even at the price of disclaiming an identity that in other contexts—political, interpersonal, or commercial—they adamantly affirm.

We take agency, like creativity, to be our own, alienable neither upward toward the heavens nor downward to the genes or the molecules of which they're made. Not that events have no causes and no higher reach or deeper roots than in the self, but in the sense that our spontaneity, in any of its forms, is a gift made possible by our nature. We act, think, and create, not in absolute freedom but in the simple sense of playing or failing to play the hand we're dealt. That's part of what it means to say that souls are real. There are cross-pressures, of course, higher imperatives than our simplest urges, and lower necessities, reflective of our makeup and environs as finite beings. This, too, belongs to what it means to say that souls are real.

The evidence we've reviewed for the reality of souls might have been expanded hundredfold. It grows daily, as the story of the soul and its brain unfolds. We embrace the evidence, unruffled by the thought that calling a nature as remarkable as the human soul not unworthy of God's workshop in nature might absolve us of responsibility for our doings or rob us of credit for our achievements. We have our measure of freedom to act and choose and our power to extend our thoughts beyond the given not because we magically breach the laws of nature but because nature, in the human person, rises beyond the reach of its elements.

If souls are to be linked with God, the reasoning, we think, should be ground-up and a posteriori, not rappelling down, from the heavens. Scripture too reasons from our world when it calls heaven and earth to witness and ascribes all forms of life, and light itself, to God's work. To regard nature and its systems as God's handiwork, or to see sublimity in a rainbow, a sunset, or the stars—or any natural marvel—is to say that it points beyond itself, toward transcendence. It's not uncommon to reason downward, casting our grappling hook heavenward, from yearnings toward the Infinite to thoughts of the more familiar realm of finitude. Dialectically there's value there—as when Malachi says, for instance, *Have we not all one Father?* (2:10). Such rhetoric makes powerful claims on hearers who already accept God's fatherhood. It invokes a moral alchemy aiming to transmute hatred or unconcern into love—as Malachi does when he pleads in the same verse: *did not the same God create us? Why do we betray one another, brother against brother, profaning the compact of our forebears?* But such appeals are lost on those who spurn a covenant with long dead ancestors or disavow the prophetic speaker's communal "we." Arguments of wider sweep need broader premises, and assumptions closer to earth

Starting out from what we know is what we find most conducive. That can't mean just what piety presumes, any more than it can mean reliance on "our" (often conflicting) "intuitions," or on the fine distinctions analysis might distill from linguistic usage or project into artificial symbolic domains. We prefer to begin with what science has been teaching us—that explanation does not always move from whole to part. Some wholes have a character of their own. Some are (in some measure) self-steering. The emergence of life lays the groundwork for the emergent selves that are not adequately explained or fully and faithfully described in language suited to the character and behavior of the atoms, molecules, and cells they're made of. Souls do rely on the properties of matter. More specifically, on the remarkable capabilities of the brain and its intricate linkage with the rest of the body, to situate us in our surroundings, including the social milieu that puts souls in touch with one another. But this reliance does not reduce souls to their roots any more than genetics reduces persons to their ancestry.

We know that souls are real because they declare themselves, not just in what they say when consciousness finds a voice in language but from what they do, on multiple planes. Human perception, consciousness and creativity, memory and moral agency, our arguments for the reality of souls, amply point toward links with something higher. There is a leap, of course, whenever one vaults from finite beauty and brilliance to an infinite Source. But science too makes such a leap when it presumes the laws of nature irrefragable. And deference to the divine need not entail any denigration of the achievement on the finite side of the springboard: The thought and agency, insight and awareness, the synthetic work of memory and perception, the emergent qualities and capabilities, are our own, facets and achievements of the nature we are given as selves and souls arise in nature. To disclaim our own agency and consciousness, creativity and freedom, would be to deny the generosity of the gift and miss the real moment and meaning of the idea of grace—generosity where there was no prior entitlement or expectation. For creation is not just the imparting of existence but the bestowal of powers and capabilities, including powers of adaptation in the case of living species, and special powers of judgment and responsibility in the human case. Without such gifts all talk of God's creative act would be empty.

Biblical poetry evokes images of the imparting of the human soul by telling of God's puffing the breath of life into the form he'd shaped from clods of earth (Genesis 2:7). That trope counters the reductive impulse. Not that earth is foreign to us. Adam still bears its name. But souls also bear the glow and warmth of their transcendent Source, most evident in their boundless aspiration. We remain dust at bottom (Genesis 3:19). If we become something more, that's not wholly our own doing. But neither is the life we find and fashion simply a dress for a bisque doll. Part of what it means for monotheists to speak of divine creation is to recognize that God does not make marionettes. As theists see it, we work in partnership with God. What religious gratitude fixes on and marks as God's glory is that God gives creatures capabilities of self-creation—as witness the fact of evolution and the general reality of emergence, of which biological evolution is a special case. The reciprocity of the link, epitomized in the meeting of insight with inspiration, finds its emblem in the image on the Sistine Chapel ceiling, where creature and Creator reach out to one another. Infinite goodness, theists argue, underwrites our delegated powers. To see our humanity—the soul that is the life and mind of each of us—as one of nature's many natural miracles is, it is true, just one way of looking at things. There are others. But that is not to say that no way of seeing things is any more respectful of the evidence than any other.

NOTES

Note: Translations throughout are Goodman's unless otherwise identified.

CHAPTER ONE: BODY AND SOUL

1. Babylonian Talmud, Sanhedrin 91ab.
2. Sorabji, *Self*, 29.
3. Ibid., 42.
4. Ibid., 48, 142, 265–97.
5. See Neisser, *The Perceived Self*, and his "Five Kinds of Self-Knowledge," 35–59; Tomasello, "On the Interpersonal Origins of the Self-Concept," and his *Cultural Origins of Human Cognition*. The thought is Galenic, reflecting Stoic teaching. The Stoic philosopher Hierocles (2nd century) anchors self-ownership (*oikeiōsis*) in the self-perception, self-concern, and social situatedness he finds in all animals. See his *Elements of Ethics*.
6. Deacon, *Incomplete Nature*, 100.
7. Bateson, *Steps to an Ecology of Mind*, 58.
8. Deacon, *Incomplete Nature*, 95.
9. Clayton and Davies, *The Re-emergence of Emergence*. See also Clayton's *Mind and Emergence*.
10. Martin et al., *Persons*, 73.
11. Weiss, "One Plus One Does Not Equal Two," 821.
12. Cf. Augustine, *De Trinitate* 10.10.14.
13. Cf. Plotinus, *Enneads* 5.5.2.
14. Descartes, *Discourse on Method* 1, 1.113.
15. La Mettrie (1709–1751), *L'Homme Machine* (1747). In *The Physical and the Moral*, Elizabeth Williams argues that French vitalism sought to show how the natural and social environment could foster the development of individuals in ways that mechanism could not adequately explain. The key thought: A science of man must regard principles beyond the elemental.
16. Descartes, *Treatise on Man*, in *Philosophical Writings*, translated by Cottingham, Stoothoff, and Murdoch, 1.100.
17. Spinoza, *Ethics* 5, preface, 2.278–80.
18. Descartes, correspondence with Princess Elisabeth, 1643–45, in *Descartes*, translated by Blom, 105–17.

19. Gazzaniga, "Neuroscience Challenges Old Ideas about Free Will." For the significance of emergence at the interface of biology with thermodynamics, see Deacon, "The Hierarchic Logic of Emergence." Clayton argues for an "iterative model" of emergence: emergent realities become "basic causal agents in their own right." See his *Mind and Emergence,* 46.
20. Maturana, "The Mind Is Not the Head."
21. Preuss, quoted in Gazzaniga, *Who's in Charge?,* 37–38.
22. Gazzaniga, "Neuroscience Challenges Old Ideas about Free Will" and *Who's in Charge?* 153–54.
23. Gazzaniga, *Who's in Charge?,* quoted in Tallis, "Rethinking Thinking."
24. Maturana, "The Mind Is Not the Head."
25. Deacon, *Incomplete Nature,* 5.
26. See Goodman, *Creation and Evolution,* esp. 138–46.
27. See Wilson, *Genes and the Agents of Life.*
28. Kauffman and Clayton, "On Emergence, Agency, and Organization."
29. Morgan, *Emergent Evolution,* chapter 2, "A Pyramidal Scheme."
30. Mill, *A System of Logic,* book 3, chapter 6, § 1, 243.
31. Morowitz, *The Emergence of Everything.*
32. Lewes, *Problems of Life and Mind,* 2.412.
33. Kim, *Mind in a Physical World,* 40–41. Quote from Kim's online précis of the book.
34. Cf. Deacon, *Incomplete Nature,* 34–35, 161–81.
35. Sperry, "Mind-Brain Interaction." Sperry, as Clayton notes, championed emergence in the 1960s, when such ideas were "not only unpopular but even anathema"—not least among neuroscientists: "he realized that consciousness is not a mere epiphenomenon of the brain; instead, conscious thoughts and decisions *do something.*" Clayton, *Mind and Emergence,* 23; cf. 57. "The subjective mental phenomena," Sperry wrote, "are conceived to influence and govern the flow of nerve impulse traffic by virtue of their encompassing emergent properties . . . just as drops of water are carried along by a local eddy in a stream or the way the molecules and atoms of a wheel are carried along when it rolls downhill." There are, Sperry insists, both top-down and bottom-up processes in the brain, just as the whirling of the eddy or rolling of the wheel involve a mutuality, whole affecting parts as well as parts affecting the whole. See Sperry, "A Modified Concept of Consciousness." Clayton tracks the rising confidence of writers like Arthur Peacocke in speaking of top-down causation in *Mind and Emergence,* 63 n. 6; cf. Campbell, "'Downward Causation' in Hierarchically Organised Biological Systems," 179–86.
36. Pomerat, "Activities Associated with Neuronal Regeneration," 371; Sin et al., "Dendrite Growth."
37. Edelman, *Second Nature,* 18, and *Wider Than the Sky.*
38. Locke, *Essay,* 2.27.15, 340. Cf. Lucretius, *De Rerum Natura* 3.843–64: even reassembly of a body just like one's own, inevitable in the ceaseless pachinko game of the atoms, matters little, since memory seems presumed to be lost. See Sorabji, *Self,* 95–99.
39. Leibniz, *Discourse on Metaphysics* § 34.
40. Hierocles, *Elements of Ethics,* apud Stobaeus, *Florilegium,* 4.671 *ll.* 7–16. See Sorabji, *Self,* 44–45.
41. Cicero, *De Officiis* 1.107–15, tr. Higginbotham, 76–80.
42. Epictetus, *Discourses* 1.1.23. See also Sorabji, *Self,* 181–97.
43. Sorabji, *Self,* 47. Twentieth-century Existentialists took a similar stance as to the self.

44. Plutarch, *On Tranquility* 473b–474b. Sorabji, *Self*, 47; 172–77 for the Plutarch passage in full, and Sorabji's discussion.
45. See Baron-Cohen et al., eds., *Understanding Other Minds*; Baron-Cohen, "Precursors to a Theory of Mind"; Sorabji, *Self*, 25–29; Tomasello, *Cultural Origins*, chapter 4.
46. Gazzaniga, *Who's in Charge?*, 185, citing numerous confirming studies.
47. Bandura, *Self-Efficacy*, 6.
48. See Martin et al., *Persons*, 77, 82. Our argument, as we've stressed here and throughout this book, rests on the conception of an integrated, socially situated, and *embodied* soul. The reasoning behind the idea of the separable soul is masterfully laid out in Stewart Goetz and Charles Taliafero's *A Brief History of the Soul*.

CHAPTER TWO: PERCEPTION

1. Democritus, fragments 9–10, apud Sextus Empiricus, *Adversus Mathematicos* 7.135–38. The Fragments of the presocratics are listed by their numbers in Diels and Kranz, *Die Fragmente der Vorsokratiker*.
2. Democritus, apud Aristotle, *Metaphysics* Gamma 1009b 10; and fragment 125.
3. Democritus, fragment 125, preserved in Galen, *On Medical Experience*, 62.
4. Cf. Epicurus apud Plutarch, *Adversus Colotem* 7.1110c.
5. Newton, *Philosophical Transactions of the Royal Society* 80, 131, quoted in Arnheim, *Art and Visual Perception*, 337.
6. Locke, *Essay*, 2.10.15, 149.
7. Ibid., 2.9.1, 143.
8. Hume, *Treatise*, 1.1.7, 17.
9. Ibid., 1.3.8, 103. Memory and imagination, Hume writes, "may mimic or copy the perceptions of the senses; but they never can entirely reach the force and vivacity of the original sentiment." *Enquiry Concerning Human Understanding*, section 2, 17.
10. Hume, *Treatise*, 1.1.1, 3.
11. Ibid.
12. Hume, *Enquiry*, section 2, 19–20.
13. Ibid., 21.
14. Ibid., 19–21.
15. Pritchard, *Knowledge and Perception*, 177.
16. James, *Principles of Psychology*, 2.7.
17. Ibid., 2.3.
18. Ibid., 2.2 n.
19. Ibid., 2.3, 2.12, 2.6–7. The fourteen pages turned over to Delabarre are found at 2.13–27.
20. See Foster, *Nature of Perception*, 148.
21. See Köhler, *Gestalt Psychology*, 3–33.
22. Edelman, *Wider Than the Sky*, 10.
23. Austin's lectures of 1947 and beyond were collated by G. J. Warnock in *Sense and Sensibilia*.
24. For vigorous defenses of sense data, see Robinson, *Perception*; Bermúdez, "Naturalized Sense Data"; Garcia-Carpintero, "Sense Data: The Sensible Approach." Teed Rockwell reviews the impact of psychological of atomism in "Effects of Atomistic Ontology on the History of Psychology," Cognitive Questions.org.
25. Köhler, *Gestalt Psychology*, 188.
26. See Metzger, *Laws of Seeing*, xvi–xxv; Spillmann's introduction, viii–ix.

27. See Brett-Green et al., "Multisensory Integration in Children," 283; Spector and Maurer, "Synesthesia."

28. Arnheim, *Art and Visual Perception*, 45; for the piano, the cocoa, and the picture, p. 11.

29. Gibson, quoted in Harris, *Hypothesis and Perception*, 249.

30. Martinez-Condé et al., "The Role of Fixational Eye Movements in Visual Perception."

31. Moore, *Principia Ethica*, 12–13, 62–69.

32. Avicenna, *Fi 'l-Nafs* from the *Najat*, tr. Rahman, 26–27; Aristotle, *De Partibus Animalium* 2.1.647a15–21.

33. Keeley, "Fixing Content and Function in Neurobiological Systems."

34. Hardin, *Color for Philosophers*, 10.

35. Berlin and Kay, *Basic Color Terms*, 109.

36. Hardin, *Color for Philosophers*, 155–56.

37. Maclaury, "From Brightness to Hue."

38. Palmer and Schloss, "Ecological Valence Theory."

39. Zentner, "Preferences for Colours."

40. Itten, *Art of Color*, 24–31.

41. Palmer and Schloss, "Ecological Valence Theory."

42. Metzger, *Laws of Seeing*, Spillmann's introduction, viii.

43. Stage lighting can change the apparent color of a scrim. But it does so by its brightness in a darkened hall; luminance in this case overpowers reflectance.

44. Hardin, *Color for Philosophers*, 83; Wallach, "Brightness Constancy and the Nature of Achromatic Colors"; Arnheim, *Art and Visual Perception*, 305–6, citing Alberti, for the paling of ivory.

45. McGinn, "Another Look at Color," 540.

46. Itten, *Art of Color*, 19.

47. Harris, *Hypothesis and Perception*, 254.

48. Hardin, *Color for Philosophers*, 24.

49. Itten, *Art of Color*, 19–20.

50. Eagleman, "Visual Illusions and Neurobiology," 920; Purves et al., "Why We See What We Do."

51. See Metzger, "Optische Untersuchungen am Ganzfeld II."

52. Hardin, *Color for Philosophers*, 24.

53. Itten, *Art of Color*, 36.

54. Ehrenstein et al., "Gestalt Issues in Modern Neuroscience," 437.

55. Itten, *Art of Color*, 36.

56. Ibid., 37, 40.

57. Ibid., 41.

58. Ibid., 64.

59. Arnheim, *Art and Visual Perception*, 369.

60. Itten, *Art of Color*, 74.

61. Shevell et al., "Misbinding of Color to Form in Afterimages."

62. Itten, *Art of Color*, 87, 92, 94.

63. Ibid., 96, 97. For laboratory validation of the emotional impact of saturation, see Camgöz et al., "Effects of Hue, Saturation, and Brightness on Preference."

64. Delacroix, *Journal*, undated remark of 1852, ed. Joubin, 1.500.

65. Itten, *Art of Color*, 104.

66. Ibid., 122.

67. See Albers, *Interaction of Color*. After leaving Europe, Albers taught at Black Mountain College in North Carolina, then at Yale from 1950, where he produced some thou-

sand paintings, drawings, prints, and tapestries in the *Homage to the Square* series over a quarter century.

68. Itten, *Art of Color*, 132–36.
69. Ibid., 136–37.
70. Ibid., 137.
71. Livingstone, *Vision and Art*.
72. See Ehrenstein, "Untersuchungen über Figur-Grund-Fragen."
73. Arnheim, *Art and Visual Perception*, 53, with 46 and 107, 145, 167–69.
74. Ibid., 43–44.
75. Palmer, *Vision Science*, 522.
76. Barry, *Fixing My Gaze*, 11; cf. 125.
77. Ibid., 63–64, 78–79, 93–94, 133, 151–52.
78. Ibid., 139–47.
79. Ibid., 124; cf. 94–95.
80. Ibid., 102, citing Ramachandran and Blakeslee, *Phantoms in the Brain*, 232–53.
81. Barry, *Fixing My Gaze*, 102, 125–26.
82. Ibid., 123 and 105.
83. Ibid., 124; cf. 98.
84. Kujala et al., "Neural Plasticity in Processing Sound Location"; Kujala et al., "Electrophysiological Evidence for Cross-Modal Plasticity."
85. Millar, *Space and Sense*, 49.
86. Ibid., 80–81.
87. Metzger, *Laws of Seeing*, Spillmann's introduction, vii.
88. Hardin, *Color for Philosophers*, 102.
89. Langer, *Mind*, 1.164.
90. Köhler, *Gestalt Psychology*; Palmer, *Vision Science*.
91. Ehrenstein et al., "Gestalt Issues in Modern Neuroscience," 434.
92. Arnheim, *Art and Visual Perception*, 12.
93. Palmer, *Vision Science*, 398–99.
94. Metzger, *Laws of Seeing*, 61–88.
95. Ehrenstein et al., "Gestalt Issues in Modern Neuroscience," 446.
96. Ibid., 441, citing von der Heydt et al., "Representation of Stereoscopic Edges in Monkey Visual Cortex."
97. Metzger, *Laws of Seeing*, xix.
98. Avicenna, *De Anima* (*The Psychology of the Shifā'*), 163–64. Translation here is Goodman's.
99. Metzger, *Laws of Seeing*, xxi.
100. Ibid., xxii.
101. Ibid., xxiii.
102. Mole, "Motor Theory of Speech Perception," 218.
103. Ibid.
104. Ikhwān al-Ṣafā', Brethren of Purity, *Case of the Animals vs. Man*, 114. The observation is confirmed in Nowak et al., "Development of Mother Discrimination by Single and Multiple Newborn Lambs"; Nowak and Lindsay, "Discrimination of Merino Ewes by Their Newborn Lambs." In "Mother Location by Newborn Lambs in Repetitive Testing," Nowak writes: "Lambs typically form a preferential relationship with their mother within 24 h after birth," 75.
105. Scruton, "Sounds as Secondary Objects and Pure Events," 62–63.
106. McDermott, "Cocktail Party Problem."

107. See Cherry, "Some Experiments on the Recognition of Speech"; Bregman, *Auditory Scene Analysis*; MacDonald and McGurk, "Visual Influences on Speech Perception Processes."
108. Smith, "Speech Sounds," 193–94.
109. Ibid., 195, citing Dehaine-Lambertz et al., "Neural Correlates of Switching from Auditory to Speech Perception"; Warren, "Perceptual Restoration of Missing Speech Sounds."
110. Harris and Lindsay, "Vowel Patterns in Mind and Sound," quoted in Smith, "Speech Sounds," 197.
111. Mole, "Motor Theory," 212.
112. Liberman, "Afterthoughts on Modularity and the Motor Theory," quoted in Mole, "Motor Theory," 212 .
113. Remez and Trout, "Philosophical Messages," 235.
114. Ibid., 236, quoting Hockett, *Manual of Phonology*, no. 11, p. 210.
115. Remez and Trout, "Philosophical Messages," 240.
116. Ibid., 242, citing Howell and Darwin, "Some Properties of Auditory Memory for Rapid Formant Transitions"; Pisoni, "Auditory and Phonetic Memory Codes in the Discrimination of Consonants and Vowels."
117. Remez and Trout, "Philosophical Messages," 257–60.
118. Ibid., 244–45.
119. Ibid., 243, citing Remez et al., "On the Perceptual Organization of Speech."
120. Remez and Trout, "Philosophical Messages," 243–44, citing Shannon et al., "Speech Recognition with Primarily Temporal Cues."
121. Remez and Trout, "Philosophical Messages," 244, citing Z. Smith et al., "Chimaeric Sounds."
122. Remez and Trout, "Philosophical Messages," 245; cf. 259.
123. Mole, "Motor Theory," 214.
124. Ibid., 215.
125. Ibid., 215–16, citing Miyawaki et al., "An Effect of Linguistic Experience," 331–40.
126. Mole, "Motor Theory," 220, citing McGurk and MacDonald, "Hearing Lips and Seeing Voices."
127. Mole, "Motor Theory," 218–19, citing Liberman and Mattingly, "Specialization for Speech Perception."
128. Scruton, *Aesthetics of Music*, 29.
129. Zatorre et al., "When the Brain Plays Music."
130. Patel, "Language, Music, Syntax and the Brain," and *Music, Language, and the Brain*.
131. Snyder, *Music and Memory*, esp. 219–24.
132. Scruton, *Aesthetics of Music*, 65–66.
133. Storr, *Music and the Mind*. Does all music carry meanings? It does, we think, if its efforts succeed. Even the most abstract and absolute musical exercises offer declarations of musical independence, celebrations of patterns of tone and melody (and their alternatives)—much as abstract art may appeal to the sheer dynamics of color and form. Cf. Rose, *Audible Signs*.
134. Scruton, *Aesthetics of Music*, 40–41.
135. Ibid., 46.
136. Ikhwān al-Ṣafā', *Rasā'il* 5, from the *Epistles of the Brethren of Purity*, in *On Music*, 6–13. The translation here is Goodman's.
137. Turin and Sanchez, *Perfumes—The Guide*, 2–3.
138. Shepherd, "Human Sense of Smell."
139. Ibid.; Aiello and Dean, *Human Evolutionary Anatomy*.

140. Herz and von Clef, "Influence of Verbal on the Perception of Odors."
141. Herz, *Scent of Desire*, 80–82.
142. Pollack, "Scents and Sensibility," *Art News*, March, 2011, 88–95.
143. Wooding, "Evolution"; Fischer, "Evolution of Bitter Taste Receptors."
144. See Stevenson, *Psychology of Flavour*, 25–60.
145. Deems et al., "Smell and Taste Disorders."
146. Stevenson, *Psychology of Flavour*, 65–66.
147. Ibid., 140–46.
148. Locke, *Essay*, 2.8.21, 139.
149. Klatzky and Lederman, "Object Recognition by Touch," 187; cf. Katz, *World of Touch*, 140.
150. Katz, *World of Touch*.
151. Ibid., 145–49.
152. Ibid., 79.
153. Klatzky and Lederman, "Object Recognition by Touch," 189.
154. Millar, *Space and Sense*, 73.
155. Katz, *World of Touch*, 76–77.
156. Ibid., 61, 62, 77.
157. Ibid., 62–63.
158. Ibid., 85–86, 158, 165–77.
159. Millar, *Space and Sense*, 72.
160. Lewis, *Analysis of Knowledge and Valuation*, 202–64.
161. Avicenna, *De Anima*, 163–64. Translation here is Goodman's.
162. Katz, *World of Touch*, 34.
163. Barry, *Fixing My Gaze*, 11–14.
164. Descartes, *Meditations*, 2.53, 61; cf. James, *Principles of Psychology*, 2.38–39.
165. Ramachandran and Blakeslee, *Phantoms in the Brain*.
166. Halligan, "Phantom Limbs."
167. Melzack, "Phantom Limbs."
168. See Spector and Maurer, "Synesthesia."
169. Brang and Ramachandran, "Survival of the Synesthesia Gene."
170. Ramachandran and Hubbard, "Phenomenology of Synaesthesia," and "Synaesthesia: A Window."
171. Ramachandran and Hubbard, "Synaesthesia: A Window."
172. Oakley and Halligan, "Hypnotic Suggestion and Cognitive Neuroscience."
173. Ramachandran and Hubbard, "The Phenomenology of Synaesthesia." Some synesthetic schizophrenics have trouble with metaphors in ways that parallel the disruption of their synesthesia by their schizophrenia. Similarly, these individuals understand puns but have difficulty with spatial metaphors in music and with expressions like "hot pink." Other impaired persons may grasp such concepts intellectually but can't relate them to what they perceive.
174. See Spector and Maurer, "Synesthesia."
175. Baron-Cohen et al., "Coloured Speech Perception"; Ramachandran and Hubbard, "Synaesthesia: A Window."
176. Smilek et al., "Binding of Graphemes and Synesthetic Colors," 87.

CHAPTER THREE: CONSCIOUSNESS
1. See Giacino et al., "The Minimally Conscious State"; Laureys et al., "Residual Cognitive Function."

2. Searle, *Rediscovery of the Mind*, 83. See also Searle, "Consciousness."
3. The 1340 work by Michael of Norwich, translates a French work of the previous century. The title, meaning The Bite of Conscience, is echoed often by James Joyce in *Ulysses*.
4. Crane, *Elements of Mind*, 71.
5. Sorabji, *Self*, 245–47, citing Aristotle, *De Anima* 3.2.426b17–23.
6. Rosch, "Mindfulness, Meditation, and the Private Self."
7. Austin, *Zen Brain Reflections*, esp. 3–19, 22–25.
8. Deacon's wheel illustration, which we also saw in Sperry, is not chosen idly. It reflects the Taoist image of the potter's wheel in the Chuang-tzu, as a symbol and paradigm of the stillness of the refined and meditative mind—and the dynamic stability of the ordered cosmos to which reflective and productive minds aspire. See Zhuangzi, translated by Graham, *The Seven Inner Chapters and Other Writings from the Book Chuang-tzu*. Cf. Flanagan, *The Boddisatva's Brain*.
9. Cf. Flanagan, *The Boddisatva's Brain*.
10. Privacy, Ryle said, relies on "the technical trick of conducting our thinking in auditory word-images, instead of spoken words." *Concept of Mind*, 35.
11. See Pylyshyn, "Return of the Mental Image"; Kosslyn et al., *Case for Mental Imagery*.
12. James, *Principles of Psychology*, 1.284–90.
13. Mangan, "Cognition, Fringe Consciousness, and the Legacy of William James," 749; Rock and Gutman, "Effect of Inattention on Form Perception."
14. Mangan, "Cognition," 747.
15. James, *Principles of Psychology*, 1.141.
16. Thompson, *Mind in Life*, 64; cf. 92, 99, 105, 124.
17. Giambrone and Povinelli, "Consciousness," 193.
18. Premack and Woodruff, "Does the Chimpanzee Have a 'Theory of Mind'?"
19. Darwin, *Descent of Man*, 48–49.
20. Premack, "Why Humans Are Unique."
21. He et al., "Understanding of False Belief"; for the chimps' failure, Hare et al., "Do Chimpanzees Know What Conspecifics Know?"; Call and Tomasello, "Does the Chimpanzee Have a Theory of Mind?"; for the false-belief test, see Wimmer and Perner, "Beliefs about Beliefs."
22. Premack and Woodruff, "Does the Chimpanzee Have a 'Theory of Mind'?"
23. Darwin, *Descent of Man*, 105.
24. De Waal, *Age of Empathy*, 74.
25. De Waal, *Good Natured*, 210–12.
26. Premack, "On the Control of Human Individual Differences," 30. Significant individual variance has been observed in some species, in intelligence, talent, and demeanor. But for most species in the wild, individual variance seems to be dwarfed by the human range.
27. For the rise of intrinsic interests, see Goodman, *Creation and Evolution*, 157.
28. Parmenides, fragment 4, apud Clement, *Stromata* 5.15.5.
29. Parmenides, fragment 7, apud Plato, *Sophist* 242a *ll.* 1–2.
30. Pindar, *Nemean Odes* 7.23f., where the blindness of gullible humans is compared with the blindness of Homer, whose art far outdistanced his experience, allowing him to seduce his audience with the winged artfulness of his sweet but solemn lies.
31. Aeschylus, *Choephori* 854; cf. *Eumenides* 103f.
32. Gorgias, *Encomium of Helen* §13, 16, in Sprague, ed., *The Older Sophists*, 50–54.
33. Plato, *Republic* 7.518, translated after Cornford in Hamilton and Cairns, *Collected Dialogues*; cf. 527de, 532b, 533d.
34. Cicero, *In Verrem*, 2.3.218: "Nam, per deos immortalis, videte, iudices, et prospicite

animis quid futurum sit"—"For in the name of the immortal gods, see, O judges, look ahead with your mind's eye at what will result"; cf. *In Catilinam*, 4.6.

35. Alexander of Aphrodisias, *De Anima* 2.54, translated after Fotinis, 79.

36. Proclus, *On Plato's "Parmenides,"* 957–58; *On Euclid Book 1*; Sorabji, *Self*, 247–51.

37. Philoponus, on *De Anima*, 464–65, translated after Wolfgang Bernard, "Philoponus on Self-Awareness," in Sorabji, *Philoponus and the Rejection of Aristotelian Science*, 156–61; Sorabji, *Self*, 253–54.

38. Philoponus on *De Anima*, 465–67; Bernard, "Philoponus on Self-Awareness," in Sorabji, *Philoponus and the Rejection of Aristotelian Science*, 157–60; Plutarch, *De Sollertia Animalium* 961a.

39. Rahman, *Avicenna's Psychology*, 104 n. 52.

40. Sorabji, *Self*, 246, 260–61.

41. See Plotinus, *Enneads* 4.3.30; Simplicius, *De Anima*, 187–88; Sorabji, *Self*, 248–52.

42. See Jaeger, *Aristotle*, 164; Nilsson, *Greek Piety*; Philo, *De Specialibus Legibus*, 1.10.44. For the prominence of the *Alcibiades* in the teaching of the Academy from the time of Iamblichus, see the opening lines of Proclus's commentary on the dialogue.

43. Plato, *Alcibiades I*, 132–33; Altmann, *Studies in Religious Philosophy and Mysticism*, 5. Plato sustains human kinship to the divine by boldly appropriating Empedocles' thesis that like is known to like.

44. Echoing *De Anima* 3.5 and Psalm 36:9.

45. Translated after Meagher.

46. Translated after Meagher.

47. Avicenna, *Shifā', De Anima*, 16.

48. Kant, *Critique of Pure Reason*, 244–47 = B 274–79, translated by Smith.

49. Ibid., B 8, 47.

50. *phygi monou pros mono*, the last words of the work, as Porphyry edited it.

51. Plato, *Theaetetus* 176ab, translated after Cornford, in Hamilton and Cairns, *Collected Dialogues*.

52. Ibn Ṭufayl, *Ḥayy Ibn Yaqẓān*; Corbin, *Avicenna and the Visionary Recital*.

53. Ibn Bājjah, *Regimen of the Solitary*. See Plato, *Republic* 7.520b, cf. 6.496de; cf. Howland, *Plato and the Talmud*, 180; al-Fārābī speaks to the same issue.

54. Pastor, *The Idea of Robinson Crusoe*.

55. See Ben-Zaken, *Reading "Ḥayy Ibn-Yaqẓān."*

56. Spinoza, *Principles of Descartes' Philosophy*, with *Ethics 2*, Proposition 5; *Cogitata Metaphysica*, chapter 1; Gebhardt, 1.145, 1.159, 1.236.

57. Spinoza, *Ethics 2*, Proposition 43, Scholium; Goodman, "An Idea Is Not Something Mute."

58. Clark and Jacyna, *Nineteenth-Century Origins of Neuroscientific Concepts*, 146–47.

59. Gasser, *Aux origines du cerveau moderne*.

60. Finger, *Origins of Neuroscience*, 248.

61. James, *Principles of Psychology*, 1.130.

62. Huxley, quoted in James, *Principles of Psychology*, 1.131.

63. Huxley, "On the Hypothesis That Animals Are Automata and Its History."

64. Richards, *Darwin and the Emergence of Evolutionary Theories of Mind and Behavior*, 430–35.

65. James, *Principles of Psychology*, 1.138.

66. Ibid., 1.136–37.

67. Bettleheim, *Freud and Man's Soul*.

68. Grünbaum, *Foundations of Psychoanalysis*; Edwin, *A Final Accounting*.

69. See Bahya, *Direction to the Duties of the Heart*.

70. Penfield, *Mystery of the Mind*.

71. Searle, *Rediscovery of the Mind*, 249 n. 9.

72. Wright, *Grammar of the Arabic Language*, 2.47–50.

73. Brentano, *Psychologie vom empirischen Standpunkt*, vol. 1, book 1, chapter 1; *Psychology from an Empirical Standpoint*, 88.

74. Searle, *Intentionality*, 24.

75. Searle, *Rediscovery of the Mind*, 155; Crane, *Elements of Mind*, 18–21. After paying due deference to Searle's distinction, Crane concludes that the connection between intension and sense in Frege's terms "shows a clear link between the idea of aspectual shape and the idea of intensionality. A state of mind's having aspectual shape is a matter of its partial presentation of a thing. . . . When ascriptions of mental states are intensional, this is a reflection of, or an expression of, their intentionality" (21).

76. Chisholm, *Perceiving*, chapter 11.

77. Quine, *Word and Object*, chapter 6 § 2.

78. Searle, *Rediscovery of the Mind*, 124.

79. Ibid., 9.

80. Ibid.

81. Searle, "Minds, Brains, and Programs."

82. Block, "The Higher Order Approach to Consciousness Is Defunct."

83. Block, "Psychologism and Behaviorism."

84. Cervantes, *Don Quixote*, part 2 (1615), chapters 62–63.

85. Tallis, reviewing Deacon's *Incomplete Nature* in the *Wall Street Journal*, November 12, 2011.

86. Searle, *Rediscovery of the Mind*, 71–73.

87. Ibid., 13.

88. Ibid., 16.

89. See Jack and Roepstorff, *Trusting the Subject*; Thompson, *Mind in Life*, 338–41.

90. Searle, *Rediscovery of the Mind*, 16; and cf. his discussion in pp. 18–20.

91. Ibid., 90 and 14.

92. Kim, "Causality, Identity and Supervenience," 47, as quoted in Searle, *Rediscovery of the Mind*, 125.

93. Searle, *Rediscovery of the Mind*, 125–26.

94. Ibid., 98.

95. Block, "Comparing the Major Theories of Consciousness."

96. Thompson, *Mind in Life*, 222–23.

97. Ibid., 232–35.

98. Crick, *Astonishing Hypothesis*, 3.

99. Edelman, *Wider Than the Sky*, 39–45, 56, 107–10.

100. Ibid., 6.

101. Ibid., 9.

102. Penrose, *The Emperor's New Mind*.

103. Tononi, "Consciousness as Integrated Information."

104. Penfield and Jasper, *Epilepsy and the Functional Anatomy of the Human Brain*; Schmid-Schonbein, "Improvements of Seizure Control."

105. Alkire, Hudetz, and Tononi, "Consciousness and Anesthesia," 876.

106. Tononi, "An Information Integration Theory of Consciousness," 42; Alkire et al., "Consciousness and Anesthesia." Philip Clayton sees Terrence Deacon as carrying on in the footsteps of Michael Polanyi when Deacon (in an unpublished paper)

argues that evolutionary biology "stands at the border between physical and semiotic science." Deacon, "Evolution and the Emergence of Spirit," quoted in Clayton, *Mind and Emergence*, 20.

107. Tononi, *Phi*.

108. Koch, *Quest for Consciousness*, 246.

109. Ibid., 304.

110. Ibid., 216.

111. Ibid., 311.

112. See Chalmers, *Conscious Mind*.

113. Koch, *Confessions of a Romantic Reductionist*, 3, 27, 57.

114. Edelman, *Wider Than the Sky*, 12.

115. Damasio, *Descartes' Error*.

116. Dunn et al., "Somatic Marker Hypothesis."

117. Damasio, *Self Comes to Mind*, 9.

118. Tallis reviewing *Self Comes to Mind* in *New Statesman*, February 24, 2011.

119. Husserl, *Ideas Pertaining to a Pure Phenomenology*, esp. §§ 41–55.

120. Thompson, *Mind in Life*, 318, 319.

121. Translation after Meagher, *Augustine on the Inner Life of the Mind*, 60; and after E. B. Pusey.

122. Radhakrishnan, *History of Indian Philosophy*, vol. 2; Potter, *Encyclopedia of Indian Philosophies*, vol. 2.

123. Unlike the Samkara school, the Nyaya were not generally atheists. One of their best-known tracts offered a detailed syllogistic argument for the existence of God. The core Nyaya project was liberation of the soul. God was an ontological and logical principle but not critical in that quest.

124. K. K. Chakrabarti, *Classical Indian Philosophy of Mind*, 22.

125. Ibid., introduction.

126. Ram-Prasad, *Knowledge and Liberation*, 65–66, 69.

127. K. K. Chakrabarti, *Classical Indian Philosophy of Mind*, 137–38.

128. Sorabji, *Self*, 245, 270–71, 292–93, citing Vâtsyâyana's commentary on Gotama's *Nyâyasûtra* 3.1.1 and 4.1.35–36; A. Chakrabarti, "I Touch What I Saw," and "The Nyaya Proofs for the Existence of the Self"; Ganeri, "Cross-Modality and the Self." Parfit, Sorabji argues, "turns selves into streams," but his "account of the streams depends on bodies and brains remaining intact and not stream-like." For Parfit's views, see his *Reasons and Persons*.

129. Ram-Prasad quoting Uddyotakara's Nyaya critique of Buddhist claims that consciousness and self are mere fleeting mental events, *Knowledge and Liberation*, 62–63.

130. Thompson, *Mind in Life*, 47.

131. Ibid., 42–43.

132. Ibid., 43, citing van Gelder, "Dynamical Hypothesis in Cognitive Science."

133. Thompson, *Mind in Life*, 421.

134. Ibid., 62.

135. Ibid., 142; cf. 431, citing Maturana and Varela, H. Haken's analysis of synergy, and Robert Rosen's rigorous distinction between living and nonliving systems (see H. Haken, Anders Karlqvist, and Uno Svedin, *The Machine as Metaphor and Tool*). Maturana and Varela devised their autopoesis theory after Maturana worked out the neuronal visual circuits of the frog. See Maturana, "The Mind Is Not the Head"; Varela et al., "Autopoiesis."

136. Thompson, *Mind in Life*, 157.

137. Ibid., 47; cf. 44.

138. Merleau-Ponty, *Structure of Behavior*, 13, quoted in Thompson, *Mind in Life*, 47.
139. Thompson, *Mind in Life*, 53–54, quoting Freeman, *Societies of Brains*, 149–50.
140. Thompson, *Mind in Life*, 58–59.
141. Ibid., 73–75.
142. Ibid., 76–77; cf. 56–59.
143. De Waal, *Good Natured*, 210.
144. Ibid., 47.
145. De Waal, *Primates and Philosophers*, 58. The "killer ape" model of human evolution, proposed by Raymond Dart (1893–1988) in "The Predatory Transition from Ape to Man" (1953), was popularized by Robert Ardrey in *African Genesis* (1963) and Konrad Lorenz in *On Aggression* (1966). Its many critics included Erich Fromm in *The Anatomy of Human Destructiveness* (1973).
146. De Waal, *Age of Empathy*, 97–98.
147. Darwin, *Descent of Man*, 70–75.
148. Cf. de Waal, *Age of Empathy*, 80. For differences of empathy from moral concern, see Goodman, *Love Thy Neighbor*, 3–6.
149. De Waal, *Age of Empathy*, 6.
150. Ibid., 12–13.
151. Ibid.
152. Ibid., 11–12, 15.
153. Ibid., 18–22, 33, 45.
154. Ibid., 47, citing the research of Jan van Hooff.
155. De Waal, *Age of Empathy*, 52, 61, 70.
156. Ibid., 72.
157. De Waal, *Primates and Philosphers*, 67.
158. De Waal, *Age of Empathy*, 75, 83.
159. Rizzolatti and Craighero, "Mirror-Neuron System"; Iacoboni et al., "Grasping the Intentions of Others"; Dobbs, "A Revealing Reflection"; Keysers, *The Empathic Brain*.
160. Neisser, "Five Kinds of Self-Knowledge," 35–59.
161. Neisser, "Roots of Self-Knowledge," 19.
162. Ibid., 19, quoting Dennett, *Consciousness Explained*, 355.
163. Neisser, "Roots of Self-Knowledge," 19.
164. Ibid., 21.
165. Van den Hoort and Ehrsson, "Being Barbie."
166. Neisser, "Roots of Self-Knowledge," 25.
167. Ibid., 29.
168. Benveniste, *Problems in General Linguistics*, 224–25.
169. See Sorabji, *Self*, 25–29, and Farroni et al., "Gaze Following in Newborns," 39–60; Frischen et al., "Gaze Cuing of Attention," 694–724.
170. Sorabji, *Self*, 26.
171. Neisser, "Roots of Self-Knowledge," 29–30.
172. Thompson, *Mind in Life*, 80; cf. 227.

CHAPTER FOUR: MEMORY

1. See Loftus et al., "Reality of Illusory Memories."
2. Vernant, *Myth and Thought among the Greeks*, 115–56; Le Goff, *History and Memory*, 58–67; Eliade, "Mythologies of Memory and Forgetting," 329–44.
3. Small, *Wax Tablets of the Mind*, 65.

4. Empedocles, Fragment 29 = Kirk, Raven, and Schofield, *Presocratic Philosophers*, #259, pp. 218–19.

5. Pindar, *The Odes*, translated by Conway.

6. Kenny, *Metaphysics of Mind*, 11.

7. Cf. Ricoeur, *Memory, History, Forgetting*. For the *ars memoriae*, Yates, *Art of Memory*. Ricoeur theorizes that memories are intrinsically associated with places, making places natural reminders. Yet often we remember a place for what happened there rather than vice versa.

8. For the "place system," see Aristotle, *Topics* 163b28, *De Anima* 427b18, *De Memoria et Reminiscentia* 452a12–16, *De Insomniis* 458b20–22. Aristotle prefers his students use dialectic flexibly rather than turn to potted arguments, as Gorgias had his students do. Aristotle values creative thinking and discovery but is not averse to students' memorizing topical paradigms as they master the art of dialectic (*Topics* 163b4–164b19), an asset not just in debate but in developing skills of mature and independent thinking. A shoe store helps if one can't learn shoemaking. But one needn't buy shoes in every style and size; *De Sophisticis Elenchis* 184b36–185a7. See Sorabji, *Aristotle on Memory*, 22–23, 27–28, 34.

9. See Plato, *Protagoras* 335a.

10. See Solmsen, *Die Entwicklung der aristotlischer Logik und Rhetorik*, 170–75.

11. Kemp, *Medieval Psychology*, 53–76.

12. Carruthers, *Book of Memory*; cf. Olson, *World on Paper*.

13. See Zetzel, "*Romane memento*," 263–84. In the electric setting of a visit to the underworld or the oracular frame of a sibylline utterance, Zetzel stresses, memory is no mere archive but an admonition to preserve Roman probity in every public and private act.

14. See e.g. Genesis 18:19, Deuteronomy 4, 6:6–9, 11:18–20, 32:46–47.

15. Dudai, "Predicting Not to Predict Too Much," 1255.

16. Milad et al., "Presence and Acquired Origin of Reduced Recall"; Schiller et al., "Preventing Fear in Humans"; cf. Schiller and Phelps, "Does Reconsolidation Occur in Humans?".

17. Locke, *Essay*, 1.10.2, 149–50.

18. Ibid., 1.10.7.

19. Bluma Zeigarnik (1901–1988) went on to become a psychiatrist and a founding figure in Soviet psychology. She described the Zeigarnik Effect in a thesis written under Lewin's supervision and published as "Über das Behalten von erledigten und unerledigten Handlungen," available in English at codeblab.com/wp-content/uploads/2009/12/On-Finished-and-Unfinished-Tasks.pdf. See Van Bergen, *Task Interruption*; cf. Masicampo and Baumeister, "Consider It Done!" Lewin (1890–1947), often called the founder of social psychology, was a student of the philosopher/psychologist Carl Stumpf (himself a student of Brentano) and of Stumpf's students Köhler and Wertheimer. As an MIT professor Lewin pioneered the study of social action and worked to help rehabilitate displaced persons after World War II, and later in combating racial prejudice by developing what became sensitivity training. As a theorist he sought to address the nature-nurture controversy rampant in his day by broadening consideration of the impact of personality.

20. Locke, *Essay*, 1.10.9.

21. Ibid., 2.27.

22. Ibid., 2.27.9.

23. Hume, *Treatise*, 1.4.2, 189–90. This and the passage quoted just below typify the

stance in Hume that Dennett echoes in the lines that rankled Neisser, as quoted above in chapter 3, Consciousness.

24. Hume, *Treatise*, 1.4.6, 251–52.

25. Hume writes: "The mind is a kind of theatre, where several perceptions successively make their appearance; pass, re-pass, glide away, and mingle in an infinite variety of postures and situations. There is properly no *simplicity* in it at one time, nor *identity* in different." He then backpedals, rejecting the suggestion of an audience in the theater: "The comparison of the theatre must not mislead us. They are the successive perceptions only, that constitute the mind." *Treatise*, 1.4.6, 253. Hume drops the comparison in the *Enquiry*.

26. Nietzsche, echoing Moliere, in *Beyond Good and Evil*, 11.

27. In *Concept of Mind*, chapter 2, Ryle, seeking to shift the idea of intelligence from substantive to adverbial application, both presses and blurs the distinction between declarative and procedural memory. Aiming to favor the procedural he underplays the interactions between *what* we know and *how* acquired dispositions enable a performance.

28. Ryle, following up on Wittgenstein's focus on language, made our most cogitative thinking a kind of unvocalized speech—lest cognition remain unresolved to behavior; *Concept of Mind*, 173–77. Rather than describe language as the expression of our thoughts, thought here becomes a special kind of language. Is memory, then, a trunk full of words and sentences? If so, how do we express the same thought in various languages—or use familiar words creatively?

29. James, *Principles of Psychology*, 1.239.

30. Ibid., 650.

31. HM's name, now in the public record: Henry Molaison.

32. Corkin, "What's New with the Amnesic Patient H.M.?"; Danziger, *Marking the Mind*, 170–71.

33. Corkin, "Lasting Consequences of Bilateral Medial Temporal Lobectomy."

34. Rosenbaum et al., "The Case of KC."

35. Tulving and Lepage, "Where in the Brain Is Awareness of One's Past?," 214.

36. Tulving, "Episodic Memory and Autonoesis," 15.

37. Ibid., 14.

38. As the mention of phlogiston and the ether signals, Tulving is addressing Paul Churchland's paper "Eliminative Materialism," which cited those long discredited notions of earlier science in branding "Folk Psychology" a "radically false" theory to be "displaced rather than smoothly reduced, by completed neuroscience" (1); Baker, "The Myth of Folk Psychology," in *Explaining Attitudes*, shows Churchland's claims to be self-refuting, reliant on the very notions they reject. Churchland and his allies confused the metaphysics of mechanism with the progress of neuroscience but offered only promissory notes. Tulving acknowledges the IOUs, but it's been clear for decades that the scrip is worthless, since the new language is not forthcoming. In trying to imagine successor notions purged of mentalistic ideas like affirmation, judgment, denial, belief, or even truth and falsity, Churchland et al. have resorted to increasingly fantastic possible worlds scenarios (see, e.g., "Eliminative Materialism," 19–20). But the roots of the issue are conceptual. As Hasker notes in *The Emergent Self*, Churchland long persisted in using the language of claims, motives, and beliefs that he finds insupportable. One might allow, Hasker writes, that in retaining language which they insist is empty, Churchland and other eliminativists are simply using "stand-ins for the names, as yet unbestowed, of the successor concepts heralded

by eliminativism." But *"this option is not available.* We simply have *no grasp* of these successor concepts, and cannot use them to make any assertions" (18). The would-be eliminativist "recognizes the untenability of this situation. She realizes that it is just not acceptable to continue writing checks on an account which has supposedly been closed out, in the hope that some day another account will be opened which will give her the resources to pay off all the debts that have accumulated" (20).

39. See Young, *Mind, Brain, and Adaptation in the Nineteenth Century;* Spillane, *Doctrine of the Nerves;* Finger, *Origins of Neuroscience.* Among primary sources, Charcot, *Lectures on Localization in Diseases of the Brain;* Ribot, *Diseases of Memory;* Ferrier, *Croonian Lectures on Cerebral Localization.*

40. Clark and Jacyna, *Nineteenth-Century Origins of Neuroscientific Concepts.*

41. See Danziger, *Marking the Mind,* 125–33; and "Hermann Ebbinghaus and the Psychological Experiment," in Traxel, *Ebbinghaus Studien* 2, 217–24.

42. Danziger, *Marking the Mind,* 128.

43. Lashley, "In Search of the Engram," 477–78.

44. Penfield, "Engrams in the Human Brain."

45. Kandel, *In Search of Memory,* fig. 15-1.

46. Andersen et al., *Hippocampus Book,* section 10.3. And see Bliss et al., *Long-Term Potentiation.*

47. Goelet et al., "Long and Short of Long-Term Memory"; Kandel, *In Search of Memory,* 270–71.

48. Kandel, *In Search of Memory,* 267.

49. Ibid., 234. Kandel assumes that species closer to the trunk of the phylogenetic tree, invertebrates, say, must be simpler than species located in the twigs. Many metabolic processes build on earlier attainments. But relative phylogenetic isolates pursue their own evolutionary paths, which may take them in directions less reliant on such a boost. We cannot assume, in any case, that today's "lower species" are less evolved than their "more advanced" contemporaries. Bacteria and insects have been evolving for far longer than mammals or birds. As Yadin Dudai writes, "there is no a priori reason to assume that parts of the brain of, say, *Drosophila* or honey bee will prove less 'complex' to resolve than some parts of the mammalian brain. . . . The early emergence of invertebrates on the phylogenetic arena does not imply that they did not evolve to an amazing complexity in parallel with the evolution of more 'advanced' species." "Why 'Learning' and 'Memory' Should Be Redefined," 112. In social species much of the work of intelligence is laid off onto instinct and social organization, not entrusted to the individual. Yet even bees and ants are neurologically advanced enough to communicate with one another and to find the route to food sources and back to the hive or nest.

50. Known for his scientific intuition, brilliant experimental design, and prodigious memory, Sutherland won the 1971 Nobel Prize for his work on hormone action. His findings as to the versatility of cAMP typify his insightful experimental work.

51. Kandel, *In Search of Memory,* 234–35.

52. Ibid., 264–66.

53. Ibid., 266–67.

54. Danziger, *Marking the Mind,* 237.

55. Kandel, *In Search of Memory,* 274.

56. Bontempi and Durkin, "Dynamics of Hippocampal-Cortical Interactions."

57. Wiltgen et al., "Towards a Molecular and Cellular Understanding of Remote Memory," 64.

58. Ibid., 64.
59. Tsien, "Organizing Principles of Real-Time Memory Encoding," 99.
60. Tsien, "Memory Code."
61. Tsien, "Organizing Principles of Real-Time Memory Encoding," 108.
62. Edelman, *Second Nature*, 59.
63. Edelman, *Second Nature*, 66. For the brain reading notion, see, for example, Kamitani et al., "Decoding the Visual and Subjective Contents of the Human Brain"; articles at http://www.technologyreview.com/energy/20380/; http://www.wired.com/medtech/health/magazine/16-06/mf_neurohacks; Norman et al., "Beyond Mind-Reading"; Langleben, "Detection of Deception with fMRI," 1–9; Kittay, "Admissibility of fMRI Lie Detection"; Rissman et al., "Detecting Individual Memories"—showing that fMRIs cannot distinguish true from false memories.
64. See Squire, "Memory and Brain Systems"; Squire and Kandel, *Memory*.
65. Dudai, "Why 'Learning' and 'Memory' Should Be Redefined," 112.
66. See Malenka, "Long-Term Potential of LTP."
67. See Dudai, "Memory," 13–14. For the argument that pan-adaptationism is Panglossian, see Gould and Lewontin, "Spandrels of San Marco."
68. Bickle, "Reducing Mind to Molecular Pathways," 432.
69. Ibid., 428.
70. Bickle, *Philosophy and Neuroscience*, chapter 3.
71. Danziger, *Marking the Mind*, 129–31.
72. Ibid., 160–61.
73. See Varela et al., *Embodied Mind*.
74. Edelman, *Second Nature*, 58.
75. On cocaine mice: http://www.time.com/time/health/article/0,8599,1952411,00.html; Schultz, "Neural Coding of Basic Reward Terms"; Wichems et al., "Cocaine Reward Models." On knockout mice as models for behavioral plasticity studies, see Winder and Schram, "Plasticity and Behavior." An excellent critique of the animal behavioral models is found in Winger et al., "Behavioral Perspectives on the Neuroscience of Drug Addiction," 667–68.
76. Kenny, *Metaphysics of Mind*, 6; Putnam gives a hilarious description of attempts to describe in molecular terms why a square peg won't fit into a round hole. See his *Mind, Language, and Reality*, 295–98.
77. Bruer, "Plasticity," 87.
78. Neisser and Hyman, *Memory Observed*, 7, 5.
79. Banaji and Crowder, "Bankruptcy of Everyday Memory," reprinted in Neisser and Hyman, *Memory Observed*, 19–20.
80. See Herz, "Naturalistic Analysis of Autobiographical Memories"; Herz and Schooler, "Naturalistic Study of Autobiographical Memories"; Hyman, "Imagery, Reconstructive Memory, and Discovery"; Oakes and Hyman, "Role of the Self in False Memory Creation."
81. Neisser and Hyman, *Memory Observed*, 11–12.
82. Nelson, "Origins of Autobiographical Memory"; Nelson et al., *Event Knowledge*; Nelson, *Narratives from the Crib*; cf. Peterson, "Childrens' Long-Term Memory for Autobiographical Events."
83. Bruner, *Acts of Meaning*, 89. Early childhood monologues are key evidence in the Wittgensteinian conception of thought as internal language. Ryle writes: "This trick of talking to oneself in silence is acquired neither quickly nor without effort; and it is a necessary condition of our acquiring it that we should have previously learned

to talk intelligently aloud and have heard and understood other people doing so." *Concept of Mind*, 28. Clearly judgments and inferences in sentential form lean on language, and language helps us order our memories (and "forgetteries") in sentential form. But thinking is protean, and language is no more necessary to every memory than it is to all other forms of mentation. Language may well be critical in the birth of thought (especially, for thinking of the most discursive kind). But the findings of genetic psychology do not fully determine the nature of every variety of thought—or memory.

84. Nadel, "Consolidation."
85. Edelman, *Second Nature*, 99.
86. Ramachandran, "Why Do Gentlemen Prefer Blondes?"
87. Edelman, *Second Nature*, 57.
88. Olson, *World on Paper*, 265, 273; cf. Stock, *Implications of Literacy*.
89. Le Goff, *History and Memory*.
90. Leroi-Gourhan, quoted in Le Goff, *History and Memory*, 98.

CHAPTER FIVE: AGENCY

1. The distinction between internal and external determination was critical in an oft misquoted and misinterpreted article, "Free Will as Involving Determination" (*Mind* 43 [1934]) by Dickinson Miller, writing under the name R. E. Hobart. As Nicholas Rescher sums up the point: "freedom is nowise at odds with motivational determinism that places the locus of causal determination in the thought process of the agent." *Free Will*, 94.

2. Kim, *Supervenience and Mind*, 280. Without the "causal closure of physics," Kim writes, "there can in principle be no complete physical theory of physical phenomena," and physics must essentially cease to be physics and open its doors to "vital principles, entelechies, psychic energies, elan vital, or whatnot." "The Non-Reductivist's Troubles with Mental Causation," 209.

3. Kim, *Supervenience and Mind*, 290 (emphasis is Kim's).

4. See Aristotle, *Metaphysics* 8.2.1042b14.

5. Democritus, apud Aristotle, *Physics* 3.4.203a33.

6. Eddington, *Nature of the Physical World* (1928 edition), 294–95.

7. See Stebbing, *Philosophy and the Physicists*.

8. Eddington, *Philosophy of Physical Science* (1938), 182.

9. Kane, *Contemporary Introduction to Free Will*, 35–36.

10. The translation here is Goodman's.

11. Cf. Lucretius's declaration of his theme: *De Rerum Natura* 2.62–66.

12. Kane, *Significance of Free Will*, 127.

13. In *Free Will: A Philosophical Appraisal*, a book dedicated to Robert Kane and Peter van Inwagen, "free-will theorists extraordinary," Rescher understands free will as the ability to choose for oneself among alternative possibilities.

14. Chrysippus, apud Aulus Gellius, *Noctes Atticae* 7.2.7–11 (= *Stoicorum Veterum Fragmenta* 2.1000 = Long and Sedley, 62D, 1.384, 2.388); Cicero, *De Finibus* 3.6.

15. Fārābī, *Commentary on "De Interpretatione,"* edited by Kutsch and Marrow, 81–100; in *Commentary and Short Treatise on Aristotle's "De Interpretatione,"* in the translation by Zimmermann, 75–95.

16. Ryle, "It Was to Be," in *Dilemmas*, 22.

17. Eccles, *The Human Mystery*, 131–32, 144.

18. Galen, *De Usu Partium*, 1.19–20, 34, translated after May, 80–81, 90.

19. *De Usu Partium*, 10.9, translated after May, 484–85.
20. *De Usu Partium* 1.7, translated after May, 74.
21. Siraisi, *Medicine and the Italian Universities*; Finger, *Origins of Neuroscience*, 193.
22. Descartes, *Treatise on Man*, in *Philosophical Writings*, translated by Cottingham, Stoothoff, and Murdoch, 1.100.
23. Ibid.
24. Ibid.
25. Galen, *De Usu Partium*, 1.10, translated after May, 81.
26. Descartes, *Treatise on Man*, in *Philosophical Writings*, 1.100.
27. Ibid.
28. Finger, *Origins of Neuroscience*, 195.
29. Krauzlis, "Control of Voluntary Eye Movements."
30. Wade and Tatler, *Moving Tablet of the Eye*.
31. See Porterfield, *A Treatise on the Eye*, book 3, chapter 7, p. 222.
32. Finger, *Origins of Neuroscience*, 197.
33. Corbetta et al., "Common Network of Functional Areas," 770. See Schall, "The Neural Selection and Control of Saccades"; Stuphorn et al., "Role of Supplementary Eye Field in Saccade Initiation"; Schall and Boucher, "Executive Control of Gaze by the Frontal Lobes."
34. Yarbus, *Eye Movements and Vision*, 171–200.
35. Ballard and Hayhoe, "Modelling the Role of Task in the Control of Gaze" (2009 and 2010); Tatler et al., "Yarbus, Eye Movements, and Vision."
36. Libet, "Do Models Offer Testable Proposals of Brain Functions?"
37. Libet et al., "Time of Conscious Intention to Act."
38. Haggard et al., "On the Perceived Time of Voluntary Actions," 291.
39. Wegner, *Illusion of Free Will*, 2, 14, 18, 55, 66, 325; cf. P. Carruthers, "The Illusion of Conscious Will," 211.
40. Hallett, "Volitional Control of Movement"; and "Volition: How Physiology Speaks to the Issue of Responsibility"; cf. Nahab et al., "Neural Processes Underlying Self-Agency."
41. K. Smith, "Neuroscience vs. Philosophy."
42. Haggard and Haynes, quoted in K. Smith, "Neuroscience vs. Philosophy."
43. Mele, *Effective Intentions*, quoting Haggard and Libet, "Conscious Intention and Brain Activity," 62.
44. Mele, *Effective Intentions*, 6; cf. 3–4.
45. Mele, *Effective Intentions*, 38, quoting Marcel, "Sense of Agency," 60.
46. See Mele, *Effective Intentions*, 36 ff.
47. James, *Principles of Psychology*, 2.496, quoted in Mele, *Effective Intentions*, 37.
48. Mele, *Effective Intentions*, 23, cf. 26–31, 36–38.
49. Ibid., 27; cf. 34–36.
50. Cantrell, *Horsemen of Israel*, 11–13.
51. Mele, *Effective Intentions*, 60.
52. Ibid., 56–59.
53. Ghazālī, *The Incoherence of the Philosophers*, translated by Marmura, paragraphs 38–46, pp. 21–24.
54. See Frankfurt, *The Importance of What We Care About*.
55. Roskies is quoted in "Taking Aim at Free Will," *Nature* 477 (September 1, 2011): 23–25.
56. Nahmias et al., "Surveying Freedom."
57. Vohs and Schooler, "The Value of Believing in Free Will"; Schooler, "What Science Tells Us about Free Will"; Baumeister and Tierney, *Willpower*.

58. Greene and Cohen, "For the Law, Neuroscience Changes Nothing and Everything."
59. Nahmias et al., "Free Will, Moral Responsibility, and Mechanism."
60. Goodman, introduction to Ibn Ṭufayl's Ḥayy Ibn Yaqẓān, 82–86.
61. Spinoza, Ethics 4, Proposition 18, Scholium.
62. Ibid., Proposition 35, Corollary and Scholium.
63. Bandura, Self-Efficacy.
64. Ibid., 5.
65. Bandura, "Toward a Psychology of Human Agency," 164–65.
66. Bandura, "Reconstrual of 'Free Will,'" 164–65, 93, 97.
67. Bandura, "Toward a Psychology of Human Agency," 165–66.
68. Bandura, in Baer et al., Are We Free? 96.
69. Ibid., 94.
70. Gallagher, "Strong Interaction and Self-Agency," 66.
71. Spinoza, Ethics 4, Proposition 18, Scholium.
72. Gallagher, "Strong Interaction and Self-Agency," 67.
73. Ryan and Deci, "Self-Regulation," 1559, 1572.
74. Ibid., 1570.
75. Ibid., 1562.
76. Dworkin, Theory and Practice of Autonomy, cited in Ryan and Deci, 1562.
77. Cf. Ryan and Deci, "Self-Regulation," 1563, 1565.
78. Ibid., 1563–64.
79. Ibid., 1566–67.
80. Ibid., 1565, quoting Walton et al., "Interactions between Decision Making and Performance Monitoring."
81. See Baumeister and Tierney, Willpower, 14, 28–29, 33–34, citing Muraven et al., "Conserving Self-Control"; Baumeister et al., "Strength Model of Self-Control"; Inzlict and Gutsell, "Running on Empty"; and the review of multiple studies in Hagger et al., "Ego Depletion and the Strength Model of Self-Control."
82. Baumeister and Tierney, Willpower, 45–48, 104–5.
83. Ibid., 42.
84. See Baumeister et al., "Free Will in Consumer Behavior."
85. Pinker, The Blank Slate, 43.
86. Ryan and Deci, "Self-Regulation," 1571.
87. Ibid., 1565, citing Bradley, Affect Regulation and the Development of Psychopathology, and Chambers et al., "Developmental Neurocircuitry of Motivation."
88. Ryan and Deci, "Self-Regulation," 1571, citing Bargh, "Automaticity of Everyday Life."
89. Thompson, Mind in Life, 436, citing Kim, Supervenience and Mind, 92–108, 280. Robert Audi, by contrast, argues that "mental properties have causal power," and "can play a causally explanatory role in broadly causal generalizations." "Mental Causation: Sustaining and Dynamic," 73.
90. Thompson, Mind in Life, 437, citing the web critique by Campbell and Bickhard, "Physicalism, Emergence and Downward Causation"; Kim, Mind in a Physical World, 84–85, and "Making Sense of Emergence."
91. Thompson, Mind in Life, 437, quoting Kim, Mind in a Physical World, 85, with Kim's emphasis omitted.
92. Thompson, Mind in Life, 437, citing Kim, "Making Sense of Emergence," 84.
93. See Bergson, Time and Free Will, especially chapter 3.
94. Goodman, God of Abraham, 249–69.
95. Thompson, Mind in Life, 40.

96. Ibid., 39–40.
97. Ibid., 49–50.
98. Ibid.
99. Doidge, *Brain That Changes Itself*; Merzenich, "Neuroscience via Computer."
100. Wolf, *Proust and the Squid*.
101. Brown and Jones, "Meditation Experience Predicts Less Negative Appraisal of Pain"; Rainville et al., "Cortical Thickness and Pain Sensitivity"; Zeidan et al., "Brain Mechanisms Supporting Modulation of Pain."

CHAPTER SIX: CREATIVITY

1. Cf. Porphyry, *De Abstinentia* 4.9.
2. Democritus, apud Aelian, *On the Nature of Animals* 12.17.
3. Democritus frg. 33, apud Clement, *Miscellanies* 4.151.
4. Democritus, apud Sextus, *Adversus Mathematicos* 7 (= *Against the Logicians* 1) 116–18. Sextus quotes Democritus here as concurring with Empedocles' view that *knowledge* is of like by like.
5. M. Root-Bernstein, "Imaginary Worldplay."
6. Runco, *Creativity*, 57–59, 377–78.
7. See Cropley et al., *Dark Side of Creativity*.
8. Rhodes, "Analysis of Creativity."
9. See Murray, *Explorations in Personality*, 59, 89, 115.
10. Runco, "Creativity."
11. Barron and Harrington, "Creativity, Intelligence, and Personality." 439–76.
12. Pasteur's famous remark was embedded in his inaugural speech as Dean of the new Faculty of Sciences at Lille, December 7, 1854. Pasteur was reflecting on the supposed role of accident in in the discovery of electromagnetism by Hans Christian Oersted. Pasteur's words: "in the fields of observation, chance favors only the prepared mind." See René Vallery-Radot, *The Life of Pasteur*, translated by R. L. Devonshire (New York: Doubleday, 1919), 76.
13. Bailin, *Achieving Extraordinary Ends*, 7, 34–35, 51–54, 59, 89, 99.
14. See Harris, *Hypothesis and Perception*, e.g. 53, 112, 272.
15. De Groot, "Perception and Memory versus Thought," in Kleinmutz, *Problem Solving*, 19–50.
16. Spinoza, *Ethics* 2, Proposition 40, esp. Scholium 2.
17. Wertheimer, *Productive Thinking*, 10.
18. See Goodman, *In Defense of Truth*, chapter 5; cf. Wertheimer, 27, citing Mendeleev to suggest what's missing in strictly empiricist accounts of induction.
19. Hume calls the linkage of sensation with expectation among animals "a strong confirmation, or rather an invincible proof" that the same nexus arises in the human case. Collapsing warrant into genesis, he finds no grounds for prediction or explanation beyond the associative linkages afforded by his Lockean psychology. *Treatise* 1.3.16. *Enquiry*, section 9 restates Hume's appeal to "custom" and "experience" on the same model, admitting the "invincible proof" to rest on an argument from analogy.
20. Wertheimer, *Productive Thinking*, 15.
21. Ibid., 18.
22. Ibid., 22–23.
23. Philoponus, Commentary on Aristotle's *Posterior Analytics* 436.22–437.2.
24. Spinoza, *Ethics* 2, Proposition 40, Scholium 2 (Gebhardt 2.122).

25. Weisberg, *Creativity: Genius and Other Myths*, 12–14, citing Greeno, "Trends in the Theory of Knowledge for Problem Solving."

26. See Kozbelt et al., "Theories of Creativity"; Weisberg, *Creativity: Genius and Other Myths*, esp. 104–208.

27. See Fruman, *Coleridge, the Damaged Archangel*.

28. Weisberg, *Creativity: Genius and Other Myths*, 19–26, citing Olton, "Experimental Studies of Incubation."

29. Weisberg, *Creativity: Genius and Other Myths*, 46–48.

30. Ibid., 49.

31. Ibid., 52, 55, citing Torrance, "Examples and Rationales," and J. P. Guilford's 1950 presidential address at the American Psychological Association, "Creativity," published in *American Psychologist* 5 (1950): 444–54, and his "Traits of Creativity." Cf. Guilford's "Creativity: Retrospect and Prospect," *Journal of Creative Behavior* 4 (1970): 149–68, from Guilford's address to the Sixteenth Annual Creative Problem Solving Institute, SUNY Buffalo, June 23, 1970.

32. Weisberg, *Creativity: Genius and Other Myths*, 59–61, citing Osborn, *Applied Imagination*.

33. Weisberg, *Creativity: Genius and Other Myths*, 62–63, citing Dunnette et al., "Effects of Group Participation."

34. Weisberg, *Creativity: Genius and Other Myths*, 63–64, citing Bouchard and Hare, "Size, Performance, and Potential in Brainstorming Groups."

35. Weisberg, *Creativity: Genius and Other Myths*, 65–66, citing Brilhart and Jochem, "Effects of Different Patterns on Outcomes."

36. Weisberg, *Creativity: Genius and Other Myths*, 77–78, citing Mackinnon, "Personality Correlates of Creativity."

37. Csikszentmihalyi, *Creativity, Flow, and the Psychology of Discovery and Invention*, 8, 10, 28–32, 76, 97–99.

38. Gruber and Wallace, *Creative People at Work*.

AFTERWORD: GOD AND THE SOUL

1. See, inter alia, Tallis, *Aping Mankind*, where Tallis describes mechanistic reductionism and its offspring, evolutionary psychology, as "a castle built on sand."

2. Tallis, "What Neuroscience Cannot Tell Us about Ourselves."

3. Ibid.

BIBLIOGRAPHY

Aiello, Leslie, and Christopher Dean. *An Introduction to Human Evolutionary Anatomy*. London: Academic Press, 1990.

Albers, Josef. *Interaction of Color*. New Haven, CT: Yale University Press, 1963.

Alexander of Aphrodisias. *De Anima*. Translated by Athanasios P. Fotinis. Washington, DC: University Press of America, 1979.

Alkire, M. T., A. G. Hudetz, and G. Tononi. "Consciousness and Anesthesia." *Science* 322 (2008): 876–80.

Altmann, Alexander. *Studies in Religious Philosophy and Mysticism*. Ithaca, NY: Cornell University Press, 1969.

Anderson, Per, Richard Morris, David Amaral, Tim Bliss, and John O'Keefe. *The Hippocampus Book*. Oxford: Oxford University Press, 2007.

Ardrey, Robert. *African Genesis: A Personal Investigation into the Animal Origins and Nature of Man*. New York: Atheneum, 1961.

Aristotle, *The Complete Works* (*The Revised Oxford Translation*), edited by Jonathan Barnes. Princeton: Princeton University Press, 1984.

Arnheim, Rudolf. *Art and Visual Perception: A Psychology of the Creative Eye—The New Version*. Berkeley: University of California Press, 1974 (1997 reprint).

Audi, Robert. "Mental Causation: Sustaining and Dynamic." In Heil and Mele, *Mental Causation*.

Austin, J. L. *Sense and Sensibilia*. Edited by G. J. Warnock. Oxford: Oxford University Press, 1962.

Austin, James H. *Zen-Brain Reflections*. Cambridge, MA: MIT Press, 2006.

Avicenna. *Avicenna's Psychology. Fi 'l-Nafs*. Translated by Fazlur Rahman. Oxford: Oxford University Press, 1952.

———. *De Anima* (*The Psychology of the Shifā'*). Oxford: Oxford University Press, 1959.

Ayala, Francisco, and Theodosius Dobzhansky, eds. *Studies in the Philosophy of Biology: Reduction and Related Problems*. Berkeley: University of California Press, 1974.

Baer, John, James C. Kaufman, and Roy F. Baumeister. *Are We Free?* Oxford: Oxford University Press, 2008.

Bahya ibn Paquda. *The Book of Direction to the Duties of the Heart*. Translated by M. Mansoor. London: Routledge and Kegan Paul, 1973.

Bailin, Sharon. *Achieving Extraordinary Ends: An Essay on Creativity*. Boston: Kluwer, 1988.

Baker, Lynne Rudder. *Explaining Attitudes: A Practical Approach to the Mind*. Cambridge: Cambridge University Press, 1995.

Ballard, Dana, and Mary Hayhoe. "Modelling the Role of Task in the Control of Gaze." *Visual Cognition* 17 (2009): 1185–1204.

———. "Modelling the Role of Task in the Control of Gaze." *Perception* 1 (2010): 7–27.

Banaji, Mahzarin R., and Robert G. Crowder. "The Bankruptcy of Everyday Memory." *American Psychologist* 44 (1989): 1185–93.

Bandura, Albert. "Reconstrual of 'Free Will' from the Agentistic Perspective of Social Cognitive Theory." In Baer et al., *Are We Free?*, 86–127.

———. *Self-Efficacy: The Exercise of Control*. New York: Freeman, 1997.

———. "Toward a Psychology of Human Agency." *Perspectives on Psychological Science* 1 (2006): 164–80.

Bargh, J. "The Automaticity of Everyday Life." In R. S. Wyler Jr., ed. *Advances in Social Cognition* 10 (1997): 1–61.

Baron-Cohen, Simon. "Precursors to a Theory of Mind: Understanding Attention in Others." In Whiten, *Natural Theories of Mind*.

Baron-Cohen, Simon, John Harrison, Laura H. Goldstein, and Maria Wyke. "Coloured Speech Perception: Is Synaesthesia What Happens When Modularity Breaks Down?" *Perception* 22 (1993): 419–26.

Baron-Cohen, Simon, Helen Tager-Flusberg, and Donald J. Cohen. *Understanding Other Minds: Perspectives from Autism*. Oxford: Oxford University Press, 1993.

Barron, Frank, and David Harrington. "Creativity, Intelligence, and Personality." *Annual Review of Psychology* 32 (1981): 439–76.

Barry, Susan R. *Fixing My Gaze*. New York: Basic Books, 2009.

Bateson, Gregory. *Steps to an Ecology of Mind: Collected Essays in Anthropology, Psychiatry, Evolution, and Epistemology*. New York: Random House, 1979.

Baumeister, Roy F., Erin A. Sparks, Tyler F. Stillman, and Kathleen D. Vohs, "Free Will in Consumer Behavior." *Journal of Consumer Psychology* 18 (2008): 4–13.

Baumeister, Roy F., and John Tierney. *Willpower: Rediscovering the Greatest Human Strength*. New York: Penguin, 2011.

Baumeister, Roy F., K. D. Vohs, and D. M. Tice. "The Strength Model of Self-Control." *Current Directions in Psychological Science* 16 (2007): 351–55.

Bechara A., A. Damasio, H. Damasio, and S. Anderson. "Insensitivity to Future Consequences Following Damage to Human Prefrontal Cortex." *Cognition* 50 (1994): 7–15.

Benveniste, Émile. *Problems in General Linguistics*. Translated by Mary Elizabeth Meek. Coral Gables: University of Miami Press, 1971.

Ben-Zaken, Avner. *Reading "Ḥayy Ibn-Yaqẓān": A Cross-Cultural History of Autodidacticism*. Baltimore: Johns Hopkins University Press, 2011.

Bergson, Henri. *Time and Free Will: An Essay on the Immediate Data of Consciousness* (1889). Translated by F. L. Pogson. London: Sonnenschein, 1910.

Berlin, Brent, and Paul Kay. *Basic Color Terms*. Berkeley: University of California Press, 1969.

Bermúdez, José Luis. "Naturalized Sense Data." *Philosophy and Phenomenological Research* 61 (2000): 353–74.

Bettelheim, Bruno. *Freud and Man's Soul*. New York: Vintage Books, 1983.

Bickle, John. *Philosophy and Neuroscience: A Ruthlessly Reductive Account*. Heidelberg: Springer, 2003.

———. "Reducing Mind to Molecular Pathways." *Synthese* 151 (2006): 411–34.

Bliss, Tim, Graham Collingridge, and Richard Morris. *Long-Term Potentiation: Enhancing Neuroscience for Thirty Years*. New York: Oxford University Press, 2004.

Block, Ned. "Comparing the Major Theories of Consciousness." In *The Cognitive Neurosciences IV*, ed. Gazzaniga.

———. "The Higher Order Approach to Consciousness Is Defunct." *Analysis* 71 (2011): 419–31.

———. "Psychologism and Behaviorism." *Philosophical Review* 90 (1981): 5–43.

Bontempi, Bruno, and T. P. Durkin. "Dynamics of Hippocampal-Cortical Interactions During Memory Consolidation: Insights from Functional Brain Imaging." In Bontempi et al., *Memories: Molecules and Circuits*.

Bontempi, Bruno, A. Silva, and Y. Christen, eds. *Memories: Molecules and Circuits*. Heidelberg: Springer, 2007.

Bouchard, Thomas, and M. Hare. "Size, Performance, and Potential in Brainstorming Groups." *Journal of Applied Psychology* 54 (1970): 51–54.

Bradley, S. J. *Affect Regulation and the Development of Psychopathology*. New York: Guilford, 2000.

Brang, David, L. Edwards, V. S. Ramachandran, and S. Coulson. "Is the Sky 2? Contextual Priming in Grapheme-Color Synaesthesia." *Psychological Science* 19.5 (May 2008): 421–28.

Brang, David, and V. S. Ramachandran. "Survival of the Synesthesia Gene: Why Do People Hear Colors and Taste Words?" *PLoS Biology* 9.11, November 22, 2011.

Bregman, A. S. *Auditory Scene Analysis: The Perceptual Organization of Sound*. Cambridge, MA: MIT Press, 1990.

Brentano, Franz. *Psychologie vom empirischen Standpunkt*. Leipzig: Duncker and Humblot, 1874. Translated by Ted Honderich as *Psychology from an Empirical Standpoint* (London: Routledge, 1973).

Brett-Green, Barbara A., Lucy J. Miller, William J. Gavin, and Patricia L. Davies. "Multisensory Integration in Children: A Preliminary ERP Study." *Brain Research* 1242 (2008): 283–90.

Brilhart, John, and Lurene Jochem. "Effects of Different Patterns on Outcomes of Problem Solving Discussions." *Journal of Applied Psychology* 48 (1964): 175–79.

Brown, Christopher, and Anthony Jones. "Meditation Experience Predicts Less Negative Appraisal of Pain: Electrophysiological Evidence for the Involvement of Anticipatory Neural Responses." *Pain* 150 (2010): 428–38.

Bruer, John T. "Plasticity: On the Level." In Roediger et al., *Science of Memory: Concepts*.

Bruner, Jerome. *Acts of Meaning*. Cambridge, MA: Harvard University Press, 1990.

Brunet, Alain, Scott P. Orr, Jacques Tremblay, Kate Robertson, Karim Nader, and Roger K. Pitman. "Effect of Post-Retrieval Propanolol on Psychophysiologic Responding during Subsequent Script-Driven Traumatic Imagery in Post-Traumatic Stress Disorder." *Journal of Psychiatric Research* 42 (2008): 503–6.

Call, Josep, and Michael Tomasello. "Does the Chimpanzee Have a Theory of Mind? Thirty Years Later." *Trends in Cognitive Sciences* 12 (2008): 187–92.

Camgöz, N., C. Yerner, D. Güvenç. "Effects of Hue, Saturation, and Brightness on Preference." *Color Research and Application* 27 (2002): 199–207.

Campbell, Donald. "'Downward Causation' in Hierarchically Organised Biological Systems." In Ayala and Dobzhansky, *Studies in the Philosophy of Biology*.

Campbell, Richard J., and Mark H. Bickhard. "Physicalism, Emergence, and Downward Causation." *Axiomathes* 21 (2011): 35–56. http://Lehigh.edu/~mhb0/physicalemergence.pdf.

Cantrell, Deborah O'Daniel. *The Horsemen of Israel: Horses and Chariotry in Monarchic Israel* (*Ninth–Eighth Centuries B.C.E.*). Winona Lake, IN: Eisenbrauns, 2011.

Carruthers, Mary. *The Book of Memory*. Cambridge: Cambridge University Press, 1990.

Carruthers, Peter. "The Illusion of Conscious Will." *Synthese* 159 (2007): 197–213.

Chakrabarti, Arindam. "I Touch What I Saw." *Philosophy and Phenomenological Research* 52 (1992): 103–16.

———. "The Nyaya Proofs for the Existence of the Self." *Journal of Indian Philosophy* 19 (1982): 211–38.

Chakrabarti, Kisor Kumar. *Classical Indian Philosophy of Mind: The Nyaya Dualist Tradition*. Albany: SUNY Press, 1999.

Chalmers, David. *The Conscious Mind*. Oxford: Oxford University Press, 1996.

Chambers, R. A., J. R. Taylor, and M. N. Potenza. "Developmental Neurocircuitry of Motivation in Adolescence." *American Journal of Psychiatry* 160 (2003): 1041–52.

Charcot, J. M. *Lectures on Localization in Diseases of the Brain*. Translated by Edward P. Fowler. New York: Wood, 1878.

Cherry, E. C. "Some Experiments on the Recognition of Speech with One and Two Ears." *Journal of the Acoustical Society of America* 25 (1953): 975–79.

Chisholm, Roderick. *Perceiving*. Ithaca, NY: Cornell University Press, 1957.

Christen, Y., ed. *Research and Perspectives in Neurosciences* (2007): 20.

Churchland, Paul. "Eliminative Materialism and the Propositional Attitudes." *Journal of Psychology* 78 (1981): 1–22.

Cicero, Marcus Tullius. *On Moral Obligation: A New Translation of Cicero's "De Officiis."* Translated by John Higginbotham. London: Faber, 1967.

———. *Rhetorica ad Herennium*. Translated by Harry Caplan. Cambridge, MA: Harvard University Press, 1954.

Clark, E., and L. S. Jacyna. *Nineteenth-Century Origins of Neuroscientific Concepts*. Berkeley: University of California Press, 1992.

Clayton, Philip. *Mind and Emergence: From Quantum to Consciousness*. Oxford: Oxford University Press, 2004.

Clayton, Philip, and Paul Davies. *The Re-emergence of Emergence: The Emergentist Hypothesis from Science to Religion*. Oxford: Oxford University Press, 2009.

Cook, Gareth. "Neuroscience Challenges Old Ideas about Free Will." *Scientific American*. November 11, 2009. http://www.scientificamerican.com/article.cfm?id=free-will-and-the-brain-michael-gazzaniga-interview.

Corbetta, M., E. Akbudak, T. E. Conturo, H. A. Drury, M. Linenweber, J. M. Ollinger, S. E. Petersen, M. E. Raichle, D. C. Van Essen, A. Z. Snyder, and G. L. Shulman. "A Common Network of Functional Areas for Attention and Eye Movements." *Neuron* 21 (1998): 761–73.

Corbin, Henry. *Avicenne et le Récit Visionnaire*. Tehran/Paris: Adrien-Maisonneuve, 1954. Translated by Willard R. Trask as *Avicenna and the Visionary Recital* (New York: Pantheon, 1960).

Corkin, S. "Lasting Consequences of Bilateral Medial Temporal Lobectomy: Clinical Course and Experimental Findings in H.M." *Seminars in Neurology* 4 (1984): 249–59.

———. "What's New with the Amnesic Patient H.M.?" *Nature Reviews: Neuroscience* 3 (2002): 153–60.

Crane, Tim. *Elements of Mind*. Oxford: Oxford University Press, 2009.

Crick, Francis. *The Astonishing Hypothesis*. New York: Simon and Schuster, 1994.

Cropley, David H., Arthur J. Cropley, James C. Kaufman, and Mark A. Runco, eds. *The Dark Side of Creativity*. Cambridge: Cambridge University Press, 2010.

Csikszentmihalyi, Mihaly. *Creativity, Flow, and the Psychology of Discovery and Invention.* New York: Harper-Collins, 1997.

Damasio, Antonio. *Descartes' Error: Reason, Emotion, and the Human Brain.* New York: Harper-Collins, 1995.

———. *The Feeling of What Happens: Body and Emotion in the Making of Consciousness.* New York: Harcourt, 1999.

———. *Self Comes to Mind: Constructing the Conscious Brain.* New York: Pantheon, 2010.

Danziger, Kurt. "Hermann Ebbinghaus and the Psychological Experiment." In Traxel, *Ebbinghaus Studien 2.*

———. *Marking the Mind.* Cambridge: Cambridge University Press, 2008.

Darwin, Charles. *The Descent of Man.* (1871) Princeton: Princeton University Press, 1981.

Deacon, Terrence. "Evolution and the Emergence of Spirit," unpublished lecture presented at Harvard's Memorial Church, October 23, 2001; comparable content is found in Deacon's essay "Giving Up the Ghost: The Epic of Spiritual Emergence." *Science and Spirit* 10 (1999): 16–19.

———. "The Hierarchic Logic of Emergence: Untangling the Interdependence of Evolution and Self-Organization." In Weber and Depew, *Evolution and Learning.*

———. *Incomplete Nature: How Mind Emerged from Matter.* New York: Norton, 2012.

Deems, Daniel A., Richard L. Doty, R. Gregg Settle, Victoria Moore-Gillon, Paul Shaman, Andrew F. Mester, Charles P. Kimmelman, Vernon J. Brightman, and James B. Snow. "Smell and Taste Disorders: A Study of 750 Patients from the University of Pennsylvania Smell and Taste Center." *Archives of Otolaryngology Head and Neck Surgery* 117 (1991): 519–28.

De Groot, Adriaan. "Perception and Memory versus Thought: Some Old Ideas and Recent Findings." In Kleinmutz, *Problem Solving.*

Dehaine-Lambertz, G., C. Pallier, W. Serniiclaes, L. Sprenger-Charolles, A. Jobert, and S. Dehaine. "Neural Correlates of Switching from Auditory to Speech Perception." *NeuroImage* 24 (2005): 21–33.

Delacroix, Eugène. *Journal.* Edited by A. Joubin. 3 volumes. Paris: Plon, 1932.

Dennett, Daniel. *Consciousness Explained.* Boston: Little Brown, 1991.

Descartes, René. *Descartes: His Moral Philosophy and Psychology.* Translated by John J. Blom. New York: NYU Press, 1978.

———. *The Philosophical Writings.* 3 volumes. Translated by John Cottingham, Robert Stoothoff, and Dugald Murdoch. Cambridge: Cambridge University Press, 1993.

De Waal, Frans. *The Age of Empathy.* New York: Crown, 2009.

———. *Good Natured.* Cambridge, MA: Harvard University Press, 1997.

———. *Primates and Philosophers.* Princeton, NJ: Princeton University Press, 2006.

Diels, Hermann. *The Older Sophists.* Translated by Rosamund Sprague. Columbia: University of South Carolina Press, 1972.

Diels, Hermann, and Walther Kranz, *Die Fragmente der Vorsokratiker.* Berlin: Weidmann, 1952.

Diogenes Laertius. *Lives of the Eminent Philosophers.* Edited and translated by R. D. Hicks. 2 volumes. Harvard University Press, 1925.

Dobbs, David. "A Revealing Reflection." *Scientific American Mind* 17 (2006): 406–22.

Doidge, Norman. *The Brain That Changes Itself: Stories of Personal Triumph from the Frontiers of Brain Science.* New York: Viking, 2007.

Dudai, Yadin. "Memory: It's All about Representations." In Roediger, Dudai, and Fitzpatrick, *Science of Memory: Concepts*, 13–16.

———. "Predicting Not to Predict Too Much: How the Cellular Machinery of Memory

Anticipates the Uncertain Future." *Philosophical Transactions of the Royal Society* 364 (2009): 1255–62.

———. "Why 'Learning' and 'Memory' Should Be Redefined (or, an Agenda for Focused Reductionism)." *Concepts in Neuroscience* 3 (1992): 99–121.

Dunn, Barnaby D., Tim Dalgleish, and Andrew D. Lawrence. "The Somatic Marker Hypothesis: A Critical Evaluation." *Neuroscience and Biobehavioral Reviews* 30 (2006): 239–71.

Dunnette, Marvin, John Campbell, and Kay Jastaad. "The Effects of Group Participation on Brainstorming Effectiveness for Two Industrial Samples." *Journal of Applied Psychology* 47 (1963): 10–37.

Dworkin, Gerald. *The Theory and Practice of Autonomy.* New York: Cambridge University Press, 1988.

Eagleman, D. M. "Visual Illusions and Neurobiology." *Nature Reviews: Neuroscience* 2 (2001): 920–26.

Eccles, C. *The Human Mystery: Gifford Lectures, 1977–1978.* Berlin: Springer, 1979.

Eddington, Sir Arthur. *The Nature of the Physical World.* Cambridge: Cambridge University Press, 1948.

———. *The Philosophy of Physical Science.* Cambridge: Cambridge University Press, 1938.

Edelman, Gerald. *Second Nature: Brain Science and Human Knowledge.* New Haven, CT: Yale University Press, 2006.

———. *Wider than the Sky.* New Haven, CT: Yale University Press, 2004.

Edwin, Erwin. *A Final Accounting: Philosophical and Empirical Issues in Freudian Psychology.* Cambridge, MA: MIT Press, 1996.

Ehrenstein, Walter M. "Untersuchungen über Figur-Grund-Fragen." *Zeitschrift für Psychologie* 117 (1930): 339–412.

Ehrenstein, Walter M., Lothar Spillmann, and Viktor Sarris. "Gestalt Issues in Modern Neuroscience." *Axiomathes* 13 (2003): 433–58.

Eliade, Mircea. "Mythologies of Memory and Forgetting." *History of Religions* 2 (1963): 329–51.

al-Fārābī. *Commentary and Short Treatise on Aristotle's "De Interpretatione."* Edited by F. W. Zimmermann. London: Oxford University Press, 1981.

———. *Commentary on Aristotle, Peri Hermeneias* (*De Interpretatione*). Edited by Wilhelm Kutsch and Stanley Marrow. Beirut: Catholic Press, 1960.

Farroni, Teresa, Stefani Massaccesi, Donatella Pividori, and Mark H. Johnson. "Gaze Following in Newborns." *Infancy* 5 (2004): 39–60.

Ferrier, David. *The Croonian Lectures on Cerebral Localization.* London: Smith-Elder, 1890.

Finger, Stanley. *Origins of Neuroscience: A History of Explorations into Brain Function.* Oxford: Oxford University Press, 1994.

Fischer, A. "Evolution of Bitter Taste Receptors in Humans and Apes." *Molecular Biology and Evolution* 22.3 (March 2005): 432–36.

Flanagan, Owen J. *The Boddisatva's Brain: Buddhism Naturalized.* Cambridge, MA: MIT Press, 2011.

Foster, John. *The Nature of Perception.* Oxford: Oxford University Press, 2003.

Frankfurt, Harry. *The Importance of What We Care About: Philosophical Essays.* Cambridge University Press, 1988.

Freeman, W. J. *Societies of Brains: A Study in the Neuroscience of Love and Hate.* Mahwah, NJ: Erlbaum, 1995.

Frischen, Alexandra, Andrew P. Bayliss, and Stephen P. Tipper. "Gaze Cuing of Attention: Visual Attention, Social Cognition, and Individual Differences." *Psychological Bulletin* 133 (2007): 694–724.

Fromm, Erich. *The Anatomy of Human Destructiveness*. New York: Holt, 1973.

Fruman, Norman. *Coleridge, the Damaged Archangel*. New York: Braziller, 1971.

Galen. *On the Natural Faculties*. Translated by Arthur John Brock. Cambridge, MA: Harvard University Press, 1916.

Galen, *On Medical Experience*, edited and translated by Richard Walzer. London: Oxford University Press, 1944. Translation reprinted in Michael Frede, *Galen: Three Treatises on the Nature of Science*. Indianapolis, IN: Hackett, 1985.

———. *De Usu Partium*. 2 volumes. Translated by Margaret Talmadge May as *On the Usefulness of the Parts of the Body* (Ithaca, NY: Cornell University Press, 1968).

Gallagher, Shaun. "Strong Interaction and Self-Agency." *Humana.Mente* 15 (2011): 55–76.

Ganeri, Jonardon. "Cross-Modality and the Self." *Philosophy and Phenomenological Research* 61 (2000): 1–19.

Garcia-Carpintero, Manuel, "Sense Data: The Sensible Approach." *Grazer Philosophische Studien* 62 (2001): 17–63.

Gasser, Jacques. *Aux origines du cerveau moderne. Localisations, langage et mémoire dans l'oeuvre de Charcot*. Collection de Penser médicine. Paris: Fayard, 1995.

Gazzaniga, Michael, ed. *The Cognitive Neurosciences IV*. Cambridge, MA: MIT Press, 2009.

———. *Who's in Charge?: Free Will and the Science of the Brain*. New York: Harper Collins, 2011.

———. "Neuroscience Challenges Old Ideas about Free Will." *Scientific American*, November 15, 2011.

al-Ghazālī, Abū Ḥāmid. *The Incoherence of the Philosophers* (*Tahāfut al-Falāsifa*), translated by Michael Marmura (Provo: Brigham Young University Press, 1997).

Giacino, J. T., S. Ashwal, N. Childs, R. Cranford, B. Jennett, D. I. Katz. "The Minimally Conscious State: Definition and Diagnostic Criteria." *Neurology* 58.3 (February 12, 2002): 349–53.

Giambrone, Steve, and Daniel J. Povinelli. "Consciousness." In *Encyclopedia of Evolution*, edited by Mark Pagel, 192–96. Oxford: Oxford University Press, 2002.

Goelet, Philip, Vincent F. Castellucci, Samuel Schacher, and Eric Kandel. "The Long and the Short of Long-term Memory—A Molecular Framework." *Nature* 322 (31 July 1986): 419–22.

Goetz, Stewart, and Charles Taliafero. *A Brief History of the Soul*. Oxford: Wiley-Blackwell, 2011.

Goodman, Lenn E. *Creation and Evolution*. New York: Routledge, 2010.

———. *God of Abraham*. New York: Oxford University Press, 1996.

———. "An Idea Is Not Something Mute Like a Picture on a Pad." *Review of Metaphysics* 62 (2009): 591–631.

———. *In Defense of Truth: A Pluralistic Approach*. Amherst, NY: Humanity, 2001.

———. *Jewish and Islamic Philosophy*. Edinburgh: Edinburgh University Press, 1999.

———. *Love Thy Neighbor as Thyself*. New York: Oxford University Press, 2008.

Gorgias. *Encomium of Helen*. Translated by George Kennedy. In *The Older Sophists*, edited by Rosamund Kent Sprague. Columbia: University of South Carolina Press, 1972; reprinted with corrections, Indianapolis, IN: Hackett, 2001. 50–54.

Gould, Stephen Jay, and Richard Lewontin. "The Spandrels of San Marco and the Panglossian Paradigm: A Critique of the Adaptationist Programme." *Proceedings of the Royal Society B Biological Sciences* 205 (1979): 581–98.

Greene, J. D., and J. D. Cohen. "For the Law, Neuroscience Changes Nothing and Everything." *Philosophical Transactions of the Royal Society of London B*, Special Issue on Law and the Brain, 359 (2004): 1775–78.

Greeno, James. "Trends in the Theory of Knowledge for Problem Solving." In Tuma and Reif, *Problem Solving and Education*.

Gruber, Howard, and Doris Wallace. *Creative People at Work: Twelve Cognitive Case Studies.* New York: Oxford University Press, 1989.

Grünbaum, Adolf. *The Foundations of Psychoanalysis: A Philosophical Critique.* Berkeley: University of California Press, 1984.

Guilford, J. P. "Creativity." *American Psychologist* 5 (1950): 444–54.

———. "Traits of Creativity." In *Creativity and Its Cultivation*, edited by H. H. Anderson, 142–61. New York: Harper, 1959.

Haggard, P., and B. Libet. "Conscious Intention and Brain Activity." *Journal of Consciousness Studies* 8 (2001): 47–63.

Haggard, P., C. Newman, and E. Magno. "On the Perceived Time of Voluntary Actions." *British Journal of Psychology* 90 (1999): 291–303.

Hagger, M. S., C. Wood, C. Stiff, and N. L. D. Chatzisarantis. "Ego Depletion and the Strength Model of Self-Control: A Meta-Analysis." *Psychological Bulletin* 136 (2010): 495–525.

Haken, H., Anders Karlqvist, and Uno Svedin. *The Machine as Metaphor and Tool.* Berlin: Springer, 1993.

Hallett, Mark. "Volition: How Physiology Speaks to the Issue of Responsibility." In *Conscious Will and Responsibility: A Tribute to Benjamin Libet*, edited by Walter Sinnott-Armstrong and Lynn Nadel. Oxford: Oxford University Press, 2010: 61–69.

———. "Volitional Control of Movement: The Physiology of Free Will." *Clinical Neurophysiology* 118 (2007): 1179–92.

Hallett, Mark, O. Bai, V. Rathi, P. Lin, D. Huang, H. Battapady, D. Y. Fei, L. Schneider, E. Houdayer, X. Chen, M. Hallett. "Prediction of Human Voluntary Movement Before It Occurs." *Clinical Neurophysiology* 122 (2010): 364–72. http://www.ncbi.nlm.nih.gov/pubmed/20675187.

Halligan, P. W. "Phantom Limbs: The Body in Mind." *Cognitive Neuropsychiatry* 7 (2002): 251–68.

Hardin, C. L. *Color for Philosophers: Unweaving the Rainbow.* Indianapolis, IN: Hackett, 1988.

Hare, Brian, Joseph Call, and Michael Tomasello. "Do Chimpanzees Know What Conspecifics Know?" *Animal Behaviour* 61 (2001): 139–51.

Harris, Errol. *Hypothesis and Perception.* London: Unwin, 1970.

Harris, J., and G. Lindsay. "Vowel Patterns in Mind and Sound." In *Phonological Knowledge: Conceptual and Empirical Issues*, edited by N. Burton-Roberts, P. Carr, and G. J. Docherty, 185–206. Oxford: Oxford University Press, 2000.

Hasker, William. *The Emergent Self.* Ithaca: Cornell University Press, 1999.

He, Zijing, Matthais Bolz, and Renee Baillargeon. "Understanding of False Belief in 2.5-Year-Olds in a Violation-of-Expectation Task." *Society for Research in Child Development*, 2007.

Heil, John, and Alfred Mele, eds. *Mental Causation.* Oxford: Oxford University Press, 1993.

Herz, Rachel S. "A Naturalistic Analysis of Autobiographical Memories Triggered by Olfactory Visual and Auditory Stimuli." *Chemical Senses* 29.3 (March, 2004): 217–24

———. *The Scent of Desire.* New York: William Morrow, 2007.

Herz, Rachel S., and J. W. Schooler. "A Naturalistic Study of Autobiographical Memories Evoked by Olfactory and Visual Cues: Testing the Proustian Hypothesis." *American Journal of Psychology* 115 (2002): 21–32.

Herz, Rachel S., and Julia von Clef. "The Influence of Verbal on the Perception of Odors: Evidence for Olfactory Illusions?" *Perception* 30 (2001): 381–91.

Hierocles the Stoic. *Hierocles the Stoic: Elements of Ethics, Fragments and Excerpts.* Edited by Ilaria Ramelli and David Konstan. Atlanta: Society of Biblical Literature, 2009.

Hockett, C. F. *Manual of Phonology.* Bloomington: Indiana University Publications in Anthropology and Linguistics, 1955.

Howell, P., and C. J. Darwin. "Some Properties of Auditory Memory for Rapid Formant Transitions." *Memory and Cognition* 5 (1977): 700–708.

Howland, Jacob. *Plato and the Talmud*. Cambridge: Cambridge University Press, 2011.

Hume, David. *An Enquiry Concerning Human Understanding and Concerning the Principles of Morals*. Edited by L. A. Selby-Bigge and P. H. Nidditch. 3rd Edition. Oxford: Oxford University Press, 1975.

———. *A Treatise of Human Nature*. Edited by L. A. Selby-Bigge. Oxford: Oxford University Press, 1896.

Husserl, Edmund. *Ideas Pertaining to a Pure Phenomenology*. (1913) Translated by F. Kersten. The Hague: Nijhoff, 1982.

Huxley, T. H. "On the Hypothesis That Animals Are Automata and Its History." *Fortnightly Review* 22 (1874): 555–89.

Hyman, Ira E. "Imagery, Reconstructive Memory, and Discovery." In *Imagery, Creativity, and Discovery*, edited by B. Roskos-Ewoldsen, M. J. Intons-Peterson, and R. E. Anderson, 99–121. Amsterdam: North Holland, 1993.

Iacoboni, Marco, Istvan Molnar-Szakacs, Vittorio Gallese, Giovanni Buccino, John C. Mazziotta, and Giovanni Rizzolatti. "Grasping the Intentions of Others with One's Own Mirror Neuron System." *PloS Biology* (2005).

Ibn Bājjah. *The Regimen of the Solitary*. In *Opera Metaphysica*. Edited by Majid Fakhry. Beirut: Dar al-Nahar, 1968.

Ibn Ṭufayl, *Ḥayy Ibn Yaqẓān*. Updated edition. Translated with introduction and notes by Lenn E. Goodman. Chicago: University of Chicago Press, 2009.

Ikhwān al-Ṣafā (The Brethren of Purity). *The Case of the Animals vs Man before the King of the Jinn*. Translated by L. E. Goodman and Richard McGregor. Oxford: Oxford University Press, 2009.

———. *On Music*. Edited by Owen Wright. Oxford: Oxford University Press, 2010.

Inzlict, Michael, and J. N. Gutsell. "Running on Empty: Neural Signals for Self-Control Failure." *Psychological Science* 18 (2007): 933–37.

Itten, Johannes. *The Art of Color: The Subjective Experience and Objective Rationale of Color*. New York: Wiley, 2004.

Jack, A. I., and A. Roepstorff, eds. *Trusting the Subject*. 2 volumes. Thorverton, UK: Imprint Academic, 2003–2004.

Jaeger, Werner. *Aristotle: Fundamentals of the History of His Development*. Translated by Richard Robinson. 2nd edition. Oxford: Oxford University Press, 1962.

James, William. *The Principles of Psychology*. 2 volumes. New York: Holt, 1890.

Kamitani, Yukiyasu, and Frank Tong. "Decoding the Visual and Subjective Contents of the Human Brain." *Nature Neuroscience* 8 (2005): 679–85.

Kandel, Eric R. *In Search of Memory*. New York: W. W. Norton, 2006.

Kane, Robert. *A Contemporary Introduction to Free Will*. New York: Oxford University Press, 2005.

———. *The Significance of Free Will*. New York: Oxford University Press, 1996.

Kant, Immanuel. *Critique of Pure Reason*. Translated by Norman Kemp Smith. New York: St. Martin's Press, 1965.

Katz, David. *The World of Touch*. Translated by L. E. Kruger. Hillsdale, NJ: Erlbaum, 1989. Originally published as *Der Aufblau der Tastwelt* (Leipzig: Barth, 1925).

Kauffman, Stuart, and Philip Clayton. "On Emergence, Agency, and Organization." *Biology and Philosophy* 21 (2006): 501–21.

Keeley, B. L. "Fixing Content and Function in Neurobiological Systems: The Neuroethology of Electrorection." *Biology and Philosophy* 14 (1999): 395–430.

Kemp, Simon. *Medieval Psychology*. Westport, CT, and London: Greenwood, 1990.

Kenny, Anthony. *The Metaphysics of Mind*. Oxford: Oxford University Press, 1992.

Keysers, Christian. *The Empathic Brain: How the Discovery of Mirror Neurons Changes Our Understanding of Human Nature*. Lexington, KY: Social Brain Press, 2011.

Kim, Jaegwon. "Causality, Identity and Supervenience." *Philosophical Studies* 41 (1979): 31–49.

———. "Making Sense of Emergence." *Philosophical Studies* 95 (1999): 3–36.

———. *Mind in a Physical World: An Essay on the Mind-Body Problem and Mental Causation*. Cambridge, MA: MIT Press, 1998.

———. "The Non-Reductivist's Troubles with Mental Causation." In Heil and Mele, *Mental Causation*.

———. *Supervenience and Mind: Selected Philosophical Essays*. Cambridge: Cambridge University Press, 1991.

Kirk, Geoffrey Stephen, John Earle Raven, and Malcolm Schofield. *The Presocratic Philosophers*. 2nd ed. Cambridge University Press, 1983.

Kittay, Leo. "Admissibility of fMRI Lie Detection—The Cultural Bias against Mind Reading Devices." *Brooklyn Law Review* 72.4 (2007): 1351–99.

Klatzky, Robert L., and Susan J. Lederman. "Object Recognition by Touch." In *Blindness and Brain Plasticity in Navigation and Object Perception*, edited by J. J. Rieser et al., 185–207. New York: Erlbaum, 2008.

Kleinmutz, Benjamin, ed. *Problem Solving*. New York: Wiley, 1966.

Koch, Christof. *The Quest for Consciousness: A Neurological Approach*. Englewood, CO: Roberts, 2004.

———. *Consciousness: Confessions of a Romantic Reductionist*. Cambridge, MA: MIT Press, 2012.

Köhler, Wolfgang. *Gestalt Psychology*. New York: Liveright, 1947 (1992 reprint).

Kosslyn, Stephen M., William L. Thompson, and Giorgio Ganis. *The Case for Mental Imagery*. Oxford: Oxford University Press, 2006.

Kozbelt, Aaron, Ronald Beghetto, and Mark Runco. "Theories of Creativity." In *The Cambridge Handbook of Creativity*, edited by James Kaufman and Robert Sternberg, 20–47. Cambridge: Cambridge University Press, 2010.

Krauzlis, R. J. "The Control of Voluntary Eye Movements: New Perspectives." *The Neuroscientist* 11 (2005): 124–37.

Kujala, T., K. Alho, M. Huotilainen, R. J. Ilmoniemi, A. Lehtokoski, A. Leinonen, T. Rinne, O. Salonen, J. Sinkkonen, C. G. Standertskjöld-Nordenstam, R. Näätänen. "Electrophysiological Evidence for Cross-modal Plasticity in Humans with Early- and Late-Onset Blindness." *Psychophysiology* 34 (1997): 213–16.

Kujala, T., K. Alho, P. Paavilainen, H. Summala, and R. Naatanen. "Neural Plasticity in Processing Sound Location by the Early Blind: An Event Related Potential Study." *Electroencephalography and Clinical Neurophsyiology* 84.5 (1992): 469–72.

La Mettrie, Julien Offray de. *L'Homme Machine* (1747). Translated by Gertrude C. Bussey as *Man a Machine* (La Salle: Open Court, 1974). Also translated by Richard A. Watson and Maya Rybalka as *Man a Machine* (Indianapolis, IN: Hackett, 1994).

Langer, Susanne. *Mind: An Essay on Human Feeling*. 3 volumes. Baltimore: Johns Hopkins University Press, 1972.

Langleben, Daniel D. "Detection of Deception with fMRI: Are We There Yet?" *Legal and Criminological Psychology* 13.1 (2008): 1–9.

Lashley, Karl. "In Search of the Engram." *Society of Experimental Biology Symposium* 4 (1950): 454–82.

Laureys, S., Fabien Perrin, Caroline Schnakers, Melanie Boly, and Steve Majerus. "Residual

Cognitive Function in Comatose, Vegetative and Minimally Conscious States." *Current Opinion in Neurology* 18 (2005): 726–33.

Le Goff, Jacques. *History and Memory*. Translated by Steven Rendall and Elizabeth Claman. New York: Columbia University Press, 1992 (1977 in Italian).

Leibniz, Gottfried Wilhelm. *Discourse on Metaphysics* (1686). Translated by Peter Lucas and Leslie Grint. Manchester: Manchester University Press, 1953.

Lewes, George Henry. *Problems of Life and Mind*. London: Trübner and Co., 1875.

Lewis, C. I. *An Analysis of Knowledge and Valuation*. La Salle: Open Court, 1946.

Liberman, Alvin M. "Afterthoughts on Modularity and the Motor Theory." In *Modularity and the Motor Theory of Speech Perception*, edited by Ignatius G. Mattingly and Michael Studdert-Kennedy, 443–46. Hillsdale, NJ: Erlbaum, 1991.

Liberman, Alvin M., and I. G. Mattingly. "A Specialization of Speech Perception." *Science* 243 (1989): 489–94.

Libet, Benjamin. "Do Models Offer Testable Proposals of Brain Functions for Conscious Experience?" In *Consciousness: At the Frontiers of Neuroscience*, edited by H. Jasper, 213–19. Philadelphia: Lippincott-Raven, 1998.

Libet, Benjamin, Curtis Gleason, Elwood Wright, and Dennis Pearl. "Time of Conscious Intention to Act in Relation to Onset of Cerebral Potential (Readiness-Potential): The Unconscious Initiation of a Freely Voluntary Act." *Brain* 106 (1983): 623–42.

Livingstone, Margaret S. *Vision and Art: The Biology of Seeing*. New York: Abrams, 2002.

Locke, John. *An Essay Concerning Human Understanding*. Edited by Peter H. Nidditch. Oxford: Oxford University Press, 1979.

Loftus, E., J. Feldam, and R. Daghiell. "The Reality of Illusory Memories." In *Memory Distortion: How Minds, Brains, and Societies Reconstruct the Past*, edited by D. Schacter, 47–68. Cambridge, MA: Harvard University Press, 1995.

Lorenz, Konrad. *On Aggression*. London: Methuen, 1966.

Lucretius. *De Rerum Natura*. 3 volumes. Edited by Cyril Bailey. Oxford: Press, 1947.

MacDonald, J., and H. McGurk. "Visual Influences on Speech Perception Processes." *Perception and Psychophysics* 24 (1978): 253–57.

Mackinnon, D. W. "The Personality Correlates of Creativity: A Study of American Architects." In *Proceedings of the Fourteenth International Congress of Applied Psychology*, edited by G. S. Nielsen, 11–39. Copenhagen: Munksgaard, 1962.

Maclaury, Robert. "From Brightness to Hue: An Explanatory Model of Color-Category Evolution." *Current Anthropology* 33 (1992): 137–86.

Malenka, Robert C. "The Long-Term Potential of LTP." *Nature Reviews: Neuroscience* 4 (2003): 923–26.

Mangan, Bruce. "Cognition, Fringe Consciousness, and the Legacy of William James." In *The Blackwell Companion to Consciousness*, edited by M. Velmans and S. Schneider, 273–85. Oxford: Blackwell, 2007.

———. "The Conscious "Fringe": Bringing William James Up to Date." In *Essential Sources in the Scientific Study of Consciousness*, edited by Bernard J. Baars, William P. Banks, and James B. Newman, 741–59. Cambridge, MA: MIT Press, 2003.

Marcel, A. "The Sense of Agency: Awareness and Ownership of Action." In *Agency and Self-Awareness*, edited by J. Rosseler and N. Eilan, 48–93. Oxford: Oxford University Press, 2003.

Martin, Jack, Jeff H. Sugarman, and Sarah Hickinbottom. *Persons: Understanding Psychological Selfhood and Agency*. New York: Springer, 2009.

Martinez-Condé, S., S. L. Macknik, and D. H. Hubel. "The Role of Fixational Eye Movements in Visual Perception." *Nature Reviews Neuroscience* 5 (2004): 229–40.

Masicampo, E. J., and R. F. Baumeister. "Consider It Done! Making a Plan Eliminates the Zeigarnik Effect." *Journal of Personality and Social Psychology* 101 (2011): 667–83.

Maturana, H. R. "Fenomenologia del Conocer: Del Universo al Multiverso." In *La Psicologia en busca del paradigma*, edited by E. Contreras. Santiago, 1985.

———. "The Mind Is Not the Head." *Journal of Social and Biological Structures* 8.4 (1986): 308–10.

McDermott, Josh H. "The Cocktail Party Problem." *Current Biology* 19 (2009): 1024–27.

McGinn, Colin. "Another Look at Color." *Journal of Philosophy* 43 (1996): 537–53.

McGurk, H., and J. MacDonald. "Hearing Lips and Seeing Voices." *Nature* 264 (1974): 746–48.

Meagher, Robert. *Augustine on the Inner Life of the Mind*. Indianapolis, IN: Hackett, 1998.

———. *An Introduction to Augustine*. New York: NYU Press, 1978.

Mele, Alfred R. *Effective Intentions: The Power of Conscious Will*. New York: Oxford University Press, 2009.

Melzack, Ronald. "Phantom Limbs: The Self and the Brain." *Canadian Psychology* 30 (1989): 1–16.

Merleau-Ponty, Maurice. *The Structure of Behavior*. Translated by A. Fisher. Pittsburgh: Duquesne University Press, 1963.

Merzenich, Michael. "Neuroscience via Computer: Brain Exercise for Older Adults." *Interactions* 14 (2007): 42–45.

Metzger, Wolfgang. *Gesetze des Sehens*. Frankfurt: Kramer, 1936.

———. *Laws of Seeing*. Translated by Lothar Spillmann, Steven Lehar, Mimsey Stromeyer, and Michael Wertheimer. Cambridge, MA: MIT Press, 2006.

———. "Optische Untersuchungen am Ganzfeld II: Zur Phänomenologie des homogenen Ganzfeldes." *Psychologische Forschung* 13 (1930): 6–29.

Milad, Mohammed R., Scott P. Orr, Natasha B. Lasko, Yudhiao Chang, Scott L. Rauch, and Roger K. Pitman. "Presence and Acquired Origin of Reduced Recall for Fear Extinction in PTSD: Results of a Twin Study." *Journal of Psychiatric Research* 42 (2008): 515–20.

Mill, John Stuart. *A System of Logic, Ratiocinative and Inductive: Being a Connected View of the Principles of Evidence and the Methods of Scientific Investigation*. (1843) London: Longmans, 1965.

Millar, Susanna. *Space and Sense*. Oxford: Taylor and Francis, 2008.

Miller, Dickinson (writing under the name R. E. Hobart). "Free Will as Involving Determination and Inconceivable without It." *Mind* 43 (1934): 1–27.

Miyawaki, Kuniko, James J. Jenkins, Winifred Strange, Alvin M. Liberman, and Robert Verbrugge. "An Effect of Linguistic Experience: The Discrimination of /r/ and /l/ by Native Speakers of Japanese and English." *Perception and Psychophysics* 18.5 (1975): 331–40.

Mole, Christopher. "The Motor Theory of Speech Perception." In Nudds and O'Callaghan, *Sounds and Perception*, 211–33.

Moore, G. E. *Principia Ethica*. Cambridge: Cambridge University Press, 1903; reprinted, 1986.

Morgan, C. Lloyd. *Emergent Evolution*. London: Williams and Norgate, 1927.

Morowitz, Harold. *The Emergence of Everything: How the World Became Complex*. New York: Oxford University Press, 2002.

Muraven, M., D. Shmueli, and E. Burkley, "Conserving Self-Control Strength." *Journal of Personality and Social Psychology* 91 (2006): 524–37.

Murray, Henry A. *Explorations in Personality: A Clinical and Experimental Study of Fifty Men of College Age*. New York: Oxford University Press, 1938.

Nadel, Lynn. "Consolidation: The Demise of the Fixed Trace." In Roediger et al., *Science of Memory: Concepts*, 177–81.

Nagel, Thomas. *Mind and Cosmos: Why the Materialist Neo-Darwinian Conception of Nature Is Almost Certainly False*. New York: Oxford University Press, 2012.

———. "What Is It Like to Be a Bat?" *The Philosophical Review* 83 (1974): 435–50.

Nahab, Fatab B., P. Kundu, C. Gallea, J. Kakareka, R. Pursley, T. Pohida, N. Miletta, J. Friedman, and M. Hallett. "The Neural Processes Underlying Self-Agency." *Cerebral Cortex*. January 21, 2011, 48–55

Nahmias, Eddy, D. Justin Coates, and Trevor Kvaran. "Free Will, Moral Responsibility, and Mechanism: Experiments on Folk Intuitions." *Midwest Studies in Philosophy* 31 (2007): 214–42.

Nahmias, Eddy, Stephen Morris, Thomas Nadelhoffer, and Jason Turner. "Surveying Freedom: Folk Intuitions about Free Will and Moral Responsibility." *Philosophical Psychology* 18 (2005): 561–84.

Negus, Victor E. *The Comparative Anatomy and Physiology of the Nose and Paranasal Sinuses*. London: Livingstone, 1958.

Neisser, Ulric. "Five Kinds of Self-Knowledge." *Philosophical Psychology* 1 (1988): 35–59.

———. *The Perceived Self: Ecological and Interpersonal Sources of Self-Knowledge*. Cambridge: Cambridge University Press, 1993.

———. "The Roots of Self-Knowledge: Perceiving Self, It, and Thou." *Annals of the New York Academy of Sciences* 818 (1997): 19–33.

Neisser, Ulric, and Ira E. Hyman Jr., eds. *Memory Observed*. 2nd ed. New York: Worth, 2000.

Nelson, Katherine, ed. *Narratives from the Crib*. 2nd edition. Cambridge, MA: Harvard University Press, 2006.

———. "The Origins of Autobiographical Memory." In Neisser and Hyman, *Memory Observed*, 309–18.

Nelson, Katherine, and Janice Gruendel. *Event Knowledge: Structure and Function in Development*. Hillsdale, NJ: Erlbaum, 1986.

Newton, Isaac. *Philosophical Transactions of the Royal Society* 80. London, 1672.

Nietzsche, Friedrich. *Beyond Good and Evil* (1886), translated by Marianne Cowan. Chicago: Regnery, 1955.

Nilsson, Martin. *Greek Piety*. Oxford. Oxford University Press, 1948.

Norman, Kenneth, S. M. Polyn, G. J. Detre, and J. V. Haxby. "Beyond Mind-Reading: Multi-Voxel Pattern Analysis of fMRI Data." *Trends in Cognitive Science* 10 (2009): 424–30.

Nowak, R. F. "Mother Location by Newborn Lambs in Repetitive Testing: Influence of First Successful Reunion." *Applied Animal Behaviour Science* 41 (1994): 75–86.

Nowak, R. F., and D. R. Lindsay. "Discrimination of Merino Ewes by Their Newborn Lambs: Important for Survival?" *Applied Animal Behaviour Science* 41 (1992): 61–74.

Nowak, R. F., P. Poindron, and I. G. Putu. "Development of Mother Discrimination by Single and Multiple Newborn Lambs." *Developmental Psychobiology* 22 (1989): 833–45.

Nudds, Matthew, and Casey O'Callaghan. *Sounds and Perception*. Oxford: Oxford University Press, 2009.

Oakes, M. A., and Ira E. Hyman. "The Role of the Self in False Memory Creation." *Journal of Aggression, Maltreatment, and Trauma* 4 (2001): 87–103.

Oakley, David A., and Peter W. Halligan. "Hypnotic Suggestion and Cognitive Neuroscience." *Trends in Cognitive Sciences* 13 (2009): 264–70.

Olson, David R. *The World on Paper*. Cambridge: Cambridge University Press, 1994.

Olton, R. M. "Experimental Studies of Incubation." *Journal of Creative Behavior* 13 (1979): 9–22.

Osborn, Alex. *Applied Imagination: Principles and Procedures of Creative Problem-solving*. New York: Scribners, 1953.

Palmer, Stephen E. "Common Region: A New Principle of Perceptual Grouping." *Cognitive Psychology* 24 (1992): 436–47.

———. *Vision Science: Photons to Phenomenology*. Cambridge, MA: MIT Press, 1999.

Palmer, Stephen E., and I. Rock. "Rethinking Perceptual Organization: The Role of Uniform Connectedness." *Psychonomic Bulletin and Review* 1 (1994): 29–55.

Palmer, Stephen E., and Karen B. Schloss. "An Ecological Valence Theory of Human Color Preference." *Proceedings of the National Academy of Sciences* 107 (2010): 8877–82.

Parfit, Derek. *Reasons and Persons*. Oxford: Oxford University Press, 1984.

Pastor, Antonio. *The Idea of Robinson Crusoe*. Watford: Gongora, 1930.

Patel, Aniruddh D. "Language, Music, Syntax, and the Brain." *Nature Neuroscience* 6.7 (2003): 674–81.

———. *Music, Language, and the Brain*. Oxford: Oxford University Press, 2008.

Penfield, Wilder. "Engrams in the Human Brain: Mechanisms of Memory." *Proceedings of the Royal Society of Medicine* 61 (August, 1968): 831–40.

———. *The Mystery of the Mind*. Princeton: Princeton University Press, 1975.

Penfield, Wilder, and H. Jasper. *Epilepsy and the Functional Anatomy of the Human Brain*. Boston: Little Brown, 1954.

Penrose, Roger. *The Emperor's New Mind*. Oxford: Oxford University Press, 1999.

Peterson, Carole. "Children's Long-Term Memory for Autobiographical Events." *Developmental Review* 22 (2002): 370–402.

Pindar, *The Odes*. Translated by G. S. Conway. London: Dent, 1972.

Pinker, Steven. *The Blank Slate: The Modern Denial of Human Nature*. New York: Viking, 2002.

Pisoni, D. B. "Auditory and Phonetic Memory Codes in the Discrimination of Consonants and Vowels." *Perception and Psychophysics* 13 (1973): 253–60.

Plato, *Collected Dialogues*. Edited by Edith Hamilton and Huntington Cairns. Princeton, NJ: Princeton University Press, 1969.

Plutarch, *Adversus Colotem*, translated as *Reply to Colotes* in Plutarch, *Moralia*, edited and translated by Benedict Einarson and Phillip H. De Lacy. London: Heineman, 1967.

Pollack, Barbara. "Scents and Sensibility." *Art News* (March, 2011): 88–95.

Pomerat, C. M. "Activities Associated with Neuronal Regeneration." *Anatomical Record* 145 (1963): 371.

Porterfield, William. *A Treatise on the Eye*. Edinburgh: Hamilton and Balfour, 1759.

Potter, Karl. *The Encyclopedia of Indian Philosophies*. Princeton: Princeton University Press, 1977.

Premack, David. "On the Control of Human Individual Differences." In *Assessing Individual Differences in Human Behavior: New Concepts, Methods, and Findings*, edited by D. J. Lubinski and R. V. Dawls, 329–40. Palo Alto: Davies-Black, 1995.

———. "Why Humans Are Unique: Three Theories." *Perspectives on Psychological Science* 5 (2010): 22–32.

Premack, David, and Peter Woodruff. "Does the Chimpanzee Have a 'Theory of Mind'?" *Behavioral and Brain Sciences* 1 (1978): 515–26.

Preuss, Todd M. "What Is It Like to Be a Human?" In *The Cognitive Neurosciences III*, edited by M. S. Gazzaniga, 5–22. Cambridge, MA: MIT Press, 2003.

Pritchard, H. A. *Knowledge and Perception*. Oxford: Oxford University Press, 1950.

Proclus. *Commentary on the First Alcibiades*. Translated by William O'Neill. The Hague: Nijhoff, 1965.

———. *Commentary on Plato's "Parmenides."* Translated by Glenn R. Morrow and John M. Dillon. Princeton: Princeton University Press, 1987.

Purves, Dale, R. Beau Lotto, and Surajit Nundy. "Why We See What We Do: A probabilistic strategy based on past experience explains the remarkable difference between what we see and physical reality." *American Scientist* 90 (2001): 936–43.

Putnam, Hilary. *Mind, Language, and Reality.* (*Philosophical Papers*, vol. 2.) Cambridge: Cambridge University Press, 1975.

Pylyshyn, Z. W. "Return of the Mental Image: Are There Pictures in the Brain?" *Trends in Cognitive Sciences* 7 (2003): 113–18.

Quine, W. V. O. *Word and Object.* Cambridge, MA: MIT Press, 1960.

Radhakrishnan, S. *A History of Indian Philosophy.* Oxford: Oxford University Press, 1953.

Rainville, Pierre, Joshua Grant, Jérôme Courtemanche, Emma Duerden, and Gary Duncan. "Cortical Thickness and Pain Sensitivity in Zen Meditators." *Emotion* 10 (2010): 43–53.

Ramachandran, V. S. "Why Do Gentlemen Prefer Blondes?" *Medical Hypotheses* 48 (1997): 19–20.

Ramachandran, V. S., and Sandra Blakeslee. *Phantoms in the Brain: Probing the Mysteries of the Human Mind.* New York: Harper-Collins, 1998.

Ramachandran, V. S., and E. M. Hubbard. "Synaesthesia—A Window into Perception, Thought, and Language." *Journal of Consciousness Studies* 8 (2001): 3–34.

———. "The Phenomenology of Synaesthesia." *Journal of Consciousness Studies* 10 (2003): 49–57.

Ram-Prasad, Chakravarthi. *Knowledge and Liberation in Classical Indian Thought.* New York: Palgrave Macmillan, 2001.

Remez, Robert E., Phillip E. Rubin, Stefanie M. Berns, Jennifer S. Pardo, and Jessica M. Lang. "On the Perceptual Organization of Speech." *Psychological Review* 101 (1994): 129–56.

Remez, Robert E., and J. D. Trout. "Philosophical Messages in the Medium of Spoken Language." In Nudds and O'Callaghan, *Sounds and Perception*, 234–64.

Rescher, Nicholas. *Free Will: A Philosophical Reappraisal.* New Brunswick: Transaction, 2009.

Rhodes, Mel. "An Analysis of Creativity." *Phi Delta Kappan* 42 (1961): 305–10.

Ribot, Theodule. *Diseases of Memory: An Essay in the Positive Psychology.* London: Kegan, Paul Trench, 1882.

Richards, Robert. *Darwin and the Emergence of Evolutionary Theories of Mind and Behavior.* Chicago: University of Chicago Press, 1987.

Ricoeur, Paul. *Memory, History, Forgetting.* Translated by Kathleen Blamey and David Pellauer. Chicago: University of Chicago Press, 2004.

Rissman, Jesse, Henry T. Greely, and Anthony D. Wagner. "Detecting Individual Memories through the Neural Decoding of Memory States and Past Experiences." *Proceedings of the National Academy of Sciences* 107 (2010): 9849–54.

Rizzolatti, Giacomo, and Laila Craighero. "The Mirror-Neuron System." *Annual Review of Neuroscience* 27 (2004): 169–92.

Robinson, Howard. *Perception.* London: Routledge, 1994.

Rock, I., and D. Gutman. "The Effect of Inattention on Form Perception." *Journal of Experimental Psychology: Human Perception and Performance* 7 (1981): 275–85.

Rockwell, Teed. "The Effects of Atomistic Ontology on the History of Psychology." Cognitive Questions.org

Roediger, Henry L., III, Yadin Dudai, and Susan M. Fitzpatrick, eds. *Science of Memory: Concepts.* Oxford: Oxford University Press, 2007.

Root-Bernstein, Michelle. "Imaginary Worldplay as an Indicator of Creative Giftedness."

In *The International Handbook on Giftedness*, edited by Larisa Shavinina, 599–616. Dordrecht: Springer, 2009.

Root-Bernstein, Robert. *Discovering: Inventing and Solving Problems at the Frontiers of Scientific Knowledge.* Cambridge, MA: Harvard University Press, 1989.

Rosch, Eleanor. "Mindfulness, Meditation, and the Private Self." In *The Conceptual Self in Context: Culture, Experience, Self Understanding*, edited by Ulric Neisser and David A. Johnson, 185–202. Cambridge: Cambridge University Press, 1997.

Rose, Michael. *Audible Signs: Essays from a Musical Ground.* New York: Continuum, 2010.

Rosenbaum, R. S., S. Köhler, D. L. Schacter, M. Moscovitch, R. Westmacott, S. E. Black, F. Gao, and E. Tulving. "The Case of KC: Contributions of a Memory Impaired Person to Memory Theory." *Neuropsychologia* 43 (2005): 989–1021.

Runco, Mark A. *Creativity: Theories and Themes—Research, Development, and Practice.* Amsterdam: Elsevier, 2007.

———. "Creativity." *Annual Review of Psychology* 55 (2004): 657–87.

Ryan, Richard M., and Edward L. Deci. "Self–Regulation and the Problem of Human Autonomy: Does Psychology Need Choice, Self–Determination, and Will?" *Journal of Personality* 74 (Dec. 2004): 1557–85.

Ryle, Gilbert. *The Concept of Mind.* Chicago: University of Chicago Press, 1949.

———. "It Was to Be." In *Dilemmas*, 15–35. Cambridge: Cambridge University Press, 1962.

Saver, J. L., and Antonio Damasio. "Preserved Access and Processing of Social Knowledge in a Patient with Acquired Sociopathy Due to Ventromedial Frontal Damage." *Neuropsychologia* 29 (1991): 1241–49.

Schall, James V. *The Life of the Mind: On the Joys and Travails of Thinking.* Wilmington, DE: ISI Books, 2006.

Schall, Jeff D. "The Neural Selection and Control of Saccades by the Frontal Eye Field." *Philosophical Transactions of the Royal Society of London B, Biological Sciences* 357 (2002): 1073–82.

Schall, Jeff D., and L. Boucher. "Executive Control of Gaze by the Frontal Lobes." *Cognitive Affective and Behavioral Neuroscience* 7 (2007): 396–412.

Schiller, Daniela, Marie-H. Monfils, Candace M. Raio, David C. Johnson, Joseph E. LeDoux, and Elizabeth A. Phelps. "Preventing the Return of Fear in Humans Using Reconsolidation Update Mechanisms." *Nature* 463 (2010): 49–53.

Schiller, Daniela, and E. A. Phelps. "Does Reconsolidation Occur in Humans?" *Frontiers in Behavioral Neuroscience* 5 (2011).

Schmid-Schonbein, C. "Improvements of Seizure Control by Psychological Methods in Patients with Intractable Epilepsy." *Seizure* 7 (1998): 261–70.

Schooler, Jonathan W. "What Science Tells Us about Free Will." In *Free Will and Consciousness: How Might They Work?*, edited by Roy Baumeister, Alfred Mele, and Kathleen Vohs, 191–218. New York: Oxford University Press, 2010.

Schultz, W. "Neural Coding of Basic Reward Terms of Animal Learning Theory, Game Theory, Microeconomics and Behavioural Ecology." *Current Opinion in Neurobiology* 14 (April 2004): 139–47.

Scruton, Roger. *The Aesthetics of Music.* Oxford: Oxford University Press, 1999.

———. "Sounds as Secondary Objects and Pure Events." In Nudds and O'Callaghan, *Sounds and Perception*, 50–68.

Searle, John R. "Consciousness." *Annual Review of Neuroscience* 23 (2003): 557–78.

———. *Intentionality: An Essay in the Philosophy of Mind.* (1983) Cambridge: Cambridge University Press, 1999.

———. "Minds, Brains, and Programs." *Behavioral and Brain Sciences* 3 (1980): 417–57.

———. *The Rediscovery of the Mind.* Cambridge, MA: MIT Press, 2002.

Shannon, R. V., F. G. Zeng, V. Kamath, J. Wygonski, and M. Ekelid. "Speech Recognition with Primarily Temporal Cues." *Science* 270 (1995): 303–4.

Shepherd, Gordon H. "The Human Sense of Smell: Are We Better Than We Think?" *PloS Biology* 2 (2004): 572–75.

Shevell, S. K., R. St. Clair, and S. W. Hong. "Misbinding of Color to Form in Afterimages." *Vision Neuroscience* 25 (2008): 355–60.

Sin, Wun, K. Haas, E. S. Ruthazer, and H. T. Cline. "Dendrite Growth Increased by Visual Activity Requires NMDA Receptor and Rho GTPases." *Nature* 419 (2002): 475–80.

Siraisi, Nancy G. *Medicine and the Italian Universities.* Leiden: Brill, 2001.

Small, Jocelyn Penny. *Wax Tablets of the Mind: Cognitive Studies of Memory and Literacy in Classical Antiquity.* London: Routledge, 1997.

Smilek, Daniel, Mike J. Dixon, and Philip M. Merikle. "Binding of Graphemes and Synesthetic Colors in Color-Graphemic Synesthesia." In *Synesthesia: Perspectives from Cognitive Neuroscience,* edited by Lynn C. Robertson and Noam Sagiv, 74–89. Oxford: Oxford University Press, 2005.

Smith, Barry C. "Speech Sounds and the Direct Meeting of Minds." In Nudds and O'Callaghan, *Sounds and Perception,* 183–210.

Smith, Kerri. "Neuroscience vs. Philosophy: Taking Aim at Free Will." *Nature* 477 (2011): 23–25. http://www.nature.com/news/2011/110831/full/477023a.html.

Smith, Z. M., B. Delgutte, and A. J. Oxenham. "Chimaeric Sounds Reveal Dichotomies in Auditory Perception." *Nature* 416 (2002): 87–90.

Snyder, Bob. *Music and Memory.* Cambridge, MA: MIT Press, 1999.

Solmsen, Friedrich. *Die Entwicklung der aristotlischer Logik und Rhetorik.* Doctoral dissertation. Berlin, 1929.

Sorabji, Richard. *Aristotle on Memory.* 2nd ed. Chicago: University of Chicago Press, 2006.

———, ed. *Philoponus and the Rejection of Aristotelian Science.* Ithaca, NY: Cornell University Press, 1987.

———. *Self: Ancient and Modern Insights about Individuality, Life, and Death.* Chicago: University of Chicago Press, 2006.

Spector, Ferrine, and Daphne Maurer. "Synesthesia: A New Approach to Understanding the Development of Perception." *Developmental Psychology* 45 (2009): 175–89.

Sperry, Roger. "Mind-Brain Interaction: Mentalism, Yes; Dualism, No." *Neuroscience* 5 (1980): 195–206.

———. "A Modified Concept of Consciousness." *Psychological Review* 76 (1969): 532–36.

Spillane, John D. *The Doctrine of the Nerves.* Oxford: Oxford University Press, 1991.

Spinoza, Baruch. *Opera.* Edited by Carl Gebhardt. 4 volumes. Heidelberg: Winters, 1927.

Squire, Larry. "Memory and Brain Systems: 1969–2009." *Journal of Neurosciences* 29 (2009): 12711–16.

Squire, Larry, and Eric Kandel. *Memory: From Mind to Molecules.* 2nd edition. Greenwood Village, CO: Roberts, 2009.

Stebbing, Susan. *Philosophy and the Physicists.* London: Methuen, 1937.

Stevenson, Richard J. *The Psychology of Flavour.* Oxford: Oxford University Press, 2009.

Stock, Brian. *The Implications of Literacy.* Princeton, NJ: Princeton University Press, 1983.

Storr, Anthony. *Music and the Mind.* New York: Free Press, 1992.

Stuphorn, Veit, Joshua W. Brown, and Jeffrey D. Schall. "Role of Supplementary Eye Field in Saccade Initiation: Executive, Not Direct, Control." *Journal of Neurophysiology* 103 (2010): 801–16.

Tallis, Raymond. *Aping Mankind: Neuromania, Darwinitis and the Misrepresentation of Humanity.* Durham, UK: Acumen, 2011.

———. *In Defense of Wonder and Other Philosophical Reflections*. Durham, UK: Acumen, 2012.

———. "A Mind of One's Own." *New Statesman*. February 24, 2011.

———. "Rethinking Thinking." *Wall Street Journal*. November 12, 2011.

———. "What Neuroscience Cannot Tell Us About Ourselves." *New Atlantis*, Fall, 2010, at http://www.thenewatlantis.com/publications/what-neuroscience-cannot-tell-us-about -ourselves.

Tatler, Benjamin W., N. J. Wade, H. Kwan, J. M. Findlay, B. M. Velichkovsky. "Yarbus, Eye Movements, and Vision." *Perception* 1 (2010): 7–27.

Thompson, Evan. *Mind in Life*. Cambridge, MA: Harvard University Press, 2007.

Tice, D. M., and R. F. Baumeister. "Self-Control as a Limited Resource: Regulatory and Depletion Patterns." *Journal of Personality and Social Psychology* 74 (1998): 774–89.

Tomasello, Michael. *The Cultural Origins of Human Cognition*. Cambridge, MA: Harvard University Press, 1999.

———. "On the Interpersonal Origins of the Self-Concept." In *The Perceived Self: Ecological and Interpersonal Sources of Self Knowledge*, edited by Ulric Neisser, 174–84. Cambridge: Cambridge University Press, 1994; online, 2010.

Tononi, Giulio. "Consciousness as Integrated Information: a Provisional Manifesto." *The Biological Bulletin* 215 (2008): 216–42.

———. "An Information Integration Theory of Consciousness." *BMC Neuroscience* 5 (2004): 42.

———. *Phi: A Voyage from the Brain to the Soul*. New York: Pantheon, 2012.

Torrance, E. P. "Examples and Rationales of Test Tasks for Assessing Creative Abilities." *Journal of Creative Behavior* 2 (1968): 165–78.

Traxel, Werner, ed. *Ebbinghaus Studien 2*. Passau: Passavia, 1987.

Tsien, J. Z. "The Memory Code." *Scientific American*. July, 2007.

———. "The Organizing Principles of Real-Time Memory Encoding: Neural Clique Assemblies and Universal Neural Codes." In Bontempi et al., *Memories: Molecules and Circuits*, 99–112.

Tulving, Endel. "Episodic Memory and Autonoesis." In *The Missing Link in Cognition: The Origins of Self-Reflective Consciousness*, edited by Herbert S. Terrace and Janet Metcalfe, 3–56. Oxford: Oxford University Press, 2005.

Tulving, Endel, and Martin Lepage. "Where in the Brain Is Awareness of One's Past?" In *Memory, Brain and Belief*, edited by Daniel L. Schacter and Elaine Scarry, 208–28. Cambridge, MA: Harvard University Press, 2000.

Tuma, D. T., and R. Reif, eds. *Problem Solving and Education*. Hillsdale, NJ: Erlbaum, 1980.

Turin, Luca, and Tania Sanchez. *Perfumes—The Guide*. New York: Viking, 2008.

Van Bergen, Annie. *Task Interruption*. Amsterdam: North Holland, 1968.

Van den Hoort, Bjorn, and Henrik Ehrsson. "Being Barbie: The Size of One's Own Body Determines the Perceived Size of the World." *PlosOne* 6 (2011) e20195.

Van Gelder, Tim. "The Dynamical Hypothesis in Cognitive Science." *Behavioral and Brain Sciences* 21 (1998): 615–65.

Varela, Francisco, Evan T. Thompson, and Eleanor Rosch. *The Embodied Mind*. Cambridge, MA: MIT Press, 1991.

Varela, Francisco, H. R. Maturana, R. Uribe. "Autopoiesis: The Organization of Living Systems, Its Characterization, and a Model." *Currents in Modern Biology* 5 (1974): 187–96.

Vernant, Jean-Pierre. *Myth and Thought among the Greeks*. Translated by Janet Lloyd with Jeff Fort. New York: Zone, 2006.

Vohs, Kathleen D., and Jonathan W. Schooler. "The Value of Believing in Free Will: Encouraging a Belief in Determinism Increases Cheating." *Psychological Science* 19 (2008): 49–54.

Von der Heydt, R., H. Zhou, and H. S. Friedman. "Representation of Stereoscopic Edges in Monkey Visual Cortex." *Vision Research* 40 (2000): 1995–97.

Wade, Nicholas J., and Benjamin W. Tatler. *The Moving Tablet of the Eye*. New York: Oxford University Press, 2005.

Wallach, Hans. "Brightness Constancy and the Nature of Achromatic Colors." *Journal of Experimental Psychology* 38 (1948): 310–24.

Walton, Mark E., Joseph T. Devlin, and Matthew F. S. Rushworth. "Interactions between Decision Making and Performance Monitoring within Prefrontal Cortex." *Nature Neuroscience* 7 (2004): 1259–65.

Warren, R. "Perceptual Restoration of Missing Speech Sounds." *Science* 167 (1970): 392–93.

Weber, Bruce, and David Depew, eds. *Evolution and Learning: The Baldwin Effect Reconsidered*. Cambridge, MA: MIT Press, 2003.

Wegner, Daniel. *The Illusion of Free Will*. Cambridge, MA: MIT Press, 2002.

Weisberg, Robert W. *Creativity: Genius and Other Myths*. New York: Freeman, 1986.

———. *Creativity: Understanding Innovation in Problem Solving, Science, Invention, and the Arts*. Hoboken: Wiley, 2006.

Weiss, Paul. "One Plus One Does Not Equal Two." In *The Neurosciences: A Study Program* edited by Gardner C. Quatron, Theodore Melnechuk, and Francis Otto Schmitt, 801–21. New York: Rockefeller University Press, 1976.

Wertheimer, Max. *Productive Thinking*. Enlarged edition, edited by Michael Wertheimer. Chicago: University of Chicago Press, 1982. (Original edition, 1945.)

Whiten, Andrew, ed. *Natural Theories of Mind: Evolution, Development, and Simulation of Everyday Mindreading*. Oxford: Basil Blackwell, 1991.

Wichems, C., N. Takahashi, X. F. Li, Z. Zeng, R. Revay, K. P. Lesch, and D. L. Murphy. "Cocaine Reward Models: Conditioned place preference can be established in dopamine- and in serotonin-transporter knockout mice." *Proceedings of the National Academy of Science* 95 (1998): 7600–704.

Williams, Ellizabeth A. *The Physical and the Moral: Anthropology, Physiology, and Philosophical Medicine in France, 1750–1850*. Cambridge: Cambridge University Press, 1994.

Wilson, Robert. *Genes and the Agents of Life. The Individual in the Fragile Sciences, Biology*. New York: Cambridge University Press, 2005.

Wiltgen, B. J., R. A. M. Brown, L. E. Talton, and A. J. Silva. "Towards a Molecular and Cellular Understanding of Remote Memory." In Bontempi et al., *Memories: Molecules and Circuits*, 59–68.

Wimmer, H., and J. Perner. "Beliefs about Beliefs: Representation and Constraining Function of Wrong Beliefs in Young Children's Understanding of Deception." *Cognition* 13 (1983): 41–68.

Winder, Danny G., and Nichole L. Schram. "Plasticity and Behavior: New Genetic Techniques to Address Multiple Forms and Functions." *Physiology and Behavior* 73 (2001): 763–80.

Winger, Gail, James H. Woods, Chad M. Galuska, and Tammy Wade-Galuska. "Behavioral Perspectives on the Neuroscience of Drug Addiction." *Journal of Experimental Animal Behavior* 84 (2005): 667–68.

Wolf, Maryanne. *Proust and the Squid: The Story and Science of the Reading Brain*. New York: HarperCollins, 2007.

Wooding, Steven. "Evolution: A Study in Bad Taste?" *Current Biology* 15.19 (2005): R805–7.

Wright, W. *A Grammar of the Arabic Language*. From the German of Caspari. 3rd edition.

Emended by W. Robertson Smith and M. J. de Goeje. Cambridge: Cambridge University Press, 1956.

Yarbus, Alfred L. *Eye Movements and Vision*. Translated by Basil Haigh. New York: Plenum, 1967.

Yates, Francis. *The Art of Memory*. Chicago: University of Chicago Press, 1966.

Young, Robert M. *Mind, Brain, and Adaptation in the Nineteenth Century: Cerebral Localization and Its Biological Context from Gall to Ferrier*. Oxford: Oxford University Press, 1969.

Zatorre, R. J., J. L. Chen, and V. B. Penhune. "When the Brain Plays Music: Auditory-Motor Interactions in Music Perception and Production." *Nature Reviews Neuroscience* 8 (2007): 547–58.

Zeidan, Fadel, Katherine Martucci, Robert A. Kraft, Nakia S. Gordon, John G. McHaffie, and Robert C. Coghill. "Brain Mechanisms Supporting the Modulation of Pain by Mindfulness Meditation." *Journal of Neuroscience* 31 (2011): 5540–48.

Zeigarnik, Bluma. "Über das Behalten von erledigten und unerledigten Handlungen." *Psychologische Forschung* (1927), translated online as "On Finished and Unfinished Tasks," at codelab.com/wp-content/uploads/2009/12/On-Finished-and-Unfinished-Tasks.pdf.

Zentner, Marcel R. "Preferences for Colours and Colour-Emotion Combinations in Early Childhood." *Developmental Science* 4.4 (2001): 389–98.

Zetzel, James E. G. "*Romane memento*: Justice and Judgment in *Aeneid* VI." *Transactions of the American Philological Association*: 119 (1989): 263–84.

Zhuangzi. *Chuang-tzu: The Seven Inner Chapters and Other Writings from the Book Chuang-tzu*. Translated by A. C. Graham. London: Allen and Unwin, 1981.

INDEX